Mozart im Haufe Dur.
Jchek.

INSIGHT GUIDES

The world's largest collection of visual travel guides

Continental Europe

Managing Editor: Roger Williams
Editorial Director: Brian Bell

APA PUBLICATIONS

L

Part of the Langenscheidt Publishing Group

INSIGHT GUIDES

Continental Europe

CONTACTING THE EDITORS: Although every effort is made to provide accurate information in this publication, we live in a fast-changing world and would appreciate it if readers would call our attention to any errors or outdated information that may occur by writing to us at Apa Publications,
P.O. Box 7910, London SE1 8ZB, England.
Fax: (44) 171-620-1074.
e-mail: insight@apaguide.demon.co.uk.

First Edition 1984
Fourth Edition (Updated) 1998

Distributed in the United States by
Langenscheidt Publishers Inc.
46–35 54th Road
Maspeth
NY 11378
Fax: (718) 784 0640

Distributed in the UK & Ireland by
GeoCenter International Ltd
The Viables Centre, Harrow Way
Basingstoke, Hampshire RG22 4BJ
Fax: (44) 1256-817988

Worldwide distribution enquiries:
APA Publications GmbH & Co. Verlag KG
(Singapore branch)
38 Joo Koon Road
Singapore 628990
Tel: 65-8651600
Fax: 65-8616438

Printed in Singapore by
Insight Print Services (Pte) Ltd
38 Joo Koon Road
Singapore 628990
Fax: 65-8616438

Barrett

Williams

The concept of "doing Europe" in a couple of weeks has become something of a joke to sophisticated Europeans. "If it's Tuesday, it must be Belgium," they chortle as coaches of dazed tourists crawl though the traffic on their way to the next sight. But the longest journey starts with just one step, and what better way is there of getting acquainted with such a diverse menu than by sampling a little of each of the many dishes on offer? There'll be other visits, after all, when individual regions can be explored in detail, and specific interests indulged.

No guidebook publisher is better equipped to offer a *menu touristique* than Apa Publications. Having published 80 *Insight Guides*, 50 *Insight Pocket Guides*, and 40 *Compact Guides* to the continent, ranging from the Algarve to the Aegean, from Venice to Vienna, the company is perfectly placed to assemble a sampler of the very best that Continental Europe has to offer. The result is this book.

Klein

Steinberg

This updated edition of *Insight Guide: Continental Europe* is a completely restructured and expanded edition of the book first published in the 1980s. It has been edited by **Roger Williams**, a highly experienced British journalist and editor whose previous work for Insight Guides has ranged from books on Catalonia to the Baltic States and who has also been working on *Over Europe*, a book of aerial photography of the continent. Building on the excellent work done by **Rolf Steinberg**, the editor of the original edition, he sought to combine the insightful text and stunning photography for which the *Insight Guide* series is renowned to create the definitive Grand Tour.

In addition to the obvious European destinations, he decided to include basic coverage of several former Eastern European destinations – Budapest, Prague, Warsaw and Cracow – since those increasingly accessible cities have become a popular addition to many tours of Europe. These chapters were written by **Rowlinson Carter**, author of *Insight*

Foster

White

Bell

Beebe

Schmetzer

Karnow

Wassman

Guide: Eastern Europe, a companion volume to this book.

After an introduction written by Williams, *Insight Guide: Continental Europe* encapsulates the complex history of the continent in three neat chapters. These were written by **Pam Barrett**, an English historian who also wrote the history section of *Insight Guide: Great Britain*.

Complementing these chapters are 26 informative short essays, alphabetically arranged, which aim to cast a light on some of the more curious aspects of European culture. These were written and compiled by Williams and **Brian Bell**, editorial director of Apa Publications and editor of *Insight Guide: Ireland*.

Many contributors to the Places section were contacts of Rolf Steinberg that he made during his many years as a foreign correspondent after graduating from the Columbia University School of Journalism. In addition to his role as editor, Steinberg also wrote the chapter on Heidelberg.

An especially prolific contributor was **Uli Schmetzer**, a German-born Australian who spent 10 years with the Reuters newsagency. He wrote the chapters on Belgium, the Rhine, Salzburg and all of Italy. The Berlin chapter was provided by **Petra Dubulski**, a journalist from the city and a contributor to *Insight Guide: Germany.*

The chapters on France involved a clutch of writers. London-born **Oliver Henderson**, who lived and worked as a travel writer in Paris for many years, wrote the Around France chapter. **Tan Chung Lee**, a Singaporean travel writer who studied in Paris, provided the chapter on that city, while Michigan-born journalist **West J. Perry**, who lives in Cannes, covered the French Riviera. **Sarah Béhar**, a teacher in Nantes, was born in Angers on the River Loire and she writes about its famous châteaux.

Lee Foster, a travel writer and photographer from California, is married to a Dutchwoman and so is a regular visitor to

the Netherlands, which he has written about for this book. **Thomas C. Lucey** is a journalist from New York who has spent much of his life living and working in Europe. For this book he has written on Bavaria and Switzerland, his areas of specialism.

Linda White graduated in English and journalism from the University of Mississippi before moving to Germany. She wrote the chapters called Around Germany, Around Austria and Vienna. **Wilhelm Klein**, the editor of *Insight Guide: Burma*, complemented the chapter on his native country Austria with an article on Innsbruck.

The work on Spain and Greece (as well as some photos) was by **F. Lisa Beebe**, an American freelance who grew up in Pennsylvania and now considers herself to be a "professional tourist".

The chapter on Albania was written for this new edition by **Paul Sullivan**, a London-based journalist who first went to the country to try to meet the partisans who had looked after his father who had been shot down over the country during World War II. The panel focusing on the troubled Yugoslavia and the chapters on Portugal were written by Insight editor Roger Williams.

One of the instantly recognisable characteristics of any *Insight Guide* is the quality of its photography, and this book was able to draw from the work of many of the top photographers who have contributed to the series over the years. Their photojournalism does more than give an idea of what destinations look like: by showing Europeans going about their everyday concerns, their work conveys what the destinations *feel* like as well.

Among regular *Insight Guides* photographers represented here are **Bill Wassman, Catherine Karnow** and **Paul Van Riel**.

This edition of *Insight Guide: Continental Europe* was produced in Apa's London editorial office, where the Travel Tips section was assembled and updated by Insight editor **Clare Griffiths**. The original text was proofread and indexed by **John Goulding**.

C O N T E N T S

CONTENTS

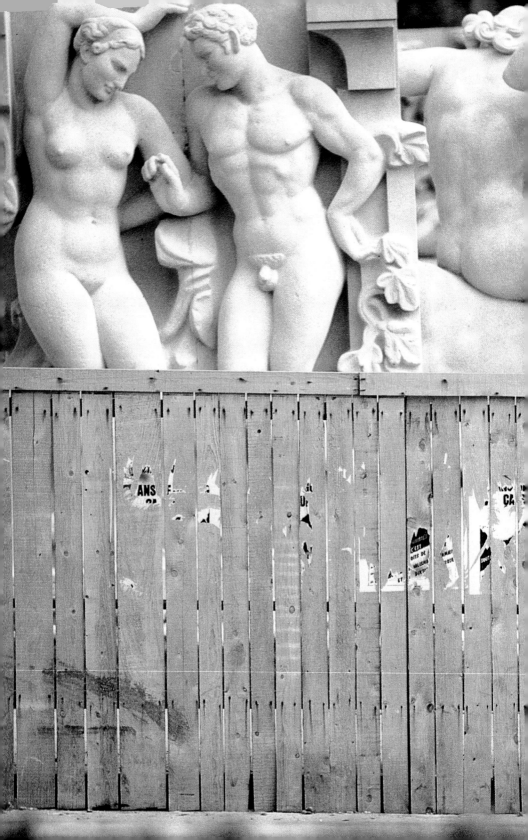

Continental Europe is the heart of Europe, nourishing the richest mix of cultures anywhere on earth. This is the world of châteaux and champagne, La Scala and Monte Carlo, gondolas and gypsy violins. It is the home of democracy, Christianity, the Renaissance, royalty, Michelangelo, Mercedes-Benz, Beethoven, Brigitte Bardot, pasta, goulash, two world wars and the common cold. Its art is admired, its wines are drunk, its clothes are copied and its languages are spoken in every corner of the world.

Europeans have always been a little hazy about the boundaries of their continent. To French politicians, it is a collection of well-off Western countries who need to get together in the interests of self-interest. To former Soviet republics, it is a fold to return to now that communism has gone. Romantics see Paris as its centre, bureaucrats see Brussels, style-setters see Milan; classicists look to Athens, Catholics to the Vatican, bankers to Bonn, while Mittel Europeans have their eyes on somewhere much mistier, further east.

The continent that begins on the Atlantic's shore and ends far beyond the horizon at the Ural mountains, has its actual centre in an unmarked field north of Vilnius in Lithuania. Only Lithuanians know this. However, like its Baltic neighbours, including all of Scandinavia, Lithuania could not be squeezed into this book. But it is fully covered in *Insight Guide: Eastern Europe*, along with Bulgaria, Romania, Moldova, Belarus, Ukraine, Georgia, Armenia, Azerbaijan and a chunk of Russia, all of which can legitimately lay claim to a place on the world's second smallest continent.

Nor can islands be added to a guide about a mainland. Malta, Cyprus, Ireland and Great Britain are thus excluded – although Britain, floating off the west coast in Atlantic waters, might have been banned through arrogance:

"Fog in Channel: Continent isolated" was a memorable headline in the London *Times*. The Channel Tunnel, of course, has consigned that attitude to history's scrapheap.

Wide divisions: Its countries may be physically attached, but Continental Europe is not homogeneous, and all efforts to unite its unruly tribes have come to nothing. Charlemagne and Napoleon failed, and so have the European Community bureaucrats.

The fact is that Europeans, in spite of all the handshaking and treaty signing, do not

see themselves as a single unity. Indeed, they often don't see themselves as part of the country to which they belong. Basques, Bretons, Catalans, Flemings, Lombards, Prussians and inhabitants of sundry former empires and city states still dream of resurrecting independent nationhood. Minorities must be heard: they vote and may lob the occasional bomb. Taking the wrong line over the question of Macedonia, a nation that has not existed for over 2,000 years, can still bring down the government of Greece.

Mistrusts run deep, and stereotypes are still used in the nations' popular newspapers to stir up feeling. In moments of sudden

Preceding pages: detail from Mozart's travel journal; Café Greco, Rome; fence-peeping in the Paris Tuileries; carnival pageant in Basel, Switzerland; in Austria's mountains; Breton fishermen. Left, celebrating Cologne's carnival. Right, a Burgundy wine confraternity meeting.

angst, they also publish reports about what other Europeans think about them. There are epigrams to sum up every nation, every region, every city, sayings to reinforce ideas about their stubbornness or *joie de vivre*, their cleverness or stupidity. Such cartoon characters are easy to sketch, from the hard working Teutonic races of the north to the excitable Latins of the south, from boisterous Bavarians and emotional Poles to arrogant French, devious Greeks, boring Belgians. "A typical Spaniard," the Viennese psychoanalyst Sigmund Freud said of the painter Salvador Dalí. "Quite mad." His statement does not bear analysis.

The north-south divide is the most noticeable: the industrious peoples of the colder climates scorn the backward and lazy siesta-seeking peasants of sunnier parts. Visually, the strapping, healthy, fair-skinned northerner gets darker, lazier, louder and smaller towards the south. Even within countries there can be divisive stereotypes: Germany's northern Prussians look down on the beer-swilling Bavarians. The richer inhabitants of northern France and Italy look down on the poorer, more rural "midday" lands of the south – the Midi in France, the Mezzogiorno in Italy. In Spain the industrious northerner has no time for "lazy" flamenco-playing Andalusia.

Such prejudices are put aside at holiday time as northerners head for the sun. The whoops from otherwise sober Germans are said to be audible as their cars cross the Alps and slip down into Italy.

Only a love a football seems to unite Europeans, though the games themselves are often replays of earlier hostilities.

Roman rule: The nearest Europe came to being united was not under one country, but under one city, ancient Rome. Pax Romana stretched all around the Mediterranean and north to the River Danube, and ruled in every country in Continental Europe. Though "Roman", it was administered by all kinds of people from sundry tribes, and many emperors were born outside the Italian peninsula.

What Rome did bequeath – apart from baths, highways, gazpacho, open-toed sandals and Christian martyrs – was a written language from which European "Romance" languages subsequently evolved, and as a result a Frenchman, an Italian, a Spaniard and a Portuguese can all roughly understand what the other is trying to say – though their hand gestures are probably equally intelligible to each other.

Teutonic tribes shaped the languages in the north, Slavs to the east, while to the west, all but pushed into the sea, are the last of the Celtic-speakers, the Bretons. Trapped in pockets in between are little-used languages such as Romansch in part of Switzerland, and Basque, spoken on the western border of France and Spain and related to Hungarian.

Language is no respecter of the borders – which have anyway failed to remain firm. At the beginning of the 20th century few countries looked the shape they do today. Italy and Germany had not long been invented. Albania, Bulgaria and Yugoslavia had not been thought of. Prussia had disappeared, Austria and Hungary dramatically deflated. Since then, Germany has divided and united, Czechoslovakia united and divided, Poland re-emerged, and Yugoslavia has been pieced together and blown apart.

It can be reassuring sometimes to be re-

Mediterranean, scattering a little of their language on their way, and giving fundamental lessons in rape and pillage. Later, the Swedish and Russian empire builders came knocking at the gates.

In the east the Ottoman Muslims held sway until the 19th century when Greece and Bulgaria re-emerged as countries after many centuries of occupation. At their height, the Turkish Ottomans pushed the Austro-Hungarian empire back to Vienna, making the city of coffee houses the crossroads of the Crusaders' cross and the Muslim's scimitar, of the croissant and the hot-cross bun.

After the death of the prophet Muhammed, a missionary zeal swept Arab tribes up

minded that Prince Hans Adam II or Prince Rainier are still quietly getting on with life in Liechtenstein and Monaco, microscopic principalities of irrevocably ancient borders straight out of a 1940s Hollywood script in which the princes would be played by the likes of Stewart Granger.

Europe has some enjoyably eccentric corners but it cannot be accused of being insular. It has been shaped and honed by neighbouring cultures. Vikings came down from the north, sailing up to Paris and round into the

Left, money-minded Swiss tram. Above, four-legged transport in Andalusia.

through Spain to Poitiers, not far from Paris. It swiftly subsided back into Spain where their caliphate produced not just an enormously rich culture and architecture in Córdoba and Granada, but affected the whole Spanish language to such an extent that a rousing roar of "*olé!*" may, some historians have suggested, be a remnant of a rallying call for "Allah!"

Europe's unparalleled architecture shows that ideas have always flowed freely across the continent. Builders, traders, businessmen, pilgrims and mercenaries – as well as visionaries – have constantly been on the move. The terracotta roof-tiles of the Romans colour all the Mediterranean's fashionable playground resorts. Italians built many of Poland's churches. Normans put up castles in northern Greece and in southern Italy. German woodcarvers left their marks on Spanish choir stalls. Dutch masters followed the Hansa traders up the North Sea to the Baltic and a visitor would be hard-pressed to tell the difference between 17th-century houses in Gdansk, Bremen and Amsterdam.

Mozart's stamping ground was a trio of neighbouring cities: Vienna, Salzburg and Prague. Opera linked Milan more to Paris than to Rome. And the royal families of all Europe were so frequently related through marriage that the surprise is not that some of

them were so mad or so bad but that they had half a brain at all.

The great architectural movements of Romanesque, Gothic, Renaissance, Baroque and Neo-classicism touched all of Europe. In the 19th century, France's art nouveau was Germany and Austria's Jugendstil, Italy's Stile Liberty and Spain's Modernismo.

Culture vultures: Europeans are very aware of the cultural heritage, which they see as a social responsibility. Public spending on the arts in France in 20 times that of the whole of the US, and French film-makers are subsidised by nearly 2 billion francs a year. No stage sets can match those in the state-backed

German theatre. Italy hosts the Venice Biennale, the most prestigious art gathering in Europe, and would no doubt spend more on its priceless monuments if half the money didn't end up in the Mafia's hands.

A fast and integrated road system makes communications between the countries easier than ever before. Germany's *Autobahns* are the densest network of roads in the world. The railway system is entirely integrated, and high-speed trains are in regular service, particularly in France where the service is modelled on airline techniques. Given Europe's overcrowded air space and overstretched airports, it's frequently faster – and certainly less fraught – to get around by train than by plane.

There is, in short, no difficulty in travelling the length and breadth of the world's second smallest continent (Antarctica is the smallest), which has proved to be quite unbeatable in its ambitions. In the past 500 years it had a good try at conquering the entire world, but the chief signs now of its glorious colonial past are its specialist restaurants: Algerian couscous in France; Indonesian rice tables in Holland, and Chinese teashops and Brazilian restaurants in Lisbon.

In recent years it has been Europe that has been colonised, by multinationals and big business from America and Japan. For years McDonald's has been opening a new hamburger house in Europe every day, and no European city is without *sushi* restaurants. France even permitted Euro Disney to be built near Paris, and Japanese work practices have penetrated the most entrenched European labour markets.

Many residents of those former colonies and outposts return looking for their roots. Names can be traced to places. Some know immediately where their ancestors came from: for example, those whose family names end "-*ian*" are from Armenia. Walt Disney's family was " d'Isigny" (from Isigny in Normandy). The late French historian Ferdinand Braudel could point to remote mountain valleys or city shopkeepers' alleyways as the place of origin for other family names. They can provide an excuse for character and temperament, too – just one more thing Europe has to answer for.

Left, performance art on Breitscheidplatz, Berlin. **Right**, France's biggest US import, Disneyland.

DECISIVE DATES

2000–1450 BC: Minoan civilisation, centred on Knossos in Crete.

1450–100 BC: Mycenean civilisation, based at Mycenae in the Peleponnese.

800–500 BC: Archaic period. Athens and Sparta emerge as major city states.

750 BC: Rome, an Etruscan trading post, said to have been founded by Romulus and Remus.

509 BC: Rome becomes a republic.

490–450 BC: Greek wars against Persia.

450–338 BC: Classical period. Parthenon built. Flowering of Greek literature and philosophy. Rome gradually takes over all Italy.

338–323 BC: Macedonia's Philip and Alexander the Great create unprecedented empires.

323–146 BC: Hellenistic period.

218 BC: The Carthaginian army attacks Rome, unsuccessfully.

146 BC: Greece falls to Rome.

48 BC: Death of Pompey the Great in civil war with Julius Caesar.

48 BC: Pax Romana spreads throughout Europe and Mediterranean during the rule of Augustus. Decline begins within 200 years.

AD 330: Constantine, the first Christian Roman emperor, establishes an eastern capital in Constantinople.

AD 527: St Benedict founds the first monastic order, at Monte Cassino, southern Italy.

6th–7th centuries: Slavs settle in Balkans.

AD 714: Spain conquered by North African Muslims.

AD 800: In Rome, Charlemagne, a Frankish leader, is crowned Holy Roman Emperor.

11th century: Romanesque architecture. This was characterised by simple vaulting and rounded arches. The style had been evolving since the fall of Rome. Pisa Cathedral, Italy, and Church of the Apostles, Cologne, are good examples.

1072: French Normans (descendants of the Vikings) conquer Sicily.

1096: First Crusade against Muslims in the Holy Land; 500,000 join up.

12th century: Gothic architecture begins to have an influence. It is identified by its pointed arches and flying buttresses. Chartres Cathedral, France, and St Stephen's Cathedral, Vienna, are prime examples.

1150–70: First universities founded.

1283: Dante Alighieri begins writing in Florence, establishing Italian language.

1286: The papacy moves from Rome to Avignon.

1325–1495: The Renaissance flourishes in Italy, an art movement that rediscoverd the classical viewpoint and celebrated the human body. It is initiated by Filippo Brunelleschi, architect of the Florence Duomo, and exemplified by Giotto, Michelangelo and Leonardo da Vinci.

1347–51: Black Death sweeps the continent, killing one-third of the population.

1337–1453: Hundred Years' War between France and England results in Joan of Arc's martyrdom and England losing all claims to French territory.

1415: Jan Hus, the Czech heretic, is burned at the stake.

1450: First printing press invented by Johannes Gutenberg in Germany. The Bible printed five years later.

1453: Ottoman Turks capture Constantinople and Byzantine empire falls.

1478: Inquisition established in Spain.

1492: Moors driven out of Spain; Jews expelled. Christopher Columbus arrives in the Americas.

1497: Vasco da Gama finds sea route to India.

1503: Leonardo da Vinci paints *Mona Lisa*.

1506–1626: Building of St Peter's, Rome, involving Michelangelo, da Vinci, Raphael and Bernini.

1519: Portuguese navigator Fernando Magellan circumnavigates the world.

1543: Poland's Nicolas Copernicus publishes theory that the earth revolves around the sun.

16th century: The Reformation is a move against the corruption of the Church of Rome. 1517:

Martin Luther nails his 95 points to Wittenberg church door. 1536: John Calvin establishes Presbyterian church in Switzerland. 1572: Protestant Huguenots purged in St Bartholomew's Day Massacre in France. The Reformation turns much of northern Europe to Protestantism, while southern Europe by and large remains Catholic. **1579:** The United Provinces established, founding the Netherlands.

1618–46: Thirty Years' War: initially a Protestant revolt against Catholicism.

1633: The Inquisition forces Italian scientist Galileo to renounce his Copernican belief that the earth revolves around the sun.

1643–1715: Louix XIV, the Sun King, creator of the Palace of Versailles in France, exemplifies a

phase of absolute monarchy and the divine right of kings.

1755: Earthquake destroys Lisbon.

17th–18th centuries: Baroque architecture is a rich style, using gold, marble, mirrors to show off wealth and power. The palace of Versailles is the best example, also the Zwinger Palace in Dresden.

18th century: Age of Enlightenment. Toleration is urged by the French writer Voltaire and others. The practice is preached by Austro-Hungarian empress Maria Theresa, "the Mother of the

Preceding pages: prehistoric cave painting from Lascaux, France. Left, Florence's literary genius, Dante. **Above,** Louis XIV, Versailles' Sun King.

Nation" (1717–80). Mozart plays at her court.

1792: The French Revolution. Louis XVI and Queen Marie Antoinette are guillotined.

1796–1815: Napoleon Bonaparte of France invades Austria, Italy, Spain, Portugal and Russia. He is defeated at Waterloo in modern Belgium.

Late 18th–19th centuries: Romanticism looks back to more idyllic times and inspires nationalist movements, encouraging local languages (Catalan, Provençal) and customs.

1822: Greece declares independence.

1848: Popular revolutions throughout Europe.

1861: Kingdom of Italy set up after Austrians ejected from the north, Spanish from the south.

1870–71: Franco-Prussian war, Paris besieged.

1874: First Impressionist exhibition held in Paris.

1885: First petrol engine vehicle produced by Karl Benz.

1912–13: Balkan Wars result in most of European Turkey being divided up.

1914–18: World War I. War of attrition fought in northern France and Belgium. It results in the break-up of the Ottoman and Austro-Hungarian empires and the formation of new countries, including Yugoslavia and Czechoslovakia.

1922: Mussolini and 25,000 Fascist Blackshirts march on Rome.

1936–39: Spanish civil war. First mobilisation of troops by air. Francisco Franco becomes dictator.

1938: Hitler invades Austria.

1939–45 World War II. France, the Netherlands, Belgium, Yugoslavia, Albania and Greece occupied by Germans and Italians. Allied landings in Normandy and southern Italy lead to end of the war. German cities destroyed. Europe is divided between Western and Soviet spheres of influence.

1956: Hungarian revolution supressed.

1958: European Common Market set up.

1961: Berlin wall built.

1968: Student unrest throughout Europe. Czechoslovakian reforms of the "Prague Spring" are crushed by Soviet Union.

1971: Women get the vote in Switzerland.

1974–75: Dictatorships in Greece, Spain and Portugal end.

1978: Poland's Cardinal Wojtyla becomes Pope John Paul II, first non-Italian pope for 400 years.

1989: Berlin wall comes down. Eastern Europe returns to democracy.

1991: Hostilities break out in Yugoslavia.

1992: Galileo is rehabilitated by the Vatican. Border controls between European Union (formerly EC) countries theoretically end.

1994: Channel Tunnel links France with Britain.

Europa, so legend has it, was the beautiful daughter of the king of Phoenicia, who was carried away by the god Zeus to the island of Crete. There she bore him three sons, one of which was Minos, after whom the Minoan civilisation was named.

It is more likely that the name Europe comes from the Assyrian word "*ereb*", the land of darkness and the setting sun ("*asu*", or Asia, was the land of the rising sun), but it is not such a romantic story. The Minoans flourished between the Middle and Late Bronze Ages, roughly 2000–1450 BC. We take this for granted now, but it was only about 100 years ago that their civilisation was discovered and the remains of their palaces, such as the most famous one at Knossos, were excavated, their layout and wall paintings suggesting a relatively sophisticated way of life – at least for the ruling classes.

The Minoans were superseded – and no one really knows how or why – by the Mycenaeans, whose civilisation on mainland Greece was also unearthed only in the late 19th century. They appear to have been dominant for some 300 years, until about 1100 BC and, again, it is unclear why such a strong and wealthy civilisation should have been toppled, although outside attack and internal dissent undoubtedly played a part. Whatever the reasons, their demise plunged the Greek world into a dark age which lasted until the beginning of what historians call the Archaic period (800–500 BC).

This was the age of the polis or city-state, of which Athens and Sparta emerged as the most powerful, and which gave us two words in common usage today: tyrant – a leader who seized power from the ruling nobility by means of a military coup – and oligarchy – a tightly-knit group who took control because of their wealth rather than their noble birth.

The Persian Empire was the greatest threat to Greek security, a threat which culminated in the Persian Wars of 490–450 BC, which are now remembered chiefly for the great Athenian victory at Marathon, and the heroic

defeat at Thermopylae. Although Athens and Sparta combined forces to vanquish the Persians, during the classical period which followed it was Athens which became most powerful. This was the age of Pericles, Athens's finest hour, when Plato sat at the feet of Socrates, before writing *The Republic*, on which much of Western philosophy is based.

It was the period when the Parthenon was built, democracy was developed, when Sophocles wrote *Oedipus Rex* and Euripides created *Medea*.

This golden age came to an end when Athens and Sparta wrestled for power during the long drawn-out Peloponnesian War, which weakened both sides and allowed Philip of Macedon to step into the breach. By 338 BC Philip had united the Greek city-states and when he was assassinated two years later, his son Alexander (the Great) took over. Although only 20 years old, he was already a seasoned soldier, as well as a pupil of Aristotle. In the 13 years before his early death he conquered the entire Persian Empire and amassed for himself an empire of unprecedented size and wealth.

As so often happens on the death of a

Left, Greek statue from Early Cycladic II era.
Right, detail from a fresco on Santorini.

strong ruler, squabbling broke out among hopeful successors and Alexander's kingdom was split into three: Egypt, Asia Minor and Macedon-Greece. In all of these, and the many smaller kingdoms, Alexander was revered as a god. This was known as the Hellenistic period, from the Greek word Hellenistes, meaning one who imitates the Greeks – which is exactly what everybody wanted to do. One thing that was imitated, or continued, was the concept of cities as political, commercial and social centres. Alexander had founded cities, named after himself, wherever he went. There were at least seven Alexandrias in the Hellenistic world and one Bucephala – named after his favourite horse.

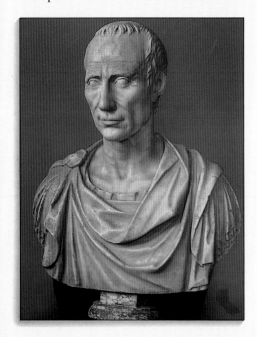

Trade and agriculture flourished in this period, but competition and war between the kingdoms weakened them and finally allowed the Romans to take control. Macedon was the first to go, in 167 BC, and Greece followed in 146 BC while Egypt held out until 31 BC.

Every Italian knows the story of Romulus and Remus, the twins abandoned on a river bank and brought up by a she-wolf, and that Romulus killed his brother, then founded Rome on the banks of the Tiber, in about 750 BC. Archaeologists agree that there was a settlement here at that time and that it grew into a flourishing city over the next century or so, but it is most likely that it was established as a trading post by the Etruscans, a highly civilised people who were also skilled craftsmen and metal workers. The Etruscans ruled Rome until 509 BC when Tarquin the Proud was ousted and a republic set up.

Rome rules: Over the next two centuries Rome conquered the rest of the Italian peninsula and in 241 BC took Sicily from the North Africa-based Carthaginians in the First Punic War. The Second Punic War began in 218 BC when Hannibal, a Carthaginian general, came up through Spain and France and made his famous crossing of the Alps with a huge army and a number of elephants. Hannibal was defeated, however, and after that there was no stopping the Romans in their quest for empire: within less than a century they had conquered Carthage and Greece and were in undisputed control of the whole Mediterranean area.

During these years the rich grew richer but the poor, ousted from their menial jobs and thrown off their land to be replaced by the slaves their masters imported from conquered provinces, grew more and more discontented. Social unrest, coupled with military threats from all over the empire, exposed the ruling class as corrupt and incompetent and led to civil war. Gnaeus Pompeius Magnus (Pompey the Great, 106–48 BC) tried to restore order, forming a Triumvirate with Marcus Crassus and Julius Caesar. But when Crassus died, the other two fell out and civil war flared again. Pompey was killed in Egypt and Caesar returned to Rome in triumph.

It was short-lived. A group of senators conspired against him and, ignoring a soothsayer's warnings about the Ides of March, Caesar was stabbed to death in the senate chamber in 44 BC. His assassins did not long outlive him. Brutus and Cassius committed suicide after defeat in Macedonia and Mark Antony (to whom Shakespeare's *Julius Caesar* gives the famous funeral oration beginning "Friends, Romans, countrymen") died at the side of Cleopatra, the Egyptian queen, after being defeated by Octavian, Caesar's heir, at the Battle of Actium.

Fortunately, Octavian, who was granted the title Augustus (the revered one), was a wise man and a strong ruler. Handling the upper classes with tact and pleasing the masses with bread and circuses, he presided over a period known as the Pax Romana – the

Roman peace – in which trade and agriculture brought prosperity and art and literature flourished, producing such great writers as Virgil and Horace.

A succession of emperors, after Augustus's death in AD 14, were soon to undo all his good works. Tiberius, Caligula and Nero were among the best-known and most eccentric villains, and they were followed by a series of weak or wicked rulers. Anarchy grew as the empire declined. In AD 286 Diocletian divided the unwieldy mass into two, the eastern and western empires. His successor Constantine, the first Christian emperor, established an eastern capital in Constantinople (Istanbul) in 330. From then

century, Pope Gregory I sent missionaries to northern Europe to convert the heathen people, and others followed their example.

But the Western Empire was disintegrating and Germanic tribes were moving in to fill the power vacuum: the Visigoths in Spain, the Ostrogoths in Italy and the Franks (who have bequeathed their name to France and Frankfurt), ruled over Gaul. It was the Franks who were to prove most powerful. Their leader Charlemagne, founder of the Carolingian dynasty, conquered the lands we know as Italy, Hungary, Germany and the Lowlands. In Rome on Christmas Day, in the year 800, the pope crowned him emperor of the west. His court at Aix-la-Chapelle (Aachen)

on the empire went two separate ways – the eastern half with more success than the west. Rome was sacked by Visigoths in 410 and the last Roman emperor deposed in 476, while the Eastern Empire, which became known as the Byzantine Empire, lasted for another thousand years.

The spread of Christianity: By the end of the 4th century Christianity had spread throughout the Empire and was gradually exported all over Europe. At the end of the sixth

became a centre of learning and culture. The title "Holy Roman Empire" was later inherited by the Austro-Hungarian Habsburgs, but as the French writer Voltaire pointed out, it was neither holy, nor Roman, nor an empire, and it was finally abolished by Napoleon. Charlemagne's own dynasty did not survive the division of lands made by his heir, Louis the Pious, and power slid into the hands of the Germanic aristocracy.

There were huge movements of people all over Europe during these years. Lombards advanced through Italy in the 6th and 7th centuries, Slavs settled in the Balkans, Muslims from North Africa attacked Spain, con-

Left, marble bust of Gaius Julius Caesar (100BC–44BC). **Above**, Cicero asks Rome to unite against the "public enemy", Cataline.

quering most of the peninsula by 714, and Arab raids on Constantinople threatened the security of the Eastern Empire. Despite this, the empire was strong enough to impose Orthodox Christianity on the Russian and Bulgar peoples, and it was only during the 11th century, when Turks overran much of Asia Minor and the Normans occupied southern Italy, that its power began to wane.

The Normans were descendants of the Vikings, who had been granted land in northern France early in the 10th century after repeated incursions into the Frankish kingdoms. They were soon integrated with the French nobility and strong enough to conquer England and sweep southwards, occupying southern Italy and seizing Sicily from the Arabs. Roger the Norman was crowned in Palermo in 1130 and, although Norman rule lasted barely 60 years, wonderful examples of the fusion of Arabic and Norman architecture still remain on the island.

The Crusades: Towards the end of the 11th century rumours spread through Christendom that the Ottoman Turks, who had held Jerusalem since the 7th century, were making life difficult for Christian pilgrims and in 1096 the First Crusade set out to liberate the Holy City. Although the Crusaders were initially successful, the Muslims retained the city and the next three centuries saw a succession of crusades, which despite occasional gains, were ultimately defeated. A huge mythology has grown up around the exploits of the Knights Templars and the Hospitallers, the members of military monastic orders who led the crusades, and the defeat of Saladin and the capture of Richard Lionheart are the stuff of heroic fairy tales. In fact, although there was genuine religious zeal at first, there was also a lot of avarice and self-interest on the part of many who went to fight for the cross against the crescent.

The Muslim world was less successful in holding on to its lands in Spain than it was in the east, although the *reconquista*, the reconquest, was a slow process. The Christian kingdoms of Castile and Aragon gained ground during the 11th century, and the fabled hero El Cid won Valencia from the Moors in 1094. Portugal was founded as a Christian kingdom in 1139 by diverted Crusaders, but it took another century before the Muslims were ousted from the whole peninsula, apart from the Emirate of Granada,

which remained a part of Islam until 1492, when Ferdinand and Isabella, the Catholic monarchs, succeeded in uniting the country under their rule. That was the same year Columbus set sail for the Americas.

It would be difficult to over-emphasise the importance of the Christian church. As the religion spread across the continent, missionary communities had been founded, centres of contemplation, self-denial and learning. St Benedict had laid down the rules for monastic life at Monte Cassino in Italy in AD 527. In the Dark Ages that followed the fall of the Western Roman Empire, the only culture that survived in any form was in the monasteries. Except in Italy, where there

was always some secular education, all learning and literacy was acquired in monastic schools. The monasteries were also the recipients of gifts of land and money from the wealthy, who hoped to lay up treasure in heaven. They therefore became not only large landowners but patrons of the arts, which is why most buildings, paintings and sculptures that survive have religious themes.

Styles in ecclesiastical architecture spread rapidly across Europe, partly because of the movement of pilgrims, who carried new ideas with them, and partly because some of the great monastic houses, such as Cluny in Burgundy, ruled strings of monasteries, stretching across the continent. Byzantine architecture had spread from Constantinople, and many examples of its domed churches can be seen in Greece. The Romanesque style – so-called by a 19th-century French art historian because it used the rounded, classical arch and had a solid grandeur which resembled that of Rome – appeared everywhere during the 11th and 12th centuries. There are many pure Romanesque churches still standing, scattered through France, Italy and Spain.

Gothic followed Romanesque, its great churches and cathedrals typified by pointed arches, vaulted ceilings, flying buttresses and numerous windows. The cathedral at

wealthy males had access to it. Nevertheless, by the 13th century, most members of the upper class, of both sexes, were able to read, even if they could not write.

A new, vernacular literature emerged, to amuse the new reading public. There were tales of courtly love, in which women are served and adored by their noble knights – an art form which began with the troubadours, travelling lyric poets from Provence, and spread through much of Western Europe. Perhaps the greatest poem in this tradition is Dante's *Divina Commedia*. Epics celebrated the deeds of real or mythical heroes, and medieval tales reached the widest audience because they could be acted out.

Chartres, southwest of Paris, is an impressive example of early Gothic, from the middle of the 12th century. Most of the surviving secular Gothic architecture is in Italy, such as the elegant Doge's Palace in Venice and the Palazzo Vecchio in Florence.

Ancient universities: During the 12th century monasteries lost their monopoly on education and secular schools were set. By the century's end, universities had been established in Oxford, Paris and Bologna. This was far from being popular education: only

Left, **Arab court painting.** **Above**, **Pope Urbain dedicates a high altar at Cluny, France, in 1095.**

But learning leads to independent thinking, and this is a dangerous thing. Inspired by the 14th-century Italian poet, Petrarch, scholars began to read Greek and Roman texts, and went on to re-examine man's role in the world. These ideas, known as humanism, spread throughout Europe and one of their most important proponents, the Dutch scholar Erasmus (1466–1536) also called for reform of the Church. In 1450 Johannes Gutenberg had set up his printing press in Mainz and the works of Erasmus, among others, reached a wide audience.

For most people in Europe in the 14th century, neither courtly love nor humanist thought were very important. They were occupied with trying to survive under circumstances even more dire than usual. The Black Death, an epidemic of the bubonic plague, arrived from the Far East in 1346 and spread quickly throughout the continent. Between 1348 and 1349 around one third of the population died and further outbreaks in the 1360s and 1370s also had huge mortality rates. Its impact was enormous.

Initially, land lay idle for lack of labour, food was scarce and prices rose sharply. In the long term the lack of manpower became a bargaining tool for the surviving peasants and contributed to the end of serfdom as well as an increase in wages and living condi-

tions. Under the feudal system, large landowners had received service from smaller ones, a system which spread from the monarch down to the lowliest peasant. At the top of the scale, knights would owe "knight service" to their masters and would have to fight when called upon. At the lower end, humble plot owners would have to work on their masters' land as well as on their own. After the plague this system gradually collapsed and peasants were able to take over some of the untended land.

None of this happened without a fight. There were peasant revolts and urban unrest everywhere, against authorities reluctant to see any power go to the people. Contributing to the unrest were royal demands for taxes to finance long drawn out wars, such as the Hundred Years' War. This was a power struggle between the English and French kings for territory in France, which actually lasted from 1337 to 1453, interrupted by a 28-year truce. It was a war littered with famous battles and heroic deeds, most importantly the leadership and martyrdom of Joan of Arc, burned at Rouen by the English as a heretic in 1431, and later canonised. The English were eventually defeated, leaving the aptly named Charles the Bold (1467–77) the undisputed ruler of what was now France.

The other great power struggle during this period was centred on the papacy. The Hohenstaufen rulers of the Holy Roman Empire had constantly threatened the security of the papal states during the late 12th and 13th century and even when the last of that dynasty was wiped out in 1268 the papacy still felt insecure and decided to move the headquarters of the Catholic Church from Rome to Avignon. This upset many Christians who believed that Rome and the Vicar of Christ should be inseparable, and worried more worldly people, who thought that a pope on French soil would be too easily manipulated by the French monarchy. Back went the pope to Rome in 1377 but almost immediately the Great Schism occurred – a period between 1378 and 1417, when two or three men, surrounded by ambitious and persuasive followers, simultaneously claimed the right to occupy the throne of St Peter.

The Church's stability was under attack from other areas, too, in part from those who believed it had become too worldly and should be relieved of some of its lands and subject to fairer taxation, and in part by the emergence of several heretical groupings. The Cathars, or Albigensians, in the south of France had been destroyed early in the 13th century by a combination of conversion – led by St Dominic who founded the Dominican order – and brute force at the hands of Crusaders, diverted from expeditions to the Holy Land, to stamp out heresy closer to home. But during the time of the Great Schism, two other heresies appeared: the Lollards, inspired by the English scholar John Wyclif, rejected both the authority of the pope and the doctrine of transubstantiation; and the Hussites, led by the Czech Jan Hus, whose beliefs were similar to those of Wyclif and who flourished for another two decades after their leader was burned at the stake in 1415.

The Reformation: All these ideas, and more, were to re-emerge and bring about the Reformation in the following century. The new printing presses rolled out copies of the scriptures, and the pamphlets issued by the new movements' leaders were widely disseminated to a reading public. Martin Luther, a German monk who led the attack on abuse of Church power, was excommunicated but his ideas spread rapidly and many Lutheran churches were established in the German states after the Peace of Augsburg (1555) gave individual princes the right to decide

St Bartholomew's Day Massacre, but they still had enough influence, when the Wars of Religion came to an end, to obtain toleration for their views under the Edict of Nantes.

The Catholic Church did not take all this lying down. The Jesuit order was founded by a zealous Spaniard, Ignatius Loyola, whose name is inextricably linked with the Inquisition. The organisation had the backing of Catholic monarchs such as Philip II of Spain, and it was responsible for investigating and stamping out heresy. Paranoia about any unorthodox beliefs led to the witch hunts which swept Europe during the late 16th and early 17th centuries, when people would be charged with witchcraft and convicted on the

the religion of their subjects – not exactly what the 20th century would call freedom of religion, but it was a start.

John Calvin was the other great leader of the Reformation. A French lawyer, he began his work in Zurich and his influence spread throughout Holland, Hungary, Poland and parts of Germany as well as his native France where his followers, known as Huguenots, were involved in the 16th-century Wars of Religion. Their strength lessened after thousands of them were killed in 1572 during the

Left, Joan of Arc. **Above**, John Calvin; officer cadet in the Thirty Years' War.

flimsiest of evidence. The Vatican and over-enthusiastic Catholic authorities may have started this craze, but Protestants also became infected with the madness: the custom was exported to the New World, where the Salem trials in Massachusetts were the best-known but not the only examples.

Decades of religious dissent eventually erupted in the Thirty Years' War, sparked off by a Protestant revolt in Prague against the Habsburg emperor Frederick II. It erupted when Hussites stormed the town hall and ejected the consuls and seven other citizens from the window, beginning the curious Prague tradition of defenestration.

From the 15th century, expansionist aims took over from religious ones. Spain resumed its on-going war with the Netherlands, the king of Sweden invaded Germany, and France took up the cudgels against her old enemy, the Habsburg empire. The main conflict ended with the Peace of Westphalia (1648), which granted Protestants freedom of worship, but by this time about a third of the population of some German states had died, due to warfare, disease or famine.

War between Spain and France rumbled on for another decade, but these were years of Spanish decline. Spain and Portugal had established the first great colonial empires, based on the early voyages of discovery by such explorers as Vasco da Gama and Christopher Columbus. Spanish power, consolidated by Ferdinand and Isabella's reconquest of the country, was given a further boost when the Habsburg Charles V of Austria came to the Spanish throne and, in 1519, was elected Holy Roman Emperor, en event viewed with some alarm by the ruling House of Bourbon in France.

Charles's empire, he said, was so vast that it was one over which "the sun never set". Habsburg tombstones were inscribed AEIOU, meaning *Austria est emperare orbi universo* (All the earth is subject to Austria), and there were few who would have disagreed – at least in public. When Charles abdicated he bequeathed all the Habsburg lands, except those in Austria itself, to his son Philip II of Spain, who went on to add the Portuguese empire to his own after the death of the king of Portugal in battle in 1578. With gold and silver flooding in from the New World to fill the national coffers this seemed to many in Spain to be a true golden age.

Spectacular successes were followed by miserable failure. Wars with France, the continued battle for independence by the Protestant Netherlands, and the defeat of the Armada by the English navy (1588), all proved extremely expensive. When recession hit the Americas in the early 17th century and the flood of silver dwindled to a trickle, it must have been clear that the balmy days were over. Catalonia revolted when asked to shoulder some of the costs of empire, and Portugal followed suit. Although Catalonia was soon recovered – to the lasting despair of its inhabitants – Portugal remained independent and the battle for supremacy over the Netherlands was finally lost.

This is not to say that the Spanish empire was not worth having. When the last of that

branch of the Habsburgs died out and the French Bourbon monarch Philip V took the throne, Charles, Archduke of Austria, was sufficiently alarmed by growing French power to take up arms in the War of the Spanish Succession (1701–13). It was a conflict which nearly brought both the Spanish and French economies to their knees but when it ended, with the Treaty of Utrecht in 1713, it confirmed the right of the Bourbon king to the throne of Spain.

Fortunately for human progress, the sorry saga of war and power grabbing is not exclusively what any country's history is about. Wonderful things were happening in the

Left, detail of a Japanese screen (*circa* **1593**) commemorating the arrival of Portuguese traders. **Right**, *The Cannon Shot*, by Dutch painter W. van de Velde de Jonge.

field of artistic endeavour during these centuries. The Renaissance began in Florence, spread to other Italian cities such as Venice and Rome, then northwards through Europe. The humanist interest in classical art forms made artists aware that Europe had a cultural past and there were wealthy patrons prepared to finance its rebirth.

Patrons of the arts: The powerful Medici banking family, who controlled so much that happened in Florence, were dominant in promoting art in the city, but it is also the wool trade which we have to thank for some of the greatest paintings, sculptures and architectural gems the world has ever known. Florence had grown rich on wool and its

wealthiest merchants, members of the Arte della Lana, or wool guild, not only provided the capital which had made their city Europe's financial capital by the end of the 14th century, but also sponsored works of art.

Their motives may have been genuine artistic interest, a desire to flaunt their wealth, or a pious wish to create and adorn churches because they felt guilty about making such huge profits. Whatever the reasons, the results were spectacular. Donatello was commissioned to work on many of the city's civic projects, Giotto designed the campanile for the new cathedral and Uccello made early experiments with perspective in his painting.

From Venice sprang Leonardo da Vinci, the archetypal Renaissance man – a scientist, mathematician and philosopher as well as an artist. In the north of Europe Albrecht Dürer changed the status of woodcuts and engravings from craftwork to an important art form. Hieronymus Bosch painted mythical monsters and Pieter Bruegel's rural scenes were a landmark in the shift from religious or allegorical themes to secular subjects.

In the late 15th and early 16th centuries the hub of the Italian Renaissance moved from Florence to Rome, as the papacy poured money into the reconstruction and embellishment of the city. Among the artistic riches this produced are Michelangelo's *Pietà* and *The Last Judgement* in the Sistine Chapel, Raphael's cartoons, also created for the Sistine Chapel, and Bramante's classical architectural designs. Later in the 16th century Palladio, who based his work on the great public buildings of ancient Rome, created a style which was emulated all over Europe.

Mannerism grew out of the Renaissance, producing such masters as the goldsmith Cellini, the Venetian artists Titian and Tintoretto, as well as the dramatic work of El Greco in Spain, and an architectural style that was so much admired by the French king François I that he used it in the construction of his château at Fontainebleau.

All artistic movements sooner or later produce reactions, and the reaction to Mannerism was the florid baroque style of the 17th century, exemplified in Italy by Guido Reni and the sculptor Bernini, in Spain by Velásquez, who won the lifelong patronage of Philip IV, but most famously of all by the Flemish painter, Rubens.

The Dutch school of painting also flourished in the 17th century, stimulated by a wave of national self-confidence following the Netherlands' deliverance from Spanish rule and its success as a trading nation. The domestic scenes painted by Vermeer and the works of Rembrandt were among the most important of the School's prolific output.

The 17th century in Europe was the age of absolute monarchy – a system under which kings dismissed any idea of consultation and held tightly to the reins of government, believing that God had granted them a divine right to rule. The concept is neatly summed up by Louis XIV's famous phrase "*L'état c'est moi*". Louis was the most famous and flamboyant of the absolute monarchs, whose ideas of personal control may have been influenced by the enormous power wielded by ministers – Cardinal Richelieu and Cardinal Mazarin – during his father's reign and his own regency, for he was still a baby when his father died.

Louis asserted his authority over the Church and created a standing army to reinforce his secular powers, and to fight against Spain and the Holy Roman Empire. Nobles were obliged to attend the newly-glorified Palace of Versailles where the king could keep an eye on them, and Louis' most able minister, Colbert, who some believe to have been the power behind the throne, created a strong

known as the Philosophes, inspired by the scientific discoveries of Sir Isaac Newton and the thinking of John Locke, began to disseminate the ideas of the Enlightenment. They believed that traditional explanations of the universe and man's place in it could no longer be taken for granted and that truth and meaning could only be discovered through reason and experience. Voltaire was the greatest exponent of Enlightenment ideals and his oft-quoted dictum "I may disagree with what you say but I will defend to the death your right to say it," encapsulates his concern for toleration and humanitarian ideals.

From this movement sprang the seemingly contradictory notion of enlightened

navy, reorganised the tax system, set up academies of science and arts and centralised the unwieldy bureaucracy. Although harvest failures, continuous wars and court extravagance undid much of his good works, France was still strong enough to impress and frighten other European nations at the time of Louis' death in 1715.

Absolutism was continued, albeit in a diluted form, by Louis XV and it was during his reign that a group of French thinkers

Left, Cosimo I by Vasari from the ceiling of Florence's Palazzo Vecchio. **Above**, Botticelli's *Judith*, from Florence's Uffizi Gallery.

despotism. Catherine the Great of Russia was influenced by its ideas when she began her programme of reform and Emperor Joseph II of Austria's attempt to abolish serfdom appears to have a humanitarian basis, although he may well have been more strongly influenced by the ideas and example of his mother, Maria Theresa (1717–80). Known as "the mother of the nation" she is said to have taken a personal interest in her subjects, opposed injustice and once claimed: "I've never had servants, only friends." The views of her servants (or friends) have not been recorded.

The court of Maria Theresa had welcomed

the child prodigy, Wolfgang Amadeus Mozart, but it was not until the year after her death that the 25-year-old musician left his home town of Salzburg to seek his fortune in Vienna. A few years later he was joined by Haydn – middle-aged and already famous – and in the 1790s the young Beethoven also arrived in the capital, making it the musical centre of an increasingly culture-conscious Europe.

The French Revolution: Music was not uppermost in the minds of the French in the late 18th century. The government was bankrupt, largely due to costly intervention in the American War of Independence. The poor were angry about the disproportionate share

This apparent success was not welcomed by other European powers, who feared that revolutionary ideas would spread across their own countries. Austria and Prussia invaded France in 1792, Britain a year later. These attacks engendered paranoia: conspiracy theories abounded and 1,000 suspected counter-revolutionaries were executed. France was declared a republic and Louis XVI was guillotined, together with his queen, Marie Antoinette, whom history has wrongly accused of suggesting that those who could not afford bread should eat cake.

Revolts by those opposed to the Revolution broke out at home. The moderates in the new government – the Girondins – were

of the taxes they were obliged to pay. The bourgeoisie were resentful of the privileges of the aristocracy, and there was growing criticism of absolutism. Louis XVI's attempt to raise taxes and reduce privileges led to the formation of a National Assembly, the establishment of a commune in Paris, peasant revolts, and the abolition of feudalism. The Declaration of the Rights of Man – *Liberté, Égalité, Fraternité* – was proclaimed in 1789 and a new constitutional government was organised. After his attempt to leave the country was foiled in 1791, Louis accepted the constitution and for a while it seemed that a bloodless revolution had achieved its aims.

overthrown by the Jacobins, and the Committee of Public Safety, led by Maximilien Robespierre, was set up. The subsequent "Reign of Terror" left thousands dead and only ended when Robespierre himself became one of its victims. The new power group, the Directory, ended the blood-letting, but was only able to keep the peace with the aid of the army and this increase in military influence led, in 1799, to the coup of 18 Brumaire (the revolution had introduced a new calendar, and Brumaire was the new name for November). The coup was led by Napoleon Bonaparte and, after serving as Consul for four years, he abolished the republic and was declared emperor, heading a military dictatorship which reversed most of the reforms achieved by the Revolution before the Terror.

Napoleon had won his stripes fighting against the Austrians in Italy. Despite subsequent defeat at the Battle of the Nile, he was still strong enough to be a hero at home, to compel Austria to accept French dominance in Italy, and to emerge the apparent victor of the Peace of Amiens in 1802. It was a fleeting peace. Britain declared war again the following year and defeated the new emperor's fleet off Cape Trafalgar in 1805. It was to be his last defeat for some years: against a coalition of Britain, Austria, Russia and Naples, Napoleon seemed invincible, notching up victory after victory, causing the downfall of the Holy Roman Empire and winning the support of Austria after his marriage to an Austrian princess. Poor Josephine, his first wife, appears to have been a casualty of war.

Small in stature, grand in his designs and one of the most brilliant generals Europe has produced, Napoleon became too greedy for his own good. His disastrous defeat in the snows of Moscow in 1812, which only one-tenth of his army survived, was compounded by his long-running conflict in Spain – the Peninsular War. Having handed the Spanish throne to his brother in 1808, he spent the next five years fighting aggrieved Spaniards and their British allies before his defeat by the Duke of Wellington at Vitoria and an allied army at Leipzig in 1813. When Paris subsequently fell he was exiled to the Mediterranean island of Elba. He staged a comeback the following year but the combined forces of Prussia and Britain brought him down at Waterloo in modern Belgium, and he was shipped off to distant St Helena, in the South Atlantic. Louis XVIII was restored to the French throne.

When the victorious allies sat round the table at the Congress of Vienna, their main aims were to stop France ever being so dominant again and, of course, to gain as much for themselves as they could. Austria kept Venice, which had previously been independent, Russia gained most of Poland, and the Netherlands became a new kingdom.

Left, Delacroix's *Liberty leading the People* captured the spirit of revolutionary France. **Right**, Napoleon Bonaparte crosses the Alps.

The most dominant man around the table may well have been Metternich, Austrian prince and statesman who spent the next three decades attempting to stem the rising tide of nationalism both in Austria and abroad. Nationalist sentiments, far from being extinguished, were strengthened by opposition and in 1848 popular revolutions broke out all over Europe. The first revolt, in Paris, inspired others in Italy and throughout the Austrian Empire, as Croats, Czechs and Hungarians demanded recognition as independent ethnic states. Optimism was high and initial gains were made, but the overthrow of the Orléans monarchy and proclamation of the Second Republic in France led

not to democracy or liberalism but to the establishment of the Second Empire. The expulsion of Austrian rulers from northern Italy and Spanish Bourbons from the south was short-lived, and independence in other parts of the Austro-Hungarian Empire was soon crushed.

Further east, the Ottoman Empire did not remain untouched by demands for self-determination and it was here that nationalism had one of its first successes. In 1822 a newly formed National Assembly declared Greece an independent state. Liberal-minded people from all over Europe pledged their support, stirred by the struggle for freedom in the land where democracy was born. European governments, of a less romantic turn of mind, tried to stay out of it, but Russian intervention in response to Turkish atrocities changed their minds. Britain and France pitched in, sunk the Turkish fleet in Navarino Bay and, together with Russia, guaranteed Greek independence in 1830. Monarchy, in the form of Otto of Bavaria, was drafted from the stock of German royalty to give the nation suitable status, a practice followed by other emergent nations.

Fear of Russian encroachment was a dominant theme in Europe in the middle of the 19th century, particularly when it involved control of the entrance to the Black Sea, the

so-called "warm water port". It did not take a great deal of political acumen to realise that the Russian doctrine of Pan-Slavism, by which Russia assumed the role of protector of smaller Slav nations who were struggling for independence, only came into play when it furthered Russia's interests. Elsewhere, in Poland for example, nationalist movements were quickly put down. Russia was also quick to intervene in the Hungarian revolution in 1848 and this, together with her occupation of Balkan territories in 1853, contributed to the outbreak of the Crimean War, a chaotic and mismanaged affair in which half a million men died.

Elsewhere in Europe, nationalism was lying low, recovering from the blows dealt to it after the 1848 revolutions, but by no means defeated. One of its strengths was its connections with Romanticism, a movement which swept the Continent during the late 18th and 19th century. It was, in part, a way of trying to make sense of the world after the enormous social dislocations brought about by the French and American revolutions; in part, a reaction against the ugliness of the Industrial Revolution. Romantics harped back to a Golden Age: for some, it was classical Greece, for others, the medieval world of courtly love and chivalry.

Cultural flowering: It was a period of cultural renaissance. In France, Rousseau idealised the "noble savage"; in Germany, Goethe and Schiller extolled spiritual freedom and the beauty of nature; literature and the local language was rediscovered and extolled in Catalonia and Provence. Beethoven's *Pastoral* symphony was a deeply Romantic work and composers such as Dvorak and Tchaikovsky were influenced by folk music and legends. Idealisation of the past and the search for ethnic origins blended smoothly with the political aspirations of people rejecting the notion that they should live under the yoke of foreign powers.

The foreign power which governed most of the Italian peninsula was that of Austro-Hungary, whose chief statesman, Prince Clemens Metternich, once described Italy as "only a geographical expression". Although the peninsula had never been one nation, a unification movement known as the *Risorgimento* (Resurrection) now pressed for one. Such romantically-named groups as the *Carbonari* were unsuccessful in uniting the 13 separate states under Italian rule, but Camillo Cavour, the prime minister of Piedmont, ejected the Austrians from northern Italy in 1859 and the following year Guiseppe Garibaldi, Italy's best-known and most colourful freedom fighter, took southern Italy from the Spanish Bourbons. The new Kingdom of Italy was formed in 1861, although the Vatican territory remained under French control until 1870.

In Germany, the situation was even more complicated, and the fact that the 39 separate states became one unified country in 1871 was mainly due to the political skill and machinations of the Prussian prime minister

Otto von Bismarck. His "blood and iron" policy involved allying Prussia with Austria against Denmark over the control of Schleswig and Holstein. The situation there had long been so tortuous that a British prime minister, Lord Palmerston, once said: "There are only three men who have ever understood it: one is Prince Albert and he is dead; the second was a German professor who became mad; I am the third and I have forgotten all about it."

Bismarck then provoked a short, sharp war with his former ally, which ended with Austria's defeat at Sadowa in 1866. Finally he engineered a war with France, the Franco-Prussian War of 1870, which he won with

Commune was brutally put down, the death toll was enormous, and all the revolutionary elements were subsequently imprisoned or exiled, which did great damage to hopes for socialism in France for several years to come. Despite this, Karl Marx may have been right in regarding it as "the dawn of a new era", for socialist parties soon developed throughout the rest of Europe.

In the newly-united Germany, the Social Democratic Party was formed in 1875, although Bismarck soon forced it underground. Socialist parties of various hues were formed in Austria, Belgium, Italy and Switzerland during the 1880s and early 1890s, by which time the German party had re-emerged and

little difficulty, enabling him to grab the border territories of Alsace and Lorraine and unite the whole Germanic area under Prussian control. Bismarck was not a man to mess with: "Nothing should be left to an invaded people except their eyes for weeping," was one of his maxims.

In Paris, the invaded people were left with little except a deep sense of humiliation, which led to the establishment of the socialist Paris Commune, modelling itself on the Jacobin-dominated Assembly of 1793. The

Left, Goethe, champion of German Classicism.
Above, Garibaldi fighting the French in 1849.

become dominant among European parties of the left.

Russia, which would be the first country to embrace state socialism was, at this stage, still troubling the other European powers by her encroachments into the Balkans. At the Berlin Congress of 1878 Russia's possession of the Caucasus was confirmed and she was given control of Bessarabia. Bulgaria was declared an autonomous province, and Serbia, Montenegro and Romania all had their independence confirmed, while poor old Bosnia-Herzogovina merely exchanged Turkish for Austro-Hungarian control.

The Berlin settlement was not satisfactory. The Ottoman Empire remained "the sick man of Europe" and complicated relationships between the six Great Powers which existed now that so many disparate states had been unified. These powers – Great Britain, France, Italy, Germany, Russia and Austro-Hungary – were also rivals for overseas colonies. During the years between 1870 and 1914, they carved up most of Africa and the Pacific between them, with Britain and France taking the lion's share. This determined drive for empire was motivated by political, strategic and, perhaps most importantly, economic factors.

Rivalries within Europe and the overseas colonies led to the alliance system, designed the French Impressionists who emerged in the 1860s and received a decidedly frosty reception. Scorned by the official Paris Salon, artists such as Monet, Renoir, Degas and Pissarro held their own exhibition in 1874, when the name Impressionist was first used by a critic as a derogatory term. They held eight such breakaway exhibitions during the next dozen years, by which time a new movement had arrived, proving perhaps that it is impossible to be new and shocking for long.

The Post-Impressionists, the most celebrated of whom were Cézanne, Gauguin and van Gogh, emphasised strong colours and powerful emotions in their works. They were followed by the Fauves – another somewhat

to create a balance of power. Germany, Austro-Hungary and Italy formed the Triple Alliance, while Russia, France and an initially hostile Great Britain became partners in the Triple Entente. It was this system which led the European governments inexorably into World War I.

Leisure pursuits: The people of Europe, meantime, were having fun exploring their countries and the continent on the new railways: learning how to ski in the Alps and how to bathe in the Mediterranean Riviera. New travel moved ideas more quickly and got artists out in the open to paint. Preeminent among the painters of nature were derogatory term meaning "wild beasts" – led by Matisse and Derain. In Austria the Vienna Secession, led by Gustav Klimt, was yet another rebellion against conventional art forms. From the Secession emerged not only Klimt's own erotic images, but the work of the Expressionist artists Egon Schiele and Oskar Kokoschka, and *Jugendstil*, the Austrian version of art nouveau, of which wonderful examples can be seen in the Austrian capital today.

The fluid, sensuous forms of art nouveau glorified Paris in the years following the 1900 Exposition Universelle, and can be seen at their most fantastic in the work of

Gaudi in Barcelona. But Brussels can claim the first nouveau building – Victor Horta's Tassel house – and is also the home of the Palais Stoclet, designed by the Austrian architect Josef Hoffmann.

At the same time Debussy, once described as a musical impressionist, was composing prolifically and Eric Satie was creating his playful, idiosyncratic music. "Realist" writers such as Zola, Chekhov and Ibsen were forcing their readers to face sometimes unpalatable truths, while the music halls of Berlin and Montmartre were never more busy or frivolous.

The end of the 19th and beginning of the 20th century was also a period when technol-

ernment had also been made in most industrialised countries by the turn of the century, including the rights to free speech and freedom of the press. Trade unions had been given full recognition in France by 1884 and in Germany soon after Bismarck's death in 1890.

Women's rights: These two countries also gave all men the right to vote in 1871, although women had to wait a lot longer – until 1918 in Germany and until the end of World War II in France. In Switzerland, women did not win the right to vote until 1971, although universal male suffrage was introduced in 1874. Belgium and Spain followed suit in the 1890s, although Portugal, Italy and the

ogy was making huge strides. Guglielmo Marconi constructed the first radio in a Bologna attic in 1894. The Paris-Orléans railway was electrified in 1900, the same year that Count von Zeppelin's dirigible made its first flight and nine years before Bleriot flew an aircraft across the English Channel. Karl Benz had produced his first petrol-engined Motorwagen in 1885 and ten years later so many cars had appeared that the 1895 Paris-Bordeaux race was run.

Moves towards democratic forms of gov-

Left, the Berlin-Potsdam railway, *circa* 1850. **Above**, a 19th-century view of Monte-Carlo.

Austro-Hungarian empire lagged behind.

Immunisation and improved sanitation were improving life expectancy rates and slums were being cleared in most major cities. Bismarck initiated a social security system, offering insurance payments for sickness, accident and old age, and during the 1880s most other European countries introduced some or all of these benefits. All in all, unless one was very poor, life was not too bad, comparatively, in Europe in the first years of the 20th century.

Then a Serb nationalist shot the Austrian Archduke Franz Ferdinand in Sarajevo in 1914, and the world changed forever.

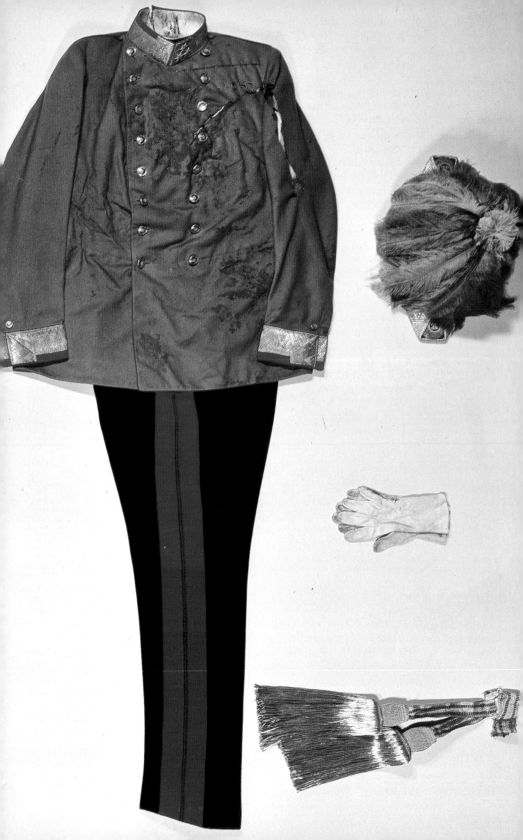

World War I, which was sparked off by the Austrian Archduke's assassination at Sarajevo, produced carnage on a scale never before imagined. An estimated 20 million people died before the Armistice was signed on 11 November 1918. This, it was said, had been the war to end all wars, and the Fourteen Point Peace Plan put forward by the American President Wilson at the Treaty of Versailles and subsequent treaties signed with Turkey and Austro-Hungary were supposed to lay the foundations for a lasting peace. In fact, they did exactly the opposite. The old empires of Germany, Russia, Austro-Hungary and Turkey were broken up and the map of Europe completely redrawn.

Alsace and Lorraine were returned to France, a new Polish state was created, with the Danzig Corridor giving it access, through German land, to the sea. Czechoslovakia also became an independent state and was awarded Bohemia and Moravia, which had been part of the Austrian empire. Hungarian-controlled land went towards the formation of Yugoslavia, while Trieste, Istria and the south Tyrol were ceded to Italy. The Ottoman empire had to relinquish much of the land it held in the Middle East, but an attempt to occupy part of Turkey itself provoked a revolt led by General Kemal Ataturk.

These divisions of land caused a great deal of bitterness and resentment. Even more doomed to failure were the restrictions imposed on the defeated German nation. The Rhineland was occupied by Allied troops, the Saarland governed by an international commission, Germany's overseas colonies were put under the control of the newly-created League of Nations, rearmament was forbidden and the size of the army strictly limited. Most painful of all were the crippling financial reparations demanded by Britain and France. They were never fully paid but they contributed to the near collapse of the German economy and engendered huge resentment, which Adolf Hitler was able to manipulate during his rise to power.

The 1920s and 1930s were decades of

totalitarian regimes and a great deal of hardship due to the severe economic recession of the Depression. But it was also a time of experiment and change and artistic expression flourished. The Italian artist de Chirico and Spanish painters, Miró and Dalí, joined the mainly French Surrealist movement. Theatre became experimental, with Bertholt Brecht in Germany, Luigi Pirandello in Italy and Jean Cocteau in France producing innovative work. Leading proponents of the newest art form, cinema, were the German Fritz

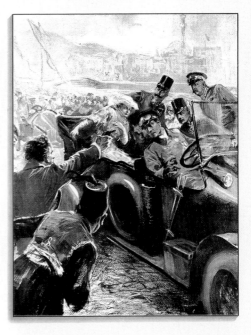

Lang, the Hungarian Alexander Korda and Luis Buñuel, a Spaniard working in France. Architecture was also taking chances: the Bauhaus school in Germany produced startling modernist designs, and art deco, which took its name from the 1925 Exposition Internationale des Arts Decoratifs in Paris produced delightfully new geometric forms.

But the ugly reality of what was happening in many parts of Europe could not be hidden behind these attractive facades. The newly created states in Eastern Europe were bedevilled by nationalist tensions and political instability. In Poland, a coup in 1926 left the country a virtual dictatorship under Marshal

<u>Left</u>, Archduke Ferdinand's blood-spattered uniform. <u>Right</u>, the assassination at Sarajevo.

Pilsudski. In Hungary, there was a fleeting period of communist control, and a much longer one under Romanian occupation. Ethnic arguments between Croats, Serbs and Slovenes in Yugoslavia culminated in the murder of King Alexander by a Croat separatist in 1934. Czechoslovakia was the most successful: under the much respected President Thomas Masaryk, democracy survived into the mid-1930s, but in the German Sudetenland a strong national socialist party dominated the latter part of the decade.

In Greece, the interwar years saw constant rivalry between republicans, led by Venizelos, and royalists, loyal to King Constantine. When the monarchy was re-

stored, in 1935, after a period of republicanism, the king could rule only with the backing of General Metaxas, a virtual dictator.

In the Iberian peninsula Portugal, a republic since the overthrow of the monarchy in 1910, came under military control in 1926, and the dictatorship of Antonio Salazar, who was to rule for the next 36 years, began in 1932. In Spain a period of military rule by General Primo de Rivera, and the abdication of King Alfonso XIII in 1931, left a shaky republic, torn with dissent between left and right. In 1936, a military revolt led by Francisco Franco initiated a civil war which lasted for three years, with Franco's nationalists

supported by Germany and Italy, the republicans by the Soviet Union and the International Brigade of volunteers.

In 1937, Guernica entered history as the first town to be bombed from the air, an event which has been immortalised by Picasso's painting *Guernica*. Franco's forces eventually defeated the republicans in 1939. He took control of a demoralised country, its people near starvation, and ruled at the head of a Falangist (neo-fascist) government until his death in 1975.

Rise of fascism: The first fascist party had arisen in Italy, where Benito Mussolini manipulated fears of communism to gain support and, in 1922, marched on Rome with his 25,000 Blackshirts. King Victor Emmanuel III reluctantly asked him to form a government, and four years later Mussolini declared himself Il Duce, the leader of the Italian people. Savagely repressing his opponents, he embarked on massive programmes of public works, forged links with the German Nazi party and, in 1935, in an attempt to build an empire, invaded Abyssinia. Emboldened by the fact that the League of Nations, the body formed to prevent war, simply imposed a few economic sanctions, he walked into Albania four years later.

In Germany, Adolf Hitler also used the fear of communism, which was rife in the years following the 1917 Bolshevik Revolution in Russia, to win support for his National Socialist party. He was also able to exploit the resentment felt by the German people over the terms of the Versailles treaty, whose effects were compounded by the economic crisis of the Depression after the 1929 Wall Street Crash.

The weak Weimar Republic could not survive and in 1933 Hitler became chancellor of Germany. When President von Hindenburg died the following year, he established himself as Führer, banning opposition parties, giving power to the Gestapo, and initiating against Germany's Jewish population the increasingly repressive measures which would culminate in the holocaust.

In 1936 Hitler reoccupied the Rhineland and two year later, with the connivance of the pro-Nazi Austrian Chancellor Seyss-Inquart, invaded Austria and proclaimed the Anschluss, the union of the two countries. Later that year, at the Munich Conference, Britain and France capitulated to Hitler's demands and allowed him control of the Sudetenland, but the "peace in our time" which the British prime minister Neville Chamberlain thought this ensured lasted less than a year. Hitler seized the rest of Czecho-slovakia, signed a non-aggression pact with the Soviet Union, then invaded Poland. It was the end of appeasement and the beginning of World War II, in which Germany, Italy and, later, Japan, took on the world.

When the conflict finally came to an end in May 1945, Europe embarked on the long, costly process of putting itself together again. Shattered cities had to be rebuilt, particularly Cologne and Dresden which the Allies had relentlessly bombed. Warsaw's historic

to keep within her sphere of interest all the areas occupied by the Red Army when the conflict ended. By the end of the decade, all these states had Soviet-dominated governments – although Yugoslavia and Romania soon installed their own brand of communism. Germany itself was divided in two, and the allied powers given zones of occupation in Berlin. In 1948 tensions between the powers resulted in the Soviet Union blockading the city and the Americans and British airlifting in supplies. Subsequent discontent in the Eastern zone, due to the marked difference in living standards, led to the construction in 1961 of the Berlin Wall, the most potent symbol of repression in the post-war world.

streets were faithfully recreated, but in most places new buildings were erected alongside the old, changing the character of many towns but, in the process, often providing better living conditions. In Greece, civil war between monarchists and communists raged for four years. Spain, ostracised by the allied powers because of her support for Hitler (even though she took no part in the war) suffered years of severe hardship, her *noche negra*, or black night.

In Eastern Europe, the USSR was allowed

Left, Hitler crosses the Czech border in 1939.
Above, World War II destruction in Warsaw.

Hungary also learned the meaning of repression in 1956, when an uprising, designed to overthrow communist rule, was brutally suppressed by the Soviet Union and its leader, Imre Nagy, executed. The Iron Curtain, as Britain's former prime minister Winston Churchill called it, was firmly drawn across Europe, and global conflict replaced by the Cold War.

Mass tourism: In Western Europe, the hardship and austerity of the post-war years began to fade and people began to enjoy more leisure and more mobility than ever before. The existence of annual paid holidays and disposable income, and the growth of commercial airlines and car ownership, all contributed to the birth of the package holiday industry in the 1960s. It transformed Europe: sleepy fishing villages turned into bustling resorts, where bikini-clad northern Europeans rubbed shoulders with black-clad Mediterranean grandmothers and high-rise hotels overshadowed whitewashed cottages. It brought prosperity to poverty-stricken areas, as well as customs and values that may not have been so welcome.

The holiday boom lined the Mediterranean with villas and hotels and contributed to the growth of motorways which now zoom business travellers and gigantic lorries, as well as tourists, across the continent. And in

versities and colleges were built. This, together with an awareness of the wider world which came with mass media, in particular as it daily showed the progress of the unpopular war in Vietnam, led to a questioning of values. Student unrest swept across Europe and the US, beginning with the student protest in Paris in May 1968, which brought France to the verge of civil war. In this same spirit of defiance came the Prague Spring, when students backed the reforming leader Alexander Dubcek against Czechoslovakia's Moscow-oriented regime. Their peaceful revolution was crushed by Soviet tanks.

The idea of a European identity was slowly growing during these decades. The Euro-

northern towns and cities mass tourism – as well as the presence of "guest workers" from less-prosperous Mediterranean countries – led to a taste for Spanish, Greek and Italian restaurants.

Skiing, a sport for the many, instead of just for the rich, came a little later than sunseeking, but soon the mountainous areas of Switzerland, Austria, Italy and France were peppered with chalets and cable cars and threatened by the ecological impact of the seasonal crowds.

The 1960s was not only the decade of mass tourism. It was, above all, a period when youth culture exploded, and when new uni-

pean Economic Community, or Common Market, was born in 1958, with France, Belgium, Luxembourg, Italy, West Germany and the Netherlands as its members. Britain, Ireland and Denmark joined in 1973.

Spain, Portugal and Greece also moved closer to the rest of Europe during the midseventies, after all three ceased to be dictatorships. In Portugal, a left-wing military coup overthrew the heirs of Salazar, but attempts at Marxist government failed and there were democratic elections in 1976. In Greece the military junta which had held power since 1967 was overthrown in 1974, and a new constitution adopted the following year. The death of Franco in Spain in 1975 also heralded a new era. The monarchy was restored, a new constitution declared and, after a rocky start and a failed military coup in 1981, Spain became a democracy and Juan Carlos a popular king.

Democracy was also in the air in Poland in the early 1980s. *Solidarnosc* (Solidarity) an independent trade union, came to prominence in the Gdansk dockyards. The union's demands frightened the authorities, who imposed martial law and arrested the union's charismatic leader, Lech Walesa. After secret talks between the Polish leader, General Jaruzelski and the Polish-born Pope John Paul II, martial law was lifted. Walesa was

led to more openness in government in the USSR, and the end of the Brezhnev Doctrine, which had given the Soviet Union the right to intervene in the affairs of all the Warsaw Pact countries, opened the floodgates throughout Eastern Europe. One by one the former satellite states renounced communism. In Czechoslovakia, a new government was formed under the playwright Vaclav Havel; and in Hungary, as in most of the other states, a democratic, multi-party government was formed. In Germany, the Berlin Wall came down, amid international rejoicing, in November 1989 and when the two halves of the divided country were reunited, it seemed like the end of a bad dream

awarded the Nobel peace prize later that year. This was progress, but it still did not seem possible that only six years later, in 1989, elections would defeat the communist party in Poland and put a Solidarity prime minister in office.

But by then, the whole face of Eastern Europe was fast changing. Mikhail Gorbachev's policies of *perestroika* and *glasnost*

Left, Czechoslovakia's Alexander Dubcek, brushed aside by the Russians in 1968; Vaclav Havel (right of picture) meets Polish leader Lech Walesa in 1968. **Above**, the Pink Floyd's "The Wall" concert in Berlin on 21 July 1990.

and a triumph for democracy and capitalism.

As a result of the collapse of the Soviet communist system, an American historian, Francis Fukuyama, wrote a bestselling book called *The End of History*. He should have known better. Poverty followed democracy in Eastern Europe, power struggles continued, racism and immigration resurfaced as crucial issues, and the peoples of the Balkans brought war to the continent again. Europe seems to be a cauldron that refuses to cool. But the very heat of its history, its conflicts and turmoil, have all been part of the process of creation and destruction that has built every character and monument in these lands.

Just why is Europe such a magnet for travellers from elsewhere in the world? What makes it so different from "home"? In 1888 James Bryce provided one answer, writing in *The American Commonwealth* that "life in one of the great European centers is capable of an intensity, a richness blended of many elements which has not yet been reached in America... In whatever country of Europe one dwells, one feels that the other countries are near, that the fortunes of their people are bound up with the fortunes of one's own, that ideas are shooting to and fro between them."

Times change, of course, but the love-hate relationship between America and Europe, born of close historical ties, still provides the most accessible mirror in which Europeans can view themselves through an outsider's eyes. Henry James called the continent "the great American sedative" and Ralph Waldo Emerson claimed: "We go to Europe to be Americanized." James Baldwin, writing in 1961, took a more balanced view: "Europe has what we do not yet have, a sense of the mysterious and inexorable limits of life, in a word, of tragedy, and we [Americans] have what they surely need: a sense of life's possibilities."

To many people, therefore, Europe is much more than a living museum, a lengthy list of monuments to be ticked off as a dutiful obligation: it is a continent whose variety and density of culture can always surprise and often enrich the inquiring visitor. On the following pages, we focus on some of the quirkier aspects of Europe which may confound the first-time visitor, from kissing customs to queueing conventions, from centres of corruption to temples of gastronomy, from driving habits to swearing skills.

This alphabetical analysis does not explain everything that goes on either in public or behind closed doors between Paris and Prague. But it may shed light on some of the shadier areas of an assortment of societies known for their curious customs, mild eccentricities and irresistible fascination to the rest of the world.

Preceding pages: glittering gala at Milan's 200-year-old La Scala opera house. **Left**, Caravaggio's Bacchus raises a weary glass to the good life.

ARCHITECTURE

A tourist in a new city is expected to take a dutiful interest in its cathedrals, palaces and great buildings from the past. But Europe also has exciting, and sometimes contentious, public buildings that have arisen this century, and they should not be overlooked in the rush to get round the historic sites.

The starting point is the Bauhaus Museum in Dessan. The Bauhaus design school, begun by Walter Gropius, set the pace in the 1920s and 1930s. Interest was added by the

Swiss architect le Corbusier, whose designs included the modular Unité d'Habitation in Marseille using units proportional to the human figure.

In the reparations of the 1950s and the boom of the 1960s several architectural heroes emerged, such as Giovanni Ponti, who designed the radical Pirelli tower block in Milan which looks down over Ulisse Stracchini's elegant white Central Station of 1931, and together they set the city's sharp style. Josep Lluis Sert, a Spaniard who had followed Gropius into the chair of architecture at Harvard University, designed two beautiful modern galleries: the Maeght in St-Paul-de-Vence in the south of France, and the Miró Foundation in Barcelona, just a short walk from the rebuilt 1929 Pavilion of Mies van der Rohe, first director of the Bauhaus.

Among many architects involved in revamping or building new museums in the 1980s was the American Richard Meier. For Frankfurt's adventurous museum expansion programme beside the River Main, he designed the first of his "white refrigerators", to house the Museum of Crafts and Allied Arts. He has also left his mark on buildings in the Hague and Barcelona.

Barcelona provided a showcase for the world's architects who were invited to make the city a star in the 1992 Olympic Games. Among the contributors were Sir Norman Foster, who went on to redesign Berlin's Reichstag, and America's I.M. Pei. Pei was the architect of the ambitious Louvre pyramid, just one of the *Grands Projets* begun during the boom years of the 1980s when grandiose building programmes throughout Europe changed the shape not only of museums, but also of business and finance districts, obsolete docklands and industrial sites. They have given many European cities the new look of the post-industrial age.
For a definition of architectural styles, see the Travel Tips section, page 399.

BEACHES

Europe has two shores, sea and ocean, and their characteristics are distinct. The wide stretches of Atlantic and North Sea beaches are churned up by two tides a day which can discolour the water and shift the sand. In the more saline, tideless Mediterranean, the beaches are spread out between small rocky coves, where the water can be stunningly translucent. Of course there is pollution, and to discourage it the European Community hands out annual Clean Beach awards.

The Atlantic's rollers are for surfing. Guincho in Portugal has reputation among the windsurfing nomads, as does Tarifa, southwest Spain. The cooler North Sea end of this bracing coast, in Germany and the Dutch Frisian islands, is where many German naturists bare themselves to the sandpapering winds and billowing seas. But tidal waters can be a hazard, especially where the shore is flat and the twice-daily tide becomes speedy, cutting off cliffs and causeways.

At Mont-St-Michel in northern France the tide is one of the fastest in the world, and can cover up to 25 miles (40 km) in six hours. The difference in height between high and low tides can reach 15 metres, an extreme exceeded only by Fundy in Canada.

The Mediterranean, on the other hand, is rather safe, but its coast and its unexpected winds still make it a rugged place. Typically, the coast is where mountains come down to the sea, and the coves are backed with dunes and umbrella pine trees. This means many resorts have half a dozen separate beaches,

CORRUPTION

"In the Mediterranean cutlure," argues Franco Ferrarotti, professor of sociology at Rome University, "stealing is not considered a serious offence, especially if you do it with manual dexterity. Corruption, if it does not entail physical offence to the persons involved, is rather considered a fine art. The same thing applies to lying, which is considered very serious in the Protestant countries. Here it is considered an expedient, part of a way of life."

for a choice of amenities and perhaps a choice of uses: family, nude, gay; or they may even be colonised by a single nationality, being wholly German or British.

The popularity of such sandy stretches as Italy's crowded lidos around Rimini on the Adriatic, prompted some resorts to import sand. The impressive 4-mile (6-km) beach at Benidorm, Spain's most notorious package-holiday destination, was established with sand shipped in from Morocco, and it is still regularly topped up.

Left, **Corbusier's Notre Dame de Haut at Ron-champ, France. Above**, *boules* on the beach.

Traditionally in Italy, says Ferrarotti, corruption was excused as a human weakness provided one eventually delivered the goods. "Now two things have gone wrong. First, the order of magnitude of the corruption. Second, corruption no longer produces. You may accept 5 per cent more on the cost of a highway but in the end you get the highway. But if you have to pay 30 per cent more and then you don't get anything at all, well, that's too much."

The attitude reached all levels of society. As the writer Umberto Eco put it: "The Italians knew who you needed to see for a favour and how much it cost. They knew how to get out of a traffic fine, how to find an easy little job with a letter of recommendation, how to win a contract without difficult competition. In short, it suited people well enough, so they held their noses and voted."

Eventually, though, the smell (and the cost of bribery) became too great. A series of anti-mafia trials began, and even Giulio Andreotti, who had headed seven of Italy's short-serving governments, faced a string of corruption charges.

The rest of Europe, though saint-like by comparison, had few grounds for complacency. The French and Spanish governments were rocked in 1993 by public-sector corruption scandals, and gangs from Eastern Europe brought large-scale racketeering to the newly united Germany.

DRIVING

Linger too long in the outside lane of a German *Autobahn* and your rear-view mirror will soon reflect the flashing headlights of a Porsche or BMW bearing down on you at 150 mph (240 kph). Germany's love of speed usually triumphs over demands for a blanket speed limit on its *autobahn* system.

When an accident occurs, of course, you're more likely to need a hearse than an ambulance, yet Germany's roads are among the safer highways of Europe. Greece tops the league table for road deaths, followed by Portugal, France and Spain. The reason is that Germany's drivers, though impatient, are disciplined: driving is a serious business, so much so that you can be fined for making an insulting gesture to another motorist.

Italians, by contrast, reflect in their driving style their anarchic attitude towards authority in general. Horns are blasted habitually and ineffectually whenever traffic stops, overtaking is instinctive, and anyone foolish enough to stop as a light turns red is likely to find several disbelieving drivers crashing into him. The philosophy was summed up by the reaction of some Italians when a seat-belt law was passed: such restraints being incompatible with their macho outlook, they tried to fool police by wearing tee-shirts with a seat-belt printed across the front.

Spanish driving, it's said, reflects the cul-ture's obsession with death. French pride can interpret overtaking as insulting behaviour. And Swiss drivers are awfully proper.

Whatever the truth of such stereotypes, the first-time visitor to Europe should bear two things in mind. One is that driving styles are generally geared to getting from A to B as fast as possible. The second is that mixing driving and alcohol carries very severe penalties, especially in northern Europe.

EUROPEAN UNION

Just after World War II, which left the Continent devastated, Britain's wartime leader, Sir Winston Churchill, declared: "We must build a kind of United States of Europe." Throughout history, visionaries from Caesar and Charlemagne to Napoleon and Hitler had tried to unite Europe, usually by force. In 1950 a French businessman, Jean Monnet, proposed a route dictated by economic self-interest. By pooling their coal and steel resources, he argued, the Continent's main industrial powers could more effectively compete in world markets.

The resulting Coal and Steel Community developed into the European Economic Community, otherwise known as the Common Market, in 1957. As it grew to its current 15-nation membership (Austria, Belgium, Denmark, Finland, France, Germany, Great Britain, Greece, Ireland, Italy, Luxembourg, the Netherlands, Spain, Sweden and Portugal), it changed its name to the European Union and gained greater aspirations. These foresaw a single currency and, broadly, a single set of laws throughout the entire community. Border controls were removed in 1992.

Unlike the United States, however, the EU shares no common language or culture and, when times get tough, its individual members, far from uniting to solve their social and economic problems, become more nationalistic and protectionist. Tariff barriers may have disappeared within the Union, but mental barriers remain. In reality, Europe's nations are still warring: the difference is that their warriors are no longer pilots and infantrymen but the battalions of officials and politicians who face each other across the floors of the EU's assemblies.

FOOD

France remains the shrine at which gourmets worship. One reason is that, for all the elaborate, sophisticated dishes concocted over the centuries – a delight for their sheer inventiveness in the use of herbs, spices, creams, cheeses and wines – the French also know the job of ingenious simplicity.

The *charcuterie* are delicious; these include cold pork cuts and sausage such as *rosette de Lyon*, ham from Auvergne or Bayonne, and *rillettes*, a rich cold mince of

mer on the Mediterranean and *bar* on the Atlantic), poached or grilled with fennel (*fenouil*). Red mullet (*rouget*), sole, sea bream (*daurade*) and turbot are other favourites. Trout (*truite*) can be sautéed in butter (*meunière*) or with almonds (*aux amandes*).

Beef steak is popular nationwide: thick *Chateaubriand* fillet, juicy *entrecôte*, tender *tournedos* fillet wrapped in bacon, and the more resilient *bavette*. Leg of lamb is *gigot*.

Outstanding poultry dishes include *poulet à l'estragon* (chicken roasted in a tarragon sauce) and duck roasted not only *à l'orange* but also with cherries, peaches, fresh figs, turnips or olives. Increasingly popular is the *magret* or *aiguillettes* of duck, fillet slices

pork or goose-meat cooked in its own fat. *Terrine* is the generic French name for *pâté*, prepared in an earthenware dish from pork, rabbit, goose, duck, or chicken livers, or fish such as salmon and pike.

Refrigeration techniques have made it safe to eat oysters at any time of the year, but the best are still served from September to April. Mussels are great served *marinière* in a white wine sauce drunk like soup. The best snails come from Burgundy. Frogs' legs taste like garlic-seasoned veal.

A favourite fish is sea bass (called *loup de*

Above, celebrated French chef Paul Bocuse.

from the breast roasted to a rare deep pink.

Regional dishes abound. Provence favours garlic, herbs, tomatoes and olives in preparing roast chicken and lamb chops. Marseille's pride and joy, *bouillabaisse*, is a fish stew of racasse, red mullet and sea perch with spiny lobster, crab and other shellfish stewed in a saffron-spiced sauce.

Besides its wines, Burgundy's great gastronomic offering is *boeuf bourguignon*, a beef stew simmered for hours in red wine with whole baby onions, mushrooms and bits of bacon.

The south-west, from Perigord to the Pyrenees, defeats the diet-conscious with its goose and duck specialities such as the truffle-studded *pâté de fois gras* and the roast *confit d'oie* (goose) or *de canard* (duck) that has been slowly cooked in its own fat.

As for cheeses, one can only recall General de Gaulle's remark about the impossibility of uniting a country capable of producing 265 kinds of different cheese. Their names are often derived from nobility: the pungent fermented cheeses with a white or yellow skin such as Camembert, Brie, Coulommiers, Pont l'Evêque, Livarot; the blues of Roquefort, Fourme d'Ambert and Auvergne; the ripe and creamy Epoisses; the hard but piquant Cantal; and the goat cheeses of Valencay or Corsica.

GESTURES

Giving a thumbs-up sign will signify approval in most countries – but not in Greece, where it is a vulgar insult, equivalent to raising the middle finger elsewhere. Flick your ear with a forefinger in Italy and you could be suggesting someone is homosexual. Jerking your forearm up and slapping your other hand into the crook of the arm would be an insult in most of Europe – which might confuse people from elsewhere in the world who regard the gesture as a sign of sexual appreciation. Make a ring with your thumb or index finger and most Europeans will interpret it as meaning OK, but others will see it as Zero or worthless, and a Greek could be referring to a bodily orifice. Another way of insulting a Greek is to extend the palms of both hands, fingers splayed.

A shrug, though less risky, can convey different things, depending on whether it is accompanied by moving the shoulders, raising the eyebrows or pursing the mouth. Is someone resigned? Indifferent? Helpless? It's sometimes hard to tell.

In France, mouth movements are important. This is partly because nine of the 16 French vowels involve rounding the lips (compared with only five in German and two in English). The French are also great gesticulators, using their hands rather than their entire arms, but their repertoire is narrower than the Italians'.

The Italians have long been regarded as Europe's most expressive people. As the English novelist Charles Dickens noted of Naples: "Everything is done in pantomime". A wide variety of hand signals are used to convey agreement, surprise, delight, disgust, and gestures familiar to Homer can still be seen today.

HUMOUR

The Euro-joke is a contradiction in terms. For one thing, language plays a large part in forming humour: thus, while French lends itself to puns, Spanish doesn't. Much French wit, therefore, is built around clever, sarcastic wordplay. On the other hand, there's a fine old tradition of slapstick in France, and the French also have an earthy humour built around sex – though it's far from sexist.

Anal humour, however, is absent in France, but is strong in Germany, where scatological references appear even in children's riddles. Is early toilet training to blame, or perhaps a rigidity in the German character? Learned theses can be written on the subject. Belgians, by contrast, are conservative about sex, so there are few sex jokes in Belgium. Really, there's only one thing regarded as funny throughout Europe: other Europeans.

IMMIGRANTS

Every year around 700,000 people seek asylum in Europe, but new laws in most countries mean their chances are increasingly slim. Since the Soviet system disintegrated and Yugoslavia broke up into warring factions, an influx of refugees has combined with high unemployment to revive racial antagonism as an ugly reality of life.

In just one year (1992), 440,000 immigrants, mostly from Yugoslavia, some from Romania and Bulgaria, settled in Germany, the National Front, led by the charismatic Jean-Marie Le Pen, has risen on a tide of racist feelings against Muslim and African immigrants, particularly from its former colonies. In Italy, where the Adriatic shores are constantly patrolled for Albanians escaping the turmoil of their own country, the neofascist Italian Social Movement has gained influence, while a group called the Ultras interrupts football matches with racist outbursts.

Especially disturbing has been the continuing attacks on Jews, whose cemeteries and synagogues are vandalised – even in liberal Holland. Do some people, pessimists wondered, ever learn anything from history?

which had one of the most liberal immigration laws in Europe. The following year, when unemployment in the recently reunited country reached 6 million, the rules were tightened up.

Meanwhile, serious attacks on immigrants had left 17 dead and 2,500 injured. In Belgium, Turks and Moroccans have been the objects of attack by the Flemish Vlaams Blok party, as much anti-French as anti-Islam. They represent Flemish speakers who want a separate, break-away state. In France,

Left, body language in Naples. <u>**Above**</u>, former East Berliners get a first taste of a united city.

JET SET

There comes a time when one simply has to have the sun and only the Caribbean will do. But, for much of the year, the curious coterie of pop singers, film stars, millionaires, aristocrats and royalty (real and ersatz) who constitute the international "glam clan" can find an acceptable venue in Europe.

After checking out the Paris fashion shows in January, it's off to the ski slopes of Klosters or St Moritz in February. After a short break, perhaps, for a southern-hemisphere safari, it's off in May to Monaco to see the Grand Prix and say hello to the Rainiers. In June, Britain beckons with Royal Ascot, the Henley Regatta and Wimbledon. Then, pausing to take in the Paris summer collections, one can follow the English in July as they head for their villas in Tuscany (which has become so English that it's been dubbed Chiantishire).

And so it continues… yachting in Cap Ferrat, villa parties on Patmos (the only really exclusive Greek island), the Prix de l'Arc de Triomph (you don't have to own a racehorse), and sundry charity balls in grand locations. Like all heavenly bodies, the jet set like to have their fixed orbits.

In Germany, by contrast, men seldom kiss the cheeks of other men, and personal space is assiduously protected. Hand-shaking is the more common form of greeting, but generally only when meeting someone by appointment. In France, on the other hand, it is common to shake hands with someone each time you meet and depart, even if you meet them several times a day.

Few generalisations are reliable, however. The Italians, for instance, are supposedly the most tactile Europeans. Yet, although two men will touch frequently when talking (perhaps implicitly to deter the other person from interrupting), and even guide each other round a corner while walking, there is noticeably

less touching between the sexes. Even married couples are less likely to walk along hand in hand than they are in Denmark or Austria. Could it be that Italian men regard hand-holding as a sign of submissiveness?

KISSING

Latin had three words for "kiss", distinguishing between a kiss of friendship on the cheek, a kiss of affection on the mouth and a lovers' kiss on the mouth. The Roman tradition lives on, for people around the Mediterranean are more spontaneously intimate than their northern cousins: they sit closer together, they touch more, they stand closer together when talking, and everyone seems to cheek-kiss enthusiastically.

LAVATORIES

Can the character of a nation's toilets give a clue to the nature of its people? Proponents of the theory would point to the Germans, whose humour is sometimes seen as tending towards the anal and whose toilet bowls often incorporate a shelf on which, before flushing, one may inspect one's faeces for tell-tale signs of potential ill-health.

Multinational manufacturing has largely eroded the varieties of bathroom fittings that once added extra spice to travelling. Modern coin-operated cabins have replaced most of Paris's old pissoirs, which enabled a gentleman to relieve himself while continuing a conversation with his companion outside. In rural France, though, you can still find some old "hole in the ground" toilets which compel you to squat over them – a healthy posture, some claim.

It's not unusual to find restaurants with common toilets, used by both men and women, and many public toilets for men have female attendants.

And what of hygiene? A survey by one roller-towel manufacturer recently revealed that 27 per cent of Europeans failed to wash their hands after using the lavatory. Another market research finding claimed that only 19 per cent of French men and 32 per cent of French women take a bath each day and only 5 per cent wash their hair every day, and that more than half the population goes to bed without cleaning their teeth. But they spend 50 per cent more on fresheners than Italians. West Germans, it appears, wash their hair twice as often as East Germans. The Spanish bathe least, but they use lots of fragrances.

What can all this mean? One view is that the French regard body odours as quite natural and fear that eliminating them might reduce sexual appeal. Many French perfumes, therefore, are designed to accentuate natural odours, not conceal them.

MONARCHIES

Hereditary kings and queens have shown remarkable endurance in an age so concerned with the spread of democracy. One country, Spain, even restored its monarchy in 1975 and, despite predictions that he would be known as "Juan Carlos the Brief", the king is still on the throne, his reputation

hugely enhanced by his successful appeal to the armed forces to avert an attempted military coup in 1981. Likewise, none of Europe's other six major crowned heads – or indeed less weighty rulers such as Prince Rainier of Monaco or Prince Hans Adam of Liechtenstein – looks imminently set to join the ranks of the jobless.

Most European monarchs are tolerated because they have no real power, and are valued mainly for providing a sense of continuity and a useful focus for ceremonial. The Swedish monarch is probably the most powerless, playing no part whatever in the parliamentary process. The Norwegian, Danish and British monarchs could theoretically

appoint prime ministers in the event of an electoral deadlock. The Dutch, although permitting their queen a great deal of power in theory, allow her almost none in practice.

In 1993, the Belgians removed King Baudouin's right to approve the appointment of a prime minster. He died soon afterwards, childless, and his younger brother Albert, who had been something of a playboy, found himself unexpectedly king at the age of 59. The monarchy was still valued as an institution, however, because it seemed virtually the only glue holding together the Dutch and French-speaking halves of a politically divided country. In contrast with

Britain, whose royal family increasingly resembles the cast of a soap opera, Belgium does not permit its media to comment on the king; indeed, one lawyer who said that the king's Christmas message to his people was boring was charged under an 1846 law of committing "outrage to royalty".

Long live the King! And long live pragmatism!

NATURE

From the eagles' eyries of the snowy alps to the lizard sunbeds of the Spanish sierras, Continental Europe supports a vast range of animal habitats. Hunting is widely permitted, and migrant birds must dodge the bullets of Italians and Spaniards who will eat anything that flaps a wing. The big-game hunters are the Germans, who like wild boar and are enthusiastic chasers of wolves and bears in the newly accessible Eastern Europe.

Boar are popular in much of Europe and in the shooting season (roughly from November to February) they are hunted, along with ducks. In France and Portugal, huntsmen dress in bright liveries, blow their bugles and give chase on horseback after foxes.

Many countries have special animals. In France, there are the long-horned black cattle of the Camargue, at the delta of the Rhône where flamingoes flock. Southern Italy has water buffalo, from which mozzarella cheese is made. Switzerland has the Chamois mountain goat, Spain the Moorish gecko, a lizard.

There is the occasional viper or adder, but in the main Continental Europe is a safe place for wild things and creepy-crawlies. Even the small brown scorpions found around the Mediterranean seem too lazy to bite. But occasionally a jellyfish in the Mediterranean will sting as fiercely as a bee.

OATHS

The Romance languages, as well as enhancing operatic arias, lend themselves particularly well to cursing and swearing. This is not a skill suitable for the linguistically uncer-

tain and its effectiveness also involves an advanced command of Gesture (*see above listing*), but a few guidelines may keep novices out of trouble.

Italy, being a Catholic country, often combines imprecations and blasphemy. Common examples are *Porco Dio!* (That pig of a god) or *Madonna puttana!* (That whore of a Virgin Mary). Oddly enough, Jesus Christ seems to have escaped relatively lightly.

Spain, another Catholic country, also embraces blasphemy. *Hostia!* (Holy bread) is mild enough, but other curses are more extreme: *Me cagoen todos los Santos*, for example, means "I defecate on all the saints." The Spanish are the acknowledged masters of the blood-freezing insult.

In Germany, the combination of pigs and dogs (as in *Schweinhund*) effectively conveys disapproval. As in many other languages, excrement crops up readily: *Scheiss* can express frustration or be an insult. The equivalent in French (*merde*) is not insulting, merely a much-used expression indicating mild annoyance.

PUNCTUALITY

The closer you get to the Mediterranean, the slower the pace of life becomes. People even walk less fast. Partly it's a matter of adapting to a hot climate, partly it's a reflection of the attitude that time serves people rather than the other way round.

To be late for an appointment in Germany or Switzerland would be regarded as rude, or at least inconsiderate. In Greece or Spain, by contrast, nobody is expected to show up on time. Indeed, being *very* late may even be a sign of status: it means you are important enough to make people wait for you.

A Belgian or an Austrian will talk of "wasting time" because, implicitly, time is money. In Greece, however, time simply passes and there's always a lot more; look too impatiently at your watch and you'll be seen to value time more than friendship. In Spain, too, people are relaxed about most things, hence the jokes about *mañana*; but some events – lunch is one of them – have a natural time and are seldom rescheduled.

In France also, lunch is important. It's not

done to discuss business at a business lunch until at least the first course has arrived; this restraint shows you know the value of friendship, not to mention food and wine, and that you are a more rounded person. And the pace of a traditional French lunch makes subsequent punctuality hard to achieve.

QUEUES

It has been said of the Englishman that, even if he is alone, he forms an orderly queue of one. This attitude is not one that is widely

ROBBERY

Most of the world's 300 million tourists a year don't get robbed or mugged. Nevertheless, the ancient tradition of highway robbery lives on in Europe, and visitors should take appropriate precautions.

Amazingly, the oldest tricks still find gullible victims. A Vespa-riding pickpocket in Rome will snatch a handbag without even slowing down. A young man in Barcelona will offer to take your photograph for you and make off with your camera as soon as

shared by his Continental neighbours. In affluent Switzerland, they'll form a line too, on the rational basis that this is the most efficient way for everyone to be served quickly and fairly. In Italy, however, the free-for-all prevails: standing in an orderly line would be regarded as both an imposition and a stifling of personal initiative.

Sociologists devote learned works to drawing parallels between such anarchic behaviour and attitudes towards government (especially disrespectful in Italy, France and Spain). But nobody queues to buy their books.

Above, for some, queueing comes naturally.

you hand it over. In Benidorm, men pose as porters and steal luggage. In Greece, men are invited into a bar, find themselves buying drinks for a number of friendly women, and then are presented with an exorbitant bill.

Robbery, like tourism, reacts to global influences. Importing a cunning ruse from Florida, French gangs steal cars and use them on a quiet stretch of autoroute to ram the back of a foreign-registered car, making it seem accidental. When the victim pulls over to inspect the damage, the gang relieves him and his family of their valuables – and possibly steals his car as well.

The French have a name for the villains:

"les pirates de la route". But their advice to potential victims is the bleak suggestion that they add a new phrase to their vocabulary; *"Prenez l'argent"* (Take the money).

STATUS

Nothing could be further from the informal way in which Americans greet people they scarcely know than the formality that is preserved in many European countries. Germans in particular put great emphasis on titles and can be seriously offended if they

are not addressed properly. As the psychologist Carl Jung once observed: "There are no ordinary human beings, you are 'Herr Professor' or 'Herr Geheimrat', 'Herr Oberrechnungsrat' and even longer things than that."

Two colleagues with much the same job status can work in the same office for 20 years and still address each other as "Herr Vogel" and "Frau Schmidt". They would feel very uncomfortable, they will tell you, using first names. The advantage of such formality is that it distinguishes acquaintances from friends, and when a friendship is finally cemented by the adoption of first names, it is a memorable occasion, usually celebrated with a few drinks.

Another method by which status is delineated is in the choice of second-person pronoun. All the main European languages except English (which dispensed with "thou" in the 17th century) have two words for "you": the familiar form (*tu* in French, *du* in German) and the formal version (*vous* in French, *Sie* in German). Again, the move from the formal to the familiar is a signal that amity has become camaraderie. In a business environment, the decision to switch is usually initiated by the person with superior status.

Such distinctions were one of the problems faced by East Germans when the country was reunited. Under Communism, they had as comrades been encouraged to address one another by the familiar *du*; now, as they come to terms with the complexities of capitalism, *Sie* is making a comeback.

TELEVISION

Switch on a TV set anywhere in Europe, turn down the sound, and you'll be amazed at how difficult it is to identify which country you're in. Here are the familiar news pictures of famine in Africa, here are the inane game shows, here is a self-satisfied political figure trying to look sincere, here is the agonised expression of the soap-opera heroine, here is... surely not *Casablanca*? Turn up the volume and you may be treated to the sound of Humphrey Bogart speaking fluent French or John Wayne dubbed into Dutch.

Many TV stations in Europe still operate under some loose form of government control, but the growth of satellite broadcasting has shifted most channels' agendas to the ruthlessly commercial question of how to gain and keep the biggest audiences. The temptation is often to go for slick, affordable and popular American series – some private French channels came close to devoting half their airtime to US programmes – but resistance has been growing at the extent of this "cultural imperialism" being pumped through millions of cathode-ray tubes. Since the US accounts for 80 per cent of the movies released in Europe, the fear is a real one.

UMBRELLAS

Except in parts of the Mediterranean in high summer, these are more often used in Europe to fend off rain than sun. The essence of the weather, however, is its unpredictability: the character of winter or summer will vary wildly from one year to another and a favourite sympathetic comment from locals as you shelter from a cloudburst or hailstorm is: "It's very unseasonal." Which is no consolation at all.

The following statistics, therefore, al-

Russia can make northern Germany in winter seem pretty arctic.

Confirming the wisdom of seeing Paris in the spring, rainfall is least in March and April. It's highest in August. In Marseille, July is clearly the driest month; the wettest are October and November. The mistral wind can bring unseasonably cold weather to the south of France in spring.

In Brussels, it rains most in July (thanks partly to thunderstorms) and December, least in March and May. Winters are wetter in the south and hill fogs occur frequently.

The Netherlands has a similar climate. It rains heaviest in July and August, least in March and April.

though no guarantee of anything, may dispel a few myths. Bear in mind, though, that a high rainfall in July, say, doesn't mean that it rains all the time – there may simply be fierce thunderstorms. But you'll still need to pack your brolly.

The driest month in Berlin is March, and the wettest July and August. In Munich, the driest is December and the wettest June and July. Being near to the Alps, southern Germany has colder and snowier winters than the north, but sharp winds blowing in from

In Italy it rains least in the extreme north of the mainland and in Sicily and Sardinia. Rome can expect least rain in July, most in November. Venice can expect least in January, most in November.

Mountainous Switzerland, affected by weather from both the Atlantic and eastern Europe, is notoriously changeable. The driest months in Zurich are March and December, the wettest June and July.

Austria has a similar climate. Most rain falls on Vienna in July, the least in January.

Greece is rightly known for its sunshine. But rainfall is heavy when it happens, which it does most notably in December. The driest

Left, French chic – but do they call each other "*tu*" or "*vous*"? **Above**, the best use for brollies.

months are July and August, when you can expect virtually no rain at all.

It's a mistake to assume that all of Spain has a Mediterranean climate; the Pyrenees give the north quite a different weather pattern. Most rain falls on Madrid in April and December, least in July. In Palma, Majorca, hardly any rain falls in July; October is the wettest month.

Coastal Portugal is at the mercy of the Atlantic. It's very dry in both Lisbon and Faro in July and August, but quite wet in December and January.

VENDETTA

Although Italy's mafia get the headlines for their acts of vengeance, most of their murders are motivated more by economic gain than personal grievance. For a cold-blooded interpretation of the Biblical "eye for an eye" principle, few have been able to match the Corsicans.

The tradition began centuries ago when the islanders retaliated against their Genoese conquerors by killing a soldier for every Corsican killed by the occupiers. The Genoese would respond and the constant retaliation meant that whole clans were wiped out. When France annexed the island in 1769, its rigorous penal code seemed to weak to the passionate Corsicans, who demanded the blood of a crime's perpetrator when family honour was at stake. A man marked by the curse of the vendetta might take refuge in the island's thorny undergrowth, but he would know that death was only a matter of time.

Prosper Mérimée, the poet who created *Carmen*, based his novella *Colomba* on a tribal drama of this kind. Balzac, Dumas and Maupassant also carved for the Corsican vendetta a place in history. Nowadays, although *vendetta corse* is still written on penknives in the island's souvenir shops, the vendetta manifests itself less in killing than in the destruction of property: the supermarket that gets burnt down the day before it's due to open, for instance, because it provides unwanted competition in a seaside resort. And, as always, the perpetrators can still be sure that the ancient code of silence observed by their fellow-citizens will protect them.

WINE

In California or Australia, the combination of an equable climate and close scientific control can ensure that the wines produced from a particular estate vary little from year to year. In Europe, by contrast, wines are at the mercy of the continent's capricious weather: one year a wine may be classed as truly great, and the next year the grapes from the same slopes will produce at best a mediocre vintage. Such uncertainty adds interest.

Most European countries have a wine in-

dustry, but the three which dominate are France, Italy and Spain.

French wine comes from eight main areas: the Bordeaux region, the most important; Burgundy in the east; Touraine, including the Loire Valley, in the west; the Rhône valley from Lyons to Avignon; the Champagne area around Rheims and Epernay; Alsace, along the left bank of the Rhine; the slopes of the Jura mountains; and the Languedoc region in the south, home of much *vin ordinaire*. The Bordeaux region produces a high proportion of the world's great wines, and Burgundy whites have become fashionable (and therefore expensive).

Italy makes prodigious amounts of wine, from the Alpine valleys down to the tip of Sicily. It tends to be lighter than French, and lacks the depth, but fine wines come from Chianti, Orvieto, Soave and Valpolicella.

Spain has made the biggest improvement in the quality of its wines in the past two decades. Many wines are now world-class, though the best-known remain Riojas from the north. Ordinary table wines from the Valdepeñas region can also be pleasant.

Although beer is more evident in most of Germany than wine, the country does produce some splendid wines, especially hocks; these white wines from the Rhineland can be either sweet or dry.

a Spaniard would first build a church, a Frenchman a fort, and a Dutchman a warehouse. In 1820, Lord Byron claimed that French courage was based on vanity, German courage on phlegm, Dutch courage on obstinacy, and Italian courage on anger. The modern version of the stereotype game is to define hell as a place where the Germans are the police, the Swedish are the comedians, the Italians are the defence force, the Frenchmen dig the roads, the Belgians are the pop singers, the Spanish run the railways, the Albanians cook the food, the Portuguese are the waiters, the Greeks run the government, and the common language is Dutch.

As so often, jokes are a means of voicing

XENOPHOBIA

Charles V of Spain claimed that he spoke Spanish to God, Italian to women, French to men, and German to his horse. The joke probably went down well in the 16th century, and Europeans haven't stopped inventing variations on the same theme ever since.

If colonising an island, it was said in 1790,

Left, nosing out a good vintage. **Above**, there are good neighbours – and less good neighbours.

inadmissable opinions. Thus the French and the Dutch make fun of the Belgians. Northern Germans mock the laziness of southern Germans, who in turn deride the stupidity of northerners. Both northern and southern Germans ridicule their new compatriots from the former East Germany. Copenhageners will make fun of somebody from Jutland. Belgium's Flemmings and Walloons joke about each other.

Images, like fashion, are subject to change. Thus the idea of the Germans as aggressive and authoritarian emerged only in the mid-19th century; previously, Machiavelli, a shrewd observer of human nature, had described them as peace-loving and rather timid.

Nicknames, mostly inoffensive, are subject to the whims of language. In English, sauerkraut-eating Germans naturally became Krauts and didn't seem to mind being compared to pickled cabbage. In the same way, spaghetti-munching Italians were Spags. How the French turned into frogs is less obvious: the term may have derived from their eating habits, but it could also have come from the three leaping toads portrayed on the coat of arms of the ancient Frankish kings (later replaced by the fleur-de-lys).

The term *dago*, on the other hand, is regarded as offensive by Spaniards, Portuguese and Italians. The reasons can't be

Cannes or St-Tropez – see the traditional *pointu* fishing boats go happily about their business alongside sleek and shining luxury vessels, the many new ports designed exclusively for private yachts have made the Riviera the world centre for a new type of craft, dubbed the "megayacht" – fully crewed private vessels over 120 ft (36 metres) long.

Riviera harbours are open to anyone wishing for a closer look at the lifestyles of the rich and famous. Between the Italian border at Menton and the port of Marseille 127 nautical miles (235 km) to the west there are 130 of these harbours, totalling over 52,000 moorings. French Riviera ports shelter a third of the world megayacht fleet of about

found in its innocent origins (the Spanish *Diego*, meaning James), and it was originally innocuous.

YACHT-WATCHING

Luxury yachting has always been part of the Riviera legend but in recent years it has become a fully-fledged industry, vital to the region's economy. Nowhere else on earth is there so much extravagant floating real estate in one place. While some harbours – like

3,500 yachts. Yachting occupies 1,500 local businesses, including many small craftsmen and tradesmen, and provides 6,000 jobs, not including crew.

Famous names still frequent Riviera ports but, except in a few cases (terrorism and taxman *oblige*), with cautious discretion. Some flamboyant owners, however, make no secret of their possession and the name of a yacht is often a clue to the ownership.

If a taste of the seafaring life sounds tempting, a used 60-ft (18-metre) displacement model can be had for about £1 million. If you want something with a bit more speed or cabin space you should be thinking in the neighbourhood of £3 million. Today, yachts worth more than £20 million are not at all uncommon and you should count on 10 percent of the boat's value as the cost of annual upkeep.

Chartering offers a cheaper solution for those on a budget and the American dollar is the trading currency. For about $4,000 a day you can hire a modest yacht, but if you plan on sailing farther afield or throwing large parties on board you'll need a bigger model at up to $20,000 a day. Prices include yacht and crew but not berthing fees, fuel, food or drink. On the Côte d'Azur more than anywhere else, a yacht truly is a hole in the water you throw money into.

antiquarian interest"? Or will the millennium give the old world a new impetus?

The preliminary diagnosis isn't good. The most cock-eyed optimist would readily concede that the mood within Europe is pretty glum. On the political front, confidence in leadership has plummeted. On the economic front, unemployment, prices and taxes are all too high. On the home front, immigration, corruption, inner city blight, poverty and crime all threaten social cohesion. On the international front, a coherent response couldn't be found to the alarming deterioration of the former Soviet Union, or to the vicious civil war being fought on Europe's doorstep, in former Yugoslavia.

ZEITGEIST

The 20th century has been popularly called the American Century. The 21st, pundits predict, will belong to Asia. So where does that leave Europe? Will the world echo the words of the American writer F. Scott Fitzgerald, who exclaimed in 1921: "God damn the continent of Europe. It is of merely

Left, yachts on the Riviera. Above, tomorrow's world – the geodesic dome at La Villette, Paris.

But that isn't the whole story. More people than ever before are educated, affluent, in good health, and able to enjoy a remarkable range of leisure pursuits. Better communications have made them more aware of the problems around them and, as they are exposed to the successes of other societies, either directly through foreign travel or indirectly through TV coverage, they are more likely to demand more of their own leaders.

Sometimes it takes an outsider to point out the silver linings on the dark clouds. And fortunately a high proportion of the millions of tourists who descend on Continental Europe each year are prepared to do just that.

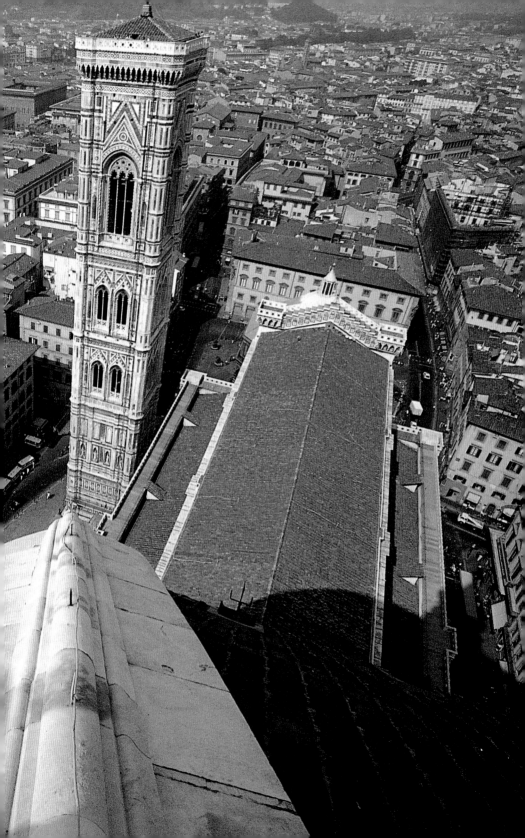

ΑΓ. ΑΘΑΝΑΣΙΟΣ Λ.Μ. 48

ι.105

·ΗΛΙΑΣ Λ.

There is something reassuringly familiar about the continent of Europe. Its snowy mountains and its beaches, its Roman remains and its cathedrals, its vineyards and cafés are all places that have figured in books and films. Yet there is such a quantity of architecture and art to absorb, so many acres of countryside to explore, so much good food to try, so many vintage wines to taste, that nobody can know it all. What follows is a full flavour of continental Europe: 15 countries that cover the land mass from Cabo de Roca, the westernmost point of Portugal, to Greece, abutting the borders with Asia in the east.

Getting around the continent is no problem. Cities are linked by road and rail, and airports are busy round the clock. Though in theory the borders between the members of the European Community were removed in 1992, the reality is that checkpoints remain in force, even though they often seem redundant and uniformed officers turn their backs on cars passing through. Crossing borders to former Eastern European countries will be more formal.

There are few places that are not used to visitors all the year round. Springtime is the time of wildflowers which cover the Alps and carpet the meadowlands. In summer many people gather in the playgrounds of the Mediterranean: most crowded are Rimini on the Adriatic coast, the French Riviera and Spain's Costa del Sol, but there are always empty beaches to seek out, on the Atlantic coast, perhaps, or among Greece's myriad islands. In the autumn the vineyards of France, Italy, Spain and the Rhine in Germany redden and the grapes are gathered in, often amid celebrations. In winter the snowy Alps attract skiers to Austria, Switzerland and France, and there are winter sports in Italy and Spain, too.

Any time of year is a good time to visit Europe's cities,which are among the most exciting in the world, a mix of architectural styles, usually starting around grand cathedrals and spreading out to modern business centres and suburbs, catering for people with an infinite variety of tastes from all over the world.

Preceding pages: driving sheep into the Schnals Valley, South Tyrol; rooftops of Florence, Italy; fishing boats, Greek Islands. Left, gathering grapes in Alsace, France.

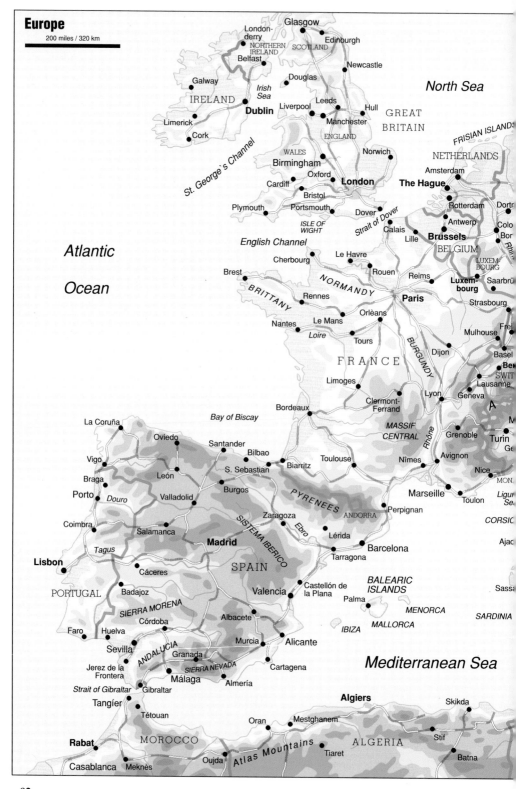

Europe

200 miles / 320 km

North Sea

Glasgow
London-derry
Edinburgh
NORTHERN IRELAND
SCOTLAND
Belfast
Newcastle
Galway
Douglas
IRELAND
Irish Sea
Leeds
Hull
Limerick
Liverpool
Manchester
GREAT BRITAIN
Cork
ENGLAND
Dublin

WALES
Norwich
Birmingham
FRISIAN ISLANDS
NETHERLANDS
Amsterdam
Cardiff
Oxford
London
The Hague
Bristol
Rotterdam
Dortr
Plymouth
Portsmouth
Dover
Antwerp
Colo
ISLE OF WIGHT
Strait of Dover
Calais
Lille
Brussels
Bor
English Channel
Le Havre
BELGIUM
Rhi
Cherbourg
Rouen
LUXEMBOURG
Brest
NORMANDY
Reims
Luxembourg
Saarbrü
Rennes
Paris
Strasbourg
BRITTANY
Le Mans
Orléans
Mulhouse
Frei
Nantes
Tours
Dijon
Basel
Loire
BURGUNDY
Ber
FRANCE
SWIT
Limoges
Lyon
Lausanne
Geneva
Bordeaux
Clermont-Ferrand
A
MASSIF CENTRAL
Grenoble
M
Bay of Biscay
Rhône
Nîmes
Turin
Ge
La Coruña
Oviedo
Santander
Avignon
Nice
Vigo
Bilbao
Biarritz
Toulouse
Marseille
MON.
Braga
León
S. Sebastian
Toulon
Ligur Se
Porto
Valladolid
PYRENEES
Marseille
CORSIC
Douro
Burgos
ANDORRA
Perpignan
Coimbra
Salamanca
Zaragoza
Lérida
Ajac
SISTEMA IBERICO
Ebro
Barcelona
Madrid
Tarragona
Lisbon
Tagus
Cáceres
SPAIN
BALEARIC ISLANDS
Sassa
PORTUGAL
Badajoz
Valencia
Castellón de la Plana
Palma
SIERRA MORENA
Córdoba
Albacete
MENORCA
SARDINIA
Faro
Huelva
Murcia
Alicante
IBIZA
MALLORCA
Sevilla
ANDALUCIA
Granada
Jerez de la Frontera
SIERRA NEVADA
Cartagena
Mediterranean Sea
Málaga
Almería
Strait of Gibraltar
Gibraltar
Tangier
Algiers
Skikda
Tétouan
Oran
Mestghanem
Rabat
MOROCCO
ALGERIA
Stif
Oujda
Atlas Mountains
Tiaret
Batna
Casablanca
Meknès

Atlantic Ocean

Mediterranean Sea

82

France

75 miles/ 120 km

United Kingdom

Calais
Boulogne
Dieppe
Cherbourg
Le Havre
Rouen
Seine
A13
Caen
Bernay
Versaille
Normandie
Rambouillet
Alençon
Chartres
Côte de Granit Rose
Perros-Guirec
Côte d'Emeraude
Mont-St-Michel
St-Malo
Rance
Brest
Bretagne
Canal
Rennes
A 81
A 11
Orléans
Quimper
Côte de Cornouaille
Lorient
Le Mans
A 10
Blois
Côte d'Amour
Canal de Nantes à Brest
Angers
Tours
Val de Loire
Che
Nantes
Loire
Indre
Marais Poitvetin
Parthenay
Poitiers
A 10
Ile de Ré
La Rochelle
Poitou-Charentes
Atlantic Ocean
Charente
Cognac
Limoges
L. de Vassivie
Angoulême
Côte des Landes
Limousi
Périgueux
Perigord
Gironde
Bordelais
Sarlat
Bordeaux
Dordogne
A63
Bergerac
Parc des Landes de Gascogne
Cahors
A 62
Garonne
Côte d'Argent
Bayonne
Toulouse
Côte d'Argent
Biarritz
Pays-Basques
S. Sebastian
Pau
P
A 64
y
Lourdes
Foix
r
Pamplona
Pic du Midi d'Ossau
é
n
é
Andorra
Spain

Bastia
Calvi
Corte
Ajaccio
Porto-Vecchio
Sartene
Bonifacio

88

France likes to think of itself as the most essential component in Europe. Foreigners think so, too. It is the place people overseas often think of first when they come to the continent, and the place many businesses initially sound out to see if it would be suitable for starting up European operations. Its attractions are well known: it has the world's best food, best wine, finest domestic architecture and a people who know how to dress. Its popularity is undeniable: the population of 57 million is just about the same as the number of visitors who arrive every year.

France is Europe's largest country (not counting European Russia) and the world's fourth richest country. Its population is spread thinly through a remarkably diverse landscape covering 211,200 sq miles (547,000 sq km), and even on major roads wayside towns and villages can seem deserted. But rural France is the real France. The French are proud of their agricultural heritage and their farmers are respected as much as the food they produce.

France is also Europe's oldest nation and, give or take the occasional small border shift, it has existed roughly in its present form since the 15th century. The nation's boundaries are largely natural ones, with the English Channel to the north, the Atlantic to the west, the Pyrenees and the Mediterranean to the south and the Alps, the Jura mountains and the Rhine to the east. These all contrive to make the French almost insular and, as a result, the overwhelmingly Catholic people are not as cosmopolitan as other European countries which have more openly shared borders. Accordingly, some visitors find them cool and uninterested in foreigners. (This is not borne out by a poll which showed 82 percent of French people would be happy to act as guides for tourists.) In spite of its insularity, this nation has had immense cultural influence on the rest of the world, and the existence of several minority languages within the country – Breton, Basque, Catalan, Alsace German and Italian – show the variety that lies within its borders.

Among the country's riches, the châteaux of the Loire stand out, buildings whose cost and craftsmanship could never be matched today. But French culture stretches through all the arts, especially to film, which is why the annual festival at Cannes is the most important event in the cinema industry's year, an event which highlights the country's stunning Riviera. All these areas are covered in the following chapters. Most of all, however, when thoughts turn to France, they turn to Paris, a vibrant city of 9 million people, whose name has become synonymous with everything chic.

Preceding pages: Villandry in the Loire Valley; checking out the *menu touristique*. **Left**, a wine farmer from Bordeaux.

AROUND FRANCE

France has an admirable network of road, rail and air transport that makes for quick, efficient and pleasant travel. The expansion of the *autoroute* (motorway) system has been accelerated in recent years. It runs from the north coast to the south and provides access to the southwest and the east by going round rather than through Paris. The link from Calais to Marseille via Reims makes the journey from north to south around 11 hours. The greatest asset of the French road network is the superlative quality of its clearly signposted secondary roads.

The railways have gained a reputation for being the best in Europe. The trains are punctual, clean and fast. The 167-mph (270-kph) TGV (*Train à Grande Vitesse*) has cut the four-hour journey from Paris to Lyon by half. The lines also run to Calais, Le Mans and Tours and a TGV Med service is underway to Marseille, Italy and Spain. The two are to link up, giving a straight-through run from the Channel Tunnel to the Côte d'Azur.

Visitors arriving by sea via the English Channel might like to stretch their legs in the port towns before continuing the journey inland. In **Boulogne**, the 13th-century ramparts of the upper town (*ville haute*) make an interesting walk. A good overall view of the town and harbour can be had from the top of the belfry of the town hall. In **Calais**' Parc St Pierre is the famous bronze statue by August Rodin of the *Burghers of Calais* who, in 1346, offered their necks to the English king if he would spare the city. He spared both.

Dieppe is the most attractive of the ports serving the Channel crossings. The Boulevard du Maréchal Foch offers a pleasant promenade along the pebble beach. The liveliest part of town is around the Place du Puits Sale with its renowned Café des Tribuneaux. Between Dieppe and Boulogne is the favourite seaside resort of **Le Touquet**, once also known as Paris-Plage.

The north of France, flat and defence-less as Belgium, has been the poignant arena of countless invasions, its place-names a veritable litany of battlefields. **Dunkirk** is famous for the providential evacuation of 200,000 British and 140,000 French troops in May 1940. From the lighthouse or the Watier locks, one can see where it happened. The English will remember glorious **Crécy** and Henry V's **Agincourt** (Azincourt in French). The French prefer to remember **Bouvines**, an important victory over an Anglo-German alliance in 1214.

Others, whether victories or defeats, soaked the fields of **Flanders** and **Picardy**, the plateau of the Ardennes and the banks of Somme and the Marne in blood. While the British cemeteries of World War I are to be found mostly in Belgium, around Ypres and Passchendaele, there are impressive monuments to the Canadian troops at **Vimy** (north of Arras), to the Australians at **Corbie** (east of Amiens) and to the Americans at **Bellicourt** (southwest of Le Quesnoy).

But the living are very much present in the architecture of the north's proud

Left, flying the flag in Burgundy. *Right*, Breton women in native costume.

civic and religious history. **St Omer**'s Basilique Notre-Dame, begun in 1200 and completed in the 15th century, is a triumphant union of Romanesque and Gothic styles, the jewel of Flanders' ecclesiastic architecture.

Lille, capital of the north, is distinguished by its civic buildings, the grand 17th-century Vieille Bourse (Old Stock Exchange) and Louis XIV's imposing fortified citadel – a massive construction of 60 million bricks demanding the labour of 2,000 bricklayers.

Arras, famous to the English for the tapestries through which Hamlet stabbed old Polonius, and to the French as the home town of revolutionary leader Robespierre, is worth a visit today for its lively squares and marketplaces, most notably Place des Héros, Grand-Place and Place du Tertre. **Amiens**'s 13th-century Gothic cathedral miraculously survived the bombardments of two world wars. Its masterpiece is the intricate wooden carving of the 16th-century choirstalls.

Further west along the coast of **Nor-**mandy are some delightful resorts and historical ports, the most picturesque of which is the harbour of **Honfleur**. The Eugène Boudin museum attests to the town's popularity with painters – Corot, Courbet, Monet and Dufy. **Deauville**, with its casino and fashionable discos, is the queen of Channel resorts, retaining much of the elegance that made it a name in the *belle époque* at the turn of the century.

Inland one should visit the superb abbey ruins in **Jumièges**, consecrated in 1067 to celebrate William's conquest of England. **Rouen**, capital of upper Normandy, is cherished by the French as the place where Joan of Arc was burned at the stake (but the British, who were responsible for her death, are allowed to visit). The 11th- and 12th-century cathedral is only one of several splendid monuments in this great medieval city and port on the River Seine.

The beaches of the **D-Day landings** of 6 June 1944 – Omaha, Utah, Gold, Juno and Sword – are to be found along the Calvados coast. One of several mu-

94

seums devoted to the landings which were the start of the Allied liberation of continental Europe is at La Madeleine, behind Utah Beach. The most important exhibition commemorating "Operation Overlord" is located at **Arromanches**. In the bay the remnants of the former artificial Mulberry harbour peek out of the water. The huge concrete construction, comprising a breakwater and piers, was towed across the Channel and installed off Arromanches in order to land supplies for the Allied forces.

The Atlantic: A swig of the fine local Calvados apple brandy might be advisable before braving the Atlantic winds along the Cotentin peninsula, where the wild Norman conquerors came from. **Caen** is the capital of lower Normandy and was the home of William the Conqueror before he moved to England. He and his wife Mathilde left two fine abbeys, *aux Hommes* and *aux Dames,* west and east of the city centre. In the cathedral at **Bayeux** hangs the exquisite tapestry depicting the events surrounding the conquest. Cannes was flattened in

The majesty of Mont-St-Michel.

the 1944 Battle of Normandy and just outside the town is the Mémorial, an impressive museum to peace.

Probably the most dramatic ecclesiastical building in all France, indeed one of the wonders of the Western world, is **Mont-St-Michel**, in a bay at the bottom of the Cotentin peninsula. The abbey, built between the 11th century and the 16th century, is perched on an island-rock that is reached by road along a dike. Try to be there at high tide.

Brittany, too, has some fine seaside resorts with sandy beaches, most notably at **Dinard** on the English Channel and **La Baule** on the Atlantic, but it is appreciated most for the beauty of its craggy coastline. The pink granite rocks of the Corniche Bretonne run from **Ploumanac'h**, via **Tregastel**'s excellent swimming beach, to **Trebeurden**.

The Bretons maintain their own Celtic language and customs, most notably the Pardons, religious processions which still see local people in their rich regional dress. Their ancient Celtic origins can be seen in the extraordinary

stone circles such as those at **Carnac**, where some 3,000 giant stones were laid out by their ancestors for some form of worship.

Further down the Atlantic coast, **La Rochelle** is a gracious port town famous for Cardinal Richelieu's ruthless siege of the Protestant population in the 17th century – the Protestants are still there. Today it's a favourite port of call for yachtsmen and the houses of the old town have retained their 17th- and 18th-century charm, particularly along the Rue du Palais.

Bordeaux, too, has an attractive old town district. Its Grand Théâtre is one of the handsomest in the country. But the real monuments are the Médocs, Margaux and Pauillacs that can be tasted in wine cellars. Nearby is the charming village of **Saint-Emilion**, which provides a closer look at the vineyards.

Biarritz, cherished resort of Emperor Napoleon III and his wife Eugénie, Bismarck and the Prince of Wales (before he became Edward VII), gives a sense of France's old-style grandeur. With a

little imagination, their reflections can still be seen in the crystal chandeliers of the wonderful old casino. The less sentimental will enjoy the oceanographical displays at the Musée de la Mer (Maritime Museum).

The southwest is also the rugged countryside of the **Auvergne**, the rolling valley of the **Dordogne** and the succulent cuisine of the **Périgord**, to be tasted in such picturesque towns as **Sarlat** or **Cahors**.

East of Périgord, in a short stretch of the Vézère Valley between Montignac and Les Ezyiers, is the world's most astonishing collection of prehistoric art. The paintings and engravings of the **Lascaux cave** are nothing less than breathtaking. Between 13,000 and 30,000 years old, the three-colour friezes of animals use a range of techniques, perspective and movement.

Further south, military history buffs will be fascinated by the complete fortified town of **Carcassonne**, though it looks as if it has more to do with fairytales than war. There is no medieval monument like it in Europe. Nearby is **Castelnaudry**, home of a famous French stew. Further east is **Albi**, another fine historical town, best-known today as the birthplace, in 1864, of the painter Toulouse-Lautrec.

The capital of these central southwestern lands of the Languedoc is **Toulouse,** which brims with character and civic pride. It has a massive red-brick fortress-church, St-Sernin, and impressive 16th- and 17th-century mansions in the old town district, also built of the region's red brick. Its museums are rich in Romanesque sculpture. Today it is the hi-tech capital of France, home of the Airbus and Concorde.

Burgundy and Bubbly: If one's taste is for Burgundy rather than Bordeaux, head east towards **Dijon** and **Beaune**. But the green and pleasant countryside of northern Burgundy makes it well worth while getting off the *autoroute* and exploring the back roads. Check out the white wine at **Chablis** and the pretty little Italianate château at nearby **Tanlay**. Further east, the abbey at **Fontenay** makes for a welcome moment of peace

Café concerns in Languedoc.

in its 12th-century cloisters. The lively city of Dijon was the capital of the 14th- and 15th-century Dukes of Burgundy. In their graceful Palais des Ducs, they rest in grandiose tombs. At the **Char-treuse** (Charterhouse) de Champenol, see the so-called Moses' Well (Puits de Moise), in fact a fine set of 14th-century statues for the cloister's water-basin, including Moses, Jeremiah, Isaiah and King David.

The wine country tour from Dijon down to Beaune goes through such illus-trious "labels" as **Gevrey-Chambertin**, **Clos de Vougeot** and **Nuits-St-Georges**. In Beaune itself, when not tasting the wine, it's worth taking a look at the elegant 15th-century Hôtel-Dieu, once a hospital, now an old peoples' home with an important museum of Flemish art.

In the Jura mountains of Franche-Comté, the town of **Besançon** nestles in a sweeping curve of the River Doubs. Visit the 16th-century Palais Granville, aristocratic home of the Chancellor to Spanish Habsburg Emperor Charles V. The town also has an impressive 70-dial astronomical clock in the cathedral and a formidable 17th-century citadel built for Louis XIV's eastern defences.

The **Champagne plains** as well as **Lorraine** and **Alsace** offer some pleas-ant stops for the eastbound traveller to Luxembourg or Germany. The Cham-pagne is the home of the greatest spar-kling drink known to man and it can be sampled in the wine grower's cellars of **Epernay** and in the historic city of **Reims**, which is also noted for the ca-thedral where the kings of France were crowned.

Lorraine and Alsace have been his-toric bones of contention between France and Germany. Here after World War I the French built the Maginot Line, an impressive line of fortifications along their eastern border. Unfortunately it was never used, for the Germans simply went round it. Some of the huge under-ground fortresses such as the Hacken-berg near **Thionville** can be visited during the summer.

Nancy, capital of Lorraine, is graced by a beautifully harmonious main square, the 18th-century Place Stanislas, its palatial pavilions flanked by mag-nificent gilded wrought-iron gates. On the way into Alsace, stop at **Ronchamp** to admire Le Corbusier's striking chapel Notre-Dame-Du-Haur, a landmark of 20th-century architecture. The moun-tain ridge of the **Vosges** embraces a charming countryside of forests, or-chards and vineyards, among which the villages of **Riquewihr** and **Kaysersberg** are true medieval gems.

Strasbourg is Alsace's dignified capi-tal and the headquarters of the **Euro-pean Parliament**. The River Ill encir-cles the lovely old town where Goethe was a happy student in 1770. The grace-ful cathedral, with its intriguing asym-metrically erected steeple, is as inspir-ing as ever, particularly for its central porch and the stained-glass rose win-dow above. **Colmar** has a quieter but irresistible charm; its 16th-century houses are the very essence of Alsatian tradition. Most cherished of its treas-ures is Grünewald's celebrated Issen-heim altar painting in the Unterlinden

Champagne maker displays his product.

Museum. **Belfort** owes its glory to its successful resistance against the Prussians in 1870, commemorated by the monumental lion designed by Auguste Bartholdi, creator of New York's Statue of Liberty.

The Rhône Valley: France's third-largest city, **Lyon**, lying on the Rivers Sâone and Rhone, is where southern France begins and it is a "must" for gourmets. Get here in the morning for the open-air market on the Quai Victor-Augagneur (and take side-trips to the gastronomic temple of Paul Bocuse at nearby Collonges). Lyon is Europe's historic silk capital, and its history can be seen in the intriguing Musée des Tissus (Cloth Museum) and the Museum of Gallo-Roman Civilisation. The old neighbourhoods of St Jean and Croix-Rousse have some fine Renaissance houses linked by strange underground passages unique to Lyon, known as *traboules.*

Provence is worth a holiday all to itself. A tour might well start at **Orange**, a favoured resort for the Romans when it was a colony of their empire, with a

population four times the size of its present day 25,000. The Roman theatre, graced by a statue of Emperor Augustus, is regarded as the most beautiful amphitheatre of the classical era.

The fascinating ruins at **Vaison-la-Romaine** provide a glimpse of the private side of Roman life in some well-preserved houses of 2,000 years ago. **Mont Ventoux** has a view over the whole of Provence down to Marseille and the Mediterranean or clear across to the Swiss Alps. One of the great attractions of this mountain region is the **Fontaine-de-Vaucluse**, where the underground River Sorgue suddenly springs into sight in a spectacular setting of grottos.

Back in the valley is the lively town of **Avignon**, offering a great summer theatre festival in and around its Palais des Papes. This 14th-century edifice was built at a time when the popes found Rome too dangerous to stay in. The famous bridge ("*l'on y danse, tous en rond*") now only reaches halfway across the River Rhône. (In fact, the people didn't dance on it as the French song says, but underneath it.)

West of Avignon is one of the great engineering and aesthetic achievements of Roman antiquity, the Pont du Gard aqueduct that carried 26,000 cubic yards (20,000 cubic metres) of water daily to the town of **Nîmes**. Nîmes itself has preserved its arena in which aficionados now watch bullfights where Roman gladiators once fought.

But the region's most picturesque site of ancient Roman life is **Arles**, which, besides its fine amphitheatre and arena, has the fascinating necropolis of Les Alyscamps in a lovely garden setting. The tree-shaped promenade of Les Lices creates a relaxed atmosphere for the many open air cafés. One wonders what made Van Gogh so miserable here.

Coming east again, **St-Rémy-de-Provence** is a delightful market town surrounded by vineyards, olive groves and almond trees. Finish the tour in **Aix-en-Provence**, serenest of university towns, with its wonderful arcade of plane trees across the Cours Mirabeau. Beyond lies the Côte d'Azur (*see pages 117–123*).

Left, autumn in Moustiers, Provence. **Right**, gilded gate pays tribute to the Sun King, Louis XIV.

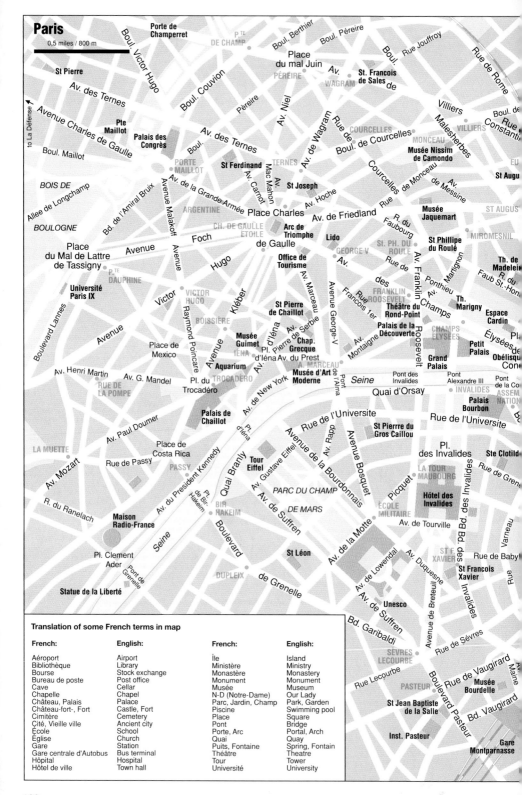

Paris

0,5 miles / 800 m

Translation of some French terms in map

French:	English:	French:	English:
Aéroport	Airport	Île	Island
Bibliothèque	Library	Ministère	Ministry
Bourse	Stock exchange	Monastère	Monastery
Bureau de poste	Post office	Monument	Monument
Cave	Cellar	Musée	Museum
Chapelle	Chapel	N-D (Notre-Dame)	Our Lady
Château, Palais	Palace	Parc, Jardin, Champ	Park, Garden
Château-fort-, Fort	Castle, Fort	Piscine	Swimming pool
Cimitère	Cemetery	Place	Square
Cité, Vieille ville	Ancient city	Pont	Bridge
École	School	Porte, Arc	Portal, Arch
Église	Church	Quai	Quay
Gare	Station	Puits, Fontaine	Spring, Fontain
Gare centrale d'Autobus	Bus terminal	Théâtre	Theatre
Hôpital	Hospital	Tour	Tower
Hôtel de ville	Town hall	Université	University

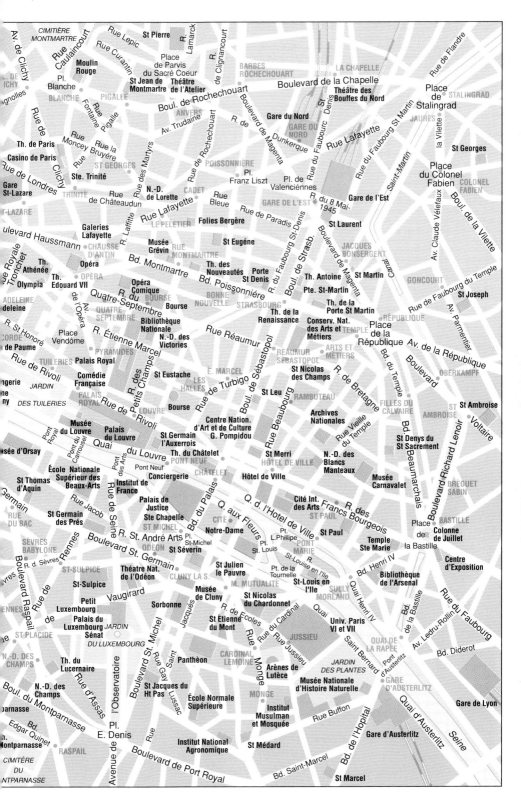

101

PARIS

Of all European capitals, Paris is undoubtedly the most glamorous. Little wonder, considering its grand architecture combined with a reputation for high living, fine cuisine and *haute couture*. Paris may not be the navel of the world any more, as the writer Henry Miller once proclaimed, but its self-assured character remains undiminished.

Paris may at first appear a really cosmopolitan city but it has maintained its quintessentially French character despite the invasion of American fast-food chains and the proliferation of Anglicisms in the French language, creating an idiom called *Franglais*. From the *clochards* sheltering in the subway stations (who are not latent poets but merely winos), to the crêpe makers and the *bouquinistes* (open-air book sellers) along the Seine, Paris offers a plethora of sights, sounds and smells.

Altogether, downtown Paris covers a circular area of 41 sq. miles (105 sq. km) and is bounded by the recreational parks of the **Bois de Vincennes** to the east and the **Bois de Boulogne** to the west. The city is divided into 20 districts called *arrondissements*, each with its own distinct character. The lower numbers up to nine designate the oldest districts of the city. *La ville de Paris*, which is the city proper (population 2.2 million), is surrounded by a belt of communities called the *banlieue* (suburbs) totalling about 8½ million people.

Born on an island: The origins of Paris are concentrated on the Île de la Cité, the largest of the two odd-shaped islands in the middle of the Seine. Here, Celtic fishermen called *Parisii* founded a village in the 3rd century BC, which they aptly named *Lutetia* – "a place surrounded by water." In 52 BC, during his Gallic War, Julius Caesar conquered the settlement. More invasions were to come from Germanic tribes; the strongest of them, the Franks, made Paris their capital in the 6th century. In the 10th century Hugo Capet ascended the throne as the first of the Capetian monarchs and made Paris a medieval centre of culture and learning.

The Renaissance monarchs were responsible for creating what today constitutes the classic beauty of Paris: some of the major streets, charming squares, the Louvre Palace with the grand Tuileries Gardens and the first stone bridge across the Seine, the Pont Neuf.

Sun King Louis XIV moved the capital to Versailles in the late 17th century but Paris continued to prosper. Luxury trades added to the prestige of the city, gaining renown among foreign visitors. The overthrow of the *ancien régime* by the legendary storming of the Bastille prison on 14 July 1789 was followed by the rise and fall of Napoleon Bonaparte, who left Paris the Arc de Triomphe and other great neo-classical monuments.

In the middle of the 19th century the urban planner Baron Haussmann laid out his *grands boulevards*. The Bois de Boulogne and Bois de Vincennes, the railway stations and the Opéra were also on his drawing board when the military defeat in the Franco-Prussian

Left, dusk in the romantic city. Right, puppy love.

War of 1870–71 brought down the Second Empire of Napoleon III.

The *belle époque* came to an abrupt end in 1914 when World War I broke out and the advancing Germans shelled Paris. They never got into the city as they did in World War II when Paris was occupied for more than four years. When the *Wehrmacht* finally retreated in August 1944, Hitler ordered the bridges over the Seine to be blown up. The German commandant saved the city by disobeying the Führer's instructions.

The postwar era again changed the face of Paris and successive presidents have left their marks on the city. André Malraux, Minister of Culture under the presidency of Charles de Gaulle, began a large-scale programme to whitewash the facades of the capital. The **Pompidou Centre** was built under President Pompidou in 1977 and President Mitterrand left his mark with the **Grande Arche**, a giant rectangular office block in the **La Défense** business quarter to the west of the city, and the glass pyramid entranceway to the Louvre.

City tour: using the city's many landmarks and riding on the easily mastered Métro, it is not difficult to find your way around the city. The right bank and the left bank of Paris grew up with a separate and distinct social tradition which is still prevalent today. The right bank has retained its established role as the mercantile centre. Here are the banks, swanky department stores, posh airline and government offices and the *Bourse*, the pompous stock exchange. The left bank, on the other hand, has been the domain of the intellectual community.

A tour of Paris may begin from any of its major landmarks. Those eager for an introductory panoramic view usually head for the Basilica of Sacré Coeur on the heights of Montmartre or the Eiffel Tower by the river, two of the classic vantage points. Others set out for the Place de l'Opéra to explore the *grands boulevards*, the *mondaine* shops along the Faubourg St-Honoré or the beautifully colonnaded Rue de Rivoli. Departing from the right bank, it may be equally tempting to take a stroll along

Left, La Grande Arche, La Défense. **Right**, modern Houdini outside the Pompidou Centre.

the Champs-Élysées. One can either walk down from the Arc de Triomphe or walk up from the **Louvre**, farther east.

Today the Louvre is the largest art museum in the world, although it was originally built as a medieval fortress to protect the River Seine. François I (1515–47) was the Louvre's first art collector. He acquired four Raphaels, one portrait of himself by Titian and three masterpieces from his friend Leonardo da Vinci, including the *Mona Lisa (La Joconde)*.

When opened to the public after the Revolution, the Louvre had 650 works of art. It now has a sparkling glass pyramid entranceway by I.M. Pei and extends over three-fifths of the palace (the rest being occupied by ministries), storing an estimated 400,000 pieces of art, only a small percentage of which are exhibited. The archaeological treasures (from Oriental, Egyptian and Graeco-Roman periods) are spread over the first two floors. Each day (except Tuesday when the Louvre and most other museums are closed) thousands of visitors

The Louvre.

pay homage to the work of an unknown sculptor from the 2nd century BC. His *Venus de Milo*, found in 1820 by a peasant on the Greek island of Melos, reveals an unsurpassed sense of harmony and feminine beauty.

From the Louvre to the Place de la Concorde extend the **Jardin des Tuileries**, some of the best examples of typically French-styled formal gardens where trees, plants and decorations are carefully laid out in a pattern. The small **Jeu de Paume** has temporary exhibitions and on the opposite (river) side of the Tuileries, the **Orangerie** offers regular retrospectives of 19th- and 20th-century artists. (Métro: Palais Royal, Louvre and Tuileries.)

The Jardin des Tuileries opens to the **Place de la Concorde**, a vast square that occupies a bloody chapter in French history. In 1793 it became the site of executions where Marie Antoinette and Louis XVI, among others, met their fate on the guillotine. In 1795 peace returned to the square, today one of the hubs of Parisian traffic, which rushes

past the oldest monument to be found in the city: the 55-foot (17-metre) Obelisk of Luxor. Dating from 1300 BC, it was taken from the Temple of Rameses in Egypt and shipped as a gift to Paris in 1836. (Métro stop: Concorde).

From the Tuileries, **Rue Castiglione** leads north to **Place Vendôme**, the queen of all squares in Paris. Shaped like an octagon, it is lined by 17th-century buildings which house some of the city's most exclusive stores, specialising in perfume, fashion and jewellery. In its centre towers a 144-foot (44-metre) column with bas-reliefs of bronze from 1,200 cannons captured in 1805 from the Austrians at the Battle of Austerlitz.

A pseudo-Greek temple stands out prominently from its position at the junction of the **Grands Boulevards** and the end of **Rue Royal**, leading from Concorde. Napoleon dedicated this monument to the glory of his Grand Armée. Better known as **La Madeleine**, it has served as a church since 1842. Opposite the church along the Boulevard de la Madeleine is a flower market and diagonally opposite the Madeleine is the world-famous caterer, Fauchon. (Métro stop: Place de la Madeleine).

Continuing west from the Place de la Concorde, one enters onto the **Champs-Elysées**. The lower stretch to the Rond-Point is a broad avenue lined with horse chestnut and plane trees. It makes an attractive promenade and has a little park, north of which lies the presidential Palais d'Élysée. Between the Rond-Point and the **Arc de Triomphe** the Champs-Élysées takes on a different character. It becomes an elegant avenue of smart shops and luxury boutiques.

Walking up the Champs-Élysées gives a magnificent view of the monumental Arc de Triomphe. Built between 1806 and 1836, this impressive monument stands 165 feet (50 metres) high and 148 feet (45 metres) wide. The Arc is noted for its frieze of hundreds of figures each 6 feet (2 metres) high and its 10 sculptures. The names of the major victories between the Revolution and the First Empire (military defeats are omitted) are inscribed under the arch, and the Tomb of the Unknown Soldier lies beneath. The eternal flame, scene of patriotic ceremonies, is rekindled every day at 6.30pm. The 284 steps to the top (there is also an elevator) give access to a spectacular view down the Champs-Élysées and to La Défense. In 1970 the Place de L'Étoile was officially named Charles de Gaulle after France's late resistance leader and state president. (Métro stops: George V and Étoile-Charles de Gaulle).

The district of **Montmartre**, the haunt of writers and artists until early this century, is still one of the liveliest spots after dark. This area is often regarded as the birthplace of modern art since Rousseau, Utrillo, Renoir, Gauguin and others spent their early years of painting here late in the 19th century. Known locally as *La Butte*, it was once unspoiled bohemian, and songs and comedies flowed from the dim cafés. Later, Montparnasse on the left bank took over as the artistic and literary centre.

At the **Place du Tertre**, however, some of Montmartre's former reputation lives on. Street artists dominate the

Montmartre artists, Place du Tertre.

scene offering tourists pencil caricatures or Parisian townscapes.

Incongruously set in Montmartre is the virginal-white **Basilica of Sacré Coeur**. Perched on a hill, its Byzantine cupolas are as much a part of the city skyline as the Eiffel Tower; when the lights are turned on at night, Sacré Coeur resembles a lit wedding cake. It can be reached by walking up 250 steps or by taking a funicular railway.

At the foot of Sacré Coeur, along **Boulevard de Clichy**, is **Pigalle**, the traditional entertainment quarter of Paris. It is symbolized by the neon-red windmill sails of the **Moulin Rouge** cabaret, home of can-can dancing since the days of Toulouse-Lautrec. Here too were once the dimly lit cabarets where the legendary Edith Piaf, the "Sparrow of Paris," sang her way to fame.

Around the red-light bars lining the side streets of **Place Pigalle**, the *belles de nuit* (beauties of the night) beckon for clients while touts try to lure strangers to a "real Parisian private party".

Visitors to Paris in the 1960s still remember their nightly excursions to Les Halles, the bustling fresh food market in the historic centre of the city. Once termed "the belly of Paris", the market which caused daily traffic congestion has been moved to Rungis in the south of Paris. On the site of the old iron constructions of the market now sprawls a multi-storey complex called **Forum des Halles,** filled with cinema halls, boutiques, galleries and restaurants.

To the east of the historic markets off Boulevard de Sébastopol looms the giant cultural machine of the **Pompidou Centre** (the Centre Nationale d'Art et de Culture Georges Pompidou, to give it its official name). Built between 1972 and 1976 by the architects Renzo Piano and Richard Rogers (winners among 681 competing designs), the futuristic structure with its multi-coloured piping and tubing resembles an oil refinery rather than a classic museum. With about 7 million visitors a year, Le Beaubourg, as it is known, has outclassed the Eiffel Tower and the Louvre as a crowd-puller.

East of the Pompidou Centre is one of

Looking down the Champs Élysées to the Arc de Triomphe.

the city's most charming quarters and home to some of the finest mansions to be found in Paris. The **Marais** was originally swampland but became a fashionable residential district in the 17th century. The Marais today is the scene of an annual festival of music and drama. In the same neighbourhood is the old Jewish quarter of Paris and a splendid little square that is the city's oldest. The 63 houses of **Place de Vosges**, with arcades, were deliberately built to look symmetrical. The writer Victor Hugo (1802-85) once lived here and his house at number 6 is a museum.

The Left Bank: In the very heart of Paris, the Seine River divides to embrace **Île de la Cité** and **Île St-Louis**. Traditionally a residence of Paris gentry, the latter has remained a patch of tranquillity in this fast-paced city. Neighbouring Île de la Cité is cluttered with historic landmarks, the most celebrated being the **Notre Dame Cathedral**. This magnificent example of Gothic ecclesiastical architecture is simply stunning viewed from any angle. It was purport-

edly built on the grounds of a Gallo-Roman temple that was first replaced by a Christian basilica and a Romanesque church. The construction of the cathedral itself began in 1133 and work was only completed in 1345.

Also to be found on Île de la Cité is the **Conciergerie**. It was once part of the Royal Palace where the warden of the kings used to live. This massive building is a beautiful sight at night when its arches are illuminated. During the French Revolution in 1789, it served as a prison for those awaiting the guillotine. Guided tours go through the courtyards where the prisoners would assemble daily. Marie Antoinette's private cell, the kitchen and the guardroom can also be seen.

The **Palais de Justice**, housing the present Paris law courts, was built on the same spot that over centuries served as the administrative quarters of the ancient Roman government and the early kings. In the courtyard is **Sainte Chapelle**, a Gothic chapel with magnificent stained-glass windows built in the 13th

Floor show at the Paradis Latin.

century by the saintly king Louis IX. (Métro stop: Cité, Châtelet.)

South of the river: From the Île de la Cité, the **Pont St Michel** leads to the left bank straight into the **Latin Quarter**. It earned its name from the dominance of Latin-speaking students who attended the nearby Sorbonne university.

The grand glass-and-iron *belle-époque* railway station of Quai d'Orsay by the river has become one of the city's great art museums, the **Musée d'Orsay.** It has a major collection of late 19th-century works, particularly by Delacroix and Ingres, as well-paintings by the later Impressionists, Monet, Manet, Renoir, Cézanne and Van Gogh.

East of **Boulevard St-Michel**, its main thoroughfare, the Latin Quarter is threaded with numerous narrow alleys such as **Rue de la Huchette**, a twisting lane of Greek restaurants, kebab corners, jazz spots and cinemas. A mini Chinatown with Chinese and Vietnamese restaurants and food stalls has sprung up. **Rue des Ecoles** gives access to the **Sorbonne**, where one can wander through its hallowed portals.

Walking down the Boulevard St-Michel and turning to the left into Rue Soufflot, one arrives at the **Panthéon**. Built as a church to fulfil Louis XV's pious vow after he recovered from an illness, the Panthéon has, since 1791, served as a national shrine to commemorate its most outstanding citizens.

On the opposite side of Boulevard St-Michel stretch the spacious **Luxembourg Gardens**. They are popular with students whiling away time between classes and children are thrilled by the adventures of Guignol (the French equivalent of the Punch and Judy Show) which are featured in the gardens' **Théâtre des Marionettes**. (Métro stop: St Michel, Odéon, Luxembourg.)

In the evening and late into the night the **Rive Gauche** becomes even more animated as crowds of people promenade along Boulevard St-Michel and **Boulevard St-Germain**, which leads from the **Pont de la Concorde** further east into the Latin Quarter. The open-air terraces of restaurants and cafés in the area are popular venues for people to sit for a drink and to soak in the ambience. Next to the pre-Gothic church of St-Germain-des-Prés are two cafés that have been elevated to the rank of institutions: the **Café Aux Deux Magots** and the **Café de Flore**. (Métro stop: Mabillon, St Germain-des-Prés.)

Heading south into **Rue de Rennes** and then changing into **Boulevard de Raspail**, one passes into the **Quartier de Montparnasse**, which replaced Montmartre as the centre of bohemian life early this century. Artists, writers, poets and revolutionaries, among them Lenin and Trotsky, flocked to live here. After World War I, American expatriate writers of the "Lost Generation", such as Hemingway, F. Scott Fitzgerald and Henry Miller, joined the locals who used to congregate in famous literary cafés like Le Dome, La Rotonde, Le Sélect or the huge dining halls of La Coupole. All these celebrated places are now surrounded by an air of nostalgia since Montparnasse has undergone extensive urban renewal in the last decade. Many of the quarter's artist studios and

The famous Café Aux Deux Magots.

small hotels have been demolished and the huge Montparnasse Tower symbolises the region's changing identity as a business centre. (Métro stop: Vavin, Raspail, Montparnasse).

Back to the Seine: The gilded Dome des Invalides faces the right bank from across Pont d'Alexandre III. Immediately beneath the vast cupola rests Emperor Napoleon I, whose body was transferred here from the island of St Helena in 1840. It is encased in seven separate sarcophagi, the exterior one being made of precious red marble. The church is surrounded by the Hôtel des Invalides built by Louis XIV as a hospital to shelter 7,000 disabled soldiers. Today it houses the **Musée d'Armée**, featuring arms, uniforms and trophies from France's military past. Just a few steps away at 77 Rue de Varenne, the former studio of sculptor Auguste Rodin (1840-1917) is now the **Musée Rodin**.

To the west of the Invalides is the École Militaire – the French Military College. It is fronted by a former parade ground, Champs de Mars, which leads

to the **Eiffel Tower**. Named after its creator Gustave Eiffel (who had designed the structure for New York's Statue of Liberty), the tower was designed as a temporary structure, slated to be dismantled in 1910, 21 years after its inauguration at the Paris World Fair. But since it proved its value as a wireless tower it remained intact. From its top platform, 800 feet (267 metres) above ground, there is a view in a radius of about 30 miles (48 km) on a clear day.

Opposite the Eiffel Tower on the right bank is the **Palais de Chaillot**, dating from the International Exposition of 1937. It has several museums and the national film library, **Cinémathèque Français**. (Métro stops: Invalides, Varenne, Trocadéro, École Militaire.)

Around the city: The most sumptuous of all châteaux in France is **Versailles**. Not to be missed, it is only 13 miles (21 km) away from the capital. Versailles was remodelled from an original manor farm by Louis XIII who used to hunt in the surrounding woods. He had the farm converted into a rose brick and stone château. This was expanded by Louis XIV, the Sun King, who took 50 years to create a palace that was so magnificent that it was copied by all over Europe.

Versailles served as capital of France on various occasions and, in its heyday, had a court population of 20,000. The palace itself housed 5,000. It was a royal residence until the Revolution of 1789.

North of Paris, on the Seine, is the house and garden of **Giverny**, created by Claude Monet who lived there until his death in 1926. Beautifully restored it has become a popular tourist spot, particularly the Japanese garden where the lilies, so famously painted by this premier Impressionist, still blossom.

A bigger attraction, though of different appeal, is **Euro Disney**, the US entertainment empire's first foothold in Europe which opened with a great fanfare in 1992. It is located at Marne-la-Vallée, 20 miles (32 km) east of Paris on a 5,000-acre (1,943-hectare) site which will not be fully developed until 2017. Although it got off to a rocky financial start, it initially attracted more than twice as many visitors as the Louvre.

Left, the Eiffel Tower. **Right**, Versailles

THE LOIRE VALLEY

The celebrated valley of the River Loire, southwest of Paris, presents itself in many facets. It has been praised as the garden of France and has been described as a melting pot of the Celtic, Roman and Nordic civilisations. Most of all, however, it was the home of kings and princes who have left a splendid mosaic of châteaux, recognised as among the finest in the world.

The whitewashed village houses along the Loire and its tributaries have a quiet charm and the valley has been an inspiration for the arts. This comes as much from the broad and reassuring river, with its hues of slate blue and subtle chalky white, as from the cities, which represent a high point of France's culture. Large and small, the prosperous towns and villages were each blessed with a handsome château or church, distinguished by artists and craftsmen.

Writers such as Rousseau, Voltaire and Molière have also been seduced by the valley's gentle life. Jean Rabelais, lusty poet of the French Renaissance, was born here, as was Honoré de Balzac, the great social historian and genius of the French 19th-century novel. Balzac's former summer home at the castle of **Saché** has been preserved as a museum.

From Paris, a tour of the Loire Valley usually begins in **Gien** or **Orléans**, an hour's drive west of the capital. The Loire proper, rising on Mont Gerbier de Joncs in the Massif Central is, at 634 miles (1,015 km), the longest river in France. It leaves its scenic valley around **Angers** to continue its journey to the Atlantic Ocean.

The road south from Orléans leads into the country of **Sologne**. Pheasants share the roadway by day and rabbits by night. The forests and marshes have been used by hunters here since time immemorial.

Beaugency, 8 miles (12 km) from Orléans, has an 11th-century dungeon, 12th-century abbey, Renaissance town hall and charming bridge. From here, **Medieval tapestry.**

the road leads on to the very heart of château country.

Altogether, the Loire region has about 3,000 castles of various periods. To visit all of them would take a lifetime. The oldest ones, such as the castle of **Loches**, began life as fortified towers and served as shelters during the strife-torn Middle Ages; the latest ones such as the opulent palace of **Cheverny** were designed for comfort rather than for defence, serving as pleasure grounds for the aristocracy during the age of absolutism. The châteaux built between the 15th and the mid-16th centuries rank as the apogee of the Renaissance.

The crown of France belonged by that time to the house of Valois so the Loire valley consequently became known as the country of the Valois.

The first Valois to seek refuge here was Charles VII in 1418. Then Dauphin (heir to the throne) of France, he had been driven out of Paris by the Duke of Burgundy who supported the claims of Henry IV of England to the French crown during the Hundred Years' War

with England. In 1429 the war took a miraculous turn when, accompanied by six men-at-arms, an 18-year-old peasant girl from Lorraine appeared at the castle of Chinon, west of Tours, which was then the seat of the royal court. She revealed to the Dauphin that divine voices had told her to aid him in the reconquest of his legitimate throne. Jeanne la Pucelle became France's national heroine, Joan of Arc, and proved her divine mission by a stunning military feat three months later when she led a royal troop of just a few hundred men to defeat the English, breaking their siege of Orléans.

Each year on 7 and 8 May her triumphant entry into the city is celebrated as the greatest event in its history. At the choir of the present cathedral the pious virgin delivered her prayers of thanks, and at Place du Martroi she can be seen in bronze, riding out to battle.

The first château to be seen when entering the Loire valley from Orléans is **Chambord**, a fantasy palace that bewitched even the most blasé of the

The Renaissance Palace at Chambord.

Venetian ambassadors to the court of France. The building is a gigantic stairway on which wings have been grafted. The stairway with its double turn is the structure's pivot. It soars to the roofs, and offers an unmistakable symbol of the power of the French king.

Everything about Chambord is colossal, but King François I, who built it, spent only 40 days there, Henri IV never came near it and Louis XIII dropped in but once. The court stopped going there in 1684, which meant that nobody troubled to complete this enormous structure, just a frozen dream set in the heart of Sologne. A *son et lumière* show celebrates its past glories.

Blois, with France's most frequented château after Versailles, is next along the valley. Without fortifications, opening on the Louis XIII wing, it has the look of a grand bourgeois dwelling offering peace, prosperity and ornament. As a vestige of its earliest years, Blois has kept its ramparts facing the Loire. Its tower of Foix provides a superb panorama over the river and suburbs.

Chaumont, on the left bank of the Loire, lies in a setting that the Prince de Broglie transformed into a veritable pastiche of the Arabian Nights. Further west, on the opposite bank, is **Amboise**, whose château, once the home of Louis XI, Charles VIII, Louis XIII, François I and Habsburg Emperor Charles V, is considered one of the finest. Much of the palace has disappeared but what is left still offers a striking contrast between the "Italianate" modifications of Charles VIII and the old medieval fortress. Leonardo da Vinci is buried in St Hubert's Chapel.

Jewel of the Renaissance: There is no clash of style about **Chenonceaux**, which achieves a perfect harmony in its Renaissance architecture. Anchored like a great ship in the middle of the River Cher, due south of Amboise, and surrounded by broad fields, Chenonceaux is a work of feminine grace, a delicate jewel set in a green casket. It was the preferred home of Diane de Poitiers, "the eternally beautiful" ravishing mistress of Henri II, and of cruel Marie de Medici, bitter enemy not only of her husband Henri IV, but also her son Louis XIII.

Chenonceaux was famous for its festivities. One of the first was the triumphal celebration on 1 March 1560 for François II and his young wife Mary Stuart. Today, the parties are all but forgotten, though there is still magic in the great classical gallery on a bridge of five arches creating a lovely reflection in the waters of the river.

About 30 miles (48 km) southwest of Tours, the capital of the Touraine region, is **Azay le Rideau**, partly built over the River Indre. This "multi-faceted diamond set in the Indre, mounted on pillars, a maske of flowers" as it was described by Balzac, offers the quintessence of the Touraine's architecture.

Chinon, 12 miles (20km) southwest of Azay, once consisted of three different fortresses. Some of the mighty fortifications as well as parts of the moat are left. A length of wall with a high Gothic chimney-piece remains from the **Grand Logis**, the hall where the court witnessed the unerring judgement of

Entrance to the Louis XII wing at Blois.

Joan of Arc when she recognized the Dauphin despite his disguise as a humble courtier.

One of the castle's towers was called Agnes Sorel after the mistress of Charles VII. In contrast to Joan of Arc, who was canonized in 1920, Agnes Sorel stands little chance of being worshipped as a saint. Her sins were so many, it is said, that her confession gave time for the priest's staff to be planted in the earth and turn into a holy tree.

In the 17th century Chinon once more became a centre of French politics when Cardinal Richelieu, first minister of France, took over the castle. His family abandoned it to become the grand ruins that can be seen today.

Beyond Chinon is **Saumur**, where the surrounding woodlands are rich in mushrooms and, in this wine country where the whites are pre-eminent, the local pride is the red Champigny and sparkling Saumur. The town's medieval castle houses the **Musée du Cheval** (Horse Museum), tracing the long history of the horse in France. As God's companion, the horse was also regarded in Gallo-Roman mythology as an embodiment of God Himself, echoes of which are to be found in local traditions. At the end of July, the *Carrousel* festivities include impressive demonstrations of dressage and horsemanship. The road from Saumur to Angers follows the riverbank, past compact white villages worth a stop for local delicacies.

At Ponts-de-Cé, a road leads north to **Angers**, town of the good King René, Duke of Anjou and of Provence. In the old town there are many fine specimens of Renaissance houses, most notably the **Logis Barrault** (housing the fine arts museum with some noteworthy works by Watteau, Chardin and Boucher), and the **Hôtel de Pincé** (also now an art museum devoted to Greek, Etruscan, Chinese and Japanese works). But pride of place among Angers' art treasures must go to the tapestries in the château, particularly the *Tenture de l'Apocalypse*, 70 pictures from a 14th-century work. The château itself is a splendid example of a medieval feudal fortress.

The château of Tanlay.

THE RIVIERA

The French Riviera was once synonymous with gambling and extravagance; a dignified daytime facade for the after-dark antics of Russian czars and British royalty. Today it is more a gaudy stage setting for sovereigns of showbiz.

It retains some aspects of the past. The number of czars has thinned out considerably, but aristocratic Britons abound and the European celebrities who don't own opulent villas in the lush hills behind Cannes or on the beach at St Tropez would be impertinent to hold their heads high among their peers.

The sun-drenched Riviera meanders lazily along the rocky Mediterranean lagoons and coves, beginning at the Italian frontier where it first captures the shimmering reflection of the 17th-century town of **Menton**. This is probably the warmest winter resort on any French coast and offers one of the most typical townscapes in Provence. In the narrow, twisting, vaulted streets overhead balconies jut out precariously over the alleyways until they almost bump balustrades.

The coastline runs southwest past the towering palisades of old **Monaco**; it then washes the stretch of golf-ball-sized pebbles that passes for a beach at Nice, and races past the tacky urban blight that has sprung up in deference to package tour operators around **Cagnes-sur-Mer**. Further on it carries a welcome puff of breeze to fill a sail or two in the magnificent yacht harbour at **Antibes**, which rests at the foot of an enormous brick citadel built in the 16th century to protect the infant town from assaults by Barbary pirates. The coast eventually graces the elegant Croisette, that celebrated boulevard at Cannes, only 40 miles (65 km) from Menton.

The Riviera ends at Cannes. The rocky coast that twists its way onward to **Marseille**, France's largest port and second largest city, is an extension of the entire coastal strip from Menton to the mouth of the River Rhône, called the Côte d'Azur. It includes **Fréjus**, a village

founded by Julius Caesar in 49 BC, where grisly bullfights still take place, appropriately enough, in an amphitheatre built by early Roman conquerors; and nearby **St Raphaël**, with the finest sweep of sandy beach on a coast which, considering that it earns its livelihood through tourism, is surprisingly devoid of that commodity.

St Tropez, where voluptuous budding starlets supposedly trade favours with high rollers for film contracts or Ferraris, and **Toulon**, the bawdy harbour city that is home port to France's Mediterranean naval fleet, are less accessible tourist frontiers down the Côte toward Marseille.

A paradise for gamblers: Many people have experienced those heady days when they get the feeling that they're worth a king's ransom. **Monte Carlo**, the ritzy resort of the principality of Monaco, is the place to put it all to the supreme test. The sumptuously decorated gaming rooms of the world's most famous gambling **Casino** are open to visitors, as is the Las Vegas-style gambling hall at the

Left, Cap d'Antibes. **Right**, street games in Grasse.

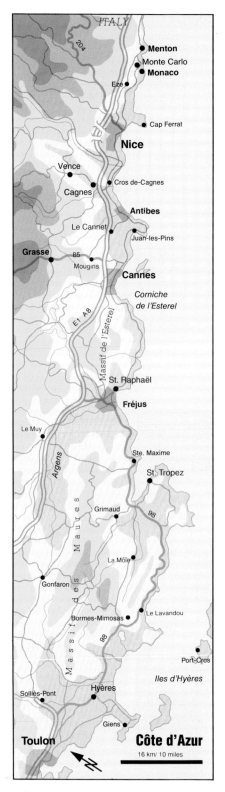

ITALY

Menton
Monte Carlo
Monaco
Eze

Cap Ferrat

Nice

Vence

Cros de-Cagnes

Cagnes

Antibes

Le Cannet

Juan-les-Pins

Grasse

Mougins

Cannes

Corniche
de l'Esterel

Massif de l'Esterel

St. Raphaël

Fréjus

Le Muy

Argens

Ste. Maxime

St. Tropez

Grimaud

La Môle

Massif des Maures

Gonfaron

Bormes-Mimosas

Le Lavandou

Port-Cros

Iles d'Hyères

Solliès-Pont

Hyères

Giens

Toulon

Côte d'Azur

16 km/ 10 miles

nearby **Loews Hotel**. Today's visitors seem to prefer the more relaxed atmosphere of the Loews when it comes to trying their luck, but Monaco's social butterflies still flutter around the famous *belle époque* wedding-cake-style Casino and its neatly trimmed gardens and terraces.

The western section, the building's oldest, was built in 1878 by the same architect who designed the stately Paris Opera House. The centre section, a tiny 529-seat rococo-styled theatre, is the home of the **Monte Carlo Opera**, which was the first to sing Wagner's *Tristan and Isolde* in French. At the **Foyer de la Dance** the Ballet Russe de Monte Carlo of Sergei Diaghilev performed its controversial *avant-garde* premiers early this century.

There is also the justly famous Monte Carlo National Orchestra which has premiered works by Berlioz, Ravel and Massenet. In July and August, it gives concerts at the doll's-house palace of Prince Rainier, a crenellated, part-Moorish, part-Italian Renaissance castle perched on a 200-foot (61-metre) rocky promontory jutting nearly half a mile (800 metres) into the sea. Visitors can tour the state apartments and throne room, and the court of honour, which sports an arcaded and frescoed gallery.

From there, the charming ancient quarter of **Monaco village**, tinted with Provençal pink, orange and yellow hues, is at hand. It surrounds the neo-Romanesque cathedral which prizes its paintings by Louis Brea, the 15th-century Nice School's most renowned artist. The aquarium in the nearby **oceanographic museum** is one of the finest and best kept in Europe, and along with the tropical gardens, which contain a remarkable collection of different species of cactus, and grottos decked with stalactites and stalagmites, attracts more than 1 million footstrong visitors a year. A climb of 558 steps is required to view the grottos properly.

From the days of its early Genoese rulers, the principality of Monaco has survived as a political curiosity on the map of Europe. It exists under the protection of France but has remained a mini-monarchy of the Grimaldi family, with its own tax privileges, national licence plates and coat of arms. This tiny principality of less than a square mile (1.5 sq. km) and a population of 30,000, has lived down its reputation as a sunny place for shady people. Today, it dotes instead on tourists – the raw material of its biggest industry. Prince Rainier III, who hit the headlines when he married the American film star Grace Kelly and who now lives somewhat in the shadow of his headline-grabbing daughters, the princesses Caroline and Stephanie, is a no-nonsense administrator of the Casino and works hard to maintain Monaco's year-round lustre.

When photographers want to capture the full panorama of Monaco on film they trudge to the tiny village of **La Turbie**, 1,575 feet (475 metres) behind the principality's yawning harbour. Here are the remains of one of the most impressive, yet little known Roman monuments, the **Alpine Trophy**.

In 6 BC Rome commemorated the final subjugation of the warriors of the Alps region by raising an enormous stone trophy where it could be seen from both directions far along the Aurelian Way (which ran from Rome to the Rhône). Although not completely restored, the impressive 114-foot (35-metre) Doric colonnade is still standing and the list of conquered tribes, which makes up the original inscription dedicated to Caesar Augustus, has survived.

La Turbie is but one of a myriad of peasant villages which, during the Middle Ages and before, sprouted like eagles' nests on mountain peaks. Inaccessible and often enclosed within a protective stone barricade and fortified gate, the villages and their villagers have often shunned outsiders. But many of the more picturesque communities, such as Eze, Peille, Roquebrune and Gourdon, tolerate tourists and some even welcome them.

Eze, the best known because it is near the sea, is easy to reach and offers a splendid panoramic overview of much of the Côte d'Azur from its 1,550-foot (470-metre) elevation. It has an intrigu-

Darling of the gossip columnists: Princess Stephanie of Monaco.

ing history of pirate assaults and Moorish massacres that can be traced back to the 1st century, when a colony of Phoenicians unnerved their Roman neighbours by consecrating a temple to their god Isis. The Romans quickly and violently replaced it with a monument more to their liking and religious persuasion. Perhaps this is what caught the imagination of Friedrich Nietzsche, who was inspired in Eze to write *Thus Spake Zarathustra*. Eze is noted today for the crumbling ramparts of its 14th-century castle; the French novelist George Sand called it the loveliest gingerbread village on the Riviera.

Winter haven of the British: "The English come and pass the winter here to take the cure, soothe their chronic spleens and live out their fantasies," wrote an observer of the budding Anglo-Saxon social scene in **Nice** in 1775. They have been doing it ever since in increasing numbers, and justifiably take credit for establishing this city as the centre for touring the Riviera. At one time it took 15 hazardous days to cross the 800 miles

(1,300 km) between London and Nice by train and ferry, the latter mostly across raging seas if contemporary commentators are to be believed. Nevertheless, by 1787, at least 115 wealthy British families had established a summer colony that marked the first blush of an enduring love affair between the English and "their" Nice.

The Promenade des Anglais, the striking waterfront dual carriageway embellished with flowerbeds and palm trees, was originally built in 1822 by the English for easier access to the sea.

Queen Victoria enjoyed her morning constitutionals along that coastal path on several occasions before the turn of this century, after which time she was carried along in her famous black and red varnished donkey cart.

Today, the Promenade skirts the pebbly Mediterranean waterfront, bedecked with luxury hotels, highrise apartment blocks and trendy cafés. A short stroll away are the narrow winding alleyways of the **vieille ville** (old town) where the visitor gets a salty taste of medieval

On show in St-Tropez.

Provençal lifestyles, heightened by the aroma of garlic, wine and pungent North African spices which emanate from a succession of *couscous* parlours.

A diminishing number of plain but traditional restaurants around the flower market on the **Cours Saleya** specialise in *soupe de poissons*, and *bourride*, a native variation of *bouillabaisse*, is usually available too. *Aioli*, a rough local mayonnaise made with olive oil and crushed garlic, is traditionally served with salted codfish on Fridays. For finer palates, there are famous restaurants nearby at Antibes, Mougins and La Napoule.

The remains of an amphitheatre, capable of seating 4,000 spectators, and three public baths dating from the Roman occupation have been uncovered at **Cimiez**, an exclusive residential quarter of Nice, located one mile (1.6 km) northeast of the city centre. The archaeological treasures taken from the site are housed in a nearby 17th-century villa, which also displays an extensive collection of paintings, sculpture, engravings and ceramics by Henri Matisse.

The International Film Festival held each May in **Cannes** is one of the highlights of an annual chain of events that attracts a set of celebrities few other cities of its size in the world could take in their stride. Kings and queens of all kinds and persuasions, sheikhs, film stars, emperors and the fabulously wealthy are all grist for a mill that has been grinding since Lord Brougham, the Lord Chancellor of England, was stranded in Cannes in 1834 because of an outbreak of cholera in Nice, where he was headed for a winter holiday. It pleased him so much that he built a house on the side of **Mont Chevalier** and encouraged other British aristocrats to do the same.

Suquet is the local name for the ancient quarter around Mont Chevalier. Its steep rocky slope leads to the 17th-century **Church of Our Lady of Good Hope**, whose clock tower is the main reference point for the city. At dinner hour in the high season, elegant women in pearls and Parisian evening gowns

The old quarter of Cannes.

and gentlemen in tuxedos emerge on to the streets, perhaps from a yacht anchored in the old harbour, and struggle up **Rue St-Antoine** to the fashionable restaurants for which the Suquet is noted.

Dinner will almost certainly be followed by a stroll along the luxurious **Boulevard de la Croisette** for the magnificent views of the Suquet silhouetted against **La Napoule Bay**, with the chunky red hills of the Esterel in the background. Starlight brings out the best in La Croisette.

Napoleon Bonaparte's first watering hole and rest-point, when he landed on the shores of France after his Elba exile, was a bivouac just to the side of what is today's Croisette. Unfortunately for Bonaparte, the mayor refused to let his troops enter the town and Napoleon was forced to begin his long march up through Grasse on to Castellane along what is now fondly called the **Route Napoleon**, which he followed to Grenoble, Paris and Waterloo.

Both **Castellane** and **Grasse** have become tourist centres in their own

rights, but Napoleon had nothing to do with it. Castellane is at the entrance to the Grand Canyon of Verdon, a local attraction, and Grasse has become the perfume manufacturing centre of France.

Inspired by sunlight: Painters have been especially fascinated by the Côte d'Azur because of its unique sunlight. The quality of the light is due largely to the Mistral, a cold, dry, strong wind that often blows in from the Rhône Valley, sweeping the sky to crystal clarity, enriching colours and deepening shadows. Matisse, Picasso, Dufy and Chagall were all devoted to the region and the products of their fidelity are displayed in museums and private collections along the Riviera.

In addition to the Matisse collection at Cimiez, the **Marc Chagall Biblical Message National Museum** there has a display of that artist's 17 monumental paintings of scenes from the Old Testament. The museum has three stained-glass windows depicting *The Creation* by Chagall, along with his 20-ft (6-metre) mosaic of Elijah in his fiery chariot. Many ceramics, engravings and sketches are also on view.

Pablo Picasso spent 27 creative years on the Côte d'Azur, more than half of them at **Vallauris** behind Cannes, where he established a ceramics studio. The **National Picasso Museum** is now housed here. He also lived at Antibes though his last years were spent at **Mougins**. The **Grimaldi Museum** in Antibes has a collection of Picasso's works, while his old studio there is maintained as a memorial.

The **Fondation Maeght** at **Saint-Paul-de-Vence**, a picturesque 16th-century walled hilltop town behind Nice, has an important collection of works by Raoul Dufy, Georges Braques, Fernand Léger, Matisse, Joan Miró and others. At the village of **Biot** between Nice and Cannes, the **Fernand Léger Museum**, shaded by cypress and olive trees, houses hundreds of the works by the artist, who contributed to the creation of Cubism.

St Paul is just one of a number of *villages perchés*, hilltop villages just behind the coast which maintain the old flavour of Provence.

Left, Portail du Peyra, one of Vence's old gateways. **Right**, terracotta hues in Villefranche.

BELGIUM

If he doesn't dally, a driver can cross Belgium in two hours. Zooming along highways agreeably lit with yellow sodium lights at night, rolling through deserted and drab industrial towns, he can reach the far border unaware that only a few miles away, off the beaten track, lie picturesque, medieval villages and towns that are among the best preserved in Europe.

This small country of 11,781 sq. miles (30,500 sq. km) has a population of 9.8 million people and 3.5 million racing pigeons. French-speaking Walloons inhabit the south and Flemings, whose language most closely resembles Dutch, live in the north. In spite of a common interest and a small domaine, they are not as neighbourly as their Catholic religion might like them to be.

The country has all the ingredients for an agreeable visit: attractive beaches, lonely mountains, rivers, lakes and, towards the east, forests. Because of its relative flatness, cycling is easy and a popular hobby as well as a profession, and the heroic race ace Eddy Merckx had both Walloons and Flemings rooting for him.

It also has some beautiful medieval towns, such as Ghent, Bruges and the diamond capital, Antwerp, which, with their canals and cobbled streets, are easy to explore. There is also an exceptional number of good museums housing, among other things, the works of the great Flemish painters. Finally (though many would say primarily) there is the cuisine which, Belgians will tell you, surpasses even that of France. Thousands on non-Belgian bureaucrats assigned to Economic Community or NATO posts in Brussels are especially grateful that the food is so good.

Although it has a distinctive flavour of its own, the country has in turn been ruled by Spain, Austria, France and Holland. It also has its own royal family, for which it acquired Leopold of Saxe-Coburg to kick off the dynasty. When King Baudouin died in 1993, most of his relations – the crowned heads of Europe – came to pay their respects. Belgians are good at pageants and some of the most colourful festivals in Europe take place here. With luck, the visitor will arrive to find the flags flying high.

Preceding pages: medieval Bruges, the "jewel of Flanders"; the Grand Place, Brussels. <u>Left</u>, masked carnival.

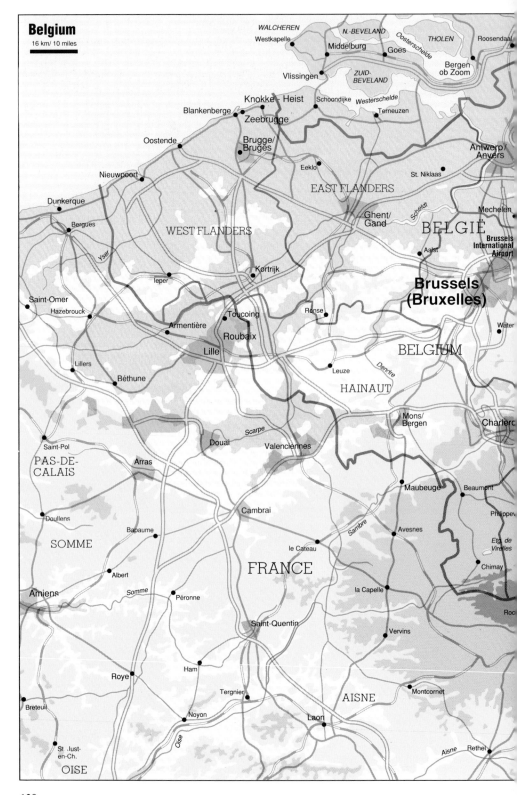

Belgium

16 km/ 10 miles

WALCHEREN
Westkapelle
N.-BEVELAND
Middelburg
Goes
Oosterschelde
THOLEN
Roosendaal

Vlissingen
ZUID-
BEVELAND
Bergen
ob Zoom

Knokke- Heist
Schoondijke
Westerschelde

Blankenberge
Zeebrugge
Terneuzen

Oostende
Brugge/
Bruges
Eeklo
St. Niklaas

Antwerp/
Anvers

Nieuwpoort
EAST FLANDERS

Dunkerque
Mechelen

Bergues
WEST FLANDERS
Ghent/
Gand
Scheldt
BELGIË

Yser
Aalst
Brussels
International
Airport

Ieper
Kortrijk
Brussels
(Bruxelles)

Saint-Omer
Ronse
Water

Hazebrouck
Toucoing

Armentière
Roubaix
BELGIUM

Lille
Leuze
Dendre

Béthune
HAINAUT

Lillers
Mons/
Bergen
Charlero

Saint-Pol
Scarpe
Douai
Valenciennes

PAS-DE-
CALAIS
Arras
Maubeuge
Beaumont

Doullens
Bapaume
Avesnes
Philippe

SOMME
le Cateau
Etg. de
Virelles

Albert
FRANCE
Chimay

Amiens
Somme
Péronne
la Capelle
Roc

Saint-Quentin
Vervins

Roye
Ham
Montcornet

Breteuil
Tergnier
AISNE

Noyon
Laon

St Just-
en-Ch.
Oise
Aisne
Rethel

OISE

130

AROUND BELGIUM

Belgium is not, as some would have it, a "pancake", except along its 40-mile (65-km) coastline washed by the North Sea. A wide ribbon of golden sands begins at **Knokke-Heist** on the Dutch border and stretches down to **De Panne** on the French frontier. The shallow beaches are safe but more suited to family holidays than water sports. They are perfect for ball games and the spectacular hybrid known as sand-yachting. The biggest and best known of the nine coastal resorts is **Ostend** where the ferries from Britain disgorge their cargoes next to a romantic fishing and yacht harbour.

The best of the Flemish towns lie at varying distances off the road on the leisurely drive from Ostend to the capital, Brussels. The route runs alongside shipping canals, lazy rivers and rolling hills, past moors, heaths and lakes and through fir and pine woods. The countryside of **Kempen** is dotted with churches. The peal of bells is a commonplace sound in the little towns and villages of Flanders.

Bruges (Brugge), the *grande dame* of the cities of Flanders, serves as a window onto Belgium's history. Miniature bridges over its delightful canals, gabled houses and verdant lawns (which Sir Winston Churchill loved to paint) have helped the city to retain a medieval atmosphere reminiscent of the time when it was one of Europe's greatest trade centres and held to be one of the most beautiful cities in the world. Bruges declined as the reputation of its rival, Antwerp, increased. Having never spilled over its 13th-century fortifications, the city, with its magnificent Gothic **Town Hall** and medieval **Cloth Hall** with a 300-ft (88-metre) Bell Tower, has become a kind of museum. To the right of the Town Hall is the **Basilica of the Holy Blood**, a reliquary carried in a magnificent procession through the city on Ascension Day.

Bruges is also famous for its Flemish art. Some of the finest paintings of the Flemish school are exhibited at the **Groeninge Museum**, among them Jan Van Eyck's controversial portrait of his wife, with the astonishingly high coiffure, and his *Canon Van Der Paelen* kneeling before the Virgin. Michelangelo's *Virgin and Child* is another prized exhibit. The enclosed village of **Beguinage**, where nuns in the days of Old Flanders secluded themselves from the world, is within the city walls.

Three miles (5 km) north of Bruges nestles the little village of **Damme**, where white windmills stand on green meadows beside tree-flanked canals. **Wingene**, 10 miles (16 km) south of Bruges, is noted for its biennial September beer festival which commemorates the 16th-century painter Pieter Bruegel.

Ghent is the city of 200 bridges and criss-crossing canals. The old medieval centre is dominated by the church of Saint Nicholas, with its Gothic belfry and 52-bell *carillon* (a mechanical bell-ring device). Next to the flamboyant Town Hall is **Saint Bavo Cathedral** which houses the Van Eyck brothers' masterpiece, *The Mystic Lamb*, and Rubens' *Conversion of Saint Bavo*. Renowned begonia fields, which come into flower between July and September, are at **Lochristi** to the northeast of Ghent.

The road to Antwerp leads past **Mechelen**, the city of belfries and carillons and home of Belgium's only school for bellringers. At the Church of Our Lady of the Dijle is the Rubens masterpiece *The Miraculous Catch of the Fishes*, and at Saint John's is another Rubens, *The Adoration of the Magi*.

City of diamonds: **Antwerp** is Europe's third largest port and has a population of 500,000. At one time, its maritime traffic – 100 ships a day and 2,000 barges – surpassed even that of Venice in its heyday. But the city lost its leading role as a trade centre in the 17th century when, under Spanish rule, its wealthy merchants fled to Holland to escape the Inquisition.

Antwerp, the home of Peter Paul Rubens (1577–1640), has become the centre of Flemish art and culture. The **Cathedral of Our Lady** is Belgium's biggest and most magnificent religious

Left, a country inn near Montagine.

building and the art collection at the **Royal Museum of Fine Arts** covers hundreds of years of Flemish art – both classical and modern. Antwerp was known as the "City of Diamonds" for its role as the cutting and trading centre of the world's diamond industry, and the precious gems can be seen at the **Diamond Centre**.

The road south from Brussels leads to a location where a watershed in European history took place: **Waterloo**. On 18 June 1815, just south of this small town, the combined Prussian and British forces imposed the final defeat on Napoleon after his escape from Elba. During the nine-hour carnage 55,000 soldiers died, 32,000 of them French. The vast battlefield is now tranquil farmland and the only reminder of the battle which changed the face of Europe is the lofty memorial standing on Lion Mound. Souvenirs, T-shirts, wineglasses, balloons and ashtrays all bear the image of Napoleon. He has been immortalized by locals, whose ancestors fought for the little French Emperor and who pretend now he won the battle – at least morally. There are no souvenirs of Wellington nor of the Prussian Marshal Blücher.

Waterloo is in French-speaking **Wallonia**, part of an industrial belt that runs from Liège to Tournai. The green woods of the **Ardennes**, the hills where some of the great battles of World War II took place, lie to the south. The most famous confrontation occurred during the winter of 1944–45 at **Bastogne** where outnumbered US forces held out against a German counter-offensive in what has become known as the **Battle of the Bulge**. The offensive cost the lives of 77,000 American soldiers and their sacrifice is commemorated at the **Mardasson Liberty Memorial** and a nearby museum commonly referred to as "Nuts" - the reply the American commander General McAuliffe gave the Germans when asked to surrender.

To the west of the industrial belt is the royal residence and capital of medieval France, **Tournai**. It is famous for its five-towered Romanesque Cathedral.

Canal trip in Bruges.

Each of the towers is crowned with a hat-like cone and the cathedral has a splendid collection of Old Masters and stained-glass windows.

Mons, east of Tournai, is another venerable Wallonian city. Its Monkey of the Grand Garde is a statuette which supposedly brings luck if kissed.

Between Mons and **Namur** lies the village of **Binche**, which is noted for its carnival procession and for the dance of the Gilles, held every Shrove Tuesday. Namur, known as the Gateway to the Ardennes, is dominated by a huge rocky peak which is the site of a 17th-century citadel accessible by cable car.

In the eastern corner of Wallonia, near the German border is **Liège**, birthplace of one of Belgium's famous sons, Georges Simenon, creator of the Maigret detective series. This city of craftsmen has established a wide reputation for Val-St-Lambert crystal, exquisitely designed jewellery and quality sporting guns. The Fine Arts Museum has an impressive collection of French Impressionists including works by Monet, Gauguin, Corot and Boudin. The Weaponry Museum exhibits more than 8,000 weapons illustrating six centuries of gunmaking at Liège.

North of Liège is the province of Limburg, a pleasant agricultural region where **Tongres** is the oldest town in the country, founded by the Romans in the 1st century AD. The region also catches the corner of **Maastricht**, which gave its name to the important EC treaty.

The Germanic east: The tiny enclave around **Eupen** and **Malmedy** skirts the German border and is inhabited by 65,000 German-speaking Belgians. The main attraction of this wild, yet passive region is a large artificial lake used for yachting and canoeing. The carnival begins on 11 November when a carnival prince is chosen by secret ballot.

In the extreme southeast of Belgium is the Province of Luxembourg, a rugged region of forests and valleys whose capital, **Arlon**, an old Roman settlement, is the site of a beautiful castle and an archaeological site. The local Luxembourg Museum contains Roman remains of great importance. Tombstones from the 2nd century depict life before the advent of Christianity.

Another historic site in the area is the fortified medieval castle built by Godfrey of Bouillon, leader of the First Crusade. Overlooking the River Semois from a wooden hill, the castle contains a museum with interesting souvenirs from the Crusades.

This region of the Ardennes was the western part of the **Grand Duchy of Luxembourg** before it became part of Belgium. The eastern part of the Grand Duchy is now Europe's smallest independent nation, Luxembourg, which has an hereditary monarchy – a fact recalled only when Europe's gossip columnists were trying to find a suitor for Princess Marie-Astrid. The capital, called **Luxembourg**, like the state, (total population approximately 305,000), was once an important fortress called "The Gibraltar of the North". It is now the seat of several European Community bodies and an international banking centre, thanks to its low taxes. It is also the smallest member of NATO.

Musician in Liège.

BRUSSELS

If you ask an old Bruxellois what makes him happy, the answer is likely to be: "My favourite beer, a plate of *frites*, a Bruegel painting and the dream that a rich Fleming will marry my daughter."

The "Capital of Europe" is where good food and good beer are considered the elixir for a long life. Here north and south, the Teuton and the Latin represented by the Dutch-speaking Fleming and the French-speaking Walloon, have been fused by hook and by crook into the Bruxellois – Europe's first urban hybrid. As befits a bilingual city, the children of Brussels attend Flemish or French speaking schools, according to the national grouping of their parents, and street and public signs are in French and Flemish (a dialect of Dutch).

Brussels is full of contrasts. Since the law prohibits the construction of two identical houses next to each other, it is not unusual to see office blocks in tinted glass squatting beside the spires of Gothic churches. Flemish baroque facades on the Grand Place recall old glories while futuristic glass "greenhouses", occupied by insurance companies or banks, line Avenue de Franklin Roosevelt. Together with the European Community Headquarters at Rond-Point Schuman, built in the shape of a four-pointed star, these buildings represent the more modern face of the city.

The city is also a capital of *Art Nouveau* (*Jugendstil* in German) whose leading local exponent was Victor Horta (1861-1947). Expressive and decorative buildings in that style have survived, wedged between shabby tenement blocks and utilitarian cement monoliths. Brussels bristles with museums such as the **Musée des Beaux Arts** (Fine Arts Museum), **Musée Instrumental** (the Musical Instrument Museum) and the **Musée d'Art Ancien** (the Museum of the Old Masters), which houses a very fine collection of Flemish painters, including works by Rubens and Bruegel, as well as Bosch and Van der Weyden from the Dutch school.

The **Grand Sablon**, with its magnificent church of **Notre-Dame-du-Sablon**, marks the location of a number of antique shops, while the **Place du Petit Sablon**, surrounded by 48 statuettes which represent traditional trades, is nearby. Other notable monuments include the **Chinese Pavilion** and the **Atomium**, a 310-foot (102-metre) high atom in the form of an iron crystal molecule. Both legacies of the 1958 Universal Exhibition stand in the Park of Laeken at Heysel, Brussels North.

For centuries the people of Brussels have shown a particular affection for **Manneken Pis**, the bronze statuette of a little boy relieving himself into the fountain at the corner of **Rue de I'Etuve** and **Rue de Chêne**, in the city centre. It incarnates the irreverent spirit and humour of the Bruxellois. During his stormy existence the little fellow has been smashed or stolen so often it is difficult to say how old the present version is. When English soldiers took him away in 1745, vigilant Bruxellois retrieved him from their camp. Two years

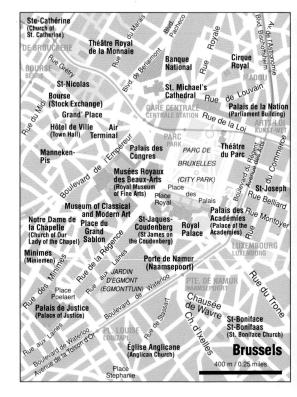

Brussels

400 m / 0.25 miles

later the populace rioted when French soldiers also tried to remove the statue. On this occasion Louis XV quickly appeased the outraged city by donating a sumptuous costume to "The Boy".

Now, with more than 160 donated costumes, including those of foreign legionnaire, Highland dancer, Sioux Indian, Texan cowboy, samurai, maharajah, Canadian hockeyplayer and fisherman of Newfoundland, Manneken Pis is probably the world's best-dressed statuette. Legend claims he represents Duke Godfrey III. In 1142, when only a few months old, the baby duke was brought to the battlefield at Ransbeke and his cradle was hung from an oak to encourage the soldiers, dejected by his father's death. At the decisive moment, when his forces were about to retreat, the young duke rose in his cradle and made the gesture reproduced later at the fountain. This, so legend goes, encouraged his troops to victory. However, a rival legend maintains that the statuette commemorates the little boy whose action inadvertently extinguished a time bomb intended to blow up the Town Hall. Whatever the truth, Manneken Pis is the oldest and most honoured bourgeois of Brussels.

Sobriety and pleasure: In this city of merchants and traders, it has been for centuries a sign of good breeding, good taste and good fortune to buy an expensive item of art and place it, properly spotlit, in a prominent part of the home – for everyone to see.

If the city's art is not merely for consumption then the beer is. In Brussels the shape of the beer glass changes to suit each of the 400 brews available in Anglicised pubs. Belgians are among the world's top beer guzzlers, not a surprise if one knows that a 1919 law prohibited the sale of spirits in public places. Spirits had to be consumed in a *cercle privé* (private club). These are often elegant and hushed places and quite accessible to "properly attired" tourists.

Perched atop the slender **Town Hall spire**, belligerent Saint Michael watches over Brussels. He reminds the visitor

Manneken Pis.

that the city is solidly Catholic and bourgeois, whose citizens respect law and order and attend mass on Sunday morning yet are liberal enough to enjoy an evening stroll down **Boulevard Jacqmain** past scantily dressed ladies beckoning from behind large windows.

With more than 1,400 so-called "Temples of Gastronomy" and countless bistros, snack bars, pull-ups and cafés, the choice of a restaurant, like the choice of a beer, can be a headache. Strolling through the picturesque **Ilot Sacré**, one finds that this central pedestrian zone is almost exclusively made up of restaurants, each seemingly more inviting than the next. The food displayed in windows and on tables lining the pavements is so appetizing it makes one's mouth water. Crabs, shrimps, mussels, shellfish, sea urchins, squid and cuttlefish are laid out for inspection on ice and framed with lemons and parsley. Once inside, the flame of an open fireplace in winter, or a cool fan in summer, provides a welcome. No wonder eating and drinking has become a daily social event for most of the 1 million Bruxellois and their guests.

Administrative capital: Perhaps it is this *joie de vivre*, this eat-drink-and-be-merry attitude which has attracted so many foreigners to Brussels. The city is the seat of the General Secretariat of the Benelux Nations, the Commission of the European Community (EC) and the Council of the North Atlantic Treaty Organization (NATO). The European Parliament holds sessions in the **Espace Léopold**. Brussels plays host to 20,000 diplomats and 15,000 EC bureaucrats. It embraces around 200 embassies and the offices of 800 multi-national companies from around the world. Entire residential communities speak English. Around the EC headquarters are scores of pubs where only English is spoken. In this polyglot city, English has effectively become the third language.

Brussels' origins go back to a fortified castle built in the 6th century on a little island in the River Senne, one of the tributaries of the Schelde. It was first mentioned in 966 under the name of *Bruoscelle* (meaning settlement in the marshes) in a chronicle of Emperor Otto I. It flourished as a trading centre along the route from Bruges to Cologne and became politically important when Duke Philip the Good of Burgundy made it his capital in the 15th century.

Shortly after, Charles V turned it into the capital of the Spanish Low Countries, later to be dominated by the Austrians, the French and the Dutch. The independence movement of 1830 against the Dutch finally gave the country its own identity.

With the progress of parliamentary democracy, the Belgian monarchy today plays a representative and ceremonial role, along the lines of their English cousins, though far less aloof. In May at the **royal residence** in **Laeken**, the glasshouses filled with exotic plants are opened to the public.

Royal business is conducted from the **Palace**, opposite the huge **Parc de Bruxelles**, which lies between the King and Parliament. The subject-King relationship is informal. The Bruxellois would hardly tolerate royalty any other way. They will tell with pride that the king dislikes curtseys, does not want to be addressed with inflated titles and will talk to anyone. As a young man, when he drove fast sports cars, the king invariably picked up hitchhikers.

The heart of Brussels is the **Grand Place**. Belgians call it the most beautiful square in the world and many visitors agree. Here, every day except Monday, a flower market is held and once a year the square is carpeted with flowers. Brussels' markets are famous and everything can be found on their stalls, from the local lace to caged birds.

Seven alleys lead into the Grand Place and a spectacle of lavishly decorated Flemish-Baroque Guild Houses. Dating from between 1695 and 1699 the facades appear to have been stamped from the same mould. Each one is different, however, yet combines in an overall harmonic effect.

Dominating the Square is the **Hôtel de Ville** (Town Hall) with a 15th-century Gothic spire. It climbs into the sky like the minaret of a mosque. Inside, fine tapestries decorate the walls.

Opposite the Town Hall is the **Maison du Roi** (King's House), though no king ever lived there. It was used as a prison for those condemned to death. Today it is a museum housing the various uniforms presented to the Manneken Pis, the soul of Brussels. Behind the King's House begins Ilot Sacré, the labyrinth of six alleys and arcades dotted with pubs, boutiques and restaurants.

Going down the Rue au Beurre from the Grand Place one runs into the **Bourse**, the city's Stock Exchange, a neo-classic building dating from 1873. Here the business heart of Brussels throbs.

For art lovers, the city has grouped together some of its best museums and galleries on **Mont des Arts**, just a short distance from the **central park**. At the park's southern end is the **Royal Palace**, built in 1820, almost a century after an earlier royal household burned down.

The new palace, which replaced the former castle of the Dukes of Brabant, is modelled in the French style of the Louis XVI period. Behind the building stands a statue of King Leopold II (1835–1909).

South from Mont des Arts, along **Rue de la Regence**, is the **Palais de Justice** (Law Court) built on the site of the former city gibbet. Its bulging cupola is 337 feet (103 metres) high and the courts occupy an area bigger than Saint Peter's Square in Rome.

Having ambled through parks, alleys and museums, the visitor can recuperate at the ancient fish market around the **Church of Saint Catherine** north of the city centre. An oblong area by the church was once a canal, along which fishing boats sailed to market. Today the site is ringed by seafood restaurants whose reputation is said to be unsurpassed in Europe.

For those who dine at one of these restaurants, it might be an idea, while digesting the sumptuous dinner, to stroll along past the shop windows of **Place Brouckère** nearby. The bawdy might like to take one last peep into the adjoining Boulevard Jacqmain for a different kind of window shopping. Brussels, the old merchant city, offers the gourmet every satisfaction.

The bird market at Brussels' Grand Place.

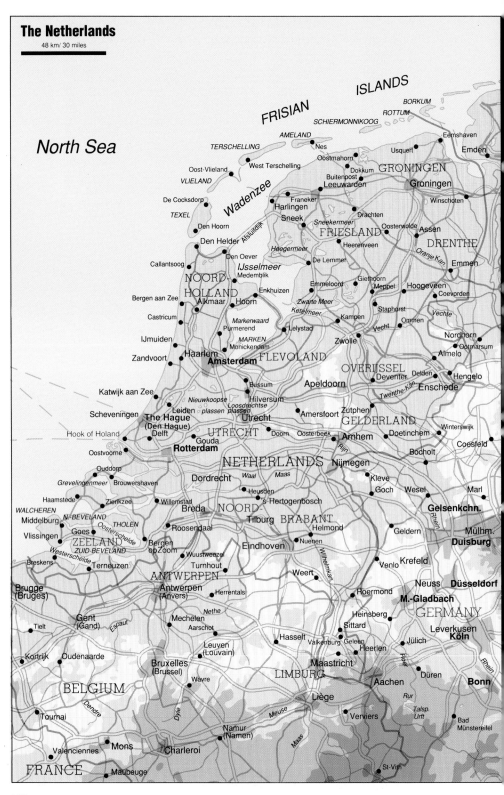

The Netherlands

48 km/ 30 miles

North Sea

FRISIAN ISLANDS

BORKUM
ROTTUM
SCHIERMONNIKOOG
AMELAND
Eemshaven
TERSCHELLING
Nes
Usquert
Emden
West Terschelling
Oostmahorn
Oost-Vlieland
Dokkum
GRONINGEN
VLIELAND
Buitenpost
Groningen
De Cocksdorp
Franeker
Leeuwarden
Winschoten
TEXEL
Harlingen
Drachten
Den Hoorn
Sneek
Sneekermeer
Oosterwolde
Assen
Den Helder
FRIESLAND
Afsluitdijk
Heegermeer
Heerenveen
DRENTHE
Callantsoog
Den Oever
De Lemmer
Oranje Kan.
Emmen
IJsselmeer
NOORD-
Medemblik
Giethoorn
Hoogeveen
HOLLAND
Emmeloord
Meppel
Coevorden
Bergen aan Zee
Enkhuizen
Zwarte Meer
Staphorst
Vechte
Alkmaar
Hoorn
Ketelmeer
Kampen
Ommen
Nordhorn
Castricum
Markerwaard
Vecht
Ootmarsum
IJmuiden
Purmerend
Lelystad
Zwolle
Almelo
MARKEN
Zandvoort
Monickendam
FLEVOLAND
OVERIJSSEL
Delden
Hengelo
Haarlem
Deventer
Apeldoorn
Enschede
Amsterdam
Bussum
Twenthe-Kan.
Katwijk aan Zee
Hilversum
Zutphen
Nieuwkoopse
Amersfoort
GELDERLAND
Scheveningen
Leiden
Loosdrechtse
Winterswijk
plassen plassen
Utrecht
The Hague
Hook of Holand
Delft
Doorn
Oosterbeek
Arnhem
Doetinchem
Coesfeld
(Den Hague)
Gouda
Rijn
Oostvoorne
Rotterdam
Bocholt
Ouddorp
NETHERLANDS
Nijmegen
Grevelingenmeer
Brouwershaven
Dordrecht
Waal
Maas
Kleve
Haamstede
Zierikzee
Willemstad
Heusden
Goch
Wesel
Marl
WALCHEREN
's-Hertogenbosch
Middelburg
N.-BEVELAND
Breda
NOORD-
Gelsenkchn.
Goes
Oosterschelde
THOLEN
Roosendaal
Tilburg
BRABANT
Vlissingen
Helmond
Geldern
Mülhm.
Breskens
ZEELAND
Bergen
Eindhoven
Duisburg
ZUID-BEVELAND
op Zoom
Nuenen
Westerschelde
Terneuzen
Wuustweezel
Venlo
Krefeld
Turnhout
Weert
Brugge
ANTWERPEN
Wilhelminakan.
Neuss
Düsseldorf
(Bruges)
Antwerpen
Herrentals
Roermond
M.-Gladbach
(Anvers)
Gent
Nethe
Heinsberg
GERMANY
Tielt
(Gand)
Mechelen
Sittard
Leverkusen
Escaut
Aarschot
Hasselt
Valkenburg
Geleen
Jülich
Köln
Kortrijk
Oudenaarde
Leuven
Heerlen
(Louvain)
Bruxelles
Maastricht
Düren
Bonn
(Brussel)
Wavre
LIMBURG
Aachen
BELGIUM
Liège
Rur
Talsp.
Tournai
Dendre
Dyle
Meuse
Verviers
Urft
Bad
Namur
Maas
Münstereifel
Valenciennes
Mons
(Namen)
Charleroi
St-Vith
FRANCE
Maubeuge

Wadenzee

Roer
Rhein
Rhein

144

THE NETHERLANDS

The Netherlands is a small country. Stretching over 15,892 sq. miles (41,160 sq. km), more than half of its area lies below sea level and almost one fifth is covered by lakes, rivers and canals. Building dykes, barriers and dams is a full-time occupation and no other nation is so acutely aware of the dangers of global warming. While the country is flat, a lush greenness is everywhere and the skies are sometimes filled with the silvery luminescence so distinctive in classic Dutch landscape painting. Of more than 10,000 windmills that once helped pump the land dry and featured so prominently among the favourite subjects of artists, about 1,000 remain. They are now regarded as national monuments and have been restored by the government in co-operation with private organisations.

English speakers call the country "Holland", but the Dutch know the country as the Kingdom of the Netherlands. Strictly, Holland refers only to the the two western provinces of North and South Holland where the majority of the 14 million population lives.

The capital, Amsterdam (pop: 750,000), is in this region, along with Rotterdam, Europe's largest port, and the administrative captital of The Hague ('s Gravenhage, or Den Haag in Dutch), where the European Court of Justice sits. The venerable university town of Leiden is here, as well as Delft, famous for its blue pottery, and Gouda, famous for its cheese.

The 10 provinces that make up the rest of the country are surprisingly varied. Zeeland in the south is a region of islands, peninsulas, sandy coastlines and bird-filled marshes which a series of huge barriers prevent from flooding. The Catholic southern provinces have a more flamboyant architecture and wooded hills. Heath, woodlands and orchards mark the northern provinces and in Drenthe, in the northeast, the wilder landscape is dotted with megaliths.

The dense network of interurban train or bus services offers a swift, comfortable means of transport in the cities while a car or even a bicycle is a good idea for the country. Exploring this varied country is made easier by the network of tourist information centres (known by the initials vvv), which are found in virtually every town. As well as handling bookings for accommodation and entertainment, they are an excellent source of local information.

Preceding pages: characteristically gabled houses line Amsterdam's canals; Holland's favourite form of transport.

AROUND THE NETHERLANDS

Less than 61 miles (99 km) from Amsterdam is **Den Haag** (The Hague), home of the royal family and also the seat of the government and of many foreign embassies. In the Peace Palace, a neo-Gothic structure donated by Scottish-American Andrew Carnegie, sits the International Court of Justice of the United Nations. The Hague, with a population of about half a million, is the third largest city of the Netherlands, often referred to as "Europe's largest and most elegant village" because of its pleasant residential character.

The historic centre around Binnenhof (Inner Court) with the 13th-century Ridderzaal (Knights' Hall) and the House of Parliament is a reminder of The Hague's origins as principal residence of the Dukes of Holland. The Royal Palace of the Princes of Orange dates from the 16th century. An exquisite art collection from the Golden Age belongs to the Royal Cabinet of Paintings exhibited at Mauritshuis. Among its treasures are such outstanding works as Rembrandt's *The Anatomy Lesson of Dr Tulp* and Vermeer's *View of Delft*.

The Seaboard: Holland's oldest bathing resort on the North Sea is **Scheveningen** which now forms a suburb of The Hague. The promenade is dominated by a pier and the *belle-époque* architecture of the Kurhaus. All year Scheveningen offers fresh air, a choice of sports and entertainment and a fashionable casino staffed by 200 croupiers.

The traditional role of the Netherlands as a maritime trading nation is illustrated by the port city of Amsterdam and the world's busiest harbour at **Rotterdam**. The volume of containerized freight shipped out from here, the barge traffic chugging up the River Rhine into Germany, and the shipbuilding and ship repairing is stunning. The entire harbour can be explored from the vantage point of an excursion boat, complete with a guide pointing out the sights in four languages.

Another vantage point from which to view the harbour and the city is the Euromast. The observation tower with a height of 591 feet (180 metres) is the landmark of modern Rotterdam. During the German invasion of May 1940, the historic centre of the city as well as the harbour suffered heavy damage from a bombing raid. That's why Rotterdam today appears as the most modern city of the Netherlands.

All the inland waterways in Zeeland, to the south of Rotterdam, have now been enclosed by dams in a massive project which ended with the installation of the Oosteschelde barrier.

Just 16 miles (26 km) west of Rotterdam lies **Hoek van Holland** (Hook of Holland), the traditional ferry harbour which has become part of the greater port of Rotterdam. The car and rail ferries leave from here for Harwich on the east coast of England (from where it is an hour's journey by rail to London).

Lovers of classical Dutch painting should not miss a trip to **Haarlem**, the provincial capital of North Holland. Here, in the Frans Hals Museum, one

Left, Keukenhof at the height of the bulb season. Right, traditional costume in Monnickendam.

can study the incisive portraits that Hals (1580-1666) painted of the Dutch at a time when the nation was at the height of its economic and political power.

He shows the faces with a marvellous complexity of character. Each is a bundle of motives, a worldly person possessed of few illusions, sometimes cynical but often ingenuous. The uniqueness of Haarlem's Frans Hals Museum extends beyond this superb collection. The structure itself, begun in 1606, was built as a home for old men. Later it became an orphanage, and in 1913 the museum was established. Artists in Hals' immediate milieu are also represented.

In the early 17th century, newly acquired bulbs from Turkey produced a "tulipmania" which swept the country. The tradition of bulb production and flower growing has flourished ever since. Worldwide distribution by air from Schiphol was introduced in the 1950s. Today, 36 countries buy 4 billion Dutch bulbs each year. A visitor can enjoy this floral world by either touring the flower regions west of Am-

sterdam in the blooming time or by going to the flower auctions held daily in **Aalsmeer** near Amsterdam, where flowers grown under grass are sold.

From the public balcony one watches the carts of flowers being brought in and the 2,000 buyers sitting below. A huge clock-like bidding wheel starts with a price higher than expected and then swirls around slowly to a lower bid. Almost every house in The Netherlands has flowers inside, partly as an antidote to the grey and rainy skies.

In the back country: Though the Netherlands is the most densely populated country in Europe, it has beautiful countryside. The coastline is a 180-mile (290-km) stretch of sandy beaches with some 55 seaside resorts. Off the north coast is a string of five islands, called the **West Friesians**, which can only be reached by boat from the naval port of **Den Helde**. The Friesians who occupy Friesland and the islands speak their own language: Rembrandt's wife and model, Saskia, was Friesian.

An alternative to the seaside is **Hoge**

Enkhuizen harbour.

Veluwe, expanses of heather and forest which make up the country's largest national park, near **Arnhem**. With the help of the local Tourist Information Office in Arnhem, one can arrange a few days of bike riding along the miles of trails here, stopping at country inns, to which luggage can be forwarded. Wild flowers in the spring and summer create a rainbow of colours on upland fields called *veluwe*.

The Netherlands has long been famous for the quality of light in its landscapes, with luminous skies a primary subject in the painting of the Golden Age. From the *veluwe* there is ample opportunity to experience the full range of greys, pinks, and whites that colour these skies.

Hoge Veluwe is also the site of the distinguished Kröller-Müller Museum, which exhibits some of the most impressive works of Van Gogh.

Another fitting destination for the naturalist, the bird watcher or the photographer is **Drenthe** which, after Zeeland, is the least populous Dutch province. An abundance of wild flowers and picnic areas, set amidst the small lakes called *vennen*, allure the traveller.

The provincial capital of **Assen**, a two-hour train ride from Amsterdam, is the starting point for a day or more of driving or cycling through the 168 miles (300 km) of bike trails and numerous back country roads.

The prehistoric stone burial mounds called *hunebedden* are scattered throughout this northeastern province and are worth a visit. The largest of the 51 sites is at **Borger**. Witnessing these large boulder burial houses (or "giant beds", as the word translates), which Stone Age or Bronze Age men built to commemorate their dead, is an awesome experience. Some recovered artifacts, such as axes and pottery from 2,500 BC can be seen at the provincial museum in Assen. As a reflection of the enduring, eternal aspirations of man to create some significant expression of what life has meant, the *hunebedden* are as moving an experience as the Acropolis or the pyramids at Chichenitza, Yucatan.

Drenthe's timeless byways.

AMSTERDAM

The first impression of Amsterdam may be its museum-like quality. Indeed, 6,700 buildings in the core of the city are protected monuments, virtually intact from the Golden Age of the 17th century, during which time the city rose to spectacular wealth, political power and cultural heights. Amsterdam's navy dominated an era when prosperity depended on ships opening trade routes to the West and East Indies. Profits from these ventures provided funds for the growth of a compact city built around a dam that had been placed on the Amstel River in the 13th century. Historic models for the modern Dutch character are common-sense merchants and businessmen, not inaccessible monarchs or ethereal clerics. The city's monuments are private houses rather than imposing public buildings.

Amsterdam, as a museum, is not at all stale. The city has the vitality of a modern metropolis while keeping a satisfying sense of age and continuity. Here one can find a gourmet Indonesian Rice Table dinner, a lively and safe night life, Europe's largest selection of antiques, some world-famous cheeses, the great paintings of the Golden Age (especially Vermeer, Rembrandt, and Frans Hals), extensive sidewalk café-idling and some exquisite flowers. To see all this requires only a good pair of walking shoes.

Amsterdam's horseshoes: A good point to begin is opposite the **railway station** at the indispensable **VVV** (the Dutch Tourist Information Office).

The main street, **Damrak**, leads to the **Dam**, a large square that is the hub of the canals and also the site of **Koninklijk Paleis** (the Royal Palace). Built in 1665 on 13,659 piles, it is now used for diplomatic receptions and parts of it are open to the public. Also situated in the square is the **Nieuwe Kerk** (New Church), dating from 1400, where the monarchs are crowned. A pause at the outdoor café in front of the **Victoria Hotel**, Damrak 1-5, provides an opportunity to watch the city pass by.

Amsterdam, built on a design of expanding horseshoe canals that fit one within the other, is unlike other cities. On a map, with the railway station at the top, the smaller numbers for canal streets begin at the upper left-hand corner and then become progressively larger as the canal swings down and then up to the right hand corner.

A round tour of the canals by boat will give a sense of what the city was like before modern roadways were built. These boats, which leave every half hour, are found on **Rokin** and on the waterway between the Dam and the railway station. Among more than 1,000 bridges, the **Magere Brug** (Slender Bridge), dating from 1670, is one of the more notable. The canals are lined with all manner of houseboats where some 10,000 people live.

An abundance of art: It is a quarter-hour walk from the Dam to the **Rijksmuseum**, the repository of much of Amsterdam's great art from the first half of the 17th century. Many of the oil paintings have been reproduced as prints

Left, Zuiderkerk. Right, a Dutch girl of Indonesian extraction.

so the museum has a sense of familiarity. Among more than a million art objects are paintings by Johannes Vermeer, including his deeply felt and quiet works of everyday events such as *Young Girl Reading* and *A Maidservant Pouring Milk*. Rembrandt's works include *The Jewish Bride*, *Syndicate of the Drapers*, and *The Nightwatch*.

To many people, Rembrandt seems to have a surprisingly modern sensibility. He rose to fame partly as a result of his ability to transform the annual "office portrait" of company executives into a striking study of their character. His fortune floundered when he didn't give equal prominence to executives in a painting for which each was paying an equal share. The **Rembrant Museum** (Rembranthuis, 4 Jodenbreestraat), his preserved town house, is where he lived and worked in the city.

From the Rijksmuseum it is a quarter-mile walk to the **Van Gogh Museum**, which focuses on only this one painter. Van Gogh's development can be traced from the haunting animalism of his early

Potato Eaters to the swirling hallucinogenic brilliance of his later *Sunflowers*. (The other major Van Gogh holdings are at the Kröller-Müller Museum, in Hoge Veluwe park near Arnhem.)

Outside and inside: The **Vondelpark**, a visionary expanse of urban greenery named after a 17th-century Dutch playwright, is a short walk from the Van Gogh Museum.

The nearby **Leidseplein** plunges one back into the lively humanity of Amsterdam and offers a contrast to the quiet and leisurely atmosphere of the Vondelpark. This square is full of pleasant surprises such as the café **Het Hok** where all the patrons play chess.

Walking through the open-air museum of Amsterdam's architecture doesn't, unfortunately, reveal anything of the insides of the canal houses. Two opportunities to see behind the buildings' facades present themselves along **Herrengracht**. At the **Willet-Holthuysen Museum** (No. 605), one can see the interior and furnishings of a 17th-century canal house. The **Toneel-**

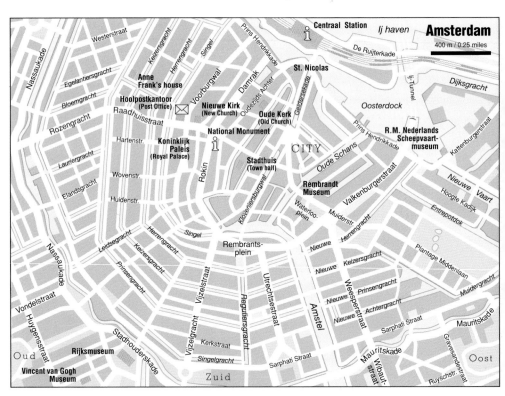

museum (No. 168) exhibits another interior, with memorabilia collected from the various performing arts.

Several canal houses have been turned into hotels. Most distinguished is the **Hotel Pulitzer**, a 10-minute walk from the Dam. The Pulitzer consists of 16 canal houses between 315 and 331 **Prinsengracht** (Prince's Canal). Tastefully conceived and deftly executed, the hotel has preserved the facades of the buildings, but modernised the compact interiors. Walk through the hotel to see an art gallery in the hallway and perhaps stop for a Heineken beer, Amsterdam's finest, in the lively **Pulitzer Bar**.

At No. 263 Prinsengracht, which can be reached down Raadhuisstraat beside the Royal Palace, is **Anne Frank Huis**. This is where the 15-year-old Jewish girl hid from the Nazis in World War II, until she was caught and sent to her death at the Bergen-Belsen concentration camp. It is now a moving and popular museum.

The **Sonesta Hotel**, in **Stroomarkt**, is a hostelry that breathes new life into an aging ecclesiastical structure. The Sonesta complex includes the **Lutheran Round Church**, whose interior now hosts meetings under an imposing dome that dignifies whatever proceedings take place. Sunday morning "coffee concerts" in the Lutheran Round Church feature classical chamber music.

Adjacent to the Sonesta is the **Amsterdam Arts and Crafts Centre**, in **Nieuwe Dijk**, where Dutch artisans can be watched at work and their artifacts bought. Diamond-cutting, pottery-making, flower-growing, Delft-ware ceramic-painting, wool-weaving, cheese-making, and leather-working are some of the activities here.

The **Jugendstil Room**, in the **American Hotel** on the Leidseplein, is a mammoth room, built in 1892, and remains a national monument to *fin-de-siècle* grandeur and the art nouveau movement. Today the room is a meeting place for the city's writers, artists and talkers.

Food from the East: Walking in Amsterdam excites a healthy appetite that can only be properly assuaged at a good

The Slender Bridge.

ethnic restaurant. For the quick snack or light lunch nothing satisfies more than the characteristic Dutch little bread, or *broodje*, filled with cheese, meat or fish. The **Broodje van Kootje**, 28 Spui, serves delicious examples of this treat. The other typical Dutch lunch, *uitsmijters*, consists of fried eggs, meat, and cheese on bread, garnished with tomatoes, lettuce, and pickles.

The two culinary glories of Amsterdam are the native Dutch winter food and the valued legacy from the Dutch colonial escapade, the Indonesian Rice Table. The **Dorrius** in Nieuwe Zijds Voorburgwal is noted for the former. Specialities include braised Dutch beef with red cabbage, Holland hunter stew, Dutch pea soup, mackerel on toast and mussels with celery.

Indonesian Rice Table consists of a large bowl of rice and perhaps 15 condiment dishes of meat, fish, fruit, vegetables and nuts to go with it. Some of the food is cooked, other dishes are served cold. The combination of spices and herbs in the dishes, including curries and peppers, and sweet-and-sour ingredients, makes the meal memorable.

There are many good Indonesian restaurants to choose from, including an old standby, **Bali**, and, top of the list in price and quality, **Samesebo**. Along **Binnenbantammerstraat** there are several good budget Indonesian restaurants. The **Manchurian** at Leidseplein is another good choice.

The Dutch, as is well known, produce a wide range of cheeses. Many people have tasted Edam, which comes from the north, or Gouda, from the south, but few have come across a cumin seed cheese or a Leidsekaas. **Abraham Kef's cheese shop** in **Marninxstraat** should be visited by those who want to learn more about Dutch cheese. It is both a shop and a tasting centre.

"Brown cafés": Amsterdam's cafés and bars, as well as being enjoyable rest places, also provide further opportunities to take in the historic atmosphere of the city. **Wynand Fockink tavern**, in the **Pijlsteeg** off the Dam, is the best of the city's "brown cafés", so named be-

Left, the city in winter. Right, cruising the canals.

cause of their brown wood panelling, often dating from the 17th and 18th centuries. In the past, a liquor purveyor named Wynand Fockink opened a little tasting room in this alley and called it **De Gekroonde Wildeman** (Crowned Wildman), and his odd image can be seen over the door. Inside is an array of old casks and ceramic flasks, plus historic artifacts of Amsterdam. The beverages to drink here are sherry, wine or *genever*, a strong gin that has become the Dutch national drink.

Hoppe's outdoor café on the Supi Plaza is a good place from which to observe the rather aged students (the Dutch tend to study at a leisurely pace and postpone taking their exams) in the heart of **Amsterdam University**.

The **Continental Bodega** on the **Brouwersgracht** off the Leidseplein is another watering hole. The Dutch and Spanish have been at each other's throats often throughout history, but they have always been of one mind when it comes to the merits of Spanish sherry. It must be said, though, that the choice of no fewer than 17 different varieties is a little overwhelming.

At stops such as Hoppe's and the Continental Bodega, the Dutch eat *satay,* an Indonesian snack of barbecued beef on a stick, dipped in peanut sauce.

Red lights and bright lights: Amsterdam has a low crime rate and is a relatively safe place, even after dark. At night the roads along the canals are lit and make for engaging routes to walk along. The Slender Bridge, also lit up at night, is one of Amsterdam's loveliest sights.

Amsterdam boasts a thriving night life. The bawdy **Zeedijk** section of the city where prostitution is an open and government-sanctioned activity, is Amsterdam's contribution to the world's oldest profession and provides an eye-opening diversion for any visitor. On balmy nights the outdoor cafés along the Rembrandtsplein and Leidseplein throb with life. Disco, jazz and folk music flourish in small clubs.

Amsterdam's famous music hall, the **Concertgebouw** (Concert Hall) offers a range of musical performances from the city orchestra to rock concerts.

Shopping in the city is easily done on foot and there are many intriguing stores tucked down side streets. The **Kalverstraat** is the busiest shopping street in the city and **P.C. Hooftstraat**, near the Leidseplein, is one of the most elegant.

Amsterdam is a centre of the European antique market and **Spiegelstraat** and **Nieuwe Spiegelstraat** house more than 20 antique shops in a small area.

The city is also a leading centre for the cutting, polishing, and mounting of diamonds. The **Van Moppes** have a complete tour and viewing room at their factory in Albert Cuypstraat. **Coster** near the Rijksmuseum offers another good diamond workshop tour and shop.

Amsterdam is also famous for its open air markets. The most elaborate is the **Waterlooplein Market** in Rapenburgerstraat. The **Albert Cuyp Market** is another lively outdoor market with a wide variety of food and merchandise. It is an especially good place to sample a Dutch delicacy – raw herring with chopped onion. Watching a native eat a herring reveals how it should be done.

A sex shop in the red-light district.

IJSSELMEER: THE RECLAIMED SEA

An excursion to the region north of Amsterdam leads one first to Volendam, on the banks of the IJsselmeer (pronounced eye-zelmeer), and then to the cheese market at Alkmaar. From both places one can continue the trip around the IJsselmeer, the former Zuiderzee, and see at first hand a human enterprise that has kept the Dutch busy throughout history: the battle of man against water.

On returning to Amsterdam, having travelled around the southern end of the IJsselmeer, one gets a good sense of this raw creation of new land.

The western shore: The Zuiderzee used to be a part of the North Sea, before a dike transformed it into a freshwater lake, the present-day IJsselmeer. **Volendam** was a Catholic village and nearby **Marken** was its Protestant counterpart. Residents of both towns have their distinctive costumes, now worn largely for the benefit of visitors. The Volendam women, in striped skirts, black aprons and lace caps are the tourism image of Dutch national costume.

At **Alkmaar**, the cheese market, which takes place in front of the **Grote Kirk** (Large Church), recreates the way cheeses were once weighed. The colourful cheese balls are carried about by members of the cheese guilds. The village of **Edam**, with its museum and 14th-century church, is nearby.

Beyond these well-travelled destinations are **Enkhuizen** and **Hoorn**. Enkuizen harbour has a particularly moving sculpture of young boys awaiting the return of their seafaring fathers, a ritual of concern because of the perils of going to sea in small boats. Hoorn has a lively **market** each week with dancers in historic regional costume. Today freshwater eel fishing has replaced the saltwater herring harvests as the living of the local fisherman.

The road around the IJsselmeer runs along the top of the 19-mile (30km) **Afsluitdijk**, which separates it from the open sea, and was originally planned to take a railway. This barrier was completed in 1932 and marked the start of the project 12 years after plans had first been drawn up. The idea for the project had first been proposed in 1893 by Cornelius Lely, a specialist engineer. For several decades the Dutch listened attentively, but failed to act. A maxim describes well the national hesitancy: "The Dutch do not like to skate over one night's ice."

Reclamation has been going on for most of this century, and the work is still not complete. The first step in the process involved building the Afsluitdijk, which formed the new freshwater lake and an area secure from sea flooding.

Within this area, four polders ("new lands") have added 408,000 acres (165,000 hectares) of land for agriculture and human habitation. Most of the rest of the enclosed area will remain a freshwater lake because the **River IJssel**, a tributary of the Rhine, runs into the sea here. The dikes are barrier walls composed of compressed sand, clay, stones and mud on willow-tree mats, all faced with basalt rock. After the dikes are

Souvenir shop in Volendam.

built, the land is drained by pumping water out to canals which have been dredged alongside the dike.

The four polders encroaching from the edges of the lake all have information centres and museums. **Wieringermeer** has a permanent photographic exhibition in Wieringerwerf town hall. The Schockland Museum on the **North-East Polder** has a museum of geology and archaeology. Lelystad on **Eastern Flevoland** has a New Land exhibition of about the whole project. **Southern Flevoland** has a migratory bird information centre on the Oostvaardersdijk.

A city is born: The first of the "new cities" to be built on the reclaimed land was **Lelystad**, named after the reclamation engineer. From the point of view of sociologists, Lelystad is an interesting application of "social engineering", employing all available modern thinking on how a city should be laid out. Lelystad was officially "born" in 1967 when the first residents moved in. Today the population is around 60,000.

Efforts have been made to combine the amenities of both city and suburban life. Single family homes with gardens are only minutes, by foot or bicycle, away from the urban centre where stores, schools, and hospitals are located. The city consists of five districts, each with its own cluster of neighbourhoods.

As you drive from Lelystad around the southern end of the IJsselmeer, both sobering and delicate images come to mind. The sobering ones are the unseen German and Allied aircraft that lie at the bottom of the IJsselmeer. Almost every year, while dredging out the polders, some new wrecks are found, some with the corpses of crew members or full bomb loads still aboard. They date from the fierce air battles that were fought over North Holland. About 700 planes are supposed to have plunged into the IJsselmeer, making it the largest single burial place in Europe for missing World War II pilots.

The lakes have abundant wildlife and white swans, swimming offshore or sunning themselves, are a reminder of how close human beings are to nature.

Inland sea of the IJsselmeer.

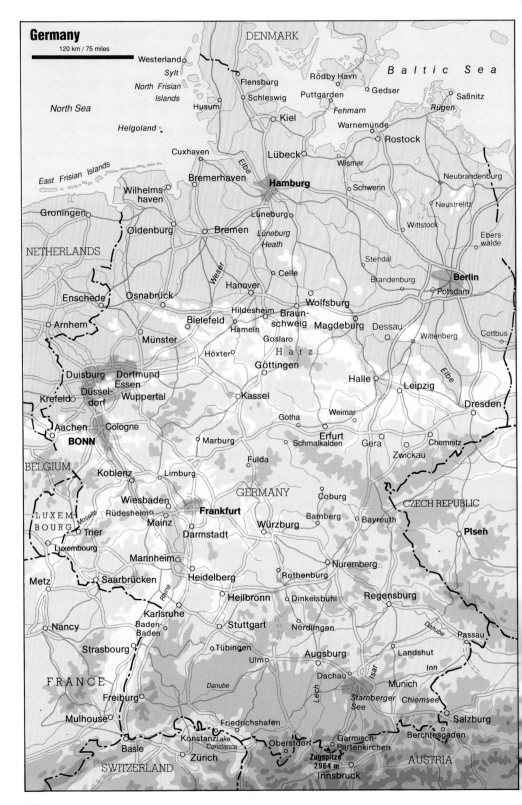

Germany

120 km / 75 miles

DENMARK

Baltic Sea

Westerland
Sylt
North Frisian Islands

North Sea

Flensburg
Schleswig
Husum
Helgoland
Cuxhaven

Rødby Havn
Puttgarden
Fehmarn
Kiel
Lübeck

Gedser
Saßnitz
Rügen
Warnemünde
Rostock
Wismar
Schwerin
Neubrandenburg
Neustrelitz
Wittstock
Eberswalde

East Frisian Islands
Wilhelms-haven
Bremerhaven
Groningen
Oldenburg
Bremen

NETHERLANDS

Enschede
Arnhem
Münster

Lüneburg
Lüneburg Heath
Celle
Hanover
Hildesheim
Bielefeld
Hameln
Höxter

Hamburg

Weser

Stendal
Brandenburg
Elbe

Berlin
Potsdam

Wolfsburg
Braun-schweig
Magdeburg
Goslaro
Harz
Göttingen

Dessau
Wittenberg
Cottbus

Duisburg
Krefeldo
Düssel-dort
Aachen
BONN

Dortmund
Essen
Wuppertal
Cologne

Kassel

Marburg

Halle
Leipzig
Elbe
Dresden

BELGIUM

Koblenz
Limburg

Gotha
Weimar
Erfurt
Schmalkalden
Gera
Zwickau
Chemnitz

LUXEM-BOURG
Moselle
Luxembourg
Trier

Wiesbaden
Rüdesheim
Mainz
Frankfurt
Darmstadt

Fulda
GERMANY

Coburg
Bamberg
Bayreuth

CZECH REPUBLIC

Plseň

Metz
Nancy

Mannheim
Saarbrücken
Heidelberg
Karlsruhe
Baden-Baden

Rhine

Würzburg
Rothenburg
Dinkelsbühl
Heilbronn

Nuremberg

Regensburg

Danube
Passau

Strasbourg

Stuttgart
Tübingen
Ulm

Nördlingen
Augsburg

Landshut
Inn

Freiburg
Mulhouse

Dachau
Lech
Isar
Munich
Starnberger See
Chiemsee
Salzburg
Berchtesgaden

FRANCE

Danube

Friedrichshafen
Konstanz
Lake Constance
Oberstdorf
Garmisch-Partenkirchen
Zugspitze 2964 m
Innsbruck

Basle
Zürich

SWITZERLAND

AUSTRIA

GERMANY

Germany may have unified east and west when the Berlin wall came down in November 1989, but the land the country occupies today is made up of peoples of greatly differing origins and characters. At the two extremes are the somber upright Prussians of the north, personified in the spike-helmeted Bismarck, and the jolly Bavarian of the south who is typified in *lederhosen* and chamois hat swilling foaming tankards of beer. In between is the Swabian who lives in a neat cottage and keeps his carefully washed Mercedes in a garage, the Ruhrgebiet miner who keeps pigeons in the colliery loft, and the Lower Saxony cattle farmer who warms his damp days with little glasses of schnapps.

They are bound together by many common elements, of politeness and punctuality and also an enjoyment of each other's company. An old saying runs: "One German makes a philosopher, three Germans make a club." And it is true that throughout the country people love forming and joining non profit-making clubs, for hobbies, for sports, for charities or neighbourhoods, electing presidents, treasurers, secretaries and committees.

The difference between east and west is most marked in the cities. Those urban areas that came under the influence of the east have grown up in dull slabs, though it is also true that many of those in the west had to be substantially rebuilt after World War II. But the new opportunities to visit Potsdam, Dresden, Weimar, the island of Rugen and the farmlands of Saxony offer new experiences for westerners which should not be missed.

It is easy to travel to any spot in Germany. The major cities have airports, but it is just as practical to travel by the intercity trains which link some 50 cities every hour, and the high-speed ICE trains have reduced travel time dramatically.

For a country that produces some of the world's most prestigious cars, it is not surprising that the road systems are good. But Germany's 8,500 miles (13,600 km) of motorway make the network one of the densest in the world and summer visitors should be prepared for delays. If the *Autobahn* pace becomes a bit nerve-racking, the secondary roads, which lead from one picturesque village to another, offer an alternative.

Preceding pages: Berlin's Brandenburg Gate; a thirsty gathering at Munich's Oktoberfest, where the beer is served in massive mugs.

AROUND GERMANY

Germany is the industrial and financial powerhouse of Europe, though its resources have been strained with unification. Whatever its fortunes, its castles and countryside remain romantic and alluring. Some of its charms may be hidden behind skyscrapers, but they are there waiting around the corner.

Nowhere is this more evident than at **Frankfurt**, geographic and financial centre, and a gateway to the country's heart. Rhein-Main Airport is Europe's second busiest, the train station is the hub of one of the best railway systems in the world, and from here the *Autobahn* (motorway) system fans out.

Yet the glass of soaring modern buildings reflects the Gothic tower of Frankfurt's cathedral; apple-wine pubs stand at cobblestone-street level in **Sachsenhausen**, the Bohemian quarter; paintings by Rubens, Rembrandt, Durer and Holbein are in the art museums. The new museum quarter on the Schumankai is the most exciting in Germany. It includes the decidedly modern Museum of Crafts and Applied Art and Hans Hollein's idiosyncratic Museum of Modern Art.

The **Romer** is a collection of three neo-Gothic buildings. It includes the church where the Holy Roman Emperors were crowned and the house where Johann Wolfgang von Goethe, Germany's greatest poet, was born in 1749.

The Main River slices through the city, on its way to join the Rhine, which runs north through Germany's wine land and provides a highway to the cities of **Koblenz**, **Cologne**, and the former West German capital of **Bonn** (*see Rhine chapter, pages 177–183*).

Germany has been producing wine since Roman times, so the art of wine making has been honed to a fine degree. Most wines are white. They come from 11 regions, stretching from the middle Rhine at Bonn to Lake Constance.

From March until November, hundreds of villages hold wine festivals when local vintners offer their wines for tasting. Two of the best are the Rheingau Festival in Wiesbaden in August and the world's biggest wine festival in Bad Dürkheim in September.

To the north of Frankfurt is the **Taunus Massif**, cloaked in green forests and dotted with mineral-water spas. To the south is the **Odenwald**, straight out of Teutonic mythology, with a road called the *Bergstrasse* running along the foothills to **Heidelberg** (*see pages 185–189*). The Main River is sometimes called the "White Sausage Equator" because to the south lies Bavaria and one of its national dishes, *Weisswurst*, is a white veal sausage.

The cliché image of Germany tends to be of **Bavaria**, the area around **Munich** in the southeast (*see pages 191–199*). This is where you might find rosy-cheeked folk in *lederhosen* and *dirndls* herding cattle on Alpine pastures. But such a sight is only part of the picture. Almost due west from Frankfurt, for example, in the heart of the Mosel valley and a short distance from Luxembourg, is **Trier**, the oldest city in Ger-

Left, the Deutsche Bank, Germany's largest. **Right**, Frankfurt's old centre.

many, founded in 16 BC by Caesar Augustus. Dominated by the Porta Nigra, the huge Roman gate, the city is a treasure chest of ruins and relics and many residents dabble in archaeology. It is said that, to store potatoes safe from winter's frost, the people simply dig down to the Roman mosaics.

Among the best of the remains are the thermal baths with part of the heating system intact, and the amphitheatre. The Basilica dates from the time of Constantine and has a vast ceiling.

To the south of Frankfurt, east of the Rhine River, is **Wiesbaden**, one of the largest and oldest spas in Germany. It has 27 hot springs, a gambling casino and a *Kurpark* (cure-park).

Moving farther south through **Mannheim** or **Heidelberg** (*see pages 185–189*) the road leads to **Stuttgart**, its sky lit by the Mercedez-Benz star. The city was the seat of the Dukes of Wurttemberg long before it became the home of the dukes of the automobile industry. The old castle stands at the Schillerplatz, the city's spacious heart.

Stuttgart is a good starting point for a tour of the vineyard-lined valley of the Neckar River and the Swabian Alps.

The Black Forest: Stretching 100 miles (160 km) along the French border, from **Karlsruhe** to the top of Switzerland, is the **Schwarzwald**, the Black Forest. For centuries, people feared this densely wooded stretch of mountains and gorges, and it was inhabited mainly by wolves, hermits and communities of monks. The ravine leading to Freiburg is known as Höllental (Hell's Valley).

Freiburg is an easy-going city, home of a university founded in 1457 and associated with such names as Erasmus (1466–1536) the humanist, and Waldseemuller, the geographer who first put America on a map. The city landmark is the lacy-spired *Münster* (cathedral) which served as a model for the greater cathedrals at Cologne and Ulm. *Bächlein*, little canals, run beside the streets as they have for centuries, early attempts at street cleaning and perhaps even medieval air conditioning.

Competing with Freiburg as beauty

Sans Souci Palace, Potsdam.

166

spot of the Black Forest is the spa city **Baden-Baden**. Many German towns are named Bad: Bad Homburg, Bad Mergentheim, Bad Kissingen. The word means "bath" and it usually indicates that the place is a spa. There are 250 registered spas and health resorts in Germany and they are popular for their *Kur* (cure). The healing waters of Baden-Baden were used by the Romans – their baths can still be seen – and rediscovered by the nobility in the 19th century.

Time seems to have stood still in the gardens of Baden-Baden, but it ticks steadily on in the higher reaches of the Black Forest. This is the land of the cuckoo clock, and a visit is not complete without a stop at **Triberg** and **Furtwangen**, where the clocks are made.

The Danube River has its source in the Black Forest, at the little town of **Donaueschingen**. The river rises here for its 1,776-mile (2,840-km) journey, through seven countries to the Black Sea: 400 miles (640 km) of that journey are through Germany.

Berlin and beyond: Visitors to the capital, **Berlin** (*see pages 171–175*), should also take in **Potsdam** and the **Sans Souci Palace** of Frederick the Great, the Prussian king whose remains were returned here in 1992, 106 years after his death, and still a potent symbol of Prussian nationalism. As grand palaces go, it is rather modest but its grounds, orangery and Chinese tea house give it great charm; among Frederick's guests here was the French writer Voltaire.

The principal cities of former eastern Germany, apart from Berlin, are Dresden and Leipzig. Much of the baroque splendour of **Dresden** was created by Augustus the Strong (1670–1733), whose claim to immortality included the siring of 352 children. It was a glittering artistic city, attracting Wagner, Weber and Schumann, but suffered appallingly in the devastating firebombing of Dresden in World War II. The musical tradition, however, is still evident in the sumptuous **Semper opera house**, though the city's focal point remains Augustus's eclectic collection of buildings, the **Zwinger**. It houses a

The Albertinum cultural centre, Dresden.

museum of Old Masters, with works by Raphael, Rembrandt and Dürer, and one of the world's largest porcelain collections. It was Augustus who founded the porcelain industry at **Meissen** in the heart of Saxony, which is still an important producer.

Leipzig, a university town, was a key place of protest in favour of unification in 1989. Today it is not the "little Paris" described by Goethe, but it remains an important publishing centre, and its name is still synonymous with trade fairs, a speciality for nearly 500 years.

Inextricably linked with the life and works of Goethe is the town of **Weimar** to the west of Leipzig, a place of literary pilgrimage. It was here, in collaboration with Schiller, that Goethe established the literary movement known as Weimar Classicism; the town has many memorials to these famous men of letters.

Hanseatic cities: Northern Germany, with its rolling heaths and two sea coasts, the North Sea and the Baltic, is no less fascinating than the southern part. Here are the great Hanseatic trading cities,

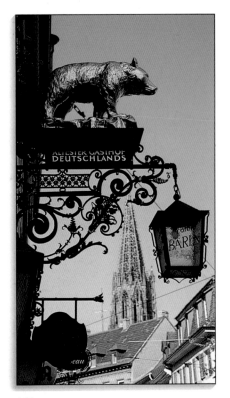

Hamburg, Bremen, Lübeck and Rostock. The first two remain city-states even today. The Hanseatic League was a commercial association set up in the Middle Ages for trade protection.

Hamburg is Germany's second largest city (population 1.7 million), and a major port, although it is 66 miles (110 km) from the sea. Cargo ships ply the River Elbe to unload bananas and venison, carpets and spices, teak and automobiles, cameras and computers. One of the most charming areas is the old warehouse district and the best way to see it is by the narrow boats that cruise the canals.

Hamburg's red-light district, the **Reeperbahn** or St Pauli, may be Europe's raunchiest, with its Eros Centres and "shop windows" along Herbertstrasse, a narrow lane closed to anyone under 18. But the area is well-policed and the tourist office takes pains to tell visitors which clubs are reputable.

Bremen is the oldest German maritime city, although its modern deep sea port is **Bremerhaven**, founded in the 19th century. The Bremen Town Musicians, from the story by the Brothers Grimm, stand near the Rathaus (Town Hall). The cavernous cellar underneath this building is a restaurant which serves all the wines of Germany.

Lübeck is on the Baltic Sea. It is a prime port for ferries to Scandinavia and **Travemünde** is its beach resort. The chubby Holstentor (Holsten Gate) leads to the old town. Beside it stand six salt warehouses, relics of the time when the "white gold" from Lüneburg was brought for shipping and was sold tax-free to the residents. Visitors should make a point of trying *Lübecker Rotspohn*, red wine imported from France and stored for a year in Lübeck's cellars. Some people say it tastes better than the wine of Burgundy.

Rostock was built up in the 1950s because the then East Germany needed access to the sea, but the modern town is still dominated by the St Mary's church. Beyond Rostock is the wildlife sanctuary of **Rügen**, Germany's biggest island where the former GDR president Eric Honecker had a summer home.

Left, "The Bear" in Freiburg is Germany's oldest inn. **Right**, biker with attitude.

168

BERLIN

Germany's re-established capital is once more a single city, but it still remains to its inhabitants a divided place. Virtually nothing is left of the Wall, but the division between the two halves of the city is a psychological scar that has yet to heal. It will take time, too, before the city finds architectural harmony: the flashy west, particularly around the famous Kurfürstendamm shopping street, contrasts with the more sombre former east, where there is much building in progress, not least to take account of the new spaces required to house the Bundestag (parliament) which will return to a refurbished Reichstag beside the Brandenburg Gate.

But the east, which encompassed Berlin-Mitte, the old city centre, is by no means a poor relation. Beyond the Brandenberg Gate is the elegant Unter den Linden boulevard, which has begun to usurp the position held by the Ku'damm as *the* street for taking a stroll, while Friedrichstrasse is busily making up for lost years by becoming the smart business address. And one of the liveliest districts in the city is Schenenviertel, further east.

There are many ways of getting around the city. The centre is not large and the public transport system is easy to use, but one of the best ways to get an idea of the place is by boat. Regular trips encircle the city, passing through Tiergarten, the city's popular park, going around the monumental buildings on Museum Island in the former east, and travelling down the River Spree.

Decadant street: Usually known as the Ku'dam, **Kurfürstendamm**, which means "The Electors' Road", only emerged 100 years ago. From the 16th century it was a broad track leading out to the country, serving as a bridle path for the electors who rode out from the royal palace in the direction of Grünewald to go hunting.

Only with Germany's rapid industrial expansion in the late 19th century did the street begin to take shape. Inspired by the Champs Élysées in Paris, Bismarck decided that he wanted just such a boulevard for the new capital of the *Reich*. Building work proceeded in "Wilhelmenian" style: generous, ornate and even florid; truly representative of the age. Proverbial Prussian frugality suffered its heaviest defeat at the hands of the Kurfürstendamm.

By the 1920s the Kurfürstendamm had become the place where everything considered bohemian was on offer. The most famous meeting-place was the Romanische Café, situated where the austere Europa Center now stands.

In 1933 all the colourful goings on were abruptly halted and, with the victimisation of Jews, the traditional centre of entertainment had become the stage for a *danse macabre*.

The street was all but wiped from the map in the second world war and despite all efforts during the rebuilding, the old splendour of the Ku'damm has never been recreated. During the postwar years, it became a symbol of western prosperity and acquired a dazzling night

Left, coffee-break on the Ku'damm. Right, the Neue Wache on Unter den Linden.

life. It was highly significant that on the night following the collapse of the Wall, it was to the Ku'damm that most of the East Berliners flocked. Many Berliners sample venues up and down the Ku'damm all night long.

At the eastern end of Ku'damm is **Breitscheidplatz** with the ruins of the **Kaiser Wilhelm Memorial Church**, together with its blue-glazed rebuilt version. Since 1983, particularly in the summer, all sorts of people have tended to gather around the **Wasserklops**, a huge fountain created by the sculptor Schmettau which stands next to the **Europa Center**.

The Europa Center is a modern shopping complex and also one of the tallest buildings in Berlin. A lift takes visitors to a viewing platform some 20-storeys up, from which there is a fine view of the city. Inside, meals are over-priced and a casino tries to emulate Monte Carlo: it is a good place to head for when it's raining, but only when you're prepared to splash out. More stylish is the **KaDeWe**, the "Store of the

West" on the adjacent **Wittenberg-erplatz**, Berlin's Harrods.

In the side streets, called **Off-Ku' damm**, are some of the better restaurants, cafés and pubs. The city has more than 8,000 places to eat and drink, more than any other city in Germany. Entertainment of a cultural nature can be enjoyed in the evening by booking seats for the **Schaubühne am Lehniner Platz**. Originally in Kreuzberg, this theatre made a name for itself through the brilliant productions of its director Peter Stein. Although this is one of the city's best theatres, since moving into its technically perfect new site, performances have tended to lack their former experimental vivacity.

Breathing space: The city is surrounded by many lakes and open spaces, such as the **Grunewald** forest to the west where there are lakes and bathing beaches. In the middle of the city is the **Tiergarten**, a wonderful park where many Berliners spend time at the weekends. The Ku'damm approaches it from the south-west where the Zoo Station, meeting

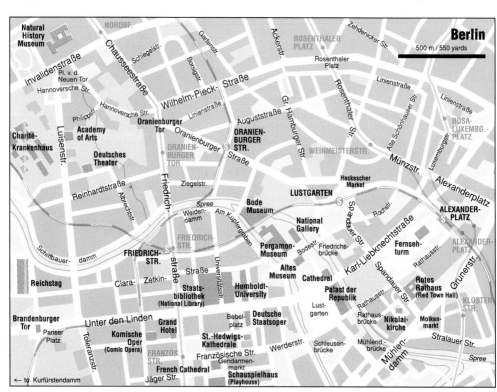

point of some of the city's more disreputable characters. The **zoo** itself is in the west off the 212-hectare (525-acre) Tiergarten. It is one of the largest zoos in the world and home to around 14,000 animals. Its aquarium houses more than 8,000 fish.

In the centre of the park is the 67-metre (223-ft) Victory Column, built in 1873 to commemorate the Prussian victory over the Danes nine years earlier. From here there is a grand view down to the Brandenburg Gate. On the north side of the gate on the edge of the park is the **Reichstag**, built in the 19th century in Italian Renaissance style and set to take its place once more as home of the national parliament. Its dome, destroyed in the famous fire of 1933 and left ruined during the post-war rebuilding, is to be replaced.

On the south side of the Tiergarten is the **Philharmonic Hall** made famous by its conductor, the late Herbert von Karajan, and the **Musical Instrument Museum**. The **New National Gallery** in Tiergarten has Realist, Impressionist

and other modern works. It was completed in 1968 after designs by Ludwig Mies Van Der Rohe (1866–1969) of the Bauhaus movement, and there is a separate **Bauhaus Museum**.

A principal museum site and the finest house in the city is the baroque **Charlottenburg Palace** in the Charlottenburg district to the west of the city. Originally built in 1695 as a country house for Sophie Charlotte, Queen of Prussia, it was elaborated in the 18th century by Frederick the Great and his successor, Frederick Wilhelm II. The Historical Rooms have been fully restored and the New Wing built under Frederick the Great contains more paintings by Antoine Watteau than any other gallery outside France. In the palace grounds are the **Museum of Antiquity** and the **Egyptian Museum**.

The greatest museum in the former west is the **Painting Gallery** at **Dahlem** to the south of the city. This has examples of every western art movement up to 1800 and it includes work by every famous artist including Canaletto, Caravaggio, Giorgione, Mantegna, Rafael, Rubens and Titian. The **Prints and Drawings Collection** is the finest in Germany with many works by Durer and Rembrandt.

Near the Dahlem museums are the 42 hectare (100-acre) **Botanical Gardens** and the **Botanical Museum**.

Historical centre: The **Brandenburg Gate** leads on to Under den Linden and the centre of the city, **Berlin-Mitte**. Since its inauguration in 1791, the Gate has been a symbol of the fate of Germany, and as such has engendered a great deal of pathos. Napoleon marched through it on his triumphant way to Russia, and slunk round it on his humiliating retreat. The Quadriga, the goddess of victory on her chariot drawn by four horses on top of the Gate, was stolen in 1806 but brought back in triumph by Marshal Blücher eight years later.

Barricades were erected at the Gate during the German Revolution of 1848. Kings and emperors paraded here. The revolutionary crowds of 1918 streamed through it on their way to the palace to proclaim the republic. The Nazis also staged their victory parades through the Brandenburg Gate, but following their downfall in 1945, Soviet soldiers hoisted the Red Flag on the Quadriga.

Following the construction of the Berlin Wall, the entire area around the monument was cordoned off, both from the east and the west. During and after the collapse of the Wall, the Gate became a central symbol of the hopes and expectations of a united Germany.

The most Prussian of Berlin's streets is undoubtedly the **Unter den Linden,** which leads from the Brandenburg Gate towards the heart of old Berlin. Here, too, much was annihilated during the war and ruined by socialist misplanning in the post-war years. However, strolling down this elegant boulevard today, the ambience of the old metropolis can almost be touched.

On the left of the street going east are the monumental buildings of the **German State Library** and the **Humboldt University**. Berlin-Mitte is more than just royal Berlin. It is also Fascist and Socialist Berlin. It was opposite the university, the old Opern Platz, now renamed Bebel Platz, where the Nazis burnt more than 20,000 books in 1933. The **Forum Fridericianum**, round this square, is graced with structures from every epoch. There is the baroque **Zeughaus**, the old arsenal decorated with 22 warriors' death masks which is now a museum. The **German State Opera House** was conceived in classical style, but has been renovated and rebuilt so many times that it now bears little resemblance to the original edifice. Behind it is **St Hedwig's Cathedral**, which is based on the Pantheon in Rome.

Berlin-Mitte was the cradle of the city, the merchants' settlement which was established on the ford on the Spree where the Mühlendamm-brücke now crosses the river. Most of the historical buildings to be seen here are not the originals and much – such as the City Palace of the Hohenzollern emperors, for example – has been lost forever. Although severely damaged during the war, it was the Stalinist authorities of the former East Germany who finished

Neptune couldn't bear to be alone.

the building off in the 1950s. The copper-coloured **Palace of the Republic**, seat of parliament and popular amusement during SED rule, now stands in its place.

It was not until the 1970s that the former regime remembered its Prussian heritage and sought to make amends. In the Nikolai District the **Church of St Nicholas**, Berlin's oldest edifice dating from the 13th century, was rebuilt in exemplary fashion, but the buildings around the church square were converted into doll's houses, into a Berlin "Disney World".

Athenean aspirations: The imposing classical structures conceived by the 19th-century architect Friedrich Schinkel, which transformed the city into "Athens on the Spree", testify eloquently to the fact that Berlin once ranked among the most beautiful European cities.

It is open to debate which of Schinkel's buildings is the most beautiful. Some maintain that it is the **Schauspielhaus** (theatre) on the **Gendarmenmarkt**. Framed by the German Cathedral and the French Cathedral the entire square is an aesthetically perfect ensemble. Others point to the **Neue Wache** near the university on Unter den Linden as being Schinkel's most complete work. It was his first building in Berlin, and it certainly possesses the harmony of classical simplicity. This is where, in DDR days, soldiers of the People's Army goose-stepped in front of the Neue Wache which served as a memorial to the victims of Fascism and militarism. As the Central Memorial of the German Federal Republic, its role has now changed to commemorate the victims of both world wars.

A third favourite candidate for Schinkel's masterpiece is the **Altes (Old) Museum** on **Museum Island**. This is indeed his most impressive building. Inside and out it was entirely designed to serve its purpose, namely to display works of art. But then the whole museum island is, in both form and content, an extraordinary artistic ensemble.

It takes more than an afternoon to visit the **Old** and **New Museums**, the **National Gallery**, the **Pergamon Museum** and the **Bode Museum**. Their treasures from antiquity are wonderful. Chief among them is the Altar of Zeus (180–160BC) from Pergamon in Turkey, which gave the museum its name. It also has the throne room facade from Nebuchadnezzar II's Babylon and the tiled market gate (604–562BC) from Miletus. The Bode Museum has Egyptian and Graeco-Roman collections.

Berlin Cathedral is a monument to the Wilhelmenian expression of splendour. The nearby equestrian statue of Frederick the Great looks beyond the Television Tower, which dominates everything on Alexanderplatz, to the Palace of the Republic.

When it was built in 1866, the **synagogue** in Oranienburger Strasse was the largest in the world, and it has been rebuilt since it was destroyed, ironically, by allied bombing. It served the largest Jewish community in Europe, who lived around the synagogue in the **Scheunenviertal** district. This has once more become one of the liveliest areas of the city, with a thriving art scene and many bustling cafés and restaurants.

Meeting up at the world clock on Alexanderplatz.

DOWN THE RHINE

More poetry, more songs and more fables have been inspired by Old Father Rhine than any other river. Legend depicts him as a grey-bearded old man, bucolic at times, urbane at others, wise with age but of a Bacchanalian disposition. Nymphs and gnomes are at his command and fabulous fortunes and secrets hide in his depths.

To the Romans he was Rhenus the river god who protected them against the savage barbarians. To medieval robber knights, who levied tolls on all passing river boats, he was a fountain of wealth. To adventurous and ravenous foreigners, the rich fiefs and towns on his banks were a coveted prize. And to German nationalists at the end of the 19th century he was a patriotic rallying cry, echoed in the song: "Dear Fatherland, fear not, fast stands the watch, the watch on the German Rhein…"

These words were chiselled into the memorial **Germania**, the sword-swinging Valkyrian symbol of Bismarck's unified Germany, which gazes defiantly west across the Rhine above Rüdesheim. The river has always been a frontier, dividing the Celtic from the Teutonic, the French from the Germans. German romanticism and German militarism are like the vineyards and the castles on the Rhine's slopes – two distinct elements in a single landscape.

Europe's longest river at 820 miles (1,320 km), the Rhine runs from the glaciers of the St Gotthard in the Swiss Alps to the twin tentacles on its last leg through the Netherlands. Neanderthals lived in the Rhine valley occasionally joined by nomadic tribes. Cities like Constance, Mainz, Cologne, and Bonn were founded by Roman legionaries who camped on the western banks, convinced that everyone across the river was barbarian. The saga of the Nibelungs (the German *Iliad*), a tale that inspired Richard Wagner, took the Rhine as the setting for its gloomy narrative.

The Rhine is also a river of industry. Flowing through Europe's greatest industrial area, the Ruhr, between Düsseldorf and Duisburg and carrying freight on 9,000 barges, it is the world's busiest waterway. Along its route are Germany's principle manufacturing towns. Important vineyards line sections of the riverbanks from the southern Kaiserstuhl to the most northern grapes, grown near Bonn, above Königswinter.

The romantic part, the 120-mile (190-km) stretch between Mainz and Cologne, has been a big attraction for tourists ever since Queen Victoria and her German husband Prince Albert journeyed down it through torrential rains in 1845. They set a trend which brought the railways and roads along both banks which in turn brought industry and such bad pollution that the name of the river derived from the German word *rein* meaning "pure", became a sad joke.

After splashing through Switzerland, the river runs into **Lake Constance**, a sprawling Alpine lake which it leaves near Schaffhausen in a spectacular 65-foot (20-metre) fall that has been harnessed for hydro-electricity by the Swiss. Navigable from **Basel** onwards, it hurries along between the far edge of the Black Forest on the eastern side and the Vosges on the French or western bank before it enters the region of Baden at **Karlsruhe** with its variety of wines. Past the old medieval city of Speyer, the Rhine reaches **Mannheim** where it joins the River Neckar.

Downriver on the left bank is the ancient city of **Worms** where the Niebelung saga claims Gunter held court. Here the villain Hagen sank the fabulous Niebelung treasure into the Rhine after murdering Siegfried, the hero of German folklore. Many a staunch wealth seeker has joined the quest to find the treasure from an era when rare swords cut steel and magic caps made their wearer invisible.

It was at Worms on 18 April 1521 that Martin Luther, addressing a diet called to make him recant his religious doctrine, shouted out his defiant message: "Here I stand, I cannot do otherwise, God help me. Amen." In this turbulent city stands one of Europe's oldest synagogues (founded in 1034) not far from the Romanesque cathedral. Outside Worms is the 13th-century **Liebfrauen-kirche** (Church of Our Dear Ladies), surrounded by gently rising vineyards which provide the grapes for the popular white wine, *Liebfraumilch* (literally, Dear Lady Milk).

Old Father Rhine's most historical stretch is between Mainz and Cologne. Here the snaking river valley is flanked by needle-sharp church spires, golden weathercocks, spic-and-span villages, gorges and hills on which terraced rows of vines climb in straight lines. This is where German poets dreamed of paradise on earth. Goethe called it "a blessed region" and Kleist labelled it "the pleasure grounds of nature." An old Roman coin, probably the first Rhine souvenir, bore the legend, "Fun on the Rhine."

For centuries, astute locals, and a few no less astute foreigners, turned Rhine houses, castles and the countryside into a kind of German Disneyland that has little to do with the original appearance. *Weinstuben* (wine rooms) and *Kneipen* (pubs or bars) bristling with copper, wrought iron, rococo ornaments and kitsch try to lure customers. The tourist boom has changed the Rhine into a make-believe land – ostentatious and often crude.

Lord Byron immortalized the river in *Childe Harold*, as did William Turner in his sketches. William Thackeray found it superfluous to write more about the river "since everyone seemed to have been there, from the ambassador to the London apprentice." The Germans discovered the beauty of the river much later, first with romanticism, then with patriotic fervour under Prussian dominance. The Rhine played a symbolic role in the founding of Germany and the victorious war against the French in 1870–71.

Castles old and new: Part of this sudden interest in Old Father Rhine manifested itself in the Prussian endeavour to preserve and renovate the castle ruins along the river. Between Mainz and Cologne there are 60 castles, most of them perched on top of vertical crags, still arrogant in their often dilapidated splendour. Nearly all the castles along the Rhine had been

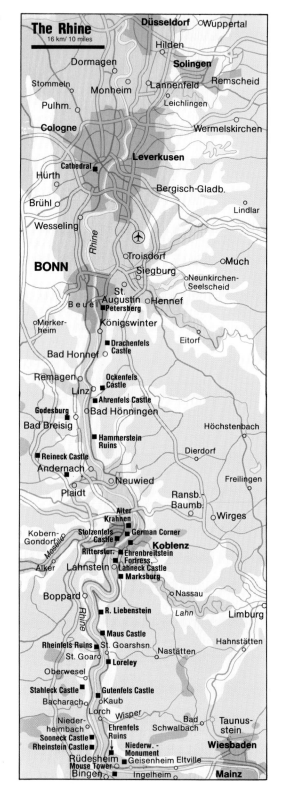

destroyed in successive campaigns by kings, emperors and local rulers who saw them as reminders of medieval days when the lofty eyries were occupied by robber knights and autocratic nobles who preyed on the domains below them. They ransacked caravans, looted villages or imposed exorbitant tolls on all navigation, dropping heavy iron chains, like boom gates, across the river.

Only one of these formidable fortresses survived this period of destruction: the mighty **Rheinfels** (Rhein Rock) above St Goar, built in the 12th century by the counts of Katzenelbogen. Rocks and burning oil greeted all assailants until, in a moment of folly, it was surrendered, without a shot being fired, to French revolutionary forces in 1794. Three years later it was demolished.

Today many of the renovated castles have been transformed into hotels, youth hostels or restaurants. Rhine castle ruins have been sold to opera singers, textile barons and dreamers with money, who spent millions making them habitable, often depleting their own fortunes in the process. Some of the castles are frauds. The **Drachenburg** (Dragon Castle) near Bonn was built by Baron Stephan von Sarten in 1879 for his paramour, a Cologne baker's daughter.

The romantic Rhine begins at the confluence of the Main and Rhine Rivers at **Mainz**, a city virtually destroyed by phosphor-bombing in the closing weeks of World War II. Its 50 churches and 100 wine rooms were rebuilt, however, with the same loving care with which its champagne makers, Kupferberg, now store their bottles in ancient Roman vaults. Mainz has a Ministry for Winegrowing, the only one in Germany, and at the **House of German Wine** many varieties can be sampled.

Further down the Rhine at **Rüdesheim**, a wine village, is the **Drosselgasse**, a narrow alley lined with ornate *Weinstuben* along its entire length. The narrowness of the lane makes it difficult for anybody who has drunk too much to fall over.

The town is the heart of the **Rheingau**, also known as the **Weingau**, an area along the famous (or infamous) Ries-

ling Route producing 27 million bottles of wine annually. Much of the Riesling boom is due to the diligence of the Benedictine monks around the **abbey of Eberbach** and the growers in the town of **Johannisberg**.

From Rüdesheim, the terraced vineyards climb, like green sheets, up the steep hills on the eastern banks of the Rhine. The hills are made of slate which retains the sun's warmth and the slopes protect the vines from the biting north winds and cold rains all year round.

A naked nymph and seven virgins: The fable of the Loreley, the siren who sits singing on the rock, luring to their death ships and knights alike, is the story of a *femme fatale*. The blonde temptress was invented in 1801 by the 23-year-old poet Clemens Brentano. In 1823, the Loreley was immortalised by the writer Heinrich Heine. Travelling down the Rhine, probably having enjoyed the hospitality of the *Weinstuben* in the Weingau, he suffered the kind of melancholy that comes with hangovers in the wake of merrymaking. This prompted

Katz Castle, near Loreley.

him to write the words: "I cannot divine what it meaneth/This haunting nameless pain/A tale of the bygone ages/Keeps brooding through my brain." This ode to the naked nymph has become the subject of more than 25 operas.

The **Loreley**, in reality, is a 400-foot (120-metre) high rock between **Kaub** and **St Goarshausen** on the right bank of the Rhine. So that tourists do not miss the famous wench, her name is even written on the rock, in Japanese. A Soviet artist was commissioned to make a statue of the siren which, unveiled in 1983, now adorns the neck of the rock.

While the Loreley has finally found a face to fit the legend, the fierce current which prompted the saga has been tamed. The notorious **Bingener Hole**, the fast-flowing treacherous gorge near the rock where ships foundered, is today equipped with an electronic guidance system that steers barges through safely.

Just before one reaches the Loreley Rock, near the town of **Oberwesel**, there are seven submerged reefs known as the **Seven Virgins** or Seven Sisters who, according to early legend, were turned into stone because they were too prudish – a tale often told by local knaves to unwilling maidens.

On the other side of the river from Rüdesheim, at **Bingen**, is the **Mäuseturm** (Mouse Tower) in the middle of the Rhine, named after the wicked bishop of Hatto who was chased by an irate populace to the tower where he was eaten by mice.

A mid-river toll station at **Kaub** remains from the days when a chain could be strung across the river to prevent any vessel from passing until the captain had paid a sum to the tollkeeper.

Beyond the Loreley, above the ancient pilgrim town of **Bornhofen**, the "enemy brothers" are two castles, **Sterrenberg** and **Liebenstein**, built next to one another but separated by a wall.

Just above them, at **Braubach**, is the **Marksburg**, one of the most spectacular and best preserved castles along the Rhine, with a reconstructed knights' hall and a museum of ancient weapons. The Marksburg looks down not only

The Mouse Tower at Bingen.

onto the Rhine but also over the picturesque Lahn River valley.

Just before the Lahn empties into the Rhine, it flows past the "gingerbread" town of **Bad Ems** which has whitewashed half-timbered houses, wisteria and lacy-iron balconies. The last stretch of the Rhine before Koblenz is literally in flames on the second Saturday of every August during the annual firework and bonfire display.

Carnival: The Rhinelanders enjoy showy celebrations and their pre-Lent carnival culminates on *Rosenmontag* (Rose Monday) in a grand parade of floats and fools. Up to 3 million people dance in a frenzy through the streets of Cologne and Mainz. The last Thursday of carnival is *Weiberfasnacht* (Wenches' carnival) when the ladies shed their inhibitions (never particularly developed in the Rhineland) and may kiss, hug and dance with the man of their choice. Some even run off into the night with him. The carnival preparations officially start at 11pm on the 11th day of the 11th month of the year and the madness ends

on Ash Wednesday when the staunchly Catholic population trudges to church to repent.

At **Koblenz**, the **Mosel**, perhaps Germany's loveliest river, joins the Rhine. The country's most delicious wines, at least to the wine lover with a gentle palate, originate from the Mosel's terraced vineyards outside such villages as Bernkastel, Piesport, Zell and Graach.

Where the two great wine-rivers meet stands an impressive monument known as **das Deutsche Eck** (the German Corner). On the opposite side of the river, high on the edge of a ridge, lies **Ehrenbreitstein**, a 13th-century fortress that has controlled this key area and has changed hands several times between the French and Germans. Just below Koblenz, before **Andernach**, Julius Caesar had the first bridge built across the Rhine in 55 BC.

Bridges have always played an important role along the Rhine, not just in communications but also in conquests. And the bridge at **Remagen** played a memorable part in the closing days of World War II. It was secured by the American Ninth Armoured Division which found it miraculously intact, while all the other 43 bridges over the Rhine had been destroyed by the Nazis.

The Americans crossed the bridge, which had already been damaged by German explosives, before it collapsed a few days later. The unexpected crossing cut several days off the war and was glorified in a Hollywood film. Memorabilia of the dramatic event are shown in the **Friedensmuseum** (Peace Museum) which is located in the only surviving pillar of the former railway bridge.

Coming from Remagen towards Bonn one can hardly miss the 1,000-foot (321-metre) high **Drachenfels** (Dragon Rock) on the right bank. On its heights the Nibelung hero Siegfried slew the dragon and bathed in its blood, thereby making himself invulnerable. This myth is commemorated by the *Drachenblut* (Dragon Blood) wine, made from the most northern grapes in Germany. The hill has a 12th-century castle ruin, pointing skywards like a thumb, and it is also known as "Holland's highest mountain" be-

Carnival time.

cause of the number of Dutch visitors it attracts. It can be conquered by donkey or in a cog-railway carriage.

Behind the Drachenfels are the mysterious **Siebengebirge** (seven mountains) built, according to legend, by seven giants who dug a channel for the Rhine and left seven mounds of earth.

The quiet capital: This legendary landscape provides a backdrop for **Bonn**, "a small town in Germany" which became, as a compromise substitute for Berlin, capital of the Federal Republic in 1949. An irreverent American correspondent who saw the city for the first time, described it bluntly as "Half the size of Chicago's central cemetery, but twice as dead."

Even Bonn's famous son, Ludwig van Beethoven, left the sleepy river town at the age of 17. Still, the house where the great musician was born has been lovingly preserved as a museum. On the **Domplatz** stands the **Beethoven statue** which was unveiled in 1845.

Founded by the Emperor Claudius as *Castra Bonnensia* in 50 AD, Bonn might have remained just another picturesque fairytale Rhine village, endowed with an old university, a fine cathedral and the **Alexander Koenig Museum** containing the cranium of the Neanderthal man, had it not gained capital status.

Before returning the status of capital to Berlin, the city housed an estimated 100,000 officials, diplomats and journalists in the tiny Rhine bank villages between Bonn and Mehlem. Embassies, consulates and other government buildings acquired the prettiest riverside spots. Up went utilitarian cement blocks such as the *Langer Eugen*, to house the parliamentary offices. The little town of narrow alleys and wooden beams has, however, remained sleepy at heart, and an amazing lethargy descends at dusk when both traffic and pedestrians disappear.

Cologne is a much livelier city with a population of about 1 million. It is not only famous for its twin-spired cathedral, exuberant Mardi Gras celebrations and religious processions, but also the courage with which it was rebuilt after

The Rhine Valley between Bonn and Mainz.

being reduced to rubble during World War II.

The spirit of Cologne is embodied in its mighty **Dom** (Cathedral) and the **Severinsbrücke** (Severinsbridge), a unique construction across the Rhine, supported by only one off-centre pillar.

The Cathedral, considered the greatest Gothic church in Christendom, contains the remains of the Wise Men of the East, the paintings of Stephan Lochner and a feeling of immense space and lofty aspirations that have an awesome effect on the visitor. Begun in 1248, its twin spires, each 515 feet (157 metres) high, were not built until 1842–80 during an era when heady ideas and monuments were in vogue.

The city also has some excellent museums, and is highly acclaimed for its theatre and music. Carnival here is celebrated with typical gay abandon and plenty of the local Kölsch beer.

Beyond Cologne the river suddenly exchanges its vineyards and castles for smoke stacks, blast furnaces and sprawling factories. At night their lights flutter like glow-worms. This is the **Ruhr** region, the country's most industrialized area. Its heart is **Düsseldorf**, nicknamed the "Paris of Germany", a city of harmonious architecture, cafés and pretty girls. The birthplace of the poet Heinrich Heine (1797–1856) it has maintained a flair for fashions, fairs and the muses.

At the edge of this industrial complex lies **Xanten**, birthplace of Siegfried and Saint Victor the martyr, a place visited by the intrepid ancient traveller Ulysses, according to the great Roman historian Tacitus.

Just before Old Father Rhine crosses the border into Holland at Emmerich, it passes **Kleve** where the **Schwanenburg** (Swan Castle) recalls the tale of Lohengrin, the silent knight, and his inquisitive spouse Elsa von Brabant.

The mighty river now splits into two. Its smaller tributaries are known as the old man's "illegitimate children". Thus divided it flows serenely through the Netherlands to empty itself, forgetful of the alcoholic indulgences en route, into the North Sea.

At work in the vineyards.

HEIDELBERG

Down from the Black Forest flows the **River Neckar**, winding for about 216 miles (360 km) through some of the most scenic areas in the southwest of Germany. East of Mannheim it finally leaves its narrow bed to spread out into the plains of the Rhine Valley. There, at the very edge of the Odenwald Mountains, nestled astride a shallow gorge along the Neckar lies Heidelberg, the epitome of romantic Germany.

Home of a 600-year-old university, it was one of the few German cities to escape bombing during World War II. High above its picturesque lanes and the maze of roofs, the ruins of **Heidelberg Castle** rise majestically. Beneath it, the six arches of the **Alte Brücke** (Old Bridge) span the river, enhancing the harmony of the valley. Its 13th-century gate is topped by the Baroque spires and leads to **Philosophenweg** (Philosopher's Way), a mountain promenade along **Heiligenberg**.

Here, on the opposite bank of the Neckar, the dramatic river panorama of **Old Heidelberg** is revealed in the shimmering rays of the late afternoon sun, as the castle's mighty facades of red sandstone turn to gold. When floodlit, the ruin seems to float on the darkness. Twice a year, on the first Saturday in June and September, it is illuminated by a magnificent display of fireworks.

Again and again, the charms of Heidelberg have inspired songs and novels. The painters and poets of German Romanticism were particularly enthralled by its beauty. Mark Twain, the author of *Huckleberry Finn*, wrote: "One thinks of Heidelberg by day – with its surroundings – as the last possibility of the beautiful; but when he sees Heidelberg by night, a fallen Milky Way, he requires time to consider upon the verdict."

Today, Heidelberg attracts about 3½ million visitors every year. More than 1½ million of these come from outside Germany; Americans rank first, followed by the Japanese and the British.

All head first for the castle. Coaches approaching from the *Autobahn* usually pass through the **Gaisberg Tunnel** and drive right up the winding **Schlossberg Strasse**. The most convenient way to reach the castle from downtown is by the **Bergbahn** which begins at the **Kornmarkt**.

The castle rests on the northern slopes of **Königsstuhl Mountain**, 328 ft (100 metres) above the town. Late in the 14th century the rulers of the Palatinate chose this site to build a fortress, which was gradually extended during the Reformation and the Peasants' Revolt. Steep ramparts and the empty shells of imposing towers bear witness to its military past. Between 1544 and 1620, a Renaissance-style castle and a magnificent pleasure garden were added. Fortifications, domestic quarters and palaces of various styles now surround the inner courtyard, from where one passes through an archway to the terrace. Some of the buildings have been left as ruins with the sky peeking through their empty windows. Other parts of the castle have been restored and are now being used, as in former times, for banquets, concerts and theatre performances.

Weddings continue to take place in the chapel, and it is particularly popular among American soldiers stationed in Heidelberg to lead their brides up to the castle's altar.

The castle also houses the **Deutsches Apothekenmuseum** (German Apothecary Museum) as well as a number of exhibitions that present a lively picture of how the Palatine nobility lived in times long gone by. The **Great Vat Building**, for example, displays the biggest barrel ever filled with wine. It had a capacity of 55,345 gallons (221,276 litres) and was guarded by Perkeo, the court fool, a most amusing dwarf whose legendary thirst far outgrew his stature.

Burned to the ground: The rulers of the Palatinate were respected as high-ranking political dignitaries within the Holy Roman Empire. Since the Middle Ages they had belonged to the elite of the powerful *Kurfürsten* (Prince Electors), who elected the German king and later the emperor. As patrons of the arts and

Heidelberg from the Philoso-phenweg.

higher learning, these rulers left their mark on Heidelberg's history. In 1386 Elector Ruprecht I founded the university, the oldest one in present-day Germany. The **Heiliggeistkirche** (Church of the Holy Ghost) was, at the time of its construction, the biggest Gothic ecclesiastical building in the Palatinate, housing one of the most valuable collections of books in the world.

During the Reformation, Heidelberg turned to Protestantism and in 1623, during the Thirty Years' War, it was stormed by troops under the command of Catholic General Tilly. The *Bibliotheca Palatina* (Palatine Library) was declared war booty, and it was loaded on carts and sent across the Alps to the Vatican. A small portion of the books were later returned.

Disastrous events were sparked off by the marriage of Liselotte Palatine to the Count of Orléans. When her younger brother died, the House of Bourbon claimed succession to the throne and went to war. In 1689 French troops invaded the Rhine valley, devastating many towns and villages, including Heidelberg. In 1693, the town was again captured by the French. This time they burned Heidelberg to the ground and blew up the castle's fortifications. When Louis XIV, the Sun King, learned about the destruction of Heidelberg he had a *Te Deum* sung in Paris's Notre Dame. The royal mint issued a memorial medal, the Latin inscription of which reads in English: "Heidelberg destroyed. The King said it and it was done."

Most of historic Heidelberg dates from the 18th century when it was reconstructed in contemporary Baroque style. In 1764, however, lightning destroyed some of the buildings, and Prince Karl Theodor (1744–99) interpreted this as a divine indication to abandon his residence for good and it fell into disrepair.

A French family finally saved the building. Count Charles de Graimberg moved in and began preservation at the beginning of the 19th century.

The two Heidelbergs: The **Altstadt** (Old Town) is now a pedestrian zone, its main artery being the **Hauptstrasse**. **The Old Bridge.**

On either side of the street lie various churches, squares and residences. Landmarks of architectural interest include the **Hotel zum Ritter**, built in 1592, with a splendid Renaissance facade that withstood the blaze of 1693 brought upon the city by the French. This renovated patrician house opposite the Church of the Holy Ghost ranks as one of the jewels of Old Heidelberg.

A rich source of information on the city's history is to be found in the former **Palais Morass**. Since 1905 it has housed the **Kurpfälzisches Museum** (Palatinate Museum) which, among other treasures, exhibits the lower jaw of the *Homo Heidelbergensis*. This piece of bone, found in the Neckar valley south of Heidelberg, is one of the oldest pieces of evidence of European man, who may have lived 500,000 years ago.

The Hauptstrasse is criss-crossed by a number of *Gassen* (narrow lanes). Turning into **Grabengasse**, one enters **University Square**. The Alte Universitat (Old University Building) of 1712 exhibits, as a public curiosity, the former **Studentenkarzer**. Up to 1914 it served as a prison for students, who, because of public drunkenness or other misdemeanours, were locked up by the University administration. This punishment was taken rather lightly by the inmates as can be seen in the prison cells, the walls of which are covered with humorous graffiti and paintings.

The modern building at the rear of the University Square was erected in 1931 with funds raised in the United States. The **Schurmann Building**, named after US Ambassador Jacob Gould Schurmann, is a memorial to the countless young Americans who spent pleasurable college days in Heidelberg. There is an unsubstantiated rumour that influential friends in the US saved the town from air raids in World War II.

Heidelberg revived its academic reputation in the 19th century. The *Ruperto Carola,* named after both its founder Ruprecht, and its renovater, Grand Duke Carl Friedrich, soon became known as the "royal residence of the intellect". It attracted a number of brilliant scholars

who taught and researched there. Today, Heidelberg plays a major role as an international centre of cancer research.

Heidelberg's modern business district stretches along **Kurfürstenanlage** from **Bismarckplatz** to the **Hauptbahnhof** (main station). The area is representative of the same sober concrete and glass architecture to be found everywhere in postwar Germany. The modern university town of clinics, institutes and student dormitories has sprouted on the right bank of the Neckar, on the **Neuenheimer plains**.

Heidelberg does not appear as a military garrison, although American soldiers, civilian employees and families living in and around the city have made it one of the largest "American" communities in western Europe. After the war the US army made undestroyed Heidelberg into its European headquarters and later some additional NATO command posts moved in. The largest US housing area, **Patrick Henry Village**, has become almost a separate town complete with its own churches, schools, cinemas, shopping and recreational facilities, though defence cuts in the 1990s have made its future uncertain.

Student princes: Heidelberg proper has a population of about 134,000, out of which every fifth person is a student attending either the university, teacher's college or the Academy of Music. Heidelberg can be thought of as an old town with a young face or a young town with an old face. The crowds of young people milling around the streets at any given hour of the day are reminders of Heidelberg's youthful side and its role as a university town.

The various coloured banners suspended from some villas in the **Old Town** are the colours of various student fraternities, some of which perpetuate 19th-century drinking rituals and even engage in traditional fencing duels to initiate new members.

The Old Town comes alive at night when the many student inns are filled to the brim with old and young alike. The most famous ones, **Roter Ochse** and **Seppl**, are located along the Haupt-

Graffiti in the Studenten-karzer.

188

strasse. The Inn of the Three Golden apples exists only in an operetta called *The Student Prince*. It is based on a German stage play, *Alt Heidelberg*, about the fairytale romance of Prince Karl Heinrich and the maid Kathie. It was a worldwide success after Hungarian-born Broadway composer Sigmund Romberg made it into an operetta. A Hollywood film, starring tenor Mario Lanza as the Student Prince, revived the myth of Old Heidelberg after the war.

During the annual August festival, this musical romance is reenacted for seven nights in and around the castle. In these surroundings the spectacle takes on an air of Old World authenticity, beginning with the hollow sound of horse hooves filling the night. Suddenly out of the shadows appears the gilded carriage of the Prince, glistening in the moonlight. Since Heidelberg normally has fine weather during August, the performance takes place outdoors in the courtyard. The open-air seating accommodates approximately 1,200 spectators and even a last-minute visitor usually finds a chair. On rainy nights, the musical takes place in the King's Hall of the castle. Since only limited seating is available there, early booking with the Heidelberg Municipal Theatre, tourist information or other ticket offices is advisable.

Exploring the surroundings of Heidelberg is a pleasure on its own. The Neckar Valley is dotted with a number of quaint towns that to this day have preserved their traditional character.

About 6 miles (10 km) upstream from Heidelberg is **Neckargemünd** which has been a favourite destination of students for centuries. Most famous among the traditional inns of the city is the **Hotel zum Ritter** where the Prince Electors regularly dined after hunting expeditions in the surrounding forests.

A well-preserved monument from the days of the Holy Roman Empire is **Eberbach**, an old imperial city of the Staufer family with old archways, cobblestone streets and half-timbered houses. The best way to visit these places is to travel along the river.

A student society's ultra-conservative members.

BAVARIA AND THE ROMANTIC ROAD

Germany's largest state, covering more than half the area of the Netherlands, is located in the south of the country, bordering the Czech Republic and Austria. It is one of the most heavily forested areas, and includes Franken (Franconia) in the north, Bayerischer Wald (Bavarian Forest), a lake-rich pre-Alpine region, and the Bayerische Alpen (Bavarian Alps).

For the true Bavarian, any place outside Bavaria is a foreign country. Both under the Prussian-led *Reich* formed in 1871 and in the present Germany, Bavaria has claimed various tokens of independence. On entering Bavaria, the traveller is welcomed by a set of border signs proclaiming *Freistaat Bayern* (Bavarian Free State). Although Bavaria no longer maintains its own army, diplomatic corps or postal service, as it did up until the end of World War I, it is the only German state with its own nationally important political party, the *Christlich-Soziale Union* (CSU – Christian Social Union). It is also the only one of the 10 *Bundesländer* (Federal States) with its own national anthem, played each night at the close of the public radio programme, as well as at all official state functions.

Bavaria also has Germany's highest mountain, the 9,721-foot (2,963-metre) Zugspitze; the world's most famous beer-hall, the Hofbräuhaus; and one of the world's most popular castles, Neuschwanstein. Its capital, Munich (population 1.3 million), lies in the south, near the Alps and the Austrian border.

Getting to and around Bavaria presents no problem. Munich has an international airport and is a main stop for express trains. Two *Autobahn* (motorway) routes converge in Munich from neighbouring states: from Frankfurt am Main via Würzburg and Nuremberg in northern Bavaria; and from Stuttgart via Ulm and Augsburg in the south. The motorway system continues south into Austria to Innsbruck and Salzburg, and on to Italy. There are other *Autobahn* routes inside Bavaria and good secondary roads. However, roads can be crowded as a result of the weekend exodus from Munich. The main *Autobahn* routes have a constant flow of international truck traffic except on Sundays and public holidays.

From Munich, it is easy to reach the castles and spectacular scenery of the nearby Bavarian Alps. It is usually easier to travel north-south, to and from Munich, than to go east-west. Distances may be deceptive. It is, for example, almost as far from Neuschwanstein castle to Berchtesgaden as from Munich to Stuttgart, and that's as the crow flies, not curving along Alpine roads.

The House of Wittelsbach: Bavaria has had a rich, but also sometimes bankrupt royal past. It was ruled for more than seven centuries by the House of Wittelsbach, one of the longest-reigning families in Europe. The blue-and-white dynasty, whose colours are still the official ones of Bavaria, was founded in 1180 by one Otto von Wittelsbach.

The southern part, Upper Bavaria

Left, Nuremberg's medieval look. Right, like father, like son.

("upper" because of the Alpine elevations), once belonged to the Roman Empire. In the 6th century the area was invaded by expanding German tribes and settled by the *Baiuvarii* or *Bajiuwaren* because they came from neighbouring *Boijerland* (later Bohemia, now across the border in the Czech Republic). Within 300 years, the new duchy had to be broken up to keep its rulers in their place. Under the Wittelsbachs, Bavaria and part of the Palatinate were ruled separately by family members until 1799. The status of "kingdom" was bestowed by Napoleon in 1806 but the Bavarians turned against the French emperor in time to be part of the victorious alliance against him.

The present borders were acquired when the Congress of Vienna redrew the map of Europe. Since then, it has included Franconia in the north and parts of Swabia in the southwest. It is said that people from these areas claim to be Bavarians only when they are in northern Germany or abroad.

The Romantic Road: Many visitors are familiar with the Romantic Road, the name given to a route through Bavaria steeped in all the riches of history, from Würzburg in the north, running down through Augsburg east of Munich to Füssen near the Austrian border.

The popularity of the Romantic Road detours many visitors from **Nuremberg**, which lies about 63 miles (105 km) east of Würzburg on the Frankfurt-Munich *Autobahn*. It is Bavaria's second largest city, with nearly 500,000 inhabitants.

Like Munich, this delightful medieval city was badly damaged during World War II. In recent years, it has made special efforts to restore some of its Old World charm in the centre of the city. The biggest attraction for visitors is the annual outdoor **Christkindlmarkt** (Christ Child Market), held in the weeks before Christmas.

The birthplace of the artist Albrecht Dürer (1471–1528) has been restored and there is the **German National Museum**, which provides a comprehensive insight into the German-speaking world. The city is also the traditional centre of the German *Spielzeug* (toy)

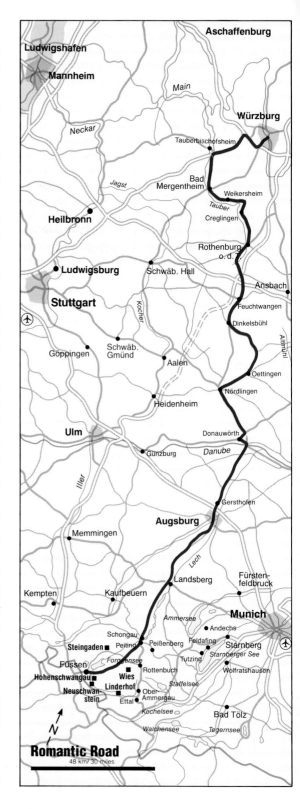

industry and there is a popular **Toy Museum**. The first steam train in Germany ran from Nuremberg to neighbouring **Fürth** in 1835, a fact commemorated by an historic collection in the **Transport Museum.**

No visit should neglect the two specialties from its hearty Franconian gastronomy: delicious grilled sausages called *Nürnberger Bratwürstchen,* and the spicy gingerbread known as *Nürnberger Lebkuchen,* particularly popular during the Christmas season.

One of the best preserved medieval towns in Germany is **Rothenburg ob der Tauber.** "Over the Tauber" describes its position on a plateau above the river on the Romantic Route to the south of Würzburg. In its medieval heyday, it was a Freie Reichstadt, a free imperial town independent in its defence and jurisdiction. From 1650 until the beginning of the last century, it was one of the myriad tiny states of central Europe. In 1802 it became part of the Kingdom of Bavaria and its once powerful role came forever to an end.

There are a number of festivities in the town. The most important is at Whitsuntide, which commemorates the town's rescue from destruction at the hands of Catholic Marshall Tilly and his troops in 1631, during the Thirty Years' War with France. The *Meistertrunk* (Master Draught) play recollects the legendary feat of Mayor Georg Nusch who, on a wager with Tilly, drank in one draft a bumper holding almost three quarters of a gallon of Franconian wine, thus saving the town which had joined the Protestant side. Nusch emptied the bumper in less than 10 minutes, slept without interruption for three days, then lived on in good health until he was 80.

Another celebration is the **Reichsstadt-Festtage** (Free Town Festival) on the second weekend of September, when the whole population, dressed in medieval costumes, joins in a pageant to revive the local history.

Other highlights in the calendar of events include the **Schäfertanze** (Shepherds' Dances) on Whit Sunday and some other Sundays during spring and

Rich variety at the baker's.

summer. They date from medieval times when members of the Shepherds' Guild danced around **Herterichsbrunnen**, the Renaissance fountain that embellishes the market square.

About 8,000 of the total population of 12,500 live within the medieval walls incorporating watch-towers, guard houses and town gates. Walking through the cobblestone streets lined with unspoiled Gothic and Renaissance facades is to step into history.

The first vantage point from which to admire the maze of red-tiled roofs, narrow lanes and quaint squares is the Gothic tower of the **Rathaus** (Town Hall) which, with its Renaissance archway and its baroque arcades, is a rich mix of architectural styles.

On the north side of the **Marktplatz** is the former **Ratsherrntrinkstube** (City Counsellor's Tavern). On its Baroque gable is the official town clock – an artistic clock that opens and shuts two windows. Here, Marshall Tilly and Mayor Nusch, the two characters of the *Meistertrunk* play, appear regularly seven times a day on the hour.

Some of Rothenburg's historic buildings now serve as museums. The **Reichstadt Museum** (Imperial Town Museum) features the medieval culture and history of the town and exhibits what is said to be the oldest kitchen in Germany.

The medieval churches are rich in ecclesiastical art, the pride of the town being the **Heiligblut-Altar** (Holy Blood Altar) in the **Church of St James**. Dating from 1504, it is one of the masterpieces of Tilman Riemenschneider, the Franconian woodcarver of whom it's been said: "he made wood speak."

Bavarian capital: Duke Henry the Lion, who preceded the Wittelsbachs, performed a historic function 800 years ago when he put a new bridge across the Isar River for the transport of salt shipments from the mines in Bad Reichenhall to Augsburg. **Munich** (München), the town that grew up around the bridge, took its name from the occupants of a nearby monastery. The city was originally called Mönchen (Little Monk) and its symbol is still a childlike monk, the

Münchner Kindl (The Munich Child). While the Wittelsbachs had a Munich residence from the early 1500s, it was not until the 19th century that the city, under the reign of Ludwig I and Ludwig II, acquired a reputation as a centre for the arts and sciences.

Much of this was due to ambitious and flamboyant architectural projects, but the city and its schools also attracted leading scientists, artists and writers. Today, Munich claims to publish more books than any other city except New York, although **Schwabing**, the traditional artists' and intellectuals' quarter, has increasingly been taken over by boutiques and tourists.

In many ways, the whole city remains a sophisticated village. Women in *dirndls*, the traditional Bavarian-Austrian rural woman's dress, sip afternoon coffee in chic cafés while men in green *loden* coats, originally woven for shepherds, drive sports cars. Country women in ankle-length dresses sell medicinal herbs from wicker baskets at the bustling Viktualienmarkt right in the city

Beer is "the bread of Bavaria".

centre, where you can also buy the finest French cheese and wine.

Visitors come from around the world to look at the **Asamkirche** (a Catholic church built by the Asam brothers) and other Baroque extravaganzas as well as the ultra-modern headquarters of the **Bayerische Motorenwerke** (BMW), shaped like an automobile cylinder. Visitors flock to the circus-size beer tents and brass bands at the annual *Oktoberfest* (October Festival) as well as to the scientific and technological exhibits in the **Deutsches Museum** (German Museum) the most popular in the country. Situated on an island in the Isar River, it includes a coal mine and a planetarium, as well as numerous exhibits from the worlds of engineering, seafaring and flight.

Munich's two famous art museums, the **Alte** and **Neue Pinakothek**, are situated to the west of the centre, as is **Königsplatz**, with its fine museum of ancient Greek and Roman sculptures, the **Glyptothek**. The Theresienwiese is the site of the world-famous Oktoberfest;

it is dominated by a statue personifying Bavaria in the form of an Amazonian woman. The traditional beer halls and restaurants are conveniently located in the centre of the city in an area framed by the Hauptbahnhof, the Stachus (also known as Karlsplatz), the Rathaus (City Hall), the Residenz and Odeonsplatz. Nearby are the **Hofbräuhaus** (the former court brewery's beer halls).

The **Hofgarten** (Court Garden) on Hofgartenstrasse is near the Residenz's small rococo gem, the **Cuvilliés Theatre**. The historic rooms can be seen in the **Residenz Museum** (entrance on Max-Joseph-Platz); while it's worth being at the **Town Hall** at 11am to view the daily performance of the mechanical figures in the tower.

The large, crowded and loud beer halls such as the **Mäthaser Beer City** (Bayerstrasse 5, off Stachus) and the **Hofbräuhaus** (Platzl 9) should be seen. Equally traditional but quieter are **Donisl** (Weinstrasse 1), **Augustiner Keller** (Amulfstrasse 52), **Franziskaner-Fuchsenstuben** (Perusastrasse 5) and

A Munich beer garden.

the **Ratskeller** in the Town Hall basement (Dienerstrasse side).

A must outside the city is **Schloss Nymphenburg**, a large castle and grounds housing a porcelain factory and the famous Schönheitsgalerie (Gallery of Beauty) with paintings of 24 women including Lola Montez, the beautiful Irish mistress of Ludwig I.

The shadows of history: The rise and fall of Adolf Hitler's Third Reich was in many ways linked with Bavaria. It was in Munich, late in 1919, that Hitler joined an obscure political party called the *Deutsche Arbeiterpartei* which became the nucleus of the Nazi movement. It was also in Munich, in November 1923, that Hitler, in a first attempt to win political power, staged his so-called "Beer Hall Putsch".

At **Bürgerbräukeller**, one of the many beer halls, he proclaimed the "national revolution" and later marched with his followers to the Feldherrnhalle. At Odeonsplatz, the Nazi caravan was stopped and Bavarian state police opened fire. Several of Hitler's followers died;

Hitler himself was arrested and imprisoned for high treason.

Even as the *Führer* (leader), when his official residence was the Chancellery in Berlin, Hitler returned to Bavaria where he owned a home called Berghof, located near **Berchtesgaden** on the Obersalzberg. In April 1945, 318 British Lancaster bombers dumped more than 1,000 tons of bombs around Berghof. However, the Royal Air Force missed its main target: Hitler was in his Berlin bunker.

The remains of Berghof were blown up after the war, though Hitler's former tea house has become a tourist attraction. The proper name of this mountain retreat is **Kehlstein**, but is more commonly known as the "**Eagle's Nest**" because it is located 6,178 feet (1,885 metres) up the mountain.

A road leads to a pedestrian tunnel cut into the mountain and to an elevator that goes up about 393 feet (120 metres) through rock and right into the house. Today, the visitor can dine there and enjoy a spectacular view, as far as Salz- **Munich's Town Hall.**

burg in clear weather, of the **Watzmann peak** (8,900 feet/2,713 metres) and **Königssee** (King's Lake) at its base.

Berchtesgaden proper has long been established as a health resort that also provides a challenge for mountain climbers and skiers. Its rival for the best skiing in the Bavarian Alps is **Garmisch-Partenkirchen**. This is also situated close to the Austrian border, but farther west, on the route to Innsbruck, 57 miles (92 km) from Munich.

Garmisch was the site of the 1936 winter Olympics, an event that put the sleepy little Alpine community on to the world stage. In the closing nighttime ceremony hundreds of torch-bearing skiers swooshed down a mountainside under a canopy of fireworks.

From Garmisch, one can go to the top of the 9,738-foot (2,966-metre) **Zugspitze**, the highest mountain peak in the country. There are two ways to get there, either by taking the cogwheel railway to **Eibsee** (Lake Eib) and changing to one of Europe's longest cableways which ascends to the summit, or by continuing on the cogwheel to **Schneefernerhaus**, a restaurant and small hotel at 8,694 feet (2,650 metres), where there is a short cableway to the top. The basis of the choice is probably the thought of being suspended in a pendulous cable-car.

A pious vow: **Oberammergau** is 12½ miles (20 km) from Garmisch. This is the site of Germany's oldest festival, the *Passionsspiel* (Passion Play), a recreation of the last days of Christ performed by local people every 10 years. An exception was made in 1984 to celebrate the 350th anniversary of the day the people of Oberammergau vowed to perform this play until the end of the world in exchange for being delivered from the plague. During the performance, the audience sits under a roof, but the stage is open to the sky and mountains.

The German press has pointed out all the earthly gain that the people of this little village (with less than 5,000 inhabitants) have been acquiring through the pious vow of their ancestors. Not only do visitors pay for theatre tickets, they must buy a package that includes an

Neuschwanstein.

overnight stay. But these controversies have not affected the popularity of the Passion Play. The next performance takes place in the year 2000, but the Passionsspielhaus, as the theatre is called, is usually open to the public.

Oberammergau is also a wood-carving town, with a wood-carving school open to visitors. The **Local History Museum** has a large collection of local work, some of it very old. The major theme of Oberammergau wood carving is religious as are the bright pictures painted on the sides of local houses.

Dreams of castles: King Ludwig II (1845-86), known as the "Mad King", had two expensive indulgences: the composer Richard Wagner and castles. He also preferred to spend his time with his dreams and allowed his servants to speak to him only from behind a screen. But the dreams became expensive realities. He was planning to add three more castles to his collection, one Chinese, one Byzantine and one Gothic, when court officials finally baulked at his excesses. In 1886 a commission de-

clared him unfit to rule and he was taken into custody. The circumstances of his death soon afterwards – he was found drowned in Lake Starnburg – have never been completely clear.

A cult of Ludwig admirers in Bavaria takes him very seriously and both celebrates the anniversary of his death every year and completely rejects the notion that he was insane. By far the most famous of his castles is his first one, **Neuschwanstein**, built between 1868 and 1886 at the southern end of the Romantic Road. The castle, which is visited by 1 million people each year, lies about 3 miles (5 km) outside **Füssen**, a health and winter sport resort on the lower slopes of the Alps.

The white marble building topping a hill was modelled after storybook illustrations. Not only has it been copied by Disneyworld, but it has been shown in so many pictures that its high, thin peaked towers are instantly recognizable. The interior is no less impressive, with an artificial cave, indoor waterfall and a two-storey throne room running the length and breadth of the building.

A short distance away, via a long detour around the mountains, lies **Linderhof**, the second of the three "fairytale" castles. Linderhof was patterned after the Petit Trianon at Versailles. This awesome setting in a marvellous park of gardens, lawns and grottos prepares the visitor for an equally awesome interior which makes extravagant use of 24-carat gold.

Ludwig's third castle is **Herren-chiemsee**, built on an island in Bavaria's largest lake, Chiemsee. Up to 9 miles (15 km) wide, the lake lies just north of the Munich-Salzburg *Autobahn*, between Rosenheim and Traunstein. Herreninsel (Men's Island), where the castle is located, is the male counterpart to Fraueninsel (Women's Island), where a Benedictine convent was set up more than 1,000 years ago.

Ludwig wanted Herrenchiemsee castle to resemble the splendour of Versailles. So naturally there is a lavish Hall of Mirrors, 321 feet (98 metres) long. On Saturday evenings in the summer, candlelight concerts are held here.

**Left,
Bavaria's
rustic style.
Right,
Rothenburg.**

198

The letters CH carried on Swiss cars stand for Confederatio Helvetica. The Helvetii were a Celtic tribe crushed by Julius Caesar and Helveticus was for five centuries the Roman name for what is now western Switzerland. The source of the word Switzerland comes from Schwyz, one of the three cantons which formed the original union at Rütli on Lake Lucerne in 1291. Today there are 23 members of the confederation and the cantons are divided into those that speak French, German and Italian.

Switzerland is only a small country, about the same size as the Netherlands but with half the population, and its largest city, Zurich, has only 706,000 people. About 1 million of its 6.3 million inhabitants are foreigners, half of them guest workers from Italy. The country is famed for its banking, neutrality and Swatch watches, and it works hard to maintain its independence: every fit male is armed and spends a number of days training each year until the age of 50. The only remnants of the *Reisege*, mercenaries who fought in Europe's wars for four centuries, are the Swiss Guard at the Vatican.

Eastern Switzerland and the lowlands, with blossoming orchards and lush meadows, are best in spring. Summer visitors head for the lakes. Autumn can be enjoyed in the vineyards of the Valais or the Vaud, in the larch forests of the Engadine and the southern valleys of the Grison, or in the Ticino where even in October the days seem to be longer and the fog thinner than in the rest of Switzerland. Finally, winter provides endless possibilities through the entire Alpine region, for skiing, or simply enjoying the beautiful, chocolate-box snow scenes.

Travel is easy in Switzerland and the visitor will get to know the country more quickly by travelling by rail, bus, cable railway or boat. Every station can provide detailed information about trips and excursions, with combination tickets for different transport.

Preceding pages: Lake Thun in the Bernese Oberland; Swiss cheesemaker. **Left,** traditional female attire in Appenzell, a German-speaking area.

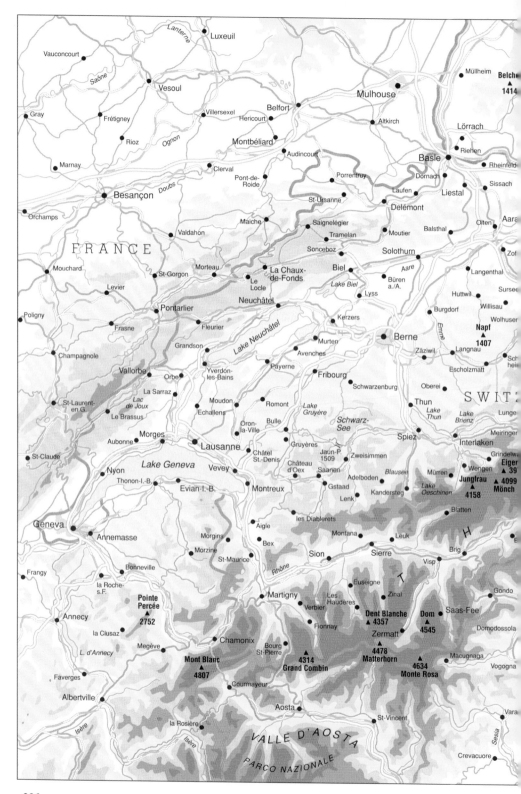

Switzerland

12 km / 7,5 miles

GERMANY

Schwenningen
Sigmaringen
Tuttlingen
Messkirch
dberg
493
Titisee
Denkingen
Schluchsee
Randen
Bad Waldsee
Memmingen
Schleithm
lasien
Radolfzell
Schaffhausen
Thayngen
Ravensburg
Leutkirch
Stein
a. Rh.
Kempten
enz
Eglisau
Constance
Friedrichshafen
Wangen i. Allg.
fenburg
Frauenfeld
Lake
Constance
g
Baden
Bulach
Romanshorn
Weinfelden
Lenzburg
Winterthur
Bischofszell
Arbon
Bregenz
Turbenthal
Rorschach
Sonthofen
Zurich
Pfäffikon
Herisau
St. Margrethen
Hittisau
Bremgarten
nlen
St. Gallen
FOREST OF
BREGENZ
1641
Feuerstätter
Kogel
Nebelhorn
▲ 2240
Oberstdorf
Muri
Affoltern
a. A.
Küsnacht
Wald
Wattwil
Altstätten
Appenzell
Hochdorf
Rapperswil
Ebnat-
Kappel
Wildhaus
Feldkirch
Schoppernau
Mädelegabel
▲
2645
Lech
Häselgehr
Zug
Unterägeri
Einsiedeln
Weesen
Buchs
AUSTRIA
Lucerne
Lake
Lucerne
Vitznau
Schwyz
Näfels
Weesen
Walenstadt
Vaduz
LIECHTENSTEIN
Lech
Arlberg
▲ 1802
Landeck
St. Anton
Stans
Muotathal
Glarus
Maienfeld
Schruns
St. Gallenkirch
Sarnen
Altdorf
Linthal
Weisstannen
Bad
Ragaz
Landquart
Schiers
Hexenkopf
▲
3033
LAND
Engelberg
Elm
Flims
Chur
Klosters
SILVRETTA GROUP
Martina
Nauders
ertkirchen
Tödi
▲
3620
3158
Hausstock
Ilanz
Vord. Rhein
Reichenau
Weisshorn
▲ 2654
Davos-Dorf
Arosa
▲ 3316
Piz Buin
Ardez
Scuol/
Schuls
Grimsel Pass
2165
Furka
2431
Wassen
GLARNER ALPS
Disentis
Safien-Platz
Thusis
Lenzerheide-
Lai
Flüela
2383
Susch
Zernez
Andermatt
Vrin
Vals
Andeer
Tiefen-
castel
Filisur
Piz Kesch
▲ 3418
Ofen Pass
2149
Glorenza
St. Gotthard
Pass 2108
Airolo
Olivone
Splügen
Savognin
Bergün/
Bravuogn
Albula Pass
2312
Zuoz
Sta. Maria
Adige
Nufenen Pass
2478
Faido
S. Bernardino
Pass
2065
St. Moritz
Samedan
Pontresina
Fusio
co Gurin
Bignasco
Malvaglia
Mesocco
Julier P. 2284
S
Bernina
2323
Bormio
Sonogno
Biasca
Castasegna
Maloja
1815
Brione
Cimalmotto
Maggia
Chiavenna
Vicosoprano
Poschiavo
Lavertezzo
Locarno
Bellinzona
Brissago
Adda
Sondrio
Tirano
Ponte
di Legno
Novaggio
Tesserete
Colico
Morbegno
Édolo
Lugano
Luino
Menaggio
Lake Como
Mezzoldo
Valbondione
Tione
di Trento
Lake
Lugano
Lake
Lecco
ITALY
Capo
di Ponte
Varese
Mendrisio
Lecco
Brembo
Clusone
Breno
Chiasso
Como
S. Pellegrino
Sesto Cal.
Lovere
Riva
Storo

207

AROUND SWITZERLAND

The shores of **Lake Geneva** and the **Bernese Alps** beyond them, are the cradle of tourism, not just in Switzerland but in all of continental Europe. The first tourists were British, and connections between Britain and this part of Switzerland are everywhere. Lord Byron's *The Prisoner of Chillon* was set in a castle on the shores of Lake Geneva, and Sir Arthur Conan Doyle's fictional creation Sherlock Holmes was to end his successful career at Reichenbach Falls in the **Bernese Oberland** at the hands of the infamous Professor Moriarty, the "Napoleon of Evil". Sir Arthur also wrote about skiing in Switzerland and started an influx of British skiers that continues up to this day.

The earliest package tours to the Continent were arranged by Thomas Cook's of London, the world's oldest travel agency. The first one, in 1863, was from London to Lake Geneva and the Bernese Oberland. The group travelled by train and channel boat to Paris, where they changed trains for the 17-hour ride to Geneva. From there they went down the **Rhône** to **Sion** and then to **Interlaken** and the region around **Lake Lucerne**.

Victorian restraints were thrown to the winds. The gentlemen dared to wear knicker-bockers with their tailcoats and top hats, and a snowball fight erupted in one of the passes. Giggling ladies protected themselves with their parasols and one gentleman lost his glass eye in the snow. The group also travelled by boat, stagecoach and mule.

Winding roads: Modern means of transportation and tunnels such as the one through **Mont Blanc** make it much easier to get into and out of Switzerland. Travel around the country has also improved and even some of the most remote areas are accessible. Direct distances between various villages and towns are short but can be greatly increased by winding mountain roads.

For travellers with time, the postal service's (PTT) national bus system is to Switzerland what the Greyhound is to the US. Curving through the highest parts of the land and through scenic valleys, these regularly scheduled, long-distance buses provide a leisurely way of seeing Switzerland. The finely graded climate of the country ranges from subtropical warmth to Arctic cold in the Alpine peaks above 12,000 ft (4,000 metres). The wide range of climates results in an equal variety of vegetation – from fertile plains in the lowlands to mountain pastures and moorland in the Jura. Vineyard slopes can be found in 19 of the 23 cantons.

Driving a car in Swiss cities is no less hectic than in other European cities. In country areas, farm vehicles and military convoys on manoeuvres slow down and even stop other traffic. Occasionally, two-way mountain roads seem barely wider than a goat path. Most Alpine passes are closed all winter, those that aren't can be crossed only by cars equipped with snow chains.

Mountains trains and cablecars take skiers and sightseers up the **Kleines Matterhorn**, **Jungfrau**, **Corvatsch** and

Left, Zermatt, in the shadow of the Matterhorn. *Right*, amateur actors portray William Tell and his son Walter.

other peaks. The Swiss continue to improve this system. They already have Europe's highest railway and the Alps' longest aerial cableway. The world's highest subway, the Metro-Alpin, 11,482 ft (3,500 metres) up in **Saas-Fee** in the canton of Valais, makes year-round skiing there possible.

Among the various means of transportation, railways and funiculars stay on the ground at all heights, cable cars and lifts do not. Anybody with a bad head for heights should ask about routes before journeying into the mountains.

Languages and lifestyles: Travelling through Switzerland clearly reveals how the linguistic and cultural background, predominantly German, French or Italian, influences everything, especially food, architecture and lifestyle.

About two-thirds of the Swiss are German-speaking. They speak *Schwyzerdütsch,* a German-Swiss dialect that is used at all social levels, including professors and company directors, and officially encouraged. Even fluent German speakers have difficulty understanding this heritage from the Alemannic tribes, and its local and regional variations. Newspapers, books and printed notices use "proper" German. The leading German-language newspaper, *Neue Zürcher Zeitung,* has been published since 1780. Its lengthy analytical articles on international events have earned it a reputation as one of the world's best newspapers. Swiss who deal with foreigners, such as shopkeepers and bankers, slip easily into conversational German and often into English.

French has worked its way into Swiss-German, too, so that people say *merci vielmals* for thank you very much. (The first word is French and the second is German.) Menus, which occasionally have quaint English translations, use German for some dishes, French for others and *Schwyzerdütsch* for the items that are the ones to try. There is no *Schwyzerfrancais* or *Schwyzeritaliano,* and the languages in the French and Italian areas are more or less identical to those spoken in France and Italy.

The German area extends from the

Savouring the alpine sun.

French-speaking west all the way east to the border with the pocket **Principality of Liechtenstein** and with Austria. Language divisions do not always follow the borders of the cantons. **Basel, Zurich** and **St Gallen** in the north, the capital of **Bern**, Lucerne, Interlaken, the ski resorts of **Zermatt** in the south and **Davos** in the east are all part of the German-speaking region. The French area, in which 18 percent of the Swiss live, runs along the French border and includes **Neuchâtel**, **Fribourg**, **Lausanne**, **Geneva** and **Montreux**.

The Italian Swiss account for 12 percent of the total population. They are found primarily around **Lago Maggiore** in the canton of **Ticino** (Tessin in German) and in parts of **Grisons** (Graubunden) in the southeastern tip of the country. Italian is also spoken in adjoining parts of the neighbouring cantons, however, a German-language "wedge" persists in the western part of Ticino. In addition more than 100 local dialects are spoken in the various regions, adding to the unmistakable char-

Left, the Davos-Parsenn skiing area. **Right**, jewel-shopping in Davos.

acteristics of their inhabitants. Romansch or Rhaeto-Romantic, the language and culture of only 1 per cent of the Swiss, survives in the large Alpine areas of Grisons, including the fashionable winter resort of **St Moritz.**

Switzerland boasts a number of interesting museums covering almost any subject including Alpinism, watchmaking, folkcraft and rifles. A major exhibition of Swiss art, culture and history is to be found in the **Swiss National Museum** (Ländesmuseum) of Zurich. A municipal art gallery, along with a large number of private art galleries, can also be found in Zurich. Basel and Bern are noted for their fine art museums, with the one in Bern exhibiting the world's largest collection of paintings by Paul Klee, who was born in nearby Munchenbuchsee in 1879.

The Swiss **Museum of Transport** (Schweizer Verkehrhaus) in Lucerne is the country's most visited museum. It is an intriguing place for nostalgia buffs as well as those interested in aeronautics and communication technology.

AROUND LAKE GENEVA

Geneva (Genève) is at the westernmost tip of **Lac Léman** (Lake Geneva) which is fed by the River Rhône. Here is the westernmost point of Switzerland; the city is surrounded by France on three sides. It has a panorama of water, mountains, parks and flowerbeds, and its elegant villas lining the lakeshore and multi-coloured sails out on the water create a truly cosmopolitan impression.

Many of the well-known sights are to be found right where the River Rhône leaves Geneva. The **Jet d'Eau** (Water Fountain) out in the harbour can send a dazzling plume of white foam 475 feet (145 metres) into the air. The first bridge to span the Rhône is the **Pont du Mont-Blanc**. From here and from the **Quai du Mont-Blanc** one can enjoy, on clear days, an unobstructed view of **Mont Blanc**, the highest peak in Europe, towering 15,781 feet (4,810 metres).

The **Jardin Anglais** (English Gar-

den) and flower clock are located here, while a little farther on is **Rousseau Island**, a place for literary pilgrims. The French philosopher Jean-Jacques Rousseau liked to stroll and meditate on the island, which can be reached by a footbridge from the **Pont des Bergues**. A statue of Rousseau stands in a setting of lawns and poplars. The Quai du Mont-Blanc is also the site of a **casino**.

On the left bank of the Rhône behind the English Garden, the well-preserved and picturesque **Vieille Ville** (Old Town) rises on a hill at the tip of the lake. Nearby is the **Reformation Monument** commemorating some of the key figures of Protestantism including John Calvin, John Knox, Oliver Cromwell and the Pilgrim Fathers.

Geneva is the capital of Swiss watchmaking. The **Clock Museum** displays timepieces, enamelled watches and music boxes dating from the 16th century.

A monument to the Reformation: As the city of Calvin (1509–64), Geneva figures prominently in the history of the Protestant Reformation. He can be praised for Geneva's nobility and blamed for its coldness. He inspired the city to turn to Protestantism in 1536, and made it the "Protestant Rome", promulgating his doctrine of rigid morality, the sovereignty of God and predestination. He closed the theatres, banned dancing and the wearing of jewellery, and considered food and drink to be necessities and not sources of enjoyment.

In Voltaire's view, the people of Geneva in his day "calculate and never laugh". The French novelist Stendhal commented: "If you see anyone jump out of a window, do not hesitate to follow his example." Nightlife was influenced by the Calvinist tradition. While staying in Geneva early in this century, Lenin remarked that he felt as though he were already in his coffin.

Calvin's influence was not entirely negative. It can be argued that it was he who made it such an international city. Protestant refugees flocked in from England, France and Italy, giving Geneva a cosmopolitan air for the first time. Calvin also made the city a centre of French learning, founding an acad- **Geneva Cathedral.**

emy that evolved into the university. He even shares some of the credit for the city's wealth. Since there were hardly any recreational activities to spend time and money on, the people had no choice but to work, prosper and accumulate wealth. Thanks to Calvin, the city regained some of its former commercial importance.

As the city of Jean-Jacques Rousseau (1712–78), Geneva was the wellspring of many of the ideas that led to the French Revolution of 1789. Rousseau's social theory of the equality of man caused the whole Western world to rethink the notion of aristocratic government. He not only laid the groundwork for the French Revolution, but also sparked the Romantic movement in literature and the arts. The city and locality of Geneva became a place of ideas because of him. The French philosopher Voltaire was also a Genevan by adoption, and Romantic writers such as Lord Byron were drawn to the area.

In the eyes of the world: Geneva is important today because of its role as the headquarters for many international organizations and the seat of diplomatic conferences. The **Palace of Nations** was built between 1929 and 1936 for the League of Nations, the predecessor to the UN, and is now its European headquarters. Several other UN subsidiary organizations, including the International Labour Organization (ILO) and the World Health Organization (WHO), are based in Geneva. Many non-Swiss staff members live across the border in France where accommodation is cheaper. Almost everyone in Geneva seems to do their Saturday shopping in France as well.

Geneva is not a modern metropolis despite its being the city of other institutions besides the UN, including the Geneva Convention, the Red Cross, the World Council of Churches and the Worldwide Fund for Nature. The city has a surprisingly small population of 175,000 – less than Switzerland's other two main cities, Zurich and Basel. Yet Geneva is linked in the public mind with the struggle for peace and brotherhood

A cruise company's sales pitch.

of man. It is from this that it derives its own unique stature.

Lake Geneva is shared between France to the south and Switzerland to the north. The Swiss side is known as the **Vaud Riviera** and the name is appropriate. The mountains protect the area from north and east winds, giving it a mild climate with 2,000 hours of sunshine a year. There is little rain and a temperature that rarely falls below 5°C (40°F), even on winter nights.

The shore, which can be visited by either car or boat, is lined with flowerbeds. There are magnolia, walnut, almond and fig trees, and behind them vineyards are backed picturesquely by snow-capped Alps.

Coppet, on the lakeshore beyond Geneva, is the location of the **Villa of Madame de Staël**, a French literary figure who was banned from Paris by Napoleon because of her liberal ideas. Her salons were attended by Lord Byron and other romantic writers of the early 19th century. The villa has been kept in its original form and is open to visitors. According to legend, *madame* was supposed to have been preserved in a vat of alcohol after she died, but the effort failed because a gardener drank it.

Farther along the lake is **Nyon**, a town clinging to a hillside crowned with a castle. Nyon is known for its rather ornate style of porcelain which was made here from 1781 to 1813. Examples of the work are on display in the castle.

A statue of Ignance Jan Paderewski (1860–1941) stands in **Morges**, a winemaking town on the edge of the lake. Paderewski was a brilliant piano virtuoso and was equally well known both for his short stay of office as Polish Prime Minister and his presence at the Versailles Peace Conference after World War I, when Poland was re-established as a sovereign state.

Lausanne, the "second city" of French Switzerland, is on the north shore of Lake Geneva between Geneva and Montreux. It enjoys a sheltered, sunny spot on the southern slopes of steep terraces and gorges.

The city of Lausanne is the capital of Vaud and has a population of 130,000.

The old quarter goes by the name of **La Cité** (the city) and is the location of the **medieval cathedral** which has the most impressive exterior in Switzerland. Lausanne also has the world-famous **Swiss Hotel School** (as well as a university and arts and technical colleges) and hosts the National Trade Fair (*Comptoire Suisse*) every September. The International Olympic Committee has its headquarters in the lakeside suburb of Vidy. In summer, the lakeside **Ouchy** area attracts a cosmopolitan crowd for boating and other water sports. Opposite Lausanne on the French bank of Lake Geneva is **Evian**, a fashionable spa with mineral springs.

Czars and festivals: The region of **Montreux-Vevey** lies 18 miles (30 km) along the lakeside highway from the southeastern end of Lake Geneva. While on a visit, the mother of Czar Alexander II wrote: "I am in the most beautiful country in the world."

The czars are gone and so is an era when the expression "idle rich" meant something; there were people who had

The lakeside castle of Chillon.

the time and the patience to pack big trunks and arrive with maids and maiden aunts to spend "the season" at a resort, to stroll along flowery promenades and admire the view.

Montreux is now seeking to attract a different kind of international clientele. Only 45 miles (72 km) away from Geneva International Airport, it has built a conference and exhibition centre and mounts international festivals such as the Golden Rose TV Festival, Montreux International Jazz Festival and the Montreux Classical Festival.

The town, with a population of only 20,000, has spread out along 4 miles (6.5 km) of lakeshore, making it the biggest resort on Lake Geneva. The pre-World War I glitter may have faded but the beautiful natural setting remains. The lush green hills still slope down to the lake, with the mountain peaks in the background. Flowers bloom easily in the unusually mild climate.

Byron and company: The literary set of the 18th and 19th centuries could not stay away. Rousseau set his 1761 novel,

La Nouvelle Héloïse, in the village of **Clarens**, now part of Montreux. Voltaire arrived, followed shortly by Lord Byron, who put Montreux on the itinerary of British tourists for the next 150 years. Charles Dickens, Leo Tolstoy, Hans Christian Andersen and Fyodor Dostoevski are some of the other literati who came. The best-known resident of nearby **Vevey** was Charlie Chaplin, who is buried there and there is a monument of his derby hat and cane.

About a mile (1.6 km) west of Montreux is **Chillon Castle**. It was built by one of the dukes of Savoy in the 9th or 10th century and expanded in the 13th century to its present appearance. The building includes large dungeons carved from the rock into which critics and plotters against the dukes were tossed. One of these was a clergyman from Geneva named François de Bonivard who spent six years at Chillon before being freed in 1536 when the Bernese conquered this area. Visitors to the castle can see the dungeon in which Bonivard is said to have been held.

Byron visited the castle in 1816 and carved his name on the pillar to which he believed Bonivard had been chained. The graffiti is still there, protected by glass. While stuck in his hotel on a rainy weekend, Byron wrote a ballad about Bonivard's ordeal called the *Prisoner of Chillon.*

Home of Gruyère: The Montreux-Vevey area provides a starting point for several excursions such as the one to the cheese-making town of **Gruyères**, home of the light yellow, very rich Gruyère cheese. A model dairy farm shows the cheese-making process (samples provided) and there is a short film.

The Gruyères district is idyllic. In addition to the famous cheese, it produces country ham, cream, strawberries and chocolate (there is a Nestlé plant in nearby Broc). The town of Gruyères has only one main thoroughfare – a wide cobblestone area from which cars have been banned and which is lined with chalets. This street, which leads up to a **castle**, is liberally planted with flowers. The hilltop location of this community ensures that it won't grow any larger.

Making friends over a cheese fondue.

THE SWISS ALPS

When people speak of the Swiss Alps they are likely to be thinking of the **Bernese Oberland**. Montreux is a starting place for journeys into this stretch of country. The mountains already begin to close in south of Montreux at **Aigle**, a town famous for its vineyards. After leaving the main road and passing through **Château d'Oex**, one comes to the resort of **Gstaad**, a meeting place for jet-setters and beautiful people.

Gstaad is less than halfway between Montreux and the twin **lakes of Thun and Brienz**, in the southeastern part of the canton of Bern. On the narrow neck of land that separates Lake Thun from Lake Brienz is the town of **Interlaken** (meaning "between the lakes").

Interlaken, the heart of the Bernese Oberland, lies near the bases of three great mountains, one of which is the **Jungfrau** at 13,642 feet (4,158 metres), second only to the **Matterhorn** as Swit-zerland's most beautiful mountain. From Interlaken one can see the 13,440-foot (4,099-metre) **Mönch** and the 13,000-foot (3,970-metre) **Eiger**. Seen by day, these peaks are pearl grey against a deep blue sky. Sunset floods them in every shade of pink and red.

Gstaad is a sprawling village of chalets, dominated by the turreted Palace Hotel, right out of Disneyland. Princess Grace and the Aga Khan had villas here. It is essentially a winter resort, but people come in the summer too. Tennis is popular and the cableway to the 9,750-foot (3,000-metre) **Diablerets glacier** allows for good skiing even in the summer. Gstaad also hosts the summer **Menuhin Music Festival**.

One fascinating attraction at Gstaad is ballooning. The weather conditions are suitable almost every day and, according to the operator's brochure, all that is required is "solid mountain boots, leisure wear, a stout heart and a bottle of champagne for the baptism." Updrafts and the absence of air traffic make the Alps ideal for ballooning.

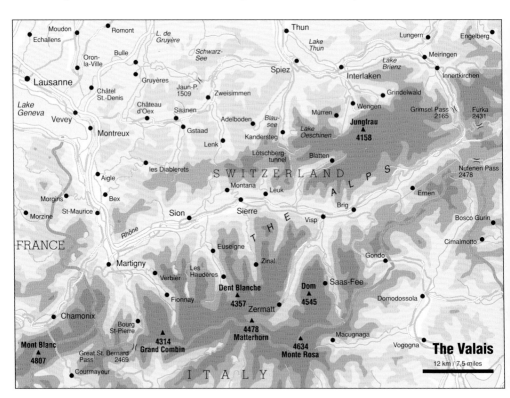

The Valais

12 km / 7.5 miles

In the middle of town is the **Höhe-matte**, 35 acres (14 hectares) of open space to provide an unspoiled view of the peaks. Far-sighted hoteliers bought the property in 1860 to keep it out of the hands of developers. The view can be enjoyed from the **Höheweg**, an elegant promenade that runs through this open area. There is a clock made of flowers in the beautiful garden here.

The **Kursaal** (spa centre) accommodates a theatre, café and a gaming room. However, in Switzerland, the players are so reserved and the stakes so small that the gambling seems closer to a church raffle than to Las Vegas.

Journey to the heavens: Interlaken is the first leg of the biggest scenic adventure of the Swiss Alps: the excursion via **Wengen**, **Kleine Scheidegg** and the **Eiger Glacier** to the 11,225-foot (3,454-metre) **Jungfraujoch**. Superlatives abound on this "journey to the heavens". The trip takes one on Europe's highest and most expensive railway and leads to Europe's highest observation point, the biggest glacier in the Alps (the

Aletsch), and the longest aerial cableway in the Alps – up the 9,650-foot (2,970-metre) **Schilthorn**. One really has to admire the engineering genius of the Swiss.

Skiing is grandiose. The trails are very long and the Jungfraujoch area has no fewer than 40 lifts: railway, cabin lifts, chair- and ski-lifts. There are plenty of opportunities to cross-country ski and to hike.

The red-and-white town of **Thun**, clustered around a castle, is next to the lake of the same name. The town's unique feature is the **Obere Hauptgasse**, which has arcades like those in Bern except the roofs of the arcades serve as a second sidewalk which are in turn lined with shops. Composer Johannes Brahms spent three summers at Thun, and his Opus 100 is known as the *Thun Sonata*.

From Thun, a scenic drive leads along the edge of the **Thuner See** (Lake Thun) to Lucerne via Spiez and Interlaken. The road from **Brienz** passes the **Sarner See** (Lake Sarnen) and **Mt Pilatus**.

LUCERNE, BERN, ZURICH AND BASLE

The French name, **Lucerne**, leaves the foreign visitor totally unprepared for the very German character of this city of about 63,000. Far better to use the same name as the locals: Luzern. It is indeed the architectural pearl of German-speaking Switzerland, with quaint lanes, red-gable houses, and a surrounding wall whose nine watchtowers are bathed in floodlight after dark.

The covered **Kapellbrücke** (Chapel Bridge), built in 1333, is Lucerne's best-known landmark. It has a distinctive red-tile roof and its interior is lined with gabled paintings which glorify the martyrs and heroes of the region. Next to the bridge is an octagonal stone tower which was originally a water tower but later became a prison and torture chamber.

A few hundred yards farther upstream a second medieval bridge with a small chapel crosses the **River Reuss**, which feeds **Lake Lucerne**. **Spreuerbrücke** (Spreuer Bridge) is made of wood and has a gable roof. The interior is decorated with paintings of Caspar Meglinger's famous *Totentanz* ("Dance of Death").

Lucerne's medieval ambience is enhanced by its breathtaking surroundings: a big mirror-like lake criss-crossed by paddle steamers, flanked on either side by the two mountain giants of the **Rigi** and **Pilatus**, the former measuring 5,888 feet (1,797 metres) and the latter 6,982 feet (2,129 metres). This majestic panorama forms what local people call their "Gate to the South".

Lucerne also has another gate to the south: an old international trade route that leads over **St Gotthard** (and through a railway tunnel to the Tessin and northern Italy). The mountain pass over **St Gotthard** was opened early in the 13th century, thereby making Lucerne an important waystation on one of the main arteries from north to south.

Excursions lead around the lake, itself situated at the foot of the Alps and considered Switzerland's most beautiful. The crystal blue waters meeting the mountain faces are reminiscent of Norwegian fjords.

Boats cruise on Lake Lucerne and stop at various points from where cable cars lead up to the surrounding peaks. The Rigi, for example, has been described as the most impressive vantage point in all of Switzerland. Following in the steps of such famous visitors as Goethe, Victor Hugo and Mark Twain it is possible to walk up from the village of **Vitznau** to the peak in about four hours. The alpine panorama is splendid and, in clear weather, stretches 186 miles (300 km) in every direction.

The cog-wheel railway on the Pilatus, with a 48 per cent gradient, is claimed to be the world's steepest. Yodelling, flag-throwing and alphorn concerts which were once a genuine part of the regional folklore, are kept alive for tourists.

The arrow and the apple: History comes alive all over Lucerne and the surrounding area. Pictures, monuments, festivals, chapels and tavern signs are reminders of the country's national hero – William Tell. It was around Lake Lucerne at places like **Uri** and **Küssnacht** that Swiss history began. In 1291, three communities around Lake Lucerne felt that their far-away Habsburg ruler was overly oppressive, especially because of the heavy taxes being demanded. So the *Waldstätte* of Uri, Unterwalden and Schwyz banded together to form a stronger, unified front.

The day they swore their legendary Oath of Unity at Rütli, a meadow outside the village of **Brunnen**, is now commemorated as Switzerland's national holiday, on 1 August. William Tell, an upright citizen of Uri, refused to show proper obedience to the king's representative, a black-hearted bailiff named Gessler. As punishment, Gessler required Tell to shoot an apple off the head of his own son, with an arrow. Needless to say, the arrow was true and the son was spared. The noble Swiss hero had his revenge later when he shot Gessler in an ambush, touching off a revolt that was to free Switzerland.

The tale of William Tell was first

immortalized in 1804 by Friedrich Schiller's drama of the same name. In 1829, it was staged again by Gioacchino Rossini in an equally famous opera.

In the world of opera, Lucerne is also known as the place where German composer Richard Wagner wrote *Die Meistersinger, Siegfried,* and *Götter-dämmerung,* three of his major works. He lived in Lucerne between 1866 and 1872 in an early Victorian mansion on the Tribschen peninsula which is now the **Wagner Museum**. This was the place where Wagner had his illicit rendezvous with Cosima von Bülow, the daughter of Franz Liszt. When Cosima's husband learned about the trysts he divorced her, whereupon she became Wagner's wife and First Lady of the music festival in Bayreuth.

Each year in August and September, Lucerne is host to famous orchestras and performers of worldwide renown at its **Internationale Musikfestwochen** (International Music Festival Weeks). The first music festival took place in 1938 at a time when the field was largely dominated by the festivals in Bayreuth and Salzburg. Some of the big luminaries of the music scene, including Arturo Toscanini and Bruno Walter, supported, for political reasons, the creation of another festival outside of what was then Nazi Germany. Switzerland appeared as an attractive alternative.

A popular feature during the Music Festival are outdoor serenades at the **Löwenplatz**. The acoustics of the water and rock and the soft illumination of the colossal lion carved from a cliff combine to provide an enchanting nocturnal experience. The lion memorial was created in 1821 in recognition of 786 Swiss soldiers who were mercenaries for the King of France. They died in Paris during the French Revolution when an angry mob stormed the Tuileries. Mark Twain, moved by the sight of the dying lion reclining in his natural grotto, commented: "His head is bowed, the broken spear is sticking in his shoulder, his protecting paw rests upon the lilies of France. Vines hang down the cliff and wave in the wind, and a clear stream

Lucerne's Chapel Bridge.

trickles from above and empties into a pond at the base… The place is a sheltered, reposeful woodland nook, remote from noise and stir and confusion – and all this is fitting, for lions do die in such places, and not on granite pedestals in public squares."

Just a few steps away at Denkmalstrasse is the **Gletschergarten** (Glacier Garden), dating from the last Ice Age some 20,000 years ago, when the valley in which Lucerne is situated was covered by a glacier. The Glacier Garden is a collection of 32 potholes, one of which is the biggest in the world. It is 30 feet (9 metres) deep.

The potholes were created by a geological process by which stones were ground into the earth by swirling water. In time, the holes created by this natural phenomenon became deeper and deeper and the stones responsible for the grinding became smoother and more round. Both surfaces became highly burnished in the process. The potholes were hidden under soil and their existence was unknown until 1872 when they were discovered by workmen while digging out a cellar.

The road from Lucerne to Bern passes through the valley of the **River Emme**, home of the famous Swiss cheese. The Swiss themselves are more likely to call their cheese Emmentaler, meaning it comes from the Emmental, the valley of the same river. **Langnau**, the main marketing centre for the cheese, is just 18½ miles (30 km) from **Bern** (population 145,000), the national capital of the Swiss Federation and also known as the town of bears. It got its name from the animal, which is translated as *Bearn* in the local dialect. Legend says that Duke Bechtold of Zähringen hunted down a bear in the area just after establishing the place in 1191. There are automated metal bears on the *glockenspiel* at the **Zeitglockenturm** and bears in the zoo.

Even the Bernese have a bear-like quality about them: slow and friendly. Never tell a Bernese a joke on Friday because he may burst out laughing in church on Sunday.

The old city is located on what the

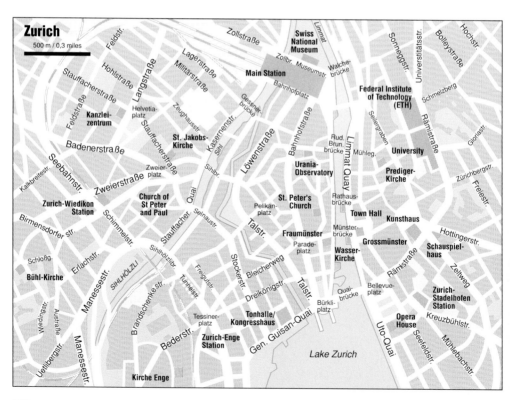

Bernese call a "peninsula", a sharp bend in the **River Aare**, with bridges heading off to the "mainland" in three directions. After a disastrous fire in 1405, the town was rebuilt with locally quarried sandstone, and the result is impressive. Gothic sandstone buildings, with elaborate bay windows, overhanging gables and red geraniums in window boxes, are ubiquitous as are squares with flower-decked fountains. There are more arcades (4 miles/6 km of them) than in any other city of Europe. The Florentine **parliament building** and a number of banking houses face each other on the same square.

Where three countries meet: Switzerland's second biggest city after Zurich is **Basel** (population 181,000), which is one of the largest ports on the Rhine and an important centre of the chemical industry. It also houses Switzerland's largest zoo and plays a leading role in the international arts and antiques trade.

Nearly all the sights of the city are in what local people call **Grossbasel**, the old town which rises steeply from the

Bern's celebrated clock tower.

Rhine's right bank. The **Dreiländereck** (Three Country Corner) is something of a novelty. By walking around a marker there, one is able to pass in a matter of seconds through Switzerland, France and Germany – and all without having to show a passport.

Tucked in between high hills on the north end of Lake Zurich is the country's largest city, **Zurich** (pop: 706,000), also one of the world's key financial centres. The region here is not yet part of the Alps but part of the Mittelland (Midland), a wide strip of land that cuts across Switzerland from the northeast to the southwest.

When the British pound hit a record low point in 1964, Britain's Chancellor of the Exchequer, George Brown, snapped: "The gnomes of Zurich are at work again." The idea that mythical little men with big heads were manipulating the affairs of the world caught the popular fancy. In addition to the gnomes in their Renaissance palace buildings on or near Bahnhofstrasse, Zurich is the national centre for most forms of business and commerce.

The River Limmat divides the **Altstadt** between the **Hauptbahnhof** on one side and **Limmatquai**, a riverside promenade, on the other. **Bahnhofstrasse**, one of Europe's most elegant shopping streets, runs south from the Hauptbahnhof parallel to the river. Price tags, if any, suggest a city of millionaires – which is what a quarter of the city's population are.

In a quiet corner on the Swiss-Austrian border, next to the cantons of St Gallen and Grisons, lies **Liechtenstein**. This independent *Fürstentum* (principality), which uses Swiss currency, is left over from the Holy Roman Empire occupying only 61 sq. miles (158 sq. km) between the River Rhine and the Vorarlberg mountains. From the Swiss town of **Buchs** on the Zurich-Vienna train route, a bus or a taxi takes the visitor to **Vaduz**, the capital with a population of 5,000. This is a tax haven for 30,000 foreign companies and a growing number of wealthy lawyers and businessmen (about a quarter of the population of 26,000 are foreigners).

AUSTRIA

"Land of mountains" is the opening line of Austria's national anthem, and that is exactly what this 32,000 sq. mile (84,000 sq. km) country is. For centuries these uplands were a bugbear, making life hard for the farmer. John Gunther, a traveller in the 1930s, remarked: "The chief crop of provincial Austria is the scenery." That scenery, combined with some of the best skiing in Europe, is now the country's highest earner, and the year-round tourist industry accounts for the largest slice of the national economy.

Nestled among the wild Alpine scenery are hundreds of mountain lakes and idyllic watercourses which are especially attractive in summer. The gentle charms of the Salzkammergut and the Carinthian Lake District are underlined by the majestic backdrop of mountains. To the east, the foothills of the Alps gradually peter out in the Vienna woods, reaching right up to the suburbs of the capital. Vienna, seat of the Babenberg dynasty for 600 years, was the centre of one of Europe's superpowers, the Austro-Hungarian empire. It is a beautiful city today, and it houses a wealth of treasures. Salzburg, on the north side of the Alps, is equally romantic, and has become almost a theme park for its most esteemed inhabitant, Wolfgang Amadeus Mozart.

Austrians are known for their courtesy and hospitality but they have their regional differences. The inhabitants of the eastern provinces reveal a mixture of German and Slavic characteristics. In Salzburg and the Tyrol, the people are like the Bavarians. The natives of Vorarlberg in the west are of Alemannic and Rhaetian descent, and are related to the inhabitants of the Engadine and Upper Rhine. Half its borders lie against eastern European countries: the Czech and Slovak republics, Hungary and former Yugoslavia, which make it feel at the centre of the changing new world. For the visitor, however, it still looks very much like the old world.

Preceding pages: Salzburg by night; a Styrian pays homage to the mountains. **Left**, a ball in Vienna.

AROUND AUSTRIA

Austria is a land of peaks and valleys, high roads and mountain passes, ski slopes and Alpine meadows which fall away eastward to the Hungarian plains. The Alps cover two-thirds of the country. The spectacular scenery, friendly people, good food and well-developed resorts have earned Austria a high reputation around the world.

Where farmers once eked out a living during the short summers, hotels and restaurants have sprung up. Networks of lifts and cable cars lace the mountain-sides taking visitors, winter and summer, to the high playgrounds.

The **Arlberg mountain region**, straddling the border of the Tyrol and Vorarlberg provinces, is considered the cradle of Alpine skiing. Here Austrian skiers refined the Scandinavian sport to suit their own steep slopes and founded a system of teaching. Hannes Schneider gave the first ski lessons to tourists in 1907 in **St Anton am Arlberg**, a village which has grown into a first-class ski resort. Others include **Kitzbühel** and **Ischul**, whose slopes lead into Switzerland, **St Johann** and **Seefeld** in Tyrol – usually sleepy villages whose population is greatly outnumbered by winter

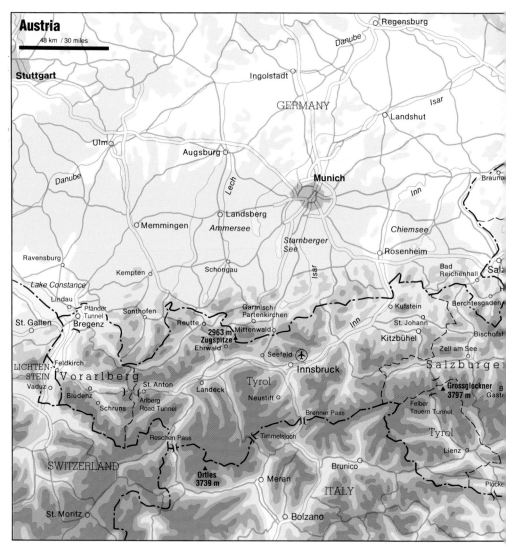

visitors. The **Tyrol** is the best known of the ski regions but good skiing is by no means limited to that province. Next to Vorarlberg is the **Montafon Valley**, gateway to the Silvretta High Alpine road, with 10,863-foot (3,312 metre) **Piz Buin** towering in the background.

The Montafon was the site of Austria's first ski championships after World War II, and the story is told of the local official who wanted to provide good food for the participants in the event. He managed to acquire two cows, even though meat was severely rationed at the time. The people dined well but the official spent six months in jail for his hospitality. Montafoners are descended from the Rhaeto-Romansch civilisation, as their dialect, place names and complexions attest.

The Tyrol and the Vorarlberg reach like an arm between Germany to the north and Switzerland and Italy to the south, so it is no wonder that the Montafon folk so closely resemble the Engadine Swiss, and the Tyroleans are hard to tell from their Bavarian cousins.

Just as the Tyrol juts between countries, the province of **Salzburgerland** juts into the Tyrol and touches the Italian border, for practical purposes cutting the East Tyrol district off from its provincial capital, Innsbruck. (The connecting section of country was chopped

off and passed to Italian control in 1919).

The East Tyrol and the provinces of Salzburgerland and Kärnten (Carinthia) converge at the **Grossglockner**, the highest point in Austria at 12,457 feet (3,797 metres). At its foot glistens the **Pasterze glacier**.

The best view of both mountain and glacier is from **Franz-Josef-Höhe**, a spur at the end of one branch of Grossglockner Road. The road is another of the great Alpine highways which snake across Austria's mountain ranges. It begins at **Bruck** and ends at the mountaineering town of **Heiligenblut**. A faster scenic route linking north and south is the **Tauern Autobahn** (motorway). Two large tunnels cut the travel time between **Salzburg** and **Klagenfurt** .

Lakes and caves: The limestone Alps of Austria are riddled with cavities; two ice caves in particular will tempt the hearty visitor. Both are in the Salzkammergut, the salt-producing region which fans out around Salzburg. One of the caves is at **Dachstein** and the other, the Eisriesenwelt (World of the Ice Gi-

ants), can be reached from the town of **Werfen**. They are open during the summer season. Huge frozen "cathedrals" and "palaces" are enhanced by the lighting. Warm clothing and good walking shoes should be worn for these cavern visits. The Alps are also dotted with lakes, emerald or lime green depending upon the rock, but the largest and most intriguing is in the plains, on the Hungarian border.

The **Neusiedler See** is strange in that it is the only steppe-type lake in central Europe; its shallow salty waters are surrounded by reeds. Sometimes the waters even disappear. When this happens, the people living beside the lake take the opportunity to enlarge their land holdings. The disputes and lawsuits that result are generally resolved when the lake mysteriously reappears. Fed from underground lakes it has only one tributary stream – the Wulka.

On the eastern shore, horses and oxen graze on the marshy flats where, in summer, the hot rays of the sun produce startling mirages. On the other side of

The Fuscher Törl on the Grossglockner Alpine Road.

the lake, however, grapevines and almond trees flourish. The villages of **Morbisch**, **Oggau** and **Rust** are known for their wines, red and white.

The **Danube River** meanders across the north of Austria, past woods and fields, through cities, in the shadow of castles, churches and abbeys. The spectacular Benedictine **Abbey of Melke** is poised in all its Baroque splendour on a promontory, and gives a fine view of the river and its valley. The allegorical painting on the ceiling of its Marble Hall is worth visiting. The Emperor's Gallery, 650 feet (198 metres) long, and the library containing 80,000 books, are also open to the public.

Austria is a Catholic country and signs of the faith can be found in humble artifacts and elegant architecture. Roofed crosses, called *Wiesenkreuz,* stand along the roadsides in the Tyrol; to the south they give way to *Bildstöcke,* posts painted with pious scenes.

A favourite patron is St Florian, usually depicted putting out a fire with his little bucket of water. The prayer to him sometimes, rather uncharitably, asks: "Spare my house and rather burn that of my neighbour."

The **Imst Schemenlaufen** (procession of ghosts) takes place only every four years in the Tyrol. The men of the village, wearing huge wooden masks, parade through the streets ringing bells to drive out winter.

The age-old tradition of "burning winter" is still carried out in many villages. The variation practised in the **Vorarlberg** on the Sunday after Ash Wednesday, with the figure of a witch filled with explosives, is particularly dramatic.

Traditional dress, too, is kept alive in Austria, although the more decorative wear is saved for festivals. Women of all ages still wear the *Dirndl,* a bright coloured apron. Men wear the traditional Tyrolean *Loden* style or leather knee-breeches and shorts with wide suspenders, and the characteristic green narrow-brimmed hats adorned with feathers or other trophies of the hunt. Even the dressiest occasions in the city will be attended by men in the *Steirer*

Winter fodder.

Anzug, a suit embroidered in green with a flared coat.

The grand tradition in Austria is music. At every turn, one is reminded of the great men in music by monuments and by the names of cafés. All summer, the festivals of music, theatre and art seem to be ubiquitous. The **Bregenz Festival** is unique among these, for the city has built an open-air stage on **Lake Constance**. The play of light and sound upon the water gives an added dimension to each performance.

The Anton Bruckner House in **Linz** is the location of the annual Bruckner Festival. The Danube flows through this town which boasts Austria's most modern port. It is an industrial city, but pretty in spite of that, especially around the **Hauptplatz** (the main square). A Holy Trinity column stands in the centre, and among the buildings surrounding the square are the Council House, built in 1513, and the Old Cathedral (Jesuit Church) with its twin spires.

A well-armed city: Far to the south is **Graz,** capital of the province of Steiermark (Styria), a grass-green, geranium-red city. Graz played an important defensive role when the Turks set out to conquer Europe in the 1500s. Austria was the outpost of the Holy Roman Empire in the wars between the Christians and the Moslems.

As the wars dragged on, it became apparent that a good stock of arms and ammunition would be needed. Iron from the Styrian **Erzberg** (Ore Mountain) was cast into heavy guns and made into swords and halberds. Armour was fashioned by Styrian craftsmen and their guildmates in Innsbruck and in Germany. A huge *Zeughaus* (arsenal) in Graz became the main storage place for these armaments. Then, around 1700, the Turks were driven back and the arms in the *Zeughaus* began to gather dust. The arsenal at Graz today contains about 29,000 arms of every kind, including 3,300 suits of armour and more than 7,800 small arms.

The last window on the top floor opens to a wonderful view of the **Landhaus** (provincial parliament), a Renaissance building dating from the mid-1500s. Behind it rises the clock tower, the city's symbol.

Graz is a serene city whose street-corner musicians usually play violin and flute music. The old town, full of romantic alleys, is the largest one intact in the German-speaking countries.

Most restaurants in town serve Styrian wines, notable for their faintly smokey taste. Austria produces other wines, mostly white, which mainly come from the provinces of Styria, Burgenland and Lower Austria. For stronger drink, *Obstler,* distilled from a mix of whatever fruits thrived during the season, is popular and powerful. Some of the best spirits are served only by private individuals, who always seem to have a secret family recipe and a special place to gather herbs, to make a few bottles each year.

Austrian cooking is not very different from German cuisine, but the food has been lightened and spiced by the many peoples who have had a hand in the kitchen – the Italians, the Turks, the Hungarians, the Czechs and the Serbs.

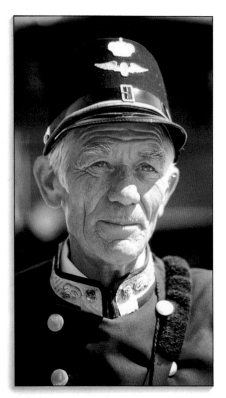

Left, giving the old uniform an airing. **Right**, looking towards the Sonnenspitze.

VIENNA

Vienna is an easy city to get to know, not because nobody ever gets lost in its maze of streets and passages (they do), but because the Viennese themselves are so helpful. They still uphold their traditional reputation of being courteous and charming, and visitors may be welcomed to the city by an elderly lady who has overheard them speaking English to a waiter in a coffee house. Strangers have also been known to get caught up in a family party at a *Beisel*, a typical local restaurant.

The diversity of people can be traced directly to the far-flung Habsburg Empire; Vienna was the seat of the ruling family for almost 650 years. Situated in the Danube Valley, it was already settled by the Celts around 400 BC, and known as *Vindobona*.

Austria's capital of 1.6 million people lies on the eastern edge of the country where East meets West – "Asia begins at the Landstrasse," Prince Metternich said. Vienna has always been something of a bulwark. It was recognised by Europe as the saviour of Christendom when it finally repelled the Turks in 1683. Today Vienna serves as a neutral meeting ground for diplomats of all political persuasions. It is the seat of OPEC (Organization of Petroleum Exporting Countries) and the third seat of the United Nations (after New York City and Geneva).

On the right bank of the Donau Kanal looms the **Vienna International Centre** which houses the International Atomic Energy Agency (IAEA), the United Nations Organization for Industrial Development (UNIDO) and other offices of the world body. UN City, serves as headquarters for some 4,000 international diplomats and employees.

For centuries, all manner of ideas were fomented and flourished among the city's cultural palaces and cafés. Art and music, theatre, medicine and psychology found the ideal climate in which to grow. Vienna has been home to some of the great composers, from Haydn to Beethoven to Schoenberg; and to some equally great architects from the historicist Heinrich von Ferstel to Otto Wagner, founder of the Viennese *Jugendstil* (Art Nouveau) movement.

Building for glory: The Habsburgs were great builders. At the heart of the old town they erected the **Hofburg** (the Imperial Palace), a town itself within the city, which was "always being built but never finished." Construction began about 1220, but it was enlarged and renovated right into the 20th century. The **Neue Hofburg** (New Hofburg) as it now stands was completed just 10 years before the collapse of the Habsburg Empire; plans for a matching wing never materialised.

The oldest part of the Hofburg is the **Schweizerhof** (Swiss Court). A chapel was added next, then the **Amalienhof**, the **Stallburg**, Leopold's imperial apartments, the **Chancellery**, the **Spanish Riding School**, the **Albertina** and the **National Library**, all of which open on to lovely courts and gardens.

Notable collections housed in the Imperial Palace are the Collection of Court Porcelain and Silver and the Imperial Treasury. The treasury contains the bejewelled crown of the Holy Roman Empire which was founded in 800 by Charlemagne and lasted until 1803, when it was broken up by Napoleon.

The crown, symbol of German kings and emperors, was carried from 1273 on by the Habsburg rulers, a role which made them one of the most influential dynasties in the political affairs of Central Europe. Among other exhibitions from the time of the Habsburg emperors is the **Albertina**, which contains a remarkable collection of graphics, most notably those of Albrecht Dürer, along with those of other masters of the Middle Ages and the Renaissance.

The **Imperial Apartments** are open to the public along with all-white Baroque confection, the **Spanische Reitschule** (Spanish Riding School). The school dates from the 17th century when Emperor Karl VI introduced the Spanish court ceremonial in Vienna. The Lipizzaner horses, originally a Spanish breed, were first raised in Lipizza (later part of Yugoslavia) and then in the Styrian town of Piber.

It is a unique experience to watch the white stallions perform the delicate steps of the *haute école* of riding to the music of classical dances such as the gavotte, quadrille, polka and waltz. The horses can be seen from March to June and from September to October. The Viennese Tourist Board has published a special bilingual leaflet on how and where to obtain tickets.

Serene residence: While the Hofburg is majestic it is also a severe edifice. It is no wonder that the rulers preferred golden **Schloss Schönbrunn** as a summer residence.

The site of this palace is the **Schöner Brunnen** (Beautiful Fountains), set in spacious grounds where Emperor Josef I wished to build a palace to rival Versailles. Because of financial difficulties, his plans did not come to fruition but the palace is still impressive.

Schönbrunn contains 1,200 rooms, 45 of which are open to the public. Also of interest in the ground are the Baroque Zoo, the English Garden and Palm House and a coach museum, the **Wagenburg** (which displays the coronation coach of Karl VI).

A third Viennese palace of sumptuous proportions is the **Belvedere**, built by Prince Eugene of Savoy who routed the Turks. It is divided into the Upper and Lower Belvedere, joined by terraced gardens and houses the **Österreichische Galerie des 19 and 20 Jahrhunderts** (Austrian Gallery for 19th century and 20th-century Art); the Lower Belvedere houses the **Museum Mittelalterlicher Kunst** (Museum of Medieval Art) and the **Barockmuseum** (Museum of Baroque Art).

The magnificent Ring: Vienna has hundreds of palaces, large and small, but the biggest building spree the city has ever seen was the **Ring**. This wide avenue, 187 feet (57 metres) across, follows the line of fortifications which stood until Emperor Franz Joseph ordered the ramparts razed in 1857. Architectural competitions were launched and the city received a brand-new face. Standing at

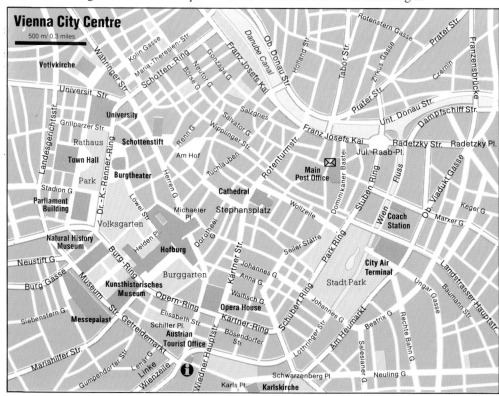

Vienna City Centre

500 m / 0.3 miles

the centre of the Ring, and the first of the buildings to be completed, is the **Staatsoper** (Opera House). The Viennese ridiculed the Romantic-Historicist style as it was being built and, stung by the criticism, one of its architects hanged himself.

It remained for the prolific architect Heinrich von Ferstel to set the traditional tone of the Ring with the **Votivkirche** (Votive Church), built in gratitude for the failure of an assassination attempt against Franz Joseph. The church is neo-Gothic down to the last detail and later buildings in the vicinity were adjusted to fit the style.

Von Ferstel's other Ring building is the **University**, built in the Italian Renaissance style. The soaring architecture continues around the circle with the **Rathaus** (Town Hall) built in imitation Gothic, and **Parliament** in Hellenistic style. The **Burg Theatre**, just steps from the University, was built in the shape of a Greek lyre, but its acoustics were so poor that it had to be reconstructed 10 years later. The **Naturkundliches Museum** (Natural Science Museum) and the **Kunsthistorisches Museum** (Fine Arts Museum), also Italian Renaissance, stand across the Ring from the New Hofburg and its parks. The Ring on the other side of the Opera is lined primarily by palaces of the rich and the City Park.

A look at a map of Vienna shows that it is laid out in concentric circles. The **Innenstadt** (Inner City), also known as I. Bezirk (first district), is enclosed by the Ring and the Danube Canal. On the other side of the Ring is the **Vorstadt**, that part of the city that grew up outside the fortifications. It is surrounded by another ring road – the Gürtel. Outside the Gürtel come the suburbs, little villages such as Grinzing, Nussdorf, Gumpoldskirchen and Severing, and their rural wine taverns called *Heurigen*.

The city subsides into the Vienna Woods where the Alps end – or begin – at the edge of the Hungarian Plains which themselves lead into the neighbouring province of Burgenland.

There are four ways to get a bird's-eye view of Vienna: an excursion to the

Horses of the Spanish Riding School.

Kahlenberg heights, from which the army watched the rout of the Turks, or a high-speed elevator to the observation platform of the **Donauturm** (Danube Tower) which was built for the 1964 Vienna Garden Show. Two revolving restaurants in the tower provide a relaxing way of viewing the city panorama below.

Another possibility for an overview of the city can be found at the **Prater**, once a playground of emperors but opened to the public as a park in 1766 by Emperor Joseph II. Its landmark is the *Riesenrad*, a giant Ferris wheel which arcs to a high point of nearly 213 feet (65 metres). Notices above the cabin windows help to identify important landmarks in the city. There is also a quiet side for strolls and picnics along the 3-mile (5-km) **Prater Hauptallee**. Bicycles can be rented and riding stables are close by.

The south tower of **Stephansdom** (St Stephen's Cathedral) is the fourth option: climb the 343 steps to the watchman's room and you are rewarded with a dramatic view of the heart of the city. As an alternative, an elevator ascends the unfinished north tower of the cathedral as far as *Pummerin* (Boomer), a copy of the giant bell which was destroyed in World War II. The original *Pummerin* was cast in 1711 from cannons captured from the Turks.

Habsburg marriages took place in St Stephen's cathedral (*Steffl* to the Viennese), following their habit of acquiring territory through marriage instead of war whenever possible. And here in the catacombs are the urns containing the entrails of the Austrian emperors. Their hearts are in the Augustinian's Church and their bodies are entombed in sarcophagi in the **Kaisergruft** (Imperial Vault). Twelve emperors and 16 empresses are buried there.

In front of the asymmetrical Steffl is the smart shopping centre of Vienna, the pedestrian zone including the **Graben** and **Kärtnerstrasse**. The latter continues on the other side of the Ring as **Mariahilferstrasse** where the large department stores can be found.

The area behind St Stephen's is called **Old Vienna** because it best retains the air of the past though it is not actually the oldest quarter. A jumble of building styles in the network of narrow lanes from the 16th and 17th centuries are well preserved.

The public transport system of Vienna is easy to use and is convenient for most journeys in the city. For a leisurely tour, though, and the entertaining patter of the driver, take a *Fiaker*. These open two-horse carriages have been operating since 1670 and the cabby, also called a *Fiaker*, lives up to tradition in both dress and charm. The fare is fixed by bargaining and the "history" of the city, as the *Fiaker* tells it, should be taken with a grain of salt.

Music until dawn: Vienna loves music and musicians of every kind thrive in Vienna. In the **Burgkapelle** (Chapel) of the Imperial Palace, the *Wiener Sängerknaben* still sing Mass on Sundays and religious holidays as they did in the times of the monarchy. The Vienna Boys' Choir was organized 400 years ago by Emperor Maximilian, but it is now a private group.

In the *Heurigen* it is still possible to hear *Schrammel* music – traditional light tunes played by small orchestras usually made up of guitar, clarinet and violins. This type of music takes its name from the Schrammel brothers, who developed it toward the end of the 19th century.

Waltzes by Johann Strauss and Franz Lehár are especially popular at Carnival season, when the elegant balls continue until dawn. For the most exclusive ones, a long evening dress for ladies is a must as are tails, or uniform with decorations, for gentlemen. The *Opernball*, one of Europe's most glamorous social affairs, can also be seen by those preferring to dress in a more relaxed way. There is a special gallery for spectators, where they have their own buffet and dancing.

Then there are the great composers like Haydn, Schubert, Mozart, Mahler, Bruckner, Schoenberg and others. Traces of them can be found in many streets throughout Vienna.

Among the houses which have been turned into small museums or memorials are: the house where Haydn wrote his *Creation* (Haydngasse 19); the apartment where Mozart is said to have spent the happiest years of his life (Figaro House, Domgasse 5); the places where Schubert was born (Nussdorferstrasse 54) and where he died (Kettenbrücken-gasse 6).

A tour of the city passes several Beethoven houses. The composer, who was born in Bonn in 1770 and who died in Vienna in 1827, had between 25 and 40 addresses, depending on the sources of research. In 1800, he moved to Heiligenstadt, then in the outskirts of Vienna, today a neighbourhood in the 19th district of Döbling.

It was here at Probusgasse 6, today the **Beethoven Museum**, that he wrote his Heilig-enstädter Testament, a moving document in which he revealed his desperate feelings about his growing deafness to all those who considered him to have become a misanthrope: "You did not know the secret reasons for the character traits you attribute to me," Beethoven wrote in 1802. "But

could I tell you: 'Speak louder, shout, I am deaf?'"

Many of the composers are buried in the Musicians' Corner of the **Zentral-friedhof** (Central Cemetery), although the graves of both Beethoven and Schubert are in Schubert Park on Währinger Strasse.

Like the homes of the composers, all sorts of museums are scattered through the city. There are the great collections such as the **Historisches Museum der Stadt Wien** (Historical Museum of the City of Vienna) and the **Militär-geschichtliches Museum** (Arms and Armour) in the New Hofburg. But there are also many just as fascinating small collections of clocks, watches, tobacco and even museums of funerals and sex.

Exploring Vienna can be followed with a trip along the Danube, although its waters are disappointingly brown. Boats operate from April to mid-October and make various journeys including day-trips to Bratislava, just inside the Czech Republic, or an overnight run to Hungary's capital, Budapest.

Schönnbrunn Castle.

INNSBRUCK AND THE TYROL

Innsbruck, city of two Winter Olympic Games, is situated in the west of Austria in a valley at the intersection of several Alpine passes, the most notable of which is the motorway to Italy over the **Brenner Pass**. Today it is the capital of the province of the Tyrol with a population of 125,000. It had its golden age as the residence of the House of Habsburg in the 15th and 16th centuries.

The town reached its prime under the reign of Emperor Maximilian I (1493–1516). Trade and manufacturing flourished, as well as architecture. Many of the city's landmarks hail from this period, including the Little Golden Roof, the Royal Palace and the Royal Church.

Maximilian I is known as the "the Last Knight" as well as "the first universal monarch" because his reign marked an age of transition between the Gothic age of knights in shining armour and the Renaissance. The Emperor borrowed money from the new leading merchants to finance his mercenary armies, and led them in battle like knights of old. His campaigns were also paid for in silver and copper from the nearby mining towns of Hall and Schwarz. To this day Tyroleans venerate Maximilian as their sovereign.

The innkeeper hero: During the Napoleonic Wars, when the province of Tyrol had to be ceded to the king of Bavaria, the Tyrolean peasants remained loyal to the Habsburgs. From their ranks rose a simple innkeeper from the Passeier Valley who became their national hero: Andreas Hofer. Moving like mountain goats on the rock faces, they inflicted on the French and their Bavarian allies one defeat after another.

The battles around historic **Bergisel** (Mount Isel) at the gates of Innsbruck have become an heroic legend. The decisive one of 1809 can be seen, exact in all details, in a huge circular panoramic fresco, measuring over 80 sq. yards (100 sq. metres), located in the **Panorama Building** next to the Hungerburg funicular station in the district of Saggen.

Despite their heroic resistance, the Tyroleans did not return to Austria until the fall of Napoleon. Andreas Hofer was caught and executed in Mantua by a French firing squad.

Innsbruck's old town is oval-shaped and constitutes a precious assembly of medieval architecture. It is bordered by the **River Inn** and the streets of **Marktgraben**, **Burggraben** and **Herrengasse**. Almost every street offers a view of the peaks of the "**die Zweitausender**" ("Two Thousand") nearby. This is not true, however, of some of the narrow lanes in the centre. Here the Gothic fronts of the houses leave so little space in between that the rays of the sun rarely reach the pavement. The city fathers wisely turned the area into a pedestrian precinct, allowing the visitor to stroll without hindrance past the pergolas, oriel windows, painted facades and stucco ornaments. Another way of viewing these architectural treasures is by hiring one of the horse-drawn carriages that wait on Rennweg, in front of the **Tiroler Ländestheater** (Tirolean Provincial Theatre).

Herzog-Friedrich-Strasse leads straight into the heart of the old town to **Goldenes Dachl** (Little Golden Roof), a magnificent oriel built around 1500 in the late Gothic style. It was added to the **Neuer Hof** (New Palace) in commemoration of the betrothal of Maximilian I and Maria Bianca Sforza, daughter of the duke of Milan. The decorative alcove, adorned with 3,450 gilt copper shingles, served as a box for spectators watching tournaments and plays in the square below. It is Innsbruck's best known landmark.

Maximilian seems to have been the first Emperor to have openly sought publicity on behalf of his dynasty. He can be seen, together with a number of adoring women, on the relief decorating the Golden Roof. On the opposite side of the street is **Helbinghaus**, adorned with rococo stuccowork, a fine example of bourgeois ostentation.

Herzog-Friedrich-Strasse is famous for a string of medieval houses amongst which **Trautsonhaus**, built during the transition from the Gothic to the Ren-

Left, Wilten Church.

aissance period, and **Katzunghaus**, with its unique reliefs on the balcony dating back to 1530, are especially noteworthy. Another landmark is the 180-foot (56-metre) **City Tower** built in 1360 as a watchtower against fire. At a height of 110 feet (33 metres) there is a little gallery with a magnificent view of the whole town and the mountains nearby. The sights include the **Ottoburg**, a residential tower on the embankment , built in 1495, and the **Burgriesenhaus** in **Hofgasse**, which Duke Siegmund built in 1490 for his court favourite Niklas Haidl, a 7 ft-10 inch (2.4-metre) giant.

In the opposite direction through Pfarrgasse is Domplatz (at the rear of Little Golden Roof). It is the location of Innsbruck's **Parish Church of Sankt Jakob**, which, with its twin towers, represents a splendid example of baroque architecture. A copy of *Mariahilf* ("Our Lady of Succour") by Lukas Cranach the Elder adorns the high altar.

At the time Vienna was concentrating its efforts on strengthening the city walls and other fortifications against the advancing Turks, Innsbruck had a boom in Renaissance building. There is no other place in Austria conveying such a vivid impression of 16th-century architecture as in the eastern part of the old town. Prime examples are the **Royal Palace**, the **Royal Church** and the **Volkskunstmuseum** (Folkcraft Museum). The 15th-century **Hofburg** (Royal Palace) was rebuilt from 1754 to 1776 in the late Rococo style. One highlight of the guided tours is the **Riesensaal** (Giant's Room), a two-storey stateroom with rococo stucco-work and portraits of the Imperial family.

An empty coffin: The Tyrolean national hero Andreas Hofer and two of his companions are buried in the **Hofkirche** (Royal Church). The church also houses the **mausoleum of Maximilian I**, however the marble sarcophagus is empty, since the emperor is buried in Wiener Neustadt, a town 35 miles (53 km) south of Vienna. In Innsbruck his bronze figure kneels on the lid of his tomb. Twenty-eight of his forebears and eminent contemporaries, all cast as larger-than-life bronze statues, stand guard around the grave, including legendary King Artus. Known as the "Black Fellows", they form the most imposing sculptural ensemble of Renaissance art north of the Alps. Busts of the Roman emperors, bronze statuettes and reliefs depicting scenes from the emperor's life round off this sepulchral monument which has become a place of pilgrimage to sculptors and lovers of the Renaissance.

To the east of the Royal Church, in an old Franciscan monastery, is the **Tiroler Volkskunst Museum** (Tyrolean Folkcraft Museum) which contains 20 rustic interiors from various periods as well as furniture, folk costumes and other folk art exemplifying the creativity of the native Tyrolean people.

Leading to the south from Herzog-Friedrich-Strasse is Innsbruck's principal thoroughfare, **Maria Theresien Strasse**, where **Anna Saule** (St Anne's Column) commemorates 26 July 1703, St Anne's Day, when the Bavarian troops forced the inhabitants out of Innsbruck during the War of the Spanish Succession (1701–14). At the end of the street

Townhouses on the Inn.

stands the **Triumphpforte** (Triumphal Arch) which the Empress Maria Theresa built in 1765 to celebrate the engagement of her son Leopold to Maria Ludovica of Spain.

Leopoldstrasse, to the south, leads both to **Stiftkirche Wilten** (Wilten Abbey Church), founded in 1138 by the Premonstratensians, and to the **Wiltener Basilika** (Wilten Basilica), built in 1755 on the foundations of a previous building. The abbey church as it stands today was completed in 1670. It is regarded as one of the loveliest churches of the early Baroque period in Austria and the Basilica ranks as highly as an example of Rococo.

It was here in the borough of Wilten that the Romans built a fort called Veldidena. It guarded a bridge over the River Inn, which subsequently gave the city its name. Like most Roman settlements in Austria the fort was swept away during the tribal migrations in the 5th and 6th centuries. *Inspruke* appeared for the first time as the name of a market place on the banks of River Inn in 1187.

The former residence of Archduke Ferdinand, **Schloss Ambras** (Ambras Castle), lies 2 miles (3.2 km) southeast of the city. Today the castle is a museum housing a substantial art and armour collection from the 16th century.

In the age of chivalry, Innsbruck was a proper jousting place where the cream of Europe's knights used to gather for their games and tournaments to seek the favour of the young ladies of the castle.

In 1964 and 1976 Innsbruck hosted a different kind of games: the Winter Olympics. At both events the Soviet Union won the largest number of gold medals, putting their Austrian hosts in second and third place.

An imposing legacy of the games just outside the city in front of Bergisel is the **Olympic ski jumps** with a stadium seating 60,000 spectators. Also remaining from the games is the **Olympic ice stadium** (open all year) and an artificial bob sleigh at **Igls**, a popular holiday resort a short distance outside the city.

Innsbruck is the gateway to a wide variety of ski regions which makes the province of Tyrol the most popular winter holiday destination in Austria. Southwest of the city, easily accessible by way of the Brenner *Autobahn*, are the **Stubai Alps**. Situated in a sunny valley about 3,300 feet (1,000 metres) above sea level are a number of cosy mountain villages, the most well-known of which is **Neustift**. This holiday resort of about 3,000 inhabitants offers excellent ski facilities because it is situated at the foot of the Stubai Glacier.

Innsbruck gives the feeling that the Alps are right around the corner. Some of the mountains of the **Nordkette** (Northern Chain) lie within the precincts of the city. The highest of these, **Mount Hafelekar**, which reaches 7,600 feet (2,335 metres), can be reached by cable car from the centre of Innsbruck, involving two changes.

On a clear day the view from the top is breathtaking, so much so that one can understand the sentiments expressed by Flemish composer Heinrich Isaak in his melancholic song "Innsbruck, I must leave you." It is with regret that one leaves this city.

The mountains around Innsbruck.

SALZBURG

Early on a Sunday morning, before the church bells beckon to Mass and the boom of the giant organ known as *Der Stier* (The Steer) echoes across the Salzach Valley, the city looks as if it might have been sleeping for centuries. Tucked in along the River Salzach, watched over by its giant fortress, the **Hohensalzburg**, its streets and squares proclaiming their long history, Salzburg at that hour might be mistaken for a small Rome of the North.

This, though, is the view from the **Kapuzinerberg**, the best panorama of the city. It is only on climbing down from this vantage point that the true face of the city is revealed; no cracks in the venerable facades, no peeled paintwork, no cobblestones out of place. All that is old has been faithfully preserved to give the city that carefully groomed Baroque look on which it thrives.

And yet this spotless Sleeping Beauty must be pitied. For a thousand years, since the days of Charlemagne, it was an independent Archbishopric ruled by autocratic Prince-Archbishops, foreigners nominated by emperors and popes, men who never allowed the city's fate to be determined by its own citizens.

One of these rulers, Prince-Archbishop Wolf Dietrich von Raitenau, a far-sighted Swabian, introduced the spacious Baroque look in 1587 by simply razing 55 town houses and allowing the old cathedral to burn down. A predecessor, Leonard von Keutschach, had already corked popular rebellion by sending the city council fathers on an icy sledge ride until they resigned their civic rights. After the last Prince-Archbishop was routed by the French in 1803, Bavarian, Austrian and German rulers toyed with the city. Finally, no longer rich from salt, gold and copper, Salzburg fell into a century-long sleep and its population declined.

A posthumous return: The prince who gave her the kiss which woke her had a brilliant idea. He turned her into a music

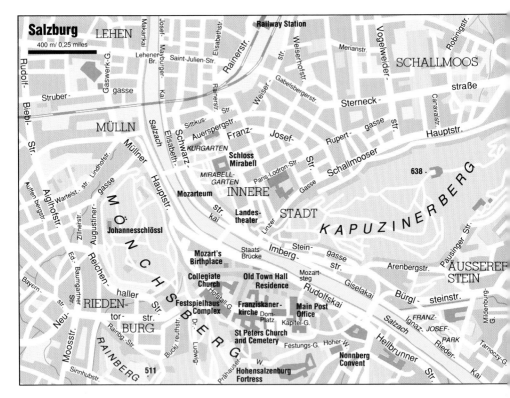

city based on the works of her more famous son, Joannes Chrysostomus Wolfgang Gottlieb Mozart, better known as Wolfgang Amadeus (or W. A.) Mozart who was born in Salzburg in 1756. The Mozart revival movement, a big success story, conveniently ignored the fact that the Maestro had been "booted" out of Salzburg. An embittered Mozart in 1778 wrote: "Salzburg is not a place for my talent… first of all people do not respect music and secondly there is no theatre, no opera… even if one wanted to play who would listen?" He died impoverished in Vienna and was interred in an unknown mass grave.

Today Mozart would turn in his grave were he told that the city which turned its back on him has achieved a new zenith of wealth and popularity trading on his name, his music and his life. Mozart is everywhere. Shop windows are clustered with chocolate spheres bearing his portrait. Sweets, cakes and squares are named after him. Every January there's a Mozart week. The annual summer Music Festival bears his indelible stamp and his birthplace in the **Getreidegasse,** now a museum bearing memorabilia from buttons to the virtuoso's violin, is crowded from morning to night. The summer festival of operas and concerts, a rendezvous for the rich, enjoys the patronage of renowned orchestra conductors. Their bickering battle over how to interpret Mozart has resulted in a plurality of styles ever since the first annual festival in 1920.

Traditionally the festival opens with Hugo von Hofmannsthal's *Jedermann* (*Everyman*), a morality play performed in the open **Domplatz** (Cathedral Square). By opening night the 135,000 festival tickets (31 percent of which go to the citizens of Salzburg but rarely stay in their hands) are long sold out to the flock of socialites (and a few genuine music lovers) who annually make the pilgrimage. To ensure the majority do not escape the city's 220,000 spare beds, no train has ever left Salzburg after the last curtain went down.

Neither the August Festival nor the Mozart week in January suffice to fill

Mozart Kugeln **(Mozart balls) are a tempting Salzburg confection.**

the city's coffers. So Salzburg invented the October Culture Days, the Advent Carols in November and December and a Whitsun and Easter Festival. The last two were run, in big-business style, by the late Herbert von Karajan, conductor of the Berlin Philharmonic and another son of Salzburg.

For many music lovers however, the saving grace of this ostentatious musical display is the Anti-Festival. This is one of Europe's most popular summer *Jugendszene* (Youth Scenes) with around 150 theatre performances, poetry readings, concerts and exhibitions. An increasing number of famous artists play gratis at **Petersbrunnhof**, the hard-seated theatre of "The Scene" – to the chagrin of society snobs who have paid small fortunes to see their idols at the Festival House.

The Old Town: None of this can be seen from the panoramic "**Kanzel**" at the top of the Kapuzinerberg on a Sunday morning. There, having climbed past the house of writer Stefan Zweig, one can only contemplate the postcard beauty of "the Teutonic Rome." In the hazy dawn the spires of the 36 churches protrude like spiked tin hats and the city's four abbeys resemble fortresses rather than ecclesiastical colleges.

Out of the fading haze, across the river on the Mönchsberg, emerges the **fortress Hohensalzburg**. It is a durable witness to the fear of the archbishops, who, caught in the power struggle between popes and emperors, built it as a refuge in the 11th century. Here in 1425, besieged by the Bavarians, the starving locals paraded a fat steer along the ramparts to make their assailants believe there was food in abundance. The trick worked and the horned steer became Salzburg's good-luck charm ever since.

Below the fortress, in the **Altstadt** (Old Town), the dominant edifice is the **Dom** (Cathedral) which shelters the bones of Saint Rupert, the assistant of Father Christmas. Built by the Italian architect Santino Solari between 1614 and 1628, the dome houses the world's largest combination of bells, seven of them, weighing a total of 32 tons.

Beyond the cathedral, nestled against the hill, is **Kloster St Peter** (Benedictine Abbey of Saint Peter's) where Mozart first conducted his *C-minor Mass* while his wife Constance sang soprano. Mozart's *Requiem* is performed here on 5 December each year, the day of the composer's death. In the cemetery outside the church, Mozart's beloved sister, Nannerl, is buried. His wife and his father, Leopold, are buried in the nearby cemetery of Saint Sebastian where the great physician and alchemist Paracelsus was also laid to rest in 1541.

Halfway down the **Dreifaltigkeitsgasse** is the **Mozarteum**, since 1914 an international foundation with a Mozart library, concert halls and a college wing. In the garden is the composer's summerhouse, brought from Vienna, where he wrote his last opera, the *Magic Flute*. Toward the river, and next to the picturesque **Makartplatz**, is Salzburg's famous **puppet theatre** and **Kammerspiele** (play-theatre). The puppet saga began in 1913 when Anton Aicker and his children staged a Mozart song-game with their puppets.

Mozart's birthplace.

A few minutes farther south on the Dreifaltigkeitsgasse stands the **Mirabell Palace**, which the Prince-Archbishop Wolf Dieter von Raitenau built for his mistress, Salome Alt, a simple and honest miller's daughter who bore the supposedly celibate archbishop 10 healthy children. A feature of this late Renaissance palace is the cherub staircase, sculptured by Raphael Donner in 1723. On its winding balustrade a score of delightful cherubs slide up and down, mischievously bare and deliciously erotic. The stairway leads to the Marble Room which today is one of the world's most splendid registries for marriages.

At this point it is best to stroll upstream towards the **Mozartsweg** (footbridge). Across it is the **Mozartplatz** (Mozart Square) into which all the alleys and streets of **Old Salzburg** discharge themselves. A walk down anyone of them leads past palaces, patrician houses and churches.

The gourmet, searching for a typical Salzburg dish, should ask for a *Jausn*. It is served with a stein of beer and made up of salted radish, ox-tongue salad, pretzels, *Mondseer* cheese, sausages – all served straight onto a wooden table, just as it was in medieval days.

Nobody should leave without calling at one of the coffee houses which, so Austrian legend claims, have been the hatcheries of literature, art, gossip and revolution. The **Café Glockenspiel** near the cathedral has a reputation for sphere-shaped ice creams and a cosy garden setting. At the casino of the **Café Winkler** up on the Mönchsberg, one can play baccarat and blackjack.

But the truly folkloric coffee house of Salzburg are the **Tomaselli** and the **Bazar**. The first, near Festival House, was founded in 1856 by an Italian tenor of that name who bequeathed it to his first born. This upset the second-born son. In opposition he opened the Bazar near the Mirabell Palace on the other side of the river. The Tomaselli became known as the headquarters of the music freaks and their entourage, the Bazar as the rendezvous of actors, writers and theatre fans.

Austrian actor Klaus Maria Brandauer as *Jedermann*.

EXCURSIONS TO THE EAST

The new destinations of continental Europe lie behind what was the old Iron Curtain. Some cities have particularly attracted tourists since it was torn down: Budapest, capital of Hungary; Warsaw and Cracow, capital and former capital of Poland; and Prague, capital of the Czech Republic, which has become awash with visitors, particularly Americans. These are exciting times in these cities.

The attractions are novelty, magnificent architecture and characteristic cafés. For Jews it may be a pilgrimage to the sites of the horrifying ghettoes created by the Nazis in World War II. For the cultured there are the haunts of Kafka, Conrad, Mozart, Chopin, Dvorak and Liszt. This is, after all, the home of the original Bohemians. And although McDonald's hamburgers have arrived, a visitor to these countries is also offered a glimpse of a different and sometimes fast disappearing way of life.

Just a look at the map is a reminder that these cities have always been central to mainstream European history and culture. They fall in a cluster, with Berlin and Vienna, over an area of around 300 miles (500 km). Prague is no further east than Naples; Warsaw and Budapest are on a line with Italy's heel. From Prague it is little more than an hour's drive to the German border, and barely twice that south to Austria's capital, Vienna, which history has treated as a next-door neighbour. From Vienna you can hitch a ride on a slow boat down the Danube to Budapest and find that coffee houses are not confined to the Austrian capital.

While Poland suffered the vagaries of history under the changing fortunes of Lithuanian, Prussian and Russian empires, Prague, Vienna and Budapest were the jewels in the Austro-Hungarian empire's crown. All of them were profoundly affected by the break-up of the former empires at the end of World War I when history once more played around with their borders.

Soviet town planning tended to leave the hearts of cities alone, and each of them have well-preserved cores; Warsaw's historic main square has been entirely rebuilt. This makes them ideal places for brief visits, as everywhere is accessible on foot.

<u>Preceding pages</u>: Prague's Tyn Church, seen from the old town hall; Bugac horseman from Hungary. <u>Left</u>, Rynek Old Town, Warsaw.

BUDAPEST

The Romans built bridges across the Danube in the 2nd century AD, yet Buda on the west bank and Pest on the east did not get one until William Tierney Clark designed and Adam Clark built the great **Chain Bridge** in the 1840s. The problem, it seems, was that the river flowed very fast and frequently flooded at this point so that there was no reliable hard ground on either side.

The first bridge cost £500,000 (US $750,000) and was regarded as an engineering wonder of the age. The two principals were British, as were many of the work force, together with Italians from Trieste and Slavs. The Hungarian nobility put up the money.

Buda, Obuda (Old Buda) and Pest became a single city in 1872, and other bridges followed. They were all blown up during World War II as the Germans prepared their last stand on Castle Hill, and the rebuilding afterwards was a long process.

The Chain Bridge reopened in 1949, exactly 100 years after its completion, but the single-span Elizabeth Bridge was not ready until 1964. The latter was named after a Habsburg royal who was genuinely popular in these parts: the Empress Elizabeth who married Franz Joseph and was universally known as Sissy. Franz Joseph had his bridge, too, but it was later renamed Szabadsaghid, or **Liberty Bridge**.

Although Buda looks older than Pest, it was in fact started only after the destruction of Pest by the Mongols in 1241. While the east bank was flat, the steep limestone hill opposite had natural defensive possibilities and moreover had the Danube between it and the direction from which these terrifying Oriental horsemen on their piebald ponies were likely to return.

The present boulevards and ring-roads were mostly laid out at the beginning of the 20th century. They cope with modern traffic reasonably well but the older

Left, the capital's Parliament building.

parts of the capital do not. This will not bother tourists. The interesting parts of the city are in concentrated clusters and public transport, including a metro, is more than adequate.

It was on one of the hills on the Buda west bank that in 1046 the worthy Swiss Bishop Gellert presumed to preach Christianity to unreceptive locals and for his pains was stuffed into a barrel studded with nails and launched down the hill into the river. The hill named after him provides an excellent panorama, one that conveys the vastness of the plain beyond the city and the way the Danube arcs through it. The hill has an old citadel and the Liberation Memorial to the dead in the siege of 1944–45.

Bela IV's plans for the new town of Buda in the 13th century began with a fortress on **Castle Hill** to protect the civilian quarter to the north of Gellert Hill. A stormy future lay ahead. The city got off lightly in the Turkish conquest of 1526 – the decisive battle was fought at Mohacs – but not in the subsequent recapture in 1686. The Turks then turned

the churches into mosques and gave the city a certain Oriental air.

Odd touches survive in some of the houses and the baths to which the Turks were so partial. The grave of Abdurrahman Ali, the last Turkish pasha to rule Buda, is in Uri Street on Castle Hill.

After the Turks were ousted, the ruined city was rebuilt in the late-baroque fashion of the times, the best examples of which are the **University Church**, the **Zichy Manor and Silk Factory** in Obuda, and **St Anne's Church** in Batthyany Square. The restoration of the monarchy in 1867 led to a second wave of celebratory building in which the fortress was transformed into a royal palace. The enthusiasm carried across the river to Pest as the Hungarians entertained the unashamed ambition of building a capital to outshine Vienna.

This rebuilding programme patched up much of the damage done by the Austrians and Russians in putting down the 1848 revolution, but there was more trouble in store. The Romanians went on the rampage in 1919, the Germans

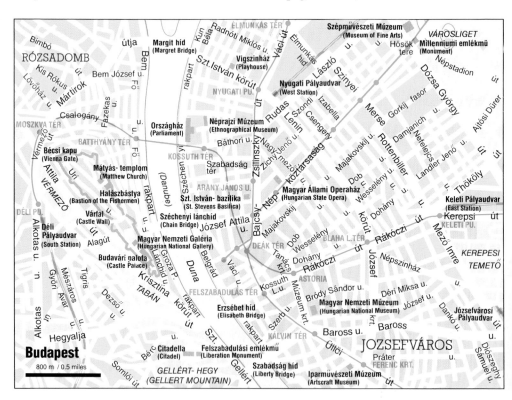

did their worst in 1944, and of course the Russians were back again in 1956. The guides who show visitors around the city seem remarkably confident about which bullet holes in the masonry belong to which army.

The destruction of almost everything that stood on Castle Hill as the Germans made their last stand in 1944 at least gave archaeologists a chance to poke about in the rubble, and this brought to light evidence of the great names of Hungarian history: the Arpads, Angevins, Mathias Corvinus and all. These remains were cleverly integrated in the reconstruction of the palace, which now houses the **Museum of Modern Hungarian History**, the **Hungarian National Gallery**, the **Budapest History Museum** and the **National Library**.

Castle Hill, which has a tunnel through its bowels, can be reached by a funicular railway from **Clark Adam Square** at the end of the Chain Bridge. The several streets on the top of the hill, linked by narrow passages, are now closed to private cars and have a fairground atmos-

phere, especially those around the **Mathias Church**.

Strictly speaking, this is the Church of Our Lady (and for a while an important Turkish mosque) but it is generally known by the name of the Hungarian king and hero Mathias Corvinus (1443-90) who was married here (twice) and remodelled it. The church was badly damaged in 1686 and was completely rebuilt in the 19th century. Franz Joseph and Charles IV, the last kings of Hungary, were both crowned here. Not much light comes through the dark windows, but as one's eyes adjust a magnificent interior of decorated pillars, walls and ceilings emerges from the gloom. The murals depict the lives of the Hungarian saints and among the sarcophagi are those of Bela III (1173–96) and his wife Anne of Chatillon, transferred from Szekesfehervar.

A short distance from the church is the **Fishermen's Bastion**, a rather weird building of winding passages and staircases built at the beginning of the 20th century and named after the medieval

Budapest's spa hotels are a big attraction.

fishermen's town which stood below.

Dwarfed by the museums in the palace complex is the curious little **Museum of Catering** in Fortuna utca, not far from the Hilton Hotel. Do not be misled by the name; this is no paean to sensible nutrition or works canteens. Several rooms are each designed to resemble the entrance halls of Budapest hotels when they were the soul of aristocratic high living. The collection of old menus and photographs of the Magyar chef's art are enough to give anyone a ripping appetite.

For another glimpse of Magyar nostalgia try the **War Museum**, in particular the 19th-century cavalry uniforms which were a large part of the swashbuckling image of the Hungarian officer class. The exhibits are mostly concerned with the Hungarian uprising of 1848 against Austria and Russia.

The arch near the War Museum is one way of getting to the newer part of Buda. The main thoroughfare is known as **Fo utca**, and at the northern end is the statue of General Joseph Bemand, a hero of 1848. It was around this statue that the demonstrations of the 1956 uprising began.

At No. 72 Fo utca are the **Kiraly baths**. The 120 or so thermal springs lining the Danube are reputed to disgorge 16 million gallons of medicinal water a day and they have been used since Roman times. Baths here serve much the same purpose as coffee-houses in Vienna. The mosque-like Kiraly baths, with a 600-year-old coloured-glass ceiling, have alternate days for men and women. More elegant are the **Gellert** or **Széchenyi** baths.

The Pest side: The fitting way to enter Pest on the east side of the river is to walk the 600 yards across the Chain Bridge: there is a pedestrian path. **Roosevelt Square** with its statues of Count Stephen Szechenyi and Lajos Kossuth is on the other side, the neo-Renaissance **Academy of Sciences** having been founded by the former. The **Corzo** running south is a pedestrian promenade leading to **Vigado Square** where, in the **Concert Hall**, all the musical giants seem to have performed

at one time or another. The roll-call begins with Brahms and Liszt.

Parallel with the Corso is **Vaci utca**, Budapest's smartest shopping street which even in the 1970s and 1980s was full of luxuries unobtainable anywhere else in Eastern Europe. This was equally true of the **Budapest market** (at the other end of Vaci utca), an amazing 19th-century building with soaring metal columns, high walkways and ramps. It is a busy place with live fish in tanks and long tables of every conceivable kind of mushroom. Red peppers by the thousand are, of course, the fabled paprikas.

Much of Pest's shopping district is now car-free, which greatly enhances the pleasure of strolling about. **Vorosmarty Square** is always a hive of activity, and it is almost obligatory to make at least one call at Gerbeaud's, the esteemed confectioners, established 1857. Most airline offices are in this area.

Just to the north of the square is the neo-Romanesque **St Stephen's Basilica** to which a steady stream of Hungarian Catholics make the pilgrimage to see

Szechenyi thermal pool.

the right hand of St Stephen. Nearby is the Opera House, and though tickets to the opera are scarce, it is worth joining a tour, even between performances.

Near the Inter-Continental Hotel is the **Inner City Parish Church** (*Belvarosi plebania templom*) whose origins pre-date the Mongol invasion. Liszt played the organ in this church regularly; in fact he lived just around the corner in a house where Richard Wagner was a regular guest at his Sunday soirées.

The huge **Parliament** imitated the British model in both its constitution and the way it is mirrored in the Danube as the British one is in the Thames. It was built between 1880 and 1902 to a design by Imre Steindl which required special concrete foundations because of the proximity of the river. There are 10 courtyards, 29 staircases and 27 gates behind the 300-yard (280-metre) facade with its 88 statues of Hungarian leaders and generals. Tours of the magnificent interior are given on certain mornings.

The **National Museum** is a must for the Apostolic Crown of St Stephen alone.

Fishermen's Bastion.

This most potent symbol in the land is apparently 12th-century Byzantine art and, while obviously a masterpiece, cannot therefore be the actual crown which Pope Sylvester II gave to Stephen, Hungary's first king who was later canonised, in the year 1000. The cross on the top was bent, and remains bent, as the result of being hastily hidden during some crisis in medieval times. The Hungarian army handed over the crown and the rest of the royal regalia to the Americans when the Red Army was on the point of entering Budapest at the end of World War II. The US relented and gave them all back only in 1978.

Close to the museum is the **Great Synagogue**, one of the largest in the world, identifiable by its onion dome

The **Millennary Monument** in **Heroes Square** commemorates the 1,000th anniversary of the Magyar conquest and has an appropriate equestrian statue of Arpad in front of the seven lesser-known Magyar chieftains who accompanied him. It was designed by Albert Schickedanz in 1896. The buildings dominating the square are the **Museum of Fine Arts** and the **Artists' House**, the former containing one of the most important collections in Eastern Europe and the latter a changing exhibition of contemporary work.

That still leaves the equally impressive **Museum of Applied Arts**, which is out on its own in the south of the city and may require a taxi. The building is an attraction in its own right, the work of Odon Lechner in the 1890s.

By far the best place for a coffee or a meal is the **Café-Restaurant Hungaria** in Erzébet Körút 9-11 on the Outer Ring road. This art-nouveau establishment, once called the Café New York, is the most splendid in the city.

Obuda, or "Old Buda", is a little distance from the centre but can be reached by the HEV train from Batthyany Square. It is mostly apartment buildings now, but there is a historic centre with the ruins of a Roman amphitheatre capable of accommodating 15,000 spectators. An 18th-century baroque mansion built by the Zichy family is the local cultural centre.

WARSAW AND CRACOW

By the end of World War II, 700,000 inhabitants of Warsaw were dead and the city was almost as devastated as Hiroshima. The easiest course of action would have been to flatten the remains and start all over again, but that would have been considered an unspeakable desecration in Poland.

Instead, Polish architects undertook a real-life jigsaw puzzle. They assembled a picture of Warsaw as it had been before the war using paintings, sketches, snap-shots, anything. They allowed themselves a little licence to brush out the more obvious blemishes, moved a building this way or that as they saw fit – and began to put it all together. Within a few years, the paint had faded on schedule to produce the desired effect and historic Warsaw was reborn. Wide boulevards, parks and new suburbs were added with an eye to future needs.

Warsaw is divided by the **River Vistula**, and it is the meticulously re-created left bank that is of most interest to visitors. According to legend, the Warsaw mermaid – the part-woman, part-fish who graces the city's coat-of-arms – once lived here. At any rate **Old Market** (Rynek Starego Miasta) was thriving on this site in the 13th century.

It is still a picturesque spot where artists sell their work on the street and numerous antique shops and galleries operate out of old patrician houses. Café umbrellas lend a dash of colour; the sound effects are provided by horse-drawn cabs on cobblestones. The **Bazyliszek**, **Swietoszek** and **Rycerska** restaurants are perennial local favourites, and there is also loyal support for the **Kaminne Schodki** coffee house, the **Krokodyl** café and the **U Fukere** wine bar. The area is floodlit at night so, as the saying goes, it stays up late.

The **Warsaw Historical Museum** in this quarter has regular showings of a short documentary which shows the city before and after rejuvenation. Ironically,

Left, old Warsaw.

these film shows are in a row of buildings, including the "Negro House", which actually survived the destruction they portray. Nearby is the Museum of Literature, which is named after the poet Adam Mickiewicz (1798–1859).

The **Cathedral of St John**, just off the Old Market, is Warsaw's oldest and most important church. Rebuilding this from scratch after World War II was an opportunity to revert to its original 14th-century form without the subsequent "improvements" of the kind which churches everywhere accumulate with the passage of time. Two of the Polish kings are buried here, as is Henryk Sienkiewicz who won a Nobel Prize in 1905 for writing, among other things, *Quo Vadis*. The figure of Christ in one of the chapels supposedly grows hair that has to be cut every year by a Warsaw virgin, the source of any number of rather predictable jokes.

Marie Curie, the discoverer of radium, was born around the corner at 16 Freta Street, now a museum dedicated to her life and work. Also worth seeing

is the **Church and Convent of the Blessed Sacrament Sisters**, founded in 1688 by the wife (and queen) of John Sobieski, the hero of the siege of Vienna.

The passage between the cathedral and the Royal Castle, along **Dziekania Street**, was roofed over as a precaution after an attempt on the life of King Sigismund III Vasa. He it was who was responsible for moving the Polish capital from Cracow to Warsaw, and fittingly his statue was the first monument to be restored after the war. The pieces of the original column are on display in the **Mariensztat Market Square**.

The **Royal Castle** was destroyed in 1944. Communism, naturally, had more urgent priorities, so rebuilding it did not commence until 1971. The scale of the job was such that it was not completed until 1984. Canaletto's views of Warsaw in the 18th century were closely consulted by architects while Warsaw was being reconstructed, as were the works of his nephew Bernardo Bellotto. An urn in the chapel contains the heart of Tadeusz Kosciuszko, who led the

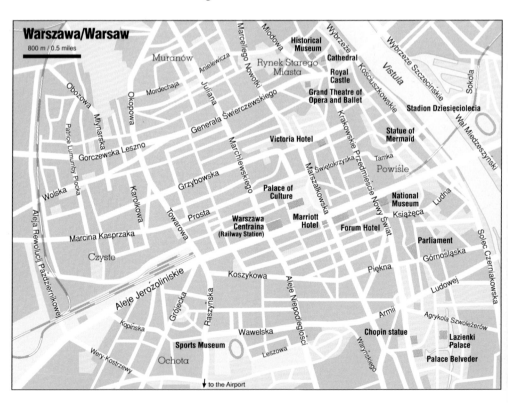

Polish assault on the Russians in an early bid for independence.

Before leaving this corner of the city, walk down **Dluga Street** to a newish-looking monument. It stands above the manhole into which, in the Warsaw uprising of September 1944, no fewer than 5,300 insurgents lowered themselves to make their way through the sewers to the city centre.

On leaving the castle square, the royal route begins by following Krakowskie Przedmiescie, in some respects the most historic street in the city. There is a statue of Copernicus (1473–1543) by the Dane, Bertel Thorvaldsen, and the route has close associations with Frédéric Chopin, whose heart was re-patriated after his death and placed in a pillar of the **Holy Cross Church**.

Before following the royal route through the change from Krakowskie Przedmiescie to Nowy Swiat (New World Street), it may be worth diverting to some of the other sights down side-streets. It will be necessary to back-track a short distance to pick up, in

A typical small shop in Warsaw.

Teatralny Square, the colossal **Grand Theatre of Opera and Ballet** and the **Monument to the Heroes of Warsaw**. The theatre was a total wreck after the war; the monument is to the civilians who died in it.

Nowy Swiat, to resume the royal route, has two claims to fame. The first is No. 45, the **birthplace of Joseph Conrad** (Korzeniowski) who wrote the first of his famous novels in English before he had ever heard the language from the lips of native-speakers. The second is **Blikle**, confectioners and pur-veyors (particularly) of widely admired doughnuts. Blikle bags are flaunted in much the same way as the Harrods equivalent in London.

The **National Museum** is a vast place filled with classical and contemporary art, although pride of place is given to the Faras frescoes discovered in the Sudan by Polish archaeologists. The attraction of the adjacent **Polish Army Museum** for military-minded Western-ers is the array of Warsaw Pact kit, often seen on TV but seldom in the flesh.

The continuation of Nowy Swiat is **Al. Ujazdowskie**, probably Warsaw's most elegant street. Most of the embas-sies are along here, as are the **Polish Parliament** (Sjem) and **Senate**.

Beyond the Trasa Lazienkowska is the **Ujazdowski Palace**, now a museum but previously the summer residence of the Wasa kings. The **Lazienki**, or Pal-ace on the Lake, on the other hand, was the private residence of Poland's last king, Stanislaw August Poniatowski, who was given the job on the strength of being one of Catherine the Great's more satisfactory lovers.

The **Orangery** is an authentic 18th-century court theatre. Regular piano re-citals are given in summer at the foot of the **Chopin Memorial**. **Belveder**, at the edge of the lake, is the official residence of the present President of Poland.

Ul. Belwederska takes the royal route out of town to **Wilanow**, the so-called Versailles of Poland and the home of the dashing King John Sobieski. His life is the subject of a *son et lumière* show. The palace is still used for state occasions and there is a good collection of posters in the museum. Visitors may like to know that there are three good restaurants at hand here: Wilanow, Kuznia Krolewska and the Café Hetmanskaya.

Until World War II, Warsaw had the world's largest Jewish community. The Monument to the Heroes of the Ghetto is a simple slab of dark granite on **ul. Zamenhofa** in the Muranow district, where the ghetto used to be. Muranow was completely flattened in retaliation for the uprising in April 1943. The site is now occupied by unremarkable high-rise blocks of flats. The only synagogue to have survived the war is situated in **Okopowa Street**.

One of the most popular excursions from Warsaw is to **Zelazowa Wola**, Chopin's birthplace. The house in which he grew up is now an inn-cum-museum. On most summer evenings, a piano recital is laid on in the adjoining park. Chopin's baptism certificate is preserved in the church at **Brochowo** were his parents were married.

Cracow: Poland's third-largest city (pop: 800,000) and former capital is an appealing town for tourists. Unlike Warsaw, it survived World War II relatively unscathed and it is on the list of UNSECO's top 12 cultural centres.

Every hour on the hour, a bugle call from the spire of the **Church of the Virgin Mary** peters out after four short notes, just as it did one day in the 13th century when the city look-out attempted to blow a warning that the Mongols were about to attack and, while doing so, took an arrow in the throat. Cracow had been a busy trading settlement on the River Vistula for 300 years before the Mongols ransacked it on that occasion. In the year 1000 it became a bishopric and from 1083 the Polish kings used Wawel Castle as their residence. The Jagiellonian University was founded in 1364, but in 1611 King Sigismund III transferred his capital to Warsaw.

The pride of Cracow is its marketplace, **Rynek Glowny**, which has at its centre a 100-yard long Gothic **Draper's Hall**, originally built in the 14th century but subsequently modified by Italian Renaissance architects. The ground floor still functions as a market, but the up-stairs section has been converted into a gallery of Polish painting.

The tower of the **Town Hall** is also 14th-century, but the hall itself was unfortunately demolished in 1820. The replacement building is now one section of the **Cracow History Museum**. It is from the tower of the church on the market square that the bugler does his stuff each hour. The altarpiece inside is quite extraordinary: a gilded and painted polyptych 36 ft (11 metres) high and 42ft (13 metres) wide, the work of Wit Stwosz in the 15th century.

Wawel Castle and **Cathedral** are on a limestone hill above the Vistula. The heart of the castle, started in the 10th century, is a rectangular Renaissance building with 71 halls and a courtyard surrounded by beautiful arcades. The state rooms, adorned with Flemish tapestries, the crown jewels and the armoury, as well as a collection of Oriental art, are open to visitors. Two of the prize exhibits are the jagged "Szczerbiec" sword held by the kings at their coronations and some fancy Turkish

One piece of history made in 1989 was Poland's victory in the Miss World contest.

tents captured by King John Sobieksi at the siege of Vienna.

The cathedral opposite the castle was begun in the 14th century, and this is where the Polish kings were crowned and buried. No fewer than 18 chapels lead off the nave, the most renowned being the Sigismund Chapelwhich has a perfect gilt dome. The **Holy Cross Chapel** contains the tombs of King Casimir and Poland's patron saint, St Stanislaw. The cathedral bell, known as Sigismund, was cast out of cannon captured in 1520 and is reserved for special occasions such as in 1983 when Cardinal Wojtyla of Cracow returned as Pope John Paul II, the first non-Italian to be elected to the post for over 400 years.

Small streets at the foot of **Castle Hill** contain some of Cracow's finest architecture. Kazimierz, further out, was once the Jewish quarter governed by a separate set of by-laws. It was a thriving place until 1941 when the inhabitants were taken to the extermination camps. They left behind seven synagogues and two cemeteries. **Boznica Stara** (the Old Synagogue) has been restored and has a small Jewish museum.

Except for the **Barbican** and **St Florian Gate**, Cracow's medieval fortifications were removed in the 19th century and replaced by the "Planty" green belt. **Ul. Florianska** was part of the royal route from the castle. The museum in this street has paintings of many scenes in Polish history by the artist Jan Matejko (1839–93) while the nearby Czartoryski in Sw. Jana boasts nothing less than a Leonardo da Vinci, and Rembrandt's *Landscape with the Good Samaritan*. The Café Jama Michalika attracts a bohemian crowd.

The **Jagiellonian University**, to which the lovely Princess Jadwiga left all her money, produced Copernicus, whose statue is in the park opposite the **Collegium Novum**. There is a special point of interest to the Jagiellonion Globe in the museum which occupies part of the university's arcaded courtyard. It was made in 1510 and, as far as anyone knows, was the first globe ever to show the American continent.

Cracow's market square and Draper's Hall.

PRAGUE

"I can see a great city, whose fame will reach the stars," declared Princess Libussa as she stood with outstretched arms on a precipice above the Vltava River. She was the mythical beauty who was reputed to have summoned an unsuspecting plough-hand, still wearing his boots, to found Bohemia's Premyslid dynasty, starting with good King Wenceslas I (903–35).

This version of events overlooks the fact that the shadowy historical figure of one Samo, the victor over the Avars in about 620, established his capital at Vysehrad a short distance away, but in any case by the 14th century Prague was the grandest city in Europe, a marvel of Gothic architecture. Three centuries later, having acquired a certain notoriety for defenestration, the fancy term for the basic business of throwing people out of windows, Prague was embellished with the finest baroque building of the age.

In spite of the city's position at the centre of all the religious and political convulsions which have surged across Europe's east-west axis, including World War II and the Soviet invasion in 1968, Prague survives in an almost pristine condition, a cross-section of all the grand themes of Western civilisation.

Removed from the mainstream of tourism for four decades, Prague proved irresistible to Westerners as soon as the Iron Curtain lifted, and it soon began attracting 4 million visitors a year, particularly Americans, as well as itinerant pedlars and stallholders from Russia and former Yugoslavia, who had to be stopped from cluttering up **Charles IV Bridge**.

This celebrated bridge, named after the enlightened king of Bohemia (1316-78) who held his court in the city, is the best place to start a city tour. High on the west bank is **Hradcany Castle**, Prague's Acropolis and the seat of political power from the 12th century onwards. Be-

Left, the city's Charles Bridge by night.

Prague 267

neath it on the same side of the river is **Mala Strana**, which means "Lesser Town"; it originally caught the civilian overflow from the castle but, after a fire in 1541, it was rebuilt in full Renaissance splendour. On the east bank just opposite the castle is **Stare Mesto**, or Old Town, whose walls enclosed the first phase of Charles IV's bold building programme.

It was obvious even then that space in the old town was limited, so Charles planned the adjacent **Nove Mesto**, or New Town, to the south as a separate district. These plans were not fully realised until the construction of modern Prague in the 19th and early 20th centuries. We shall here track down the sights of Prague in that order.

The Charles Bridge was thrown across the river at what was a traditional crossing point. Archaeological finds confirm human settlement along the banks as early as the 4th century BC, which predates the shadowy Samo with his settlement at Vysehrad. Whether or not Princess Libussa and her ploughman husband existed, there is no doubt about the Premyslids developing the Hradcany site or Charles IV building his castle, modelled on the Louvre, on top of an older one.

The king's principal architects were Master Matthew of Arras, whom Pope Clement recommended, and after his death in 1352 a young Swabian named Peter Parler, who was not only an architect but a sculptor and wood-carver. Together they produced St Vitus's Cathedral and the Charles Bridge. The other great works of Charles's reign were the castle of Karlstein outside Prague and the Benedictine monastery of Emmaus.

Much of their work was destroyed or damaged in 1541 in a fire which began in the Mala Strana and worked up the hill. Legend has it that the fire was started deliberately by Ferdinand I, the first Habsburg king of Bohemia, as a massively indiscriminate way of destroying some embarrassing public records. In any case, a large part of Prague had to be rebuilt afterwards.

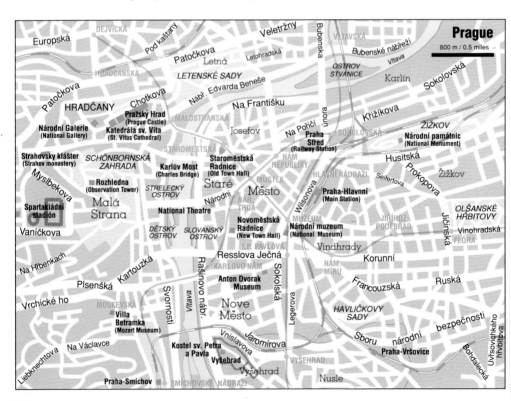

The main entrance to the castle complex is on **Hradcanske Namesti**, or Castle Square. Entry through the gate, guarded by Titans which are 1912 copies of 1768 originals, leads to a series of courtyards. Off the second of these is the **Castle Gallery** with a collection of Rubens, Titian, Tintoretto and others which once belonged to Charles I of England and were acquired by Rudolf II. They were presumed lost until found by accident in 1962.

The third courtyard is dominated by the towering Gothic spires of the **St Vitus's Cathedral**. Construction started in 1344 on top of the remains of 10th- and 11th-century churches. It was again interrupted by the Hussite rebellion, again by the 1541 fire and the Turkish wars, and eventually finished only in 1929. The Wenzel chapel with walls studded with semi-precious stones and ancient frescoes survived the fire. The ring on the door is reputed to be from an earlier church in which St Wenceslas was murdered by his brother Boleslav in 935. It is said he clung to this ring as life ebbed away. His tomb and relics are in the chapel; his statue, by Peter Parler's nephew, is dated 1373.

The adjoining Martinic chapel contains the remains of one of the councillors defenestrated in 1618, while the Sternbeck chapel has the tombs of Ottokar I (1230–53) and II (1253–78). The principal royal mausoleum, however, is in the centre of the Cathedral (before the high altar).

To one side of the cathedral behind a deceptively modest entrance is the great **Vladislav Hall**, built at the end of the 15th century as an indoor arena for tournaments. The hall gives access to the Statthalterei (council room) where the Protestant nobles gathered in 1618 to remonstrate with Catholic councillors. A certain Count Thurni suggested that the two Catholic ringleaders, Councillors Martinic and Slavata, be thrown out of the window.

Across the square behind the cathedral is the **St George's Church and Monastery** whose towers are relics of 970. It contains early and baroque Bo-

Old Town Square.

hemian art. Beyond is the **Zlata Ulicka** (Golden Lane), a row of small houses built into the castle walls after the 1541 fire and now lively with antique and book shops. These were occupied by palace craftsmen, and they were joined for a while by the writer Franz Kafka.

The **castle keep** at the end of the lane was named after an unfortunate knight who was locked up in the dungeon below, Dalibor of Kozojed. At the end of Jirska street, which runs parallel with Zlata Ulicka, are the **palace gardens** where there is an astounding collection of marble garden architecture culminating in a flight of stairs with a water basin at the bottom.

Although it is possible to leave the Hradcany via the Old Castle Staircase, it is worth returning to the square at the main entrance for the baroque **Archbishop's Palace**, the **National Gallery** in the Sternbeck Palace and the **Museum of Military History** in the Schwarzenberg (formerly Lobkovic) Palace. The summer tournaments held in the courtyard of the military museum

are thoroughly good entertainment.

A narrow lane leads to the **Loretto Square** with the **Loretto Church** and shrine on one side and the **Cernin Palace** on the other. The church was the gift of a Czech noblewoman who knew that the miraculous transfer of the Holy House of Nazareth, Christ's birthplace, to Loretto in the 13th century saved the Italian town from the infidel. She felt Prague needed a copy and commissioned the younger Dienzenhofer. The church contains a monstrance, the "Sun of Prague", set with 6,222 diamonds.

The main road through Mala Strana down to the Charles Bridge is **Mostecka** (Bridge Street), flanked by winding streets and small houses which survived the 1541 fire and by the mansions (many now embassies and diplomatic residences) which replaced those that did not. The most impressive of the latter is the **Wallenstein Palace** (1623–45) with its art gallery and the gardens in which concerts are sometimes staged. The **Church of the Infant of Prague** (Prazskeho Jezulatko) has a wax effigy

Left, a goldsmith's shop. **Right**, artist at work.

figurine of the infant Jesus which receives a change of costume according to the Christian calendar. When the infant started performing miracles, replica churches sprang up all over the world.

The **Charles Bridge** which links the Castle and Lesser Town to the Old Town is as a tourist attraction. The 30 statues lining either side were not in Parler's original 1357 design; most were added in the early 18th century. That of St John Nepomuk, Bohemia's patron saint, was the victim of a variation on Prague's tradition of defenestration. A marble slab and cross mark the spot where Nepomuk plunged on the orders of King Wenceslas IV in 1393. The other notable depontification concerned Jaroslav Hasek, the hell-raising creator of *The Good Soldier Schweik*. His was actually a faked suicide to throw creditors off his scent.

The most famous landmark on the east bank of the river, **Wenceslas Square**, is a broad and sloping boulevard that links Old Town and New Town. Charles IV planned it as the horse market. **Na prikope**, which runs

at right-angles across the bottom, follows the line of the old city moat, and the 1475 **Powder Tower,** rebuilt in the 19th century, is part of the fortifications.

Celetna Street, running past the tower, was once on the royal processional route which filed through the Old Town and across the Charles Bridge up to the Hradcany. Celetna Street is now closed to traffic and its buildings restored, so visitors could do worse than follow the old route. It is generously lined with specialist shops, coffee bars and wine cellars.

Celetna Street enters the delightful Old Town Square and its adjacent Little Square, the latter famous for the astronomical clock on the **Old Town Hall** (Staromestská radnice). Nikolaus von Kadan made the original clock in 1410 and, although it has been restored several times, the Gothic detailing is 15th and 16th century. The fact that the clock often broke down between the aborted Prague Spring and Havel's Velvet Revolution was regarded as heavily symbolic. The Old Town Hall was built

The National Museum from Wenceslas Square.

in 1338. The groups of statues in the centre of the square were erected in 1915 to commemorate the 500th anniversary of the burning to death of the religious reformer Jan Hus. The setting is appropriate because the **Tyn Church** on the square was the symbol of the Hussites who subsequently precipitated a civil war. The interior of the church is highly baroque. The nearby **Kinsky Palace** is the work of the famous Fisher von Erlach.

It is worth backtracking to the left from the Old Town Square in order to see the **Carolinum**, or Charles University. The main part of the modern university has been moved elsewhere, but a few faculties remain here where, in one of the lecture rooms, Jan Hus, who was rector in 1402, conducted his "disputations" of current religious orthodoxy.

Resuming at the Old Town Square, either Parizska or Maislova streets leads to the **Prague ghetto**, the oldest in Europe. It dates back to at least the 10th century, in other words to the time of St Wenceslas and some four centuries be-

fore Prague took on its recognisable form under Charles IV. The synagogue was built about 1270 and the old cemetery presents the extraordinary sight of more than 12,000 graves crammed into layers one on top of another.

The walls which separated the ghetto from the rest of the city were pulled down in the late 18th century. Its history is told in the **Jewish State Museum**; the **Pinkas Synagogue** contains the names of the 77,000 Bohemian and Moravian Jews who were murdered by the Nazis.

The former Red Army Square between the ghetto and the river is now named after Jan Palach, the student who burnt himself to death in protest against the 1968 Soviet invasion. Further along the river, just beyond the Charles Bridge, is the highly impressive **Krizovnicke Namesti**, or Square of the Knights of the Cross, with its bastion of Catholicism, the Clementinum. This was the Jesuit headquarters and is now the **State Library**. The more modest baroque church is that of St Francis, also known and the **Church of the Crusaders**.

To climb the hill of **Wenceslas Square** towards the statue of St Wenceslas and the National Museum is to enter the New Town. The square is an entertainment in itself. This is where everyone congregates and people-watching is accordingly fruitful. Of the numerous vantage points, the **Hotel Europa** is incomparably the best.

The main museums, theatres, shops and hotels are in the New Town and attest to Prague's illustrious musical past. In Lazenska 2 a **Museum of Musical Instruments** is the second largest of its kind in the world. Villa Amerika, built in 1720 in Ke Karluva 20, contains the **Anton Dvorak Museum**. The **Mozart Museum** is in Villa Bertramka where the composer lived, on the opposite bank, south of Mala Strana.

The magnificently restored **National Theatre** is in the New Town on the river. Coach parties are invariably dropped off at **U Kalicha**, the inn associated with the Good Soldier Schweik. His admirers will feel obliged to look in, although there are any number of other bars and inns.

Left, the Tyn Church. **Right**, typical steps in the Malá Strana.

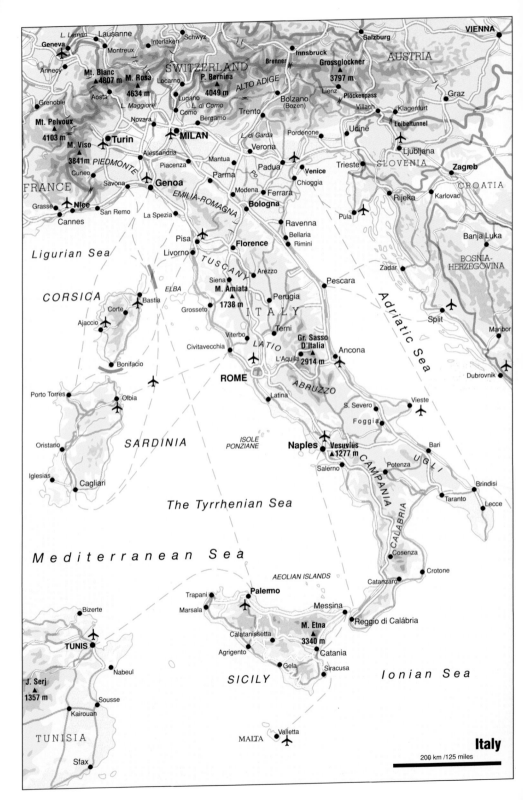

Italy

200 km /125 miles

ITALY

The traveller in Italy will frequently have the feeling of *déjà vu,* for many of its landmarks are well known and many of its medieval towns and city centres look as if they have been built as copies of Renaissance paintings. But the traveller will not feel alone: in summer the major attractions, such as Rome, Florence and Venice, are a heady mix of heat, noise and tourists, and if possible visitors should come at other times of the year.

Italy is also a lively, modern country (Milan is the fashion centre of Europe) and the pace, particularly on the roads, can be fast. The cities are all best explored on foot. If you are driving, head for the Centro Storico (historic centre) or Duomo (cathedral), and find a *parcheggio* to park.

The 116,500 sq. mile (301,000 sq. km) Italian boot which dips its toes into the middle of the Mediterranean has the Appenine hills as its backbone and is divided between the more businesslike north and the Mezzogiorno, the poorer, agricultural south. It is said that a man's assets in the north are his shares and property. In the south a man's only asset is his honour: thus even a poor man can be rich. The two halves are divided by Rome, which is on roughly the same parallel as New York.

There are few idle pastimes more rewarding than observing Italians going about their lives. They are past-masters at showing off, at preserving *la bella figura*. Both their public and social life is intricate and intriguing. Governments lurch from one crisis to another and scandals regularly invade public lives, usually in the form of corruption and the Mafia. And while women visitors may find young men oppressively predatory, a woman's role is crucial at home. "No Italian who has a family is ever alone," wrote Luigi Barzini in *The Italians*. "He finds in it a refuge to lick his wounds after defeat, or an arsenal and a staff for his victorious drives."

Preceding pages: Florence's skyline at dusk; traditional costumes at the Quintana Festival.

AROUND ITALY

The majority of travellers crossing the Alps into Italy use the **Brenner Pass** from Austria; its alpine landscape of wooden chalets and onion-domed churches is more German than Italian. The people of **Bressanone**, **Merano** and **Bolzano** are South Tyroleans. The majority speak German, their cuisine is Austrian and their manners Teutonic. Fiercely independent, they have been granted a measure of autonomy by the Italian government.

Farther to the east is the Vittorio Veneto region with the raking Dolomites, an alpine idyll of isolated valleys, villages, wood carvers, hermits and picturesque ski resorts such as **Cortina d'Ampezzo** and the **Marmolata**.

The Brenner Highway runs past castles, fortifications and independence monuments to medieval **Trento** with its 12th-century cathedral. The highway leaves **Lake Garda** on the right before it reaches **Verona**, the gateway to Italy, and the city in which Romeo and Juliet are said to have lived and loved.

South of Verona begins the great Italian plain in the Po Valley, with its irrigation channels and ghostly poplar trees. This fertile region between Milan in the west and Rovigo in the east is Italy's larder as well as its fruit and vegetable garden.

The Brenner Highway links up with the Autostrada del Sole (the Sun Motorway) near **Modena**. This 780-mile (1,200-km) artery, beginning at Milan, runs the length of the peninsula right down to Reggio di Calabria on the Strait of Messina at Italy's toe.

Crossing the Alps over the **St Gothard Pass** and under its 10-mile (16-km) tunnel or over the **St Bernard Pass** (where Hannibal supposedly entered Italy with elephants) leads one down to Milan on a road wedged between the scenic lakes **Maggiore** and **Como**.

Milan, with 4 million inhabitants, is Italy's biggest city. It is also the most industrialised city, a bastion of Italian fashion, a citadel of music (La Scala Opera House) and noted for its cathedral, the biggest Gothic construction in Italy.

Milan, **Turin** and **Genoa** form Italy's industrial triangle, the largest concentration of industry in the country. Genoa, the ancient sea republic near the chic resort of **Portofino**, is still the country's busiest port. Between the three cities trucks shunt goods back and forth on a network of highways.

Roads are the most popular means of transport in Italy (Italians are passionate drivers), though railways are cheaper.

The Adriatic coast: Italy's "Adria" begins at **Trieste** on the border of Slovenia in former Yugoslavia. The city has been subjected to constant ownership disputes. Its lively harbour and shipyards have quietened in recent years. Past **Venice**, south of the Po, is **Ravenna**, the 4th-century capital of the western Roman Empire under Theoderic the Goth, whose mausoleum still stands. The city is a gem of Byzantine art. Its 6th-century Basilica San Vitale, a domed octagonal structure, is a masterpiece. Dante

Left, Catholic Italy has loosened up. **Right**, St Francis of Assisi.

is buried beside the Basilica in a touchingly simple grave.

Barely half an hour's drive inland from **Rimini**, the Adriatic's principal resort, lies the world's smallest republic – **San Marino**. This mini-country has just 18,000 inhabitants and was made famous by its fierce independence and the variety of its stamps (which, together with tourism and farming, provide the main revenue).

Small it may be, but since the 5th century San Marino has managed, with wile and guile, to maintain its sovereign status, while other republics on the peninsula have lost theirs.

In 1861 Abraham Lincoln accepted honorary citizenship of the republic though this did not prevent the Americans from bombing it during World War II when Germans troops were in occupation.

The capital, also called San Marino, has just over 3,000 residents, and it is run by its Grand Council, whose 60 members are elected every five years. Women were given the right to vote and the right to hold public office in 1960 and 1973 respectively.

The Adriatic Highway, which follows the coast, leads past the buzzing port of **Ancona**, and then bypasses the panoramic **Gargano**, the spur on the Italian "boot", a promontory of white beaches and forests.

The coastal stretch from the Gargano to **Otranto** on the heel of Italy's boot is the province of Apulia, the most romantic part of the Adriatic. In **Barletta**'s main street stands the Colossus, the 15-foot (5-metre) bronze statue of an unknown Roman emperor, washed ashore from a Venetian shipwreck in the Middle Ages.

Trani has a fine Romanesque seaside cathedral; **Bari** is a bustling port; and at **Brindisi**, a departure point for ferries to Greece, a column marks the end of the Via Appia, the first and greatest of the ancient roads that lead to Rome. **Lecce** is the city of baroque, nicknamed "the Florence of Apulia"; **Alberobello** is the home of the dome-shaped "trulli" houses; and **Taranto**, on the gulf bear-

Left, a Renaissance warrior. **Right**, the Bay of Naples.

ing its name, was founded by the Spartans.

The south of Italy is the magic land of Magna Graecia, the ancient Greek colonies whose style and culture influenced the old Romans so much. What survives, apart from the legends, are the impressive skeletons of the old temples. The best of them are on the west coast on the plain of **Paestum**, south of **Salerno**, where the Greeks founded a medical school, not far from the famous Roman ruins at **Pompeii**.

Calabria, at the foot of the boot, is a jigsaw of villages and towns, a land where people eke out a miserable existence from a rocky soil and a few haphazard industries.

The islands: From **Reggio di Calabria** ferries cross the strait to **Messina** in **Sicily**. This fertile island has always been at the confluence of the Mediterranean world, serving as a springboard for ambitious conquerors. It is best seen by road: though the ever-smouldering volcano **Etna** provides the most dramatic single vantage point. Around the central

town of Enna, the country is one rolling plain of golden cornstalks. Near **Piazza Armerina**, in the heart of the island, some of the finest Roman mosaics have been found at the Villa Romana at Casale. One mosaic, proving that there's nothing new under the sun, shows a group of young women playing beachball and wearing bikinis. **Palermo**, Sicily's capital, is a turbulent place, famous both for its Mafia connections and for some wonderful architecture.

Off **Milazzo**, on Sicily's northeastern tip, are the **Aeolian islands**, where the ancient Greeks believed the god Aeolus kept the winds imprisoned. Now a popular holiday resort, the scattered islands include **Stromboli**, which spews lava into the night.

It takes from 8 to 12 hours to reach **Sardinia** by ferry. The major port of embarkation is **Civitavecchia**, 37 miles (60 km) north of Rome. A good but lonely road circles this island where steep coastlines, crystalline bays and jagged mountains vie for attention. Its culture is closer to Spain.

Villa Romana's "bikini girls" in action.

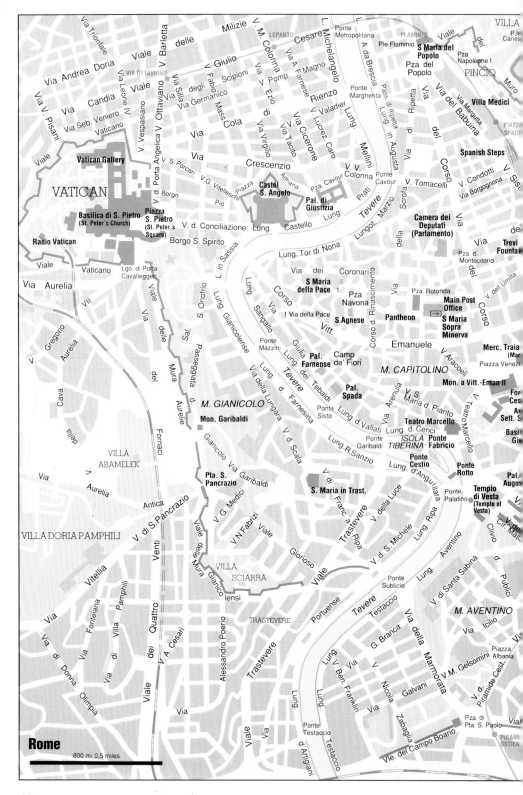

Rome

800 m/ 0.5 miles

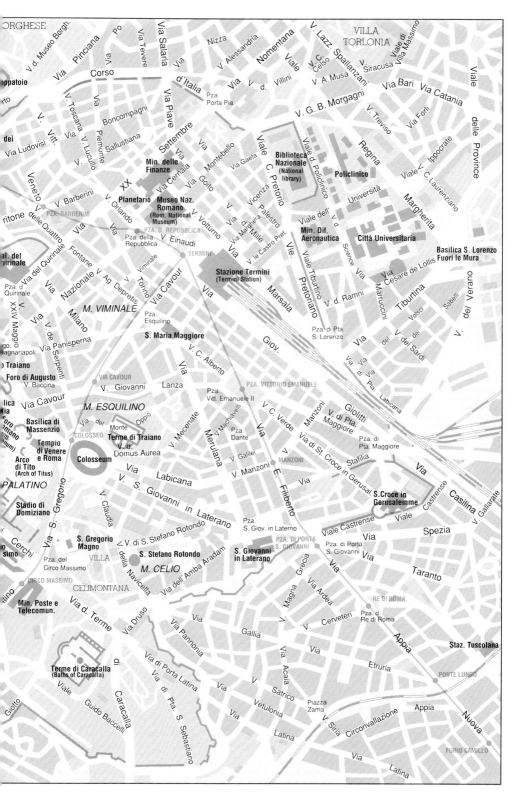

ROME

Watching the sunset from the Pincio lookout, three men heatedly discussed her charms and faults. The first cursed her as a tramp and a vamp, the second called her a coquette and the third, ecstatically gazing down at her, cried that she was the Mother of All, that she was eternal.

The object of their dispute was Rome, a city which has its magnificent and its seamy sides. They are ensconced in the stumps of ruins, broken walls, crumpled cornices and proud quarterstones. These can be found in the forums, the decorative squares built by various emperors, the tombstones along the **Via Appia Antica**, the road that leads to the Adriatic port of Brindisi, the circuses of Maxentius and Maximus, the arched and elevated aqueducts that carried water into the ancient city, the remnants of the Aurelian wall which circled Rome, a barrier against invaders. Some are like giant sets of decayed teeth, upon which one stumbles suddenly.

At times the city smells, mouldy with decay and damp, littered with refuse, her walls smeared with graffiti.

The city has many faces: the imperial face of the Caesars, the Renaissance and Baroque facade of the **Centro Storico**, the historical centre of the city, the cement face of rabbit warren apartment blocks on the fringes and the face of piety, tolled in a morning Mass, the midday Angelus and the Ave Maria in the evening.

Stairs and statues: In the heart of the city, at the southern end of the **Piazza Venezia**, two stairways lead to **Campidoglio** (Capitol Hill), aptly symbolising the rivalry between State and Church. On the right is the gently rising ramp, designed by Michelangelo in 1536 for the reception of the Emperor Charles V. On the left, 120 steep steps lead to the **Church of Aracoeli**, built in 1348 in gratitude for Rome's delivery from the plague. The latter suggests that life is a weary pilgrimage that leads eventually to Heaven, the former, theatrical and

worldly, is far easier to climb. Capitol Hill reflects Michelangelo's passion for antiquity. He designed the square to rise, almost imperceptibly, towards a bronze statue of emperor Marcus Aurelius (161–180 AD).

The **Senatorial Palace** faces the stairway. Today it is still a town hall and together with the two palaces on either side (both of them museums), it creates a visual harmony worthy of the hill from which the ancient world was once ruled. Justly, the **Capitoline museums** contain some of the greatest treasures prised from ancient Rome, among them the *Dying Gaul*, the *Marble Faun* (which prompted Hawthorne's novel of the same name), the comely *Capitoline Venus*, and the *Lupa* (the She-Wolf who suckled Romulus and Remus). This bronze sculpture of the symbol of Rome was, until her fall, mounted on a column above the city.

When the night steals up, spreading a velvet mantle over the city, it is time to squeeze through the archway between the Senatorial Palace and the Palazzo

Nuovo for a glimpse into Rome's glorious past.

Ghosts of past glory: On a terrace lookout behind the **Town Hall** and below the **Tarpeian Rock** (from which traitors were hurled) one has the best view of the **Forum Romanum**. Over the last century this great centre of Rome was rescued from rubble and dung from below the fields on which cows, sheep and goats had been grazing in tranquillity for generations.

In the fading light, and with some imagination, the stark columns and ghostly white blocks of weather-beaten marble take on flesh and life. The Forum emerges for a few minutes again as the magnificent commercial, religious and social centre of the world. And if there are pieces missing the blame must be placed on successive popes and the noble families of Rome, who, for more than a millennium, have used the Forum as a convenient quarry, providing the stones for their palaces.

The foreground is dominated by the columns of the **Temple of Saturn** with their broken architraves. On the left is the arch built to honour the emperor Septimius Severus. In front of it are the remnants of the two Rostrae from which the great orators addressed the populace, men like Cicero or Mark Antony who (according to Shakespeare) made from here his impassioned funeral speech after Caesar's assassination, beginning: "Friends, Romans, countrymen, lend me your ears…"

On the very far left, sombre, square and red-bricked, stands the last curia, the Roman Senate, Parliament and voice of the people until the emperors reduced it to the task of rubber-stamping their edicts. Halfway between the **Arch of Septimius Severus** and the Colosseum in the background is the **Temple of Antoninus and Faustina**, built by the pious emperor to honour the virtuousness of his wife Faustina, though he was said to be the only man in Rome unaware he was constantly being cuckolded. In the centre of the Forum stands the rotund Temple of the Vestal Virgins whose task it was to keep the Eternal

Rome 2,000 years ago.

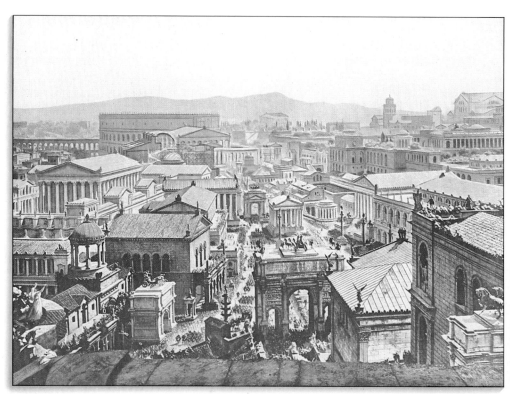

Flame burning. If they broke their 30-year vow of chastity, they were punished with life entombment. If they behaved, their privileges were many, their social status equal to that of the empress herself.

A symbol of oppression: At the far end of the Forum rises the **Arch of Titus**. For Jews it has been a symbol for almost 2,000 years of their enslavement and humiliation at the hand of the pagan and later Christian world. Erected to commemorate Titus's capture of Jerusalem in AD 70, it marks the start of the Jewish exodus from their homeland. The troops of Titus brought back in chains thousands of Jews as slaves. They were settled in what became the world's first Jewish ghetto, behind the **Teatro Marcello**, the towering wall on the right side of Capitol Hill.

The ghetto still buzzes with Jewish culture and commerce, inhabited today by the descendants of a people who can, proudly or sadly, trace their ancestry back to the days of ancient Rome. The Jews have always given the Arch a wide berth. It not only reminds them of the harsh Roman rule but the spite of the popes. Whenever a pope was elected and driven in triumph through the ancient city, he expected to be greeted by a garlanded Jewish convert to Christianity. The tradition prompted ever sceptical Romans to whisper that the token convert under the Arch was "always the same Jew".

Nearby stands the **Arch of Constantine**, built at a time when Roman art and culture had declined so badly that its ornaments had to be scavenged from the monuments of previous emperors.

The Colossus: Next to that arch, like a huge battleship cast in stone, rises the **Colosseum** which in its heyday seated 50,000 spectators in open stands. Sailors of the imperial navy worked ropes that moved enormous linen sails to shade and fan the excitable mob. The Colosseum, completed half a century after Nero's death, is inaccurately identified as the arena where the Christians were hurled to the lions. In reality the early martyrs (and the historian Gibbon main-

Constantine's Arch.

tained there were rather fewer than the Church would have people believe) died in the garden and circus of Nero across the Tiber in the Vatican. The Christians were eventually commemorated with a church, then a basilica and finally the headquarters of the Holy See – the Vatican State of today.

The Colosseum, on the other hand, was principally used for gladiatorial duels and elaborate water games with naked or scantily clad nymphs, sea monsters, huge floating orchestras and exhibitions of fornication. The ever more carnivalesque games pointed to the decadence and impending doom of imperial Rome.

But even today this brooding colossus is considered an enviable feat of architecture and engineering, designed with such foresight that the huge and unruly crowd could find their seats and disperse with ease through the 80 strategically located exits called *vomitoria*. As was the case with the Forum, popes and the aristocracy used the Colosseum as a quarry for their own constructions. Cannibalised, ransacked and abused, it still remains as Byron described in his poem *Childe Harold:*

Arches on arches! as it were that Rome, collecting the chief trophies of her line, would build up all her triumphs in one dome,
her Colosseum stands...

For the first Romans the **Tiber River** separated their "civilised" city from the barbarians on the other bank, known as **Trastevere** (across the Tiber). The Roman Empire – the expansion of Roman rule – began when the people of Rome crossed the river and subjugated the tribes and towns on the other side. They built bridges and a harbour where corn ships from the port of Ostia disgorged their precious cargos.

Today there is a lighthouse on the Trastevere side of the Tiber, on top of the **Gianicolo Park**. It flashes the green, white and red colours of Italy at night. The parapet in front of the lighthouse is a lookout and a rendezvous point for lovers. It provides a panorama of the city below in a state of suspended animation: silent, without traffic, like a

mirage. This impression can be quickly shattered by the shouts from the prisoners in the jail of Regina Coeli, just below the hill, communicating with relatives on the hill.

Beyond the river in a sea of churches, palaces and parks, pieced together like a mosaic, ochre, white and patchy pink, lies the Rome that is identified with the popes. They ruled it, some benevolently, some perfidiously, some with an iron fist, from the fall of the Roman Empire in the 5th and 6th centuries AD, to its reinstatement as capital of a unified Italy just over 100 years ago. Like ancient emperors they used the money of the Church, and sometimes their own, to embellish their prestige (and that of God) with temples, monuments and art.

The popes turned Rome into the Mecca of the arts, the Hollywood of the 15th, 16th and 17th centuries, a must for every artist who coveted fame and money. The Church, popes, cardinals and religious orders became the chief employers of the artists, together with the rich who might build or decorate a

Catering for a sweet tooth.

church in order to pave their way into paradise. These patrons demanded from the artists religious motifs, sometimes tempered with allegories from mythology. Only Florence and Venice, when their trade fortunes made them scoff at the ecclesiastical riches of Rome, offered equal or better pecuniary rewards to artists who were principally egoists, secondly narcissists and thirdly – with a few exceptions – opportunists.

Through this labyrinth of narrow alleys and convivial squares, rattled the gilded carriages of cardinals – the Princes of the Church. Through it drove *Il Bambino* (The Child), the wooden statuette of the baby Jesus, which is taken in its own velvet coach to the dying (today the *Bambino* uses a taxi). Through it drove the beautiful Vanozza Cattanei, mistress of Rodrigo Borgia who became Pope Alexander VI (1492–1503), the mother of Lucrezia and Cesare Borgia. Here popes and cardinals died mysteriously and he who greased the most palms (a practice known as simony) was often made pope. The profane and

the sacred were never closer than in Rome.

But there is also the little man's Rome, embodied in the *bottega*, the ground-level artisan and tradesmen shops that exist all over the historical centre, a tradition still alive today and which gives Rome that quaint air of village provinciality. Each *quartiere* (locality) in the city seems to have its own shoemaker, plumber, carpenter, laundry, grocer and fruit shop, all making it a self-contained unit in the maze of old Rome. Some Romans, like old villagers, never venture out of their *quartiere* where social life, as it has done for centuries, takes place in the piazza.

Rome is not remembered for the foibles of its people but those of its popes and artists. The people, rebelling in 1305 against papal tax levies and cruelty, forced Clement V to escape to Avignon in France – not the first nor the last time a pope fled popular wrath.

In 1527, Clement VII was forced to watch the sack of Rome from **Castel Sant' Angelo**, the mausoleum of the

The Colosseum.

emperor Hadrian on the bank of the Tiber. The mausoleum was first converted into a church, and later into a fortress to which the popes fled in times of popular unrest or war. When in danger, they simply ran along a walled-in passage connecting the castle with the Vatican.

Clement is said to have wept while the 30,000 German *Landsknechte* (mercenaries) of the Constable of Bourbon rampaged through Rome for 90 days in an outburst of senseless slaughter, unequalled by even the most savage of the barbarian invaders who plundered the city during the Dark Ages. According to one chronicler: "No female of any age or condition, nun or not, was left untouched in Rome."

Naked saint in the city of art: The years before and after the sack of Rome were the richest in the history of Italian art. They were the years of the High Renaissance, the era of Michelangelo, Leonardo da Vinci and Raphael. They were followed 100 years later by the genius of Bernini, Borromini, and others who,

rearranging the ancient sites and monuments, decorated Rome with some of the world's finest Baroque fountains, exciting churches and harmonious squares and palaces which have made the city so attractive: the Piazza Navona, the Campo de' Fiori, the Piazza Venezia, the Spanish Steps, Piazza Popolo, Piazza della Rotonda, Piazza Barberini and St Peter's Square.

The most notable of these is undoubtedly the **Piazza Navona**, a perfect blend of antiquity with baroque – the old and the new. Its horseshoe design faithfully adheres to the shape of the emperor Domitian's stadium (81–96 BC) used for athletic displays and chariot racing. Its baroque monuments are enveloped with legends of the rivalry between stormy Gianlorenzo Bernini, sculptor, architect and idol of 17th-century Rome, and the brooding, brilliant Borromini. The latter was the architect of the **Church of Saint Agnese** built on the spot where the 13-year-old saint was allegedly stripped naked in a brothel by a cheering crowd (in 1944 the church

Left, the Spanish Steps. Right, Piazza Navona.

belfry served as a hideout for a partisan radio station reporting on Nazi troop movements to the allies). Bernini designed the **Fountain of the Four Rivers** in the centre of the piazza and it is said he raised the hand of the River Plate so as to ward off the "falling" facade of the church built by his rival. To finance the church and fountain, Pope Innocent X levied a highly unpopular bread tax on the people of Rome which prompted the famous wall slogan: "If only the stones could turn to bread."

From the Piazza Navona one can walk down the **Via Giustiniana**, alongside the **Palazzo Madama**, which is the Italian Senate or Upper House. A little farther on is the **Piazza della Rotonda** with its Renaissance fountain obelisk of Rameses II and the Pantheon.

A Roman proverb says that people who visit Rome and do not see the **Pantheon** are asses. That may be so, the Romans are known not only for their arrogance but, like their ancestors, for their superstition.

Superstition prompted the Romans to build the Pantheon, a temple for all the gods, the known and the unknown ones. This they thought would make sure no strange foreign god harboured a grudge against them.

Although an inscription credits "Marcus Agrippa, son of Lucius, consul for the third time" for the construction of what has been called "this perfectest of all the antiquities", it was not until 1892, when French archaeologists were working on the base of the columns, that evidence came to light, in the form of coins, that Hadrian, one of the most brilliant Roman emperors, had designed it after the old Pantheon burned down. With a modesty so typical of this emperor he had left the ancient inscription.

Hadrian is also the architect of the vast villa that was named after him and which is outside Tivoli, 16 miles (30 km) from Rome. The villa boasts lavish decor and far-sighted architecture and engineering skill all set in idyllic surroundings.

The Pantheon's great wonder is its cupola, until this century the largest in

Below and right, Rome's "village life".

THE VATICAN

Rome and the Vatican have lived for more than one and a half millennia in symbiosis, not always perfect, not always happy, but always mutually rewarding. Rome is where the Church gained fame through its martyrs, where the emperor Constantine made Christianity the predominant religion in 337 AD. In return, the Vatican eventually gave Rome another empire, a spiritual one, at times almost as powerful as the worldly one lost to the barbarians.

Vatican is the name given to a hill on the right bank of the Tiber. There the emperor Nero completed a circus which Gaius had built and adorned with an obelisk brought from Egypt (the one which now rises in the middle of St Peter's Square). There Nero staged the cruel spectacle he succeeded in dreaming up by turning Christians into human torches. As a symbolic gesture Constantine awarded "the hill of martyrs" to the church where, over the grave of St Peter, the church built its first temple, which

was later enlarged and eventually replaced by the vast complex that exists today: St Peter's is the largest church in Christendom.

Some 700 million Catholics are governed from this walled-in hill known as **Vatican City**, whose boundaries were defined by a the Lateran Treaty of 1929. It is a sovereign state with just 365 citizens but nearly 2,000 employees. It has its own supermarkets, petrol stations, banks, a radio network in 37 languages, its own number plates, passports, postal service, railway station, heliport.

It is virtually impossible for the ordinary visitor to penetrate the walled-in Vatican City. He may climb the 244 stairs to the top of **St Peter's Dome** for a glance, not only over Rome, but into the Vatican gardens; he may buy the coveted Vatican stamps and mail postcards at the Vatican post office; he may visit the **Vatican Museum** or, if he is lucky, obtain a ticket for the weekly Wednesday audience with the Pope; and he may attend the Angelus blessing at midday on Sundays in **St Peter's Square**.

What the visitor may see, at a price, is the treasure of the Vatican. Its vast museums contain the world's greatest artistic treasure chest, including the papal coaches and the Collection of Modern Religious Art laid out in 55 rooms from the Borgia Apartment to the floor below the Sistine Chapel.

The Sistine Chapel is a source of wonder and awe. On the wall of the chapel where popes are still elected, Michelangelo painted the *Last Judgement* in which the good ascend to Heaven and the bad are cast into Hell. And on the ceiling he painted the *Creation*, where God's and Adam's fingers touch.

The library contains 65,000 manuscripts, among them the oldest new testament from the 4th century and original manuscripts from Virgil.

At the age of 72 Michelangelo designed the cupola of Saint Peter's to cover the sky above the bones of the first apostle and those of his successors, the popes, in their subterranean tombs. In the central nave is the seated bronze statue of a black Peter whose foot has been almost eroded by the innumerable touches and kisses.

The papal summer residence at **Castel Gandolfo** in the Alban hills is also an enclave of the Vatican State. Fleeing Rome at its hottest period, the Pope lives here from mid-July until early September. ■ A papal audience.

the world. The impression of immense space it creates is due to the fact that its 142-foot (43-metre) diameter is equal to its height. The cupola's huge weight was sustained with an intricate system of relieving arches and by the use of light tufa and pumice stone at the top and heavy material, concrete, travertine and brick, at the bottom. The cupola tapers from 19 feet (5.9 metres) at the base to 5 feet (1.5 metres) around the oculus, the central all-seeing eye, the symbol of a divinity that is superior to all men.

Steps and shops: The Spanish Steps leading up to the **Church of the Trinità dei Monti** are associated with a different era of Rome's history. In the last century, the Steps became the haunt for artists and writers who lived and worked on or near them and met for cups of coffee or *digestivi* at the **Café Greco** in the **Via Condotti**.

The American author and sculptor W.W. Story vividly described the famous scene in the 19th century: "There you may see every night representatives of art from all parts of the world, in all kinds of hats, from the conical black felt with its velvet ribbon to the French stovepipe, and in every variety of coat from the Polish and German nondescript, all befrogged and tagged, to the shabby American dress coat, with crumpled tails, and with every cut of hair and beard from that of Peter the Hermit, unkempt and uncut, to the moustache and beard of Anthony Vandyck…"

Shelley, Keats, Byron, Ludwig of Bavaria (king and artist), Hans Christian Andersen and many others sat there. Samuel F.B. Morse even rested there after humping his painting pack across the Alban hills in the days before he invented the telegraph. These were the times when a model cost 50 cents a day, and when John S. Saratt, a key figure in the conspiracy against President Lincoln, was discovered under a false name in the Papal Guards. Future American President James A. Garfield called Rome "my country forevermore," James Fenimore Cooper wrote "to leave Italy was like quitting one's own home" and Quaker and artist Benjamin West

shocked the Roman snobs at a party when he exclaimed, on viewing the "divine" Belvedore torso: "How like a Mohawk warrior."

The Spanish Steps were once dominated by Beppe, the legless beggar-king of Rome. Here artists hired their models, some of whom were durable old pros like the famous Mincucci who, at the age of 70, had posed for three generations of artists and could still hold a steady pose for hours. In his *American in Rome* Henry P. Leland lamented: "They do want a new model for the Madonna, for Giacinta is growing old and fat and Stella, since she married that cobbler, has lost her angelic expression. The small boy who used to pose for angels has smoked himself too yellow and the man who stood for charity has gone out of business…"

A century has gone by since then, but some things have changed very little. The Romans are still endowed with a nonchalance (and often ignorance) about their city that comes from being satiated. Theatre audiences still cheer the

On the steps of the Church of the Trinità dei Monti.

hero, malign the villain and identify each actor in real life with his or her stage role. Soothsayers and clairvoyants still frequent alleys and squares, only today they speak English, French and German. The peddlers are present too, but their numbers are so great there is no time for the traditional initiation ceremony during which they were dragged, feet first, down the stairs of the church of Sant' Agnese in Piazza Navona and half drowned in Bernini's famous fountain.

The merciless lampooning of the authorities, a favourite Roman pastime, is done in satirical newspapers now, instead of notes pinned to the antique torso known as Pasquino. The Café Greco is still active though it hardly caters for artists today but the footsore foreign shoppers who invade the boutiques in the popular shopping areas around the **Via Condotti** and **Via della Croce**, opposite the Spanish Steps. The artists are still there but today their models pay to be sketched.

The eye of a visitor from the last century might encounter few visible changes in the structure of the old city, despite significant differences in style. In the old days purists dismissed the **Trevi Fountain** as a rococo hotchpotch of marble stuck against the walls of the State Copperplate Engraving Gallery. But today it has become a shrine for romantic "pilgrimages" after Hollywood made it immortal with the soap opera *Three Coins in the Fountain* and Anita Ekberg bathed in it in *La Dolce Vita*.

Not only a favourite meeting place for lovers, the fountain is now the unofficial headquarters of the *Papagalli* (parrots), the term for the slick gigolos and hangabouts who haunt the Trevi in search of foreign women and their favours. No lovely lady in Rome has to go farther than the Trevi Fountain for company. The "King" of the *Papagalli* is Gianni, a nattily dressed young gentleman whose blue open sports car (a gift from a grateful "client") is parked below the church steps opposite the fountain whenever its owner is on the prowl. Gianni stalks his victims with the aid of

The Trevi Fountain.

a white poodle, trained (by a tug on the leash) to make contact with the lady his master has in his sights.

The Trevi Fountain, off the **Via Tritone**, is only a 2-minute walk from the **Quirinale**, the former summer palace of the popes on the hill bearing the same name. Today the sprawling palace with its fabulous garden is the seat of the Italian President, head of state, and the site for Rome's most glamorous state receptions. The daily change of the guards, accompanied by snappy marching music, between 3pm and 4pm, attracts a big audience.

The modern face: Walking up the Via Tritone, past the **Piazza Barberini** with its fountain of conch shells, one comes to the beginning of the **Via Veneto**, synonymous with the *La Dolce Vita* (The Sweet Life) as represented by the exploits of Scandinavian actresses and smooth, curly-haired Italian male stars of the 1950s and 1960s. Visitors to Rome inevitably head for the pavement cafés of this Italian-style Hollywood Boulevard. There they search for the stars, starlets, the rich, the famous and the kinky who once paraded up and down. The sidewalk cafés are still there, along with the white-aproned waiters and bumper-to-bumper traffic. The tourists, however, sipping cappuccinos, martinis and campari sodas, search in vain for a famous face.

It is the old Rome that remains a living monument to history. It is still provincial, its bars and restaurants close before midnight and life fizzles out after sunset. Though it has been the capital of Italy since 1871 it is not a worldly city, unlike the much younger Milan, vigorous, cosmopolitan and a centre of modern European culture and art.

Travel fever has made Rome more crowded, cars have made her more congested, commercial enterprise has made her less attractive. The nooks and niches, into which the sound of traffic has not penetrated yet, retain something of the past. There, where messages are still shouted rather than telephoned and washing is strung across the alley, live the artists and writers of tomorrow.

Via Appia.

VENICE

Sometimes, in the morning, when the mist still lingers over the lagoon and the water cannot be seen, only heard, one may be forgiven for thinking that Venice is not real, that it is really only a *fata morgana*, an illusion that will dissolve in time and space.

Nothing in Venice is ever quite what it seems. The placid lagoon is in reality gnawing at the foundations, having already gobbled up all but 30 of the 490 islands that existed a thousand years ago. The *palazzi* with their glistening gilded facades are like slums at their rear ends. Yesterday's Venetians defended their city for 986 years with bluff, bluster, cunning and masterly diplomacy – and then let it fall without a blow. The city itself, once the bazaar of the world and the centre of cosmopolitan life, today is really no more than a vast cavernous museum with only echoes of its former splendour.

Endless curiosity: The republic reached its peak in 1203 with an act of treachery as wicked as it proved expedient. In exchange for allowing the Crusaders to use his port, the blind Doge Enrico Dandolo, a man of enormous size and appetite, persuaded the flotilla of 500 ships to ransack Constantinople, the richest city in the world, whose power and seafaring influence had long been a thorn in the side of Venice.

In 1203, the pious Crusaders sacked Constantinople, murdering the city's inhabitants. As booty, Venice was awarded the legendary "quarter and a half of a quarter" of the eastern Roman Empire. Her sailors carried off to Saint Mark's Square Constantinople's finest monuments, among them the Quadriga of Horses from the emperor's box at the Hippodrome and the Ikon of Nikopoeia. Venice became the chief depository of Byzantine art.

Europe's Drawing Room: There are no more clerics in the aviary over **St Mark's Square**, but as in the old days, the square is still invaded by entertainers, vendors and café orchestras who keep the crowd amused. Foreigners still stroll across the Piazza as they did at the height of the city's glory. Napoleon, seeing the gossiping multitudes and the lavish decor for the first time, called it "the finest drawing room in Europe."

Today they come for pleasure, not for business. They still visit the **Cathedral** to see gold-backed mosaics, carved galleries and the bones of Saint Mark, stolen from the Middle East. They wander through the oriental **Doge's Palace**, where the Doge lived more like a puppet than a ruler.

Behind the palace is the **Bridge of Sighs**, so named because the prisoners led from the Palace to the dungeons on the other side drew their last breath of free air on it.

At the lagoon end of the square is the **wharf** dominated by two columns bearing Saint Theodorus and the Lion of Venice. Where pleasure boats today set out for a trip around the lagoon, merchant ships used to ride at anchor. The *vaporetti* (water buses) and speedboat taxis stop there along with the few hundred gondolas remaining from the flotilla that was once 20,000 strong.

The Islands: **San Francesco** is just one of many islands that make up the complex waterways of Venice. Now a honeymoon island, it takes its name from Saint Francis who was shipwrecked in 1220. His name is remembered for a miracle he performed by poking his walking stick in the ground and producing a larch tree.

Sombre **San Michele**, with its dark cypress trees, is the lagoon's cemetery island. Black-draped gondola hearses, manned by black-robed gondoliers, still row the coffins to this last resting place. **San Clemente** is the island for the mentally disturbed, and fertile **Vignole** supplies fruit and vegetables for the city.

Murano has become the island of the glass blowers. Its inhabitants developed a technique for making the fragile, almost air-thin Murano glass which has become a trademark all over the world. The island was a retreat for the Venetian nobility who built luxury villas and gardens which have since fallen into disrepair. Women painstakingly stitch lace on Burano. The lagoon's oldest church, the **Basilica of Santa Maria Assunta**, built in 639 AD by the north Italian traders who fled to the islands from Atilla the Hun, is on **Torcello**. This was Ernest Hemingway's favourite island.

A practical people: Ideally situated at the crossroads of Europe and the east, Venetians not only acted as merchants but as go-betweens to settle disputes. Venetian ships sailed anywhere. Venice had ears everywhere. Men like Marco Polo and his father opened up new trade routes, contacted new empires and brought back to Venice; and the world, new products, new techniques and new ideas. (Marco Polo is credited with bringing back to Italy from China the technique of making spaghetti.)

Only twice did the city's diplomacy fail, against the Turks and against Napoleon who, sailing down her Grand Canal in 1797 simply announced: "The Republic has ended," then tossed her, like a worn-out strumpet, to Austria. The gesture of the little Corsican prompted the 120th Doge, Lodovico Manin, to take off his fisherman's cap (the ancient symbol of the Doges) and hand it over to his valet with the words: "Hang it up, I won't need it any more." The words were typical of the nonchalance and practical sense that had guided the republic through its ups and downs.

Museum, haven and ghetto: Venetians, aware that their city is a showpiece museum, have become experts in gaining maximum benefit from the millions of tourists who flood through the "turnpikes" each summer and are inundated with kitsch: straw hats, miniature gondolas, churches and palaces with musical clocks inside, glass and toy figures whose origin is always given as Murano but more likely is somewhere in Asia.

Venetian liberalism was regarded by the rest of Europe as depraved or at least "Bohemian". Though fighting under the winged lion of Saint Mark for Catholicism, she permitted all creeds to live on her lagoon. At one stage she flirted with Protestantism and the pope temporarily excommunicated the entire city. She was a haven to Jews escaping from

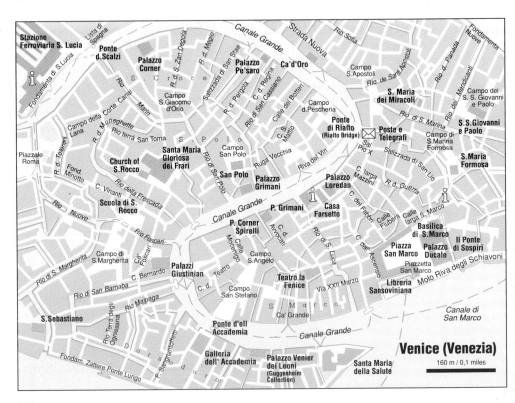

persecution in the 17th century, though her so-called tolerance had a price. In a practice known as the "cash-register" policy, the Jews paid rent for their *ghetto* (a Venetian word meaning "mould").

The price of money ruled Venice. At least once a day a Venetian went to the **Rialto**, the area around the built-up drawbridge over the **Grand Canal**, to visit his bank. The Rialto was the Wall Street of Europe. Venetians still go to the Rialto every day, to shop in its popular stores and the market on the western bank.

The Grand Canal is the Champs Elysées of Venice. At times this unique waterway is as congested as an urban road. Speedboats, made from polished mahogany wood, jostle for space with the *vaporetti*. Dodging in and out between them are the freight barges, the postman's barge, the milkman, the debt collector, the tourist gondolas, the gondolas training for the annual race down the canal, and the flat-bottomed barges that ferry pedestrians across it. The Grand Canal was one of Europe's larg-est ports until the Portuguese navigator Vasco da Gama found a new sea route to the Indies around the Cape of Good Hope in the 16th century. The discovery ruined the overland spice traffic which had filled Venetian treasuries with revenue far greater than the income of the papacy or the empires of the time.

The Grand Canal remains the core of the city. Along its winding 2.6-mile (4-km) route stand 200 palaces and seven churches. A score of vegetable and fruit markets make it the centre of daily social life. When Venetians embark on a "walk" they invariably have themselves rowed down the Grand Canal.

The more energetic row their own boats (a sport known as "water jogging") in the peculiar style of the gondolier. Their black lacquered gondolas, half rowed, half punted with the aid of a viola-shaped oar, were multi-coloured until 1562 when the City Council decreed that they all had to be black. This, the city fathers claimed, was the proper colour for the vehicles of a serious city.

The architecture along the Grand

Left, the symbol of Venice. **Right**, a water taxi.

Canal is influenced by both East and West. Departing from the railway station, at the end of the modern causeway spanning the lagoon, the first striking sight is the **Church of San Geremia** at the point where the **Canal Canaregio** enters the Grand Canal. The church contained the bones of St Lucy, kidnapped from the Middle East and returned only a few years ago.

On the left, before a bend in the canal exposes the Rialto Bridge, is Venice's most famous palace, the **Ca' d'Oro** (Golden Palace). It was here that Shakespeare set up Desdemona, the wife of Othello. Shylock lived nearby according to the bard's *Merchant of Venice.* The **Palazzo Loredan**, where Wagner lived within earshot of the gondolier songs which inspired him so much is beyond the Rialto. Next door is the **Ca' Farsetto**,the former family seat of the blind old Doge Dandolo of Constantinople fame and today the Town Hall.

At the end of the Grand Canal, **Santa Maria della Salute** squats like a fat dove. This church was built in the 17th century by the city's fathers in gratitude for the relief of Venice from the plague.

Beside the church run shipping channels on which portly tankers and freighters sail towards **Porto Marghera**, which is the harbour for **Mestre**, the industrial satellite city of Venice. From Porto Marghera passenger and car ferries travel to Greece, Turkey and the Middle East.

The Carnival Queen: In the 17th and 18th centuries, as Venice declined, she lived in style, as if on an endless carnival parade, debauched and indifferent. *La Serenissima,* as Venice was known, became a boudoir for painters, after having been for centuries a warehouse of art collected by sailors who knew how to recognise a masterpiece.

The love for the arts has survived today with the **Biennale Art Exhibitions** and the annual **Lion of Venice film festivals.** The men who made Venetian painting, frescoes and mosaics famous, are many and their works can be admired in churches and galleries around the city. High on the list are the names of Jacopo Bellini (1400–70)

Canal-side dining.

and his sons Gentile (1429–1507) and Giovanni (1430–1516). Others are Giorgione (1475–1510), Titian (1488–1576), Paolo Veronese (1528–88), Tintoretto (1518–94) and Tiepolo (1696–1770). Naturally, Venetians were quick to commercialise on their artists and they created family "art" companies that offered high quality products.

When a larger number of well-to-do tourists started to arrive in the 18th century, a Venetian school of skilled "view" painters sprang up with, Giovanni Antonio Canal becoming the dominating figure. Later known as Canaletto (1697–1768), he was mostly absorbed in meeting foreign demands for souvenir views and pressure upon him was such that he was ultimately forced to work largely from drawings or even from other artists' engravings. The old assertive merchant of Venice may have died out but those who remained went down with great spirit, coupled with the enormous joy of staring at their own vain glory in the mirror of art.

This was the Venice fascinated and haunted by the amorous exploits of Casanova, the Venice Lord Byron praised as being (next to the East) "the greenest island of my imagination," a place he loved so much that he swam the 2½-mile (4-km) Grand Canal from end to end. It was the city of the Vivaldi (1675–1741) and Wagner who sat at the famous **Café Florian**, still the best place for a coffee on Saint Mark's Square.

This century Thomas Mann brooded here and wrote *Death in Venice* and Ernest Hemingway guzzled down six bottles of wine a night while he wrote some of his best prose in a room above **Harry's Bar**. Generations of Americans, lured by the drinking exploits of Papa Hemingway, turned Harry's Bar into a prosperous chain across the peninsula as a result.

Today Venice is supposed to be sinking, and in winter planks are needed to cross St Mark's Square, but the orchestras play on and on, a little out of tune maybe, a little shabby even, but determined to see the Grand Old Lady dance to her grave.

The Campanile and the Doge's Palace.

FLORENCE

After midnight, when Florence has gone to sleep, a ghostly spectacle appears in the central **Piazza della Signoria**. That is the time when "The Great White Man" climbs from his fountain, walks across the Piazza and talks to his friends housed in the **Loggia d'Lanzi**, one of whom is "The Giant", a symbol of how a small country can defeat a huge enemy. Another friend is "The Tyrant" who symbolises the victory of the Medici family over Republican Florence.

Florentines have believed for centuries that spirits are imprisoned in their marble statues. They believe the spirits begin to move and talk as soon as the **Palazzo Vecchio** and **Uffizi**, one of the world's greatest art galleries, close down at night and the visitors have disappeared from the streets.

"The Great White Man" is Ammannati's imposing Neptune which dominates the fountain in the Piazza della Signoria. Florentines believe he is really the river god Arno, famous for spurning the love of women. "The Giant" is Michelangelo's *David* and "The Tyrant" is Cellini's *Perseus* who holds up the bloody head of Medusa.

In the days when the city went to war, the most beloved of the statues were carried ahead of the troops. After World War II the city launched a frenetic search for the missing head of "Spring", a vital member of the Four Seasons quartet guarding each end of the **Bridge of Santa Trinità**. Its wartime loss, they thought, would bring bad luck. In the end it was found at the bottom of the River Arno, into which it had fallen after having been struck by an artillery shell. In a noisy procession it was taken back to the bridge – and peace was restored in the spirit world.

The Medicis: Florence was founded by the Romans at the time of Sulla and settled by the veterans of Julius Caesar's army. By the 3rd century AD it was a provincial capital of the Roman Empire. It came into prominence in the 11th and 12th centuries when the city-republic emerged as a leading power in its region of Tuscany. Constitutionally, 6,000 of the city's 50,000 citizens had the right to hold public office in the 300-member Popular Council and the 200-member Town Council.

In 1433, Cosimo Medici, often referred to as *Il Vecchio* (the Old Man), whose father had become the city's richest banker, gathered around him 700 opportunists and dependents to form a party of law and order with which he swept into power. His arrival ended the republic and for the next 304 years a succession of Medicis ruled Florence and Tuscany, interrupted only by two brief, ill-fated spells of republicanism.

Between 1865 and 1871, it was the provisional capital of the United Kingdom of Italy but eventually had to relinquish this title to Rome. During these and the succeeding years much of Florence's past was seriously jeopardised. The medieval walls were pulled down, the ancient centre was laid waste. The city's boundaries and the population continued to grow chaotically into the

Outside San Lorenzo church.

20th century, when order and sense were slowly restored to the renovations.

The River Arno has been an occasional adversary to Florentine life by destroying the bridges and flooding the city. The most devastating occurrence was the flood of November 1966, when the city's cultural heritage was seriously damaged. In some places the water rose as high as 20 feet (6 metres), submerging sculpture, paintings, mosaics and manuscripts in the city's libraries. A host of international experts, financed by contributions from around the world, arrived to save the treasures, damaged by water and muck.

Artistic pinnacle: Florence has remained a mammoth monument to the Renaissance. No city in Italy has produced such an avalanche of genius: Leonardo da Vinci, Michelangelo, Dante, Brunelleschi, Donatello, Machiavelli, Botticelli, Fra Angelico, Fra Filippo Lippi, Ghirlandaio, Giotto, Ghiberti, Ucello. No city has so reshaped modern thought and art, nor gathered within its walls such a treasure of local art and architecture. Florentines ushered in the Renaissance and took the arts to heights not even the Greeks had reached.

The humanist movement began here, upsetting the fire and brimstone belief that man was a miserable worm. The humanists contended instead: "Man is God's finest work." Dante Alighieri (1265–1321) wrote the *Divina Comedia* (Divine Comedy), a journey to heaven via hell and purgatory. One of the world's most translated authors, he wrote in an everyday language for all to understand, thus marking the beginning of modern Italian literature.

Florentines discovered perspective and painted the first nudes of the Renaissance. The first humanist, Petrarch, was born there; Boccaccio initiated literary criticism and wrote the first modern love story; Machiavelli became the father of political science; Giotto originated the new painting style; Michelangelo perfected it. The Tuscan language became the language of Italy, and even the New World, America, took its name from a Florentine traveller,

Left, the Cathedral. Right, Neptune's Fountain.

Amerigo Vespucci, who was an agent for the bank of the Medici.

The list of achievements and marvels is as crowded as the city itself. Florence today can hardly breathe. It swelters in the stink of mopeds and buses with hardly a tree or hedge to dissipate the summer heat, and although the city is saturated with history and art, a step back to snatch a better look might well lead into the path of an oncoming car.

The visitor may have to stand in line to see Michelangelo's *David* at the **Academy**, though good copies are in the Piazza della Signoria and the **Piazza di Michelangelo** situated on the left bank of river. From here, there is a splendid view over the Arno valley and the skyline of Florence which is marked by the slender tower of the **Palazzo Vecchio** to the left and the church of **Santa Croce** to the right. In the centre looms the cupola of the **Duomo**.

The famous Duomo (Cathedral) with Brunelleschi's dome lies a short distance along the Via Calzaioli. This free-hanging cupola has astonished archi-tects and builders for centuries. Florentines refer to it as **Il Cupolone**, the dome of domes. The endless stairway leads to the lantern gallery right inside Brunelleschi's building secret: the "two" domes, one shell inside the other and mutually supporting

The man who perhaps best symbol-ises both the greatness and the parochi-alism of this city was Michelangelo, who supposedly never washed and al-ways went to bed in his long gaiters. He was, like many Florentines of his time, thrifty and endowed with a dose of inso-lence, which prompted Pope Clement VII to write that one had to ask Michelangelo to sit down immediately or else he would do so anyway, and leave others standing.

Another indication of his character is in a wall of the Palazzo Vecchio, the stately central palace of government, in the form of a head chiselled into stone. Tradition has it that, to win a bet, Michel-angelo carved the head with his hands behind his back and facing away from the wall.

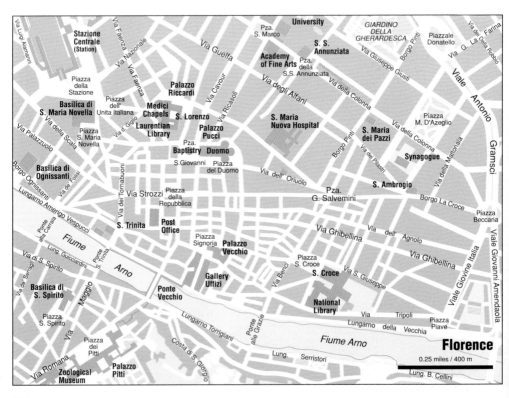

A firm republican, Michelangelo mourned the public burning in 1498 of the Florentine Dominican monk Girolamo Savonarola, who had wrested power from the Medici. The fiery monk held Florence under his spell from 1494 to 1497. During that time he headed a "Rule for the Poor" administration which ended when he was arrested, tortured, hung and burned on the orders of the pope. On the Piazza della Signoria a **plaque** on the spot where the great monk was burned pays reluctant tribute to a man badly maligned by local historians.

A manly city: The people of Florence burned people in effigy and drew the portraits of criminals on the jail wall in the belief that portraits contained the spirit of people. On Easter Sunday, a wire dove is lit in the Cathedral and sent burning into the street, where it must ignite an ox-cart piled with fireworks if the next harvest is to be prosperous. At the end of June, Florentine youth play a bone-crushing 23-men-a-side football game in ancient costumes in honour of St John.

The American writer Mary McCarthy described Florence as "a manly town". In her book, *The Stones of Florence – Venice Observed,* she wrote: "The great sculptors and architects who stamped the outward city with its permanent image or style – Brunelleschi, Donatello, Michelangelo – were all bachelors. Monks, soldier-saints, prophets and hermits were the city's heroes..." She added however, that homosexuality in old Florence was an accepted practice, especially among painters who loved to depict sturdy male legs and buttocks encased in tights.

Tradition is honoured in many ways. Florence today, with a population of half a million people, is still a city of craftsmen, shopkeepers, artisans, farmers and professors. On the **Ponte Vecchio**, the historic bridge across the Arno which dates in its present form from 1345, some of Italy's finest silver jewellery is made and sold in kiosks lining the bridge. In boutiques in the old city, a tradition of leather goods and textiles still flourishes.

Ponte Vecchio.

TUSCANY AND UMBRIA

Tuscany, neat, regimented and functional, resembles its capital, Florence. The farmland has a linear pattern and is edged by hedgerows. The houses, rectangular and frugal like the inhabitants, stand on conical hills or, like soldiers on parade, along well-planned streets. The pointed cypresses, the tall "males" and dishevelled "females", are planted with geometrical exactitude, picketing the hills, delineating borders, flanking gateposts, dividing plots of land or simply giving shade to a crop. Everything has its purpose. Everything is arranged to please the eye, yet while the Tuscan countryside, where man's hand has heavily rearranged nature, is exalted, Tuscans direct their real reverence to God.

Tower power: During the Renaissance Tuscan cities were carefully planned with bylaws to ensure everything matched. No house had a wrong colour, wrong window, wrong shape, height or width. The houses of the Tuscans are inward-looking, bristling against entry. They have been compared to safe deposit boxes, a fortification in which possessions can be defended. Before the aestheticism of the approaching Renaissance awakened a civic consciousness for orderly but beautiful cities, the urban skyline of Tuscany was marked by huge towers, some of which were 160 ft (50 metres) tall, from which feuding Guelph (pro-pope) or Ghibelline (pro-emperor) factions fought against each other constantly.

South of Florence is **San Gimignano**, the "Manhattan of Tuscany", where as in any other of the feuding towns it had been a matter of prestige to build the tallest tower possible. Out of 72 stone towers, 15 still stand, a reminder of the days when street battles were conducted between "tower empires".

The towns of Tuscany are gems: Siena, Pisa, Lucca, San Gimignano, Volterra, Arezzo and Pistoia. This last was so vehemently republican and the aristocracy so despised that ordinary people guilty of a crime were punished by being "ennobled" – turned into aristocrats.

The **Leaning Tower** in **Pisa** is famous if only for its sense of suspense. Many people come to see the 12th-century edifice before it topples over. Generations of experts have been unable to agree whether the tower is leaning more or whether it is indeed leaning less. The latest diagnosis is that it will fall in 100 years' time. One plain fact is that when last measured the 177-ft (54-metre) tower had an inclination of 14 ft (4.25 metres).

Pisa is not only famous for its Leaning Tower. It is one of Italy's great cities of art. The old maritime republic, once a flourishing sea port on the River Arno's estuary, was an ally of the Normans during their conquest of Sicily, and its ships carried the First Crusade to the Holy Land, a journey that gave Pisa trading posts in the East. A Ghibelline city, Pisa's links with Hohenstaufen Emperor Frederic Barbarossa gave it a leading position in Tuscany during the 12th century which ended with the city's

Left, the well-ordered Tuscan landscape. **Right**, the Leaning Tower of Pisa.

defeat by Genoa in 1284. In 1406 it was taken by Florence after a long siege. During World War II the city was badly damaged but faithfully reconstructed. Other historical buildings in this city, whose most famous son was Galileo Galilei (1564–1642), are the **Campo dei Miracoli** (The Square of Miracles), the Baptistry and the Cathedral beside the leaning tower.

Wild horsemen of Siena: If Florence is the living monument to the Renaissance then **Siena** is the jewel of medieval Italy. Its banks and commerce flourished and a merchant-nobility engaged in business all over Europe. In 1260 Siena imposed a dreadful defeat on its rising rival Florence in which 10,000 Florentines died, 15,000 were imprisoned and the general of the Florentine army was dragged, tied to an ass, through the city-republic. In 1559, however, it lost its independence to Florence.

The life story of Silvio Piccolomini who became Pope Pius III in 1458 is wonderfully told by Pintoricchio on the walls of **Piccolomini Library** in the **Duomo**. Siena's great attraction is its central square built in 1347 and known simply as **Il Campo**. The shell-shaped piazza is one of Europe's most harmonious and scenic squares, particularly on a moonlit night when the silhouettes of the **Palazzo Pubblico** and the **Great Tower** below a velvet blue sky give it the aura of an unearthly place.

Twice a year during summer, the square is covered in sand and lined with barricades for one of the wildest horse races in the world. The stake is a simple piece of cloth, *Il Palio*. A colourful procession of pages, knights, flagtossers and men-at-arms, dressed in 15th-century costumes, opens the spectacle. The race is between the various districts of the city, each represented by a horse which is blessed in the local church before the start. Riding bareback, the riders risk life and limb.

To the east of Tuscany is the province of **Umbria**. Its best-known community is **Assisi**, the home of St Francis (1182–1226), the saint who spoke to the animals, resurrected brotherly care and love

San Gimignano.

and dedicated himself to chastity, abstinence and the cause of poverty. The city long ago turned itself into a shrine dedicated to its best-known son, though it is now also an important market place.

Today, the city offers millions of pilgrims a glittering array of souvenirs, from religious trinkets and sacred memorabilia to embossed copper, wrought iron and embroidery. In the friary, above the tomb, sandalled Franciscan monks and lay staff conduct a booming bazaar in Franciscan software. This briskness echoes in the voices of the friars who, acting as tourist guides, gallop through the history of Assisi in most languages.

Francesco Bernardone was born in the winter of 1182, the son of an affluent textile merchant. As a young man, Francesco showed no inclination towards piety. Initially he sought glory as a soldier in the perpetual war with Perugia before exchanging his rich garbs for beggars' rags and his free life for an existence as a hermit. His own father took him to court for selling cloth from the family warehouse and giving the

proceeds for the rebuilding of a church.

A walk along the **Via Merastrasio** (Assisi is strictly pedestrian) leads below balconies ringed with geraniums to the **Porta San Giacomo**, a gateway famous for the tall cypress tree on its turreted top.

Around one last twisting bend the eye meets the *pièce de résistance* of Assisi, the **Basilica of Saint Francis**, the first, the most impressive and the most famous of the many temples dedicated to *Il Poverello* (the Pauper). It comprises two superimposed churches, the **Lower and the Upper Church**, both built upon a plateau known by the ancients as "The Hill of Hell" but quickly renamed by the Franciscans "The Hill of Heaven". In the crypt of the Basilica rest the remains of the saint, taken in 1230, four years after his death, from their burial place in the church of Saint George, despite bitter protests that the ostentatious tomb was contrary to his vows of poverty.

Among those who have come to pay homage were the Florentine pioneers of Renaissance painting, Giotto and Cima-

bue, who chronicled his life in frescoes. Giovanni Cimabue (1240–1302), the older of the two, decorated the vaults of the Lower Church with scenes from the life of Jesus Christ and St Francis. Cimabue came across the young Giotto (1266–1337) guarding sheep for his father while etching into rock with a pointed stone the life-like portraits of the animals.

Giotto became Cimabue's pupil and soon surpassed his master in the ability to copy from nature, to bring life-like qualities to his paintings. In the gallery below the windows of the Upper Church, Giotto painted 32 frescoes and even during his lifetime contemporaries marvelled at the animation in the faces of his figures and the details and colours of their garments.

The oak and the olive: Over the plain on the next hill from Assisi lies the Umbrian capital of **Perugia** (pop: 180,000). The city reflects the bellicose side of a region where the martial and the mystical are inextricably intertwined, where the harsh oak and the gentle olive grow side by side on the same hillside and where the shepherd cuts the sheep's gullet then plays the flute to mourn it. Perugia's churches were never completed in the same generation since the citizens were too busy with wars, feuds, pillage and murder. The old town bristles with battlements, and legend has it that the church walls of **San Ercolane** had to be washed with wine at times of water shortage to clean away the blood left by the nocturnal massacres.

Perugia has a more creative side. In 1307 it opened what is one of Europe's oldest and most famous universities. Within its walls is the **University for Foreigners** where Italian migrants, who made fortunes in America, Australia and Canada, have traditionally sent their children.

In this barbed hilltop fortress the "divine" Raphael studied under the great Pietro Perugino who squandered his great talent on making copies of his most popular works just for the money. The young Raphael helped the master with the cycle of frescoes in the **Sala del Cambio**, Perugino's largest, but not finest, work, and at the **Church of San Severino** one can admire Raphael's earliest frescoes, completed years later by the aged Perugino after his pupil had died at the age of 37. Here the "divine" Fra Angelico worked, and Nicola and Giovanni Pisano decorated Italy's most famous marble and bronze fountain with sculptured saints, prophets and legends. **The Fonte Maggiore** squats in the centre of Perugia, as a symbol of the power and culture of the city.

From the vantage point of the **Giardino del Frontone** (which Dante called the "Garden of the Peninsula") one can see some of the seven cities of Umbria – the Umbrian Beauties. **Spoleto's** proud turrets lie to the south. Lucrezia Borgia reigned here and Pintoricchio worked on the cathedral frescoes – the same frescoes on which Fra Fillipo Lippi spent the last years of his turbulent life. After his death the wall paintings were completed by his virtuoso 12-year-old son, Fillipo Lippi, the product of the scandalous relationship between the former monk and the nun Lucrezia.

The town of **Gubbio**, built on a mountainside, is striking in its well-preserved medieval splendour. Tucked away in the backwoods of Umbria, it is removed from the mainstream of trade and travel routes and is accessible only by a tortuous hilltop road.

The most famous of the Umbria hilltop settlements is **Orvieto**, which sits on a slender outcrop of tufa rock above the Tiber valley as if being held aloft on the palm of a giant hand. Its **cathedral** is best approached from the **Via Maitani** at midday when the sun turns the fabulous gilded facade into a shimmering gold. In the **Chapel of the Madonna di San Brizio** are the frescoes of Luca Signorelli and Fra Angelico which form an invaluable part of the Italian artistic heritage. They are most favourably viewed when the sun strikes them in the morning. Signorelli's scenes of the Last Judgement, with the damned flying on the backs of propellered devils, is said to have inspired Michelangelo some years later to his own interpretation of the Last Judgement.

Right, the church of Assisi.

THE BAY OF NAPLES

Naples has mesmerised its visitors and many foreign masters: the Phoenicians, Greeks, Romans, Goths, Vandals, Saracens, Turks, Normans, Germans, Spaniards, French and British.

Down the centuries her troubles have been great and but so have been her charms. They still are. A Neapolitan thief will relieve victims of their valuables with a smile and a politeness that will make it all quite painless. If porters, taxidrivers, merchants and vendors cheat a little they do so while raining titles: "*Dottore*", "*Professore*", "*Generale*" and "Your Excellency."

Founded by Greek colonists who named it "Neapolis" (the New City), the city was once part of Magna Graecia, the ancient Greek colonies. It was captured by the Romans in 326 BC who enriched the settlement with temples, gymnasiums, aqueducts, hippodromes arenas and numerous catacombs outside the city. It became the favourite residence of many of the emperors and this is where the infamous Nero made his stage debut.

After the fall of the Roman Empire Naples became a Byzantine dukedom in the 7th century, and early in the 12th century it fell to the feudal Norman Kingdom of Sicily. Since then European monarchies have converted it into the flourishing capital of a kingdom, inhabited by a people who quickly learned to adjust to the whims of their foreign rulers. Wily, ingenious, devious, roguish yet loyal and proud, they are sons of a city where politics and business are a blend of Machiavellian realism and Byzantine intrigue. In this atmosphere laws were never taken too seriously; after all they were made by foreign bosses to benefit themselves and rob poor Neapolitans.

A quarter of a million Neapolitans live, directly or indirectly, from smuggling, chiefly cigarettes. To confiscate the truck which daily picks up the smuggled cartons from the fleet of boats bringing them into the bay from freighters on the high sea would deprive every fourth Neapolitan home of its source of income. Nevertheless the Guardia di Finanza patrol boats bobbing in the harbour now and then do sally forth to show the flag.

Of blood and saints: The **Piazza del Mercato** in the centre of Naples is a run-down parking lot surrounded by a crumbling church and derelict houses. Until the 19th century, however, it was the site of executions. In 1268 the German dynasty of the Hohenstaufens ended with the beheading of the 16-year-old heir, Conradin. The execution established the supremacy of the French house of Anjou in Naples. The piazza is one of many spots in a city buzzing with legends, and superstitions.

At the **Castel Nuovo** for instance, it is said that Pope Celestine V, known as the "old hermit" and the resident of the castle, decided to abdicate, a decision prompted by "the voice of an angel" which urged him every night to do so. The voice, so Neapolitans say, drifted down a speaking tube belonging to

Left, fishing boats at Naples. **Right**, basking by the bay.

Benedict Caetani who, as Boniface VIII, became Celestine's successor in 1764.

The **Duomo** (Cathedral) of Naples is sandwiched between family apartments in the northern part of the historic centre. In its **crypt** rests the relic Neopolitans treasure most: a phial containing the blood of Saint Januarius (San Genaro) who was martyred in AD 305. The blood must liquefy and boil three times a year – on the first Sunday in May, on 19 September and on 16 December – if Naples is to escape disaster. Though the Vatican eliminated San Genaro from the official list of saints during a recent purge, the liquefication ceremonies are the highlights of the Neopolitan ecclesiastical year. If the miracle is slow in happening and the blood refuses to liquefy, then Neapolitans have their own ways of coaxing the saint into action: in fact the cursing of San Genaro became so coarse that the Archbishop of Naples has banned swearing in church.

It is hardly surprising Neopolitans have been less than impressed with authority when one considers their overlords. Ferdinand IV, for example, who reigned in the mid-18th century, was illiterate and known as "King Nosey". He preferred to shoot, skin and gut huge amounts of game and to roam the city with fishermen than attend to the affairs of state. After his daily slaughter, Ferdinand had himself rowed around the Bay in the royal barge followed by an entire string orchestra in a second boat. Ferdinand's favourite was the British ambassador, Sir William Hamilton, a dilettante archaeologist and writer (and an excellent shot), who married the beautiful young mistress of his nephew when he was almost 60 and she just 19. The girl, Emma Hart, was a blacksmith's daughter from London who, after elocution lessons in *My Fair Lady* style, became the darling of Naples and eventually the mistress of Admiral Horatio Nelson. She died impoverished and abandoned in Paris.

The great sentinel: The eyes of the people living on the Bay of Naples are imperceptibly drawn every day towards

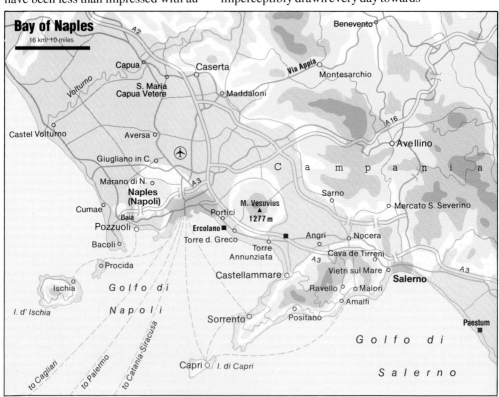

the giant sentinel who stands ominously above them to check and comment on his mood. They refer to him simply as "he", never as **Vesuvius**. The height of the cone is 4,198 feet (1,280 metres), but it varies after each eruption. He last erupted in 1944 and his "vomit" (as the locals call it) is still scattered in a vast slag heap around the crater. His lava became the fertile Vesuvian soil where the finest vines and olive grow, the main reason why peasants for thousands of years have stubbornly clung to the precarious slopes.

Still life of lovers: His most famous explosion occurred in 79 BC at a time when everyone thought he was extinct, when woods brimming with wild boar covered his very summit. Spartacus and his rebellious slaves withdrew into these woods to escape the first punitive expeditions of the Roman legions.

The eruption, elaborately described by Pliny the Younger, buried the flourishing cities of **Herculaneum** and **Pompeii** under the mountains of ashes and brimstone. The life and last drama of these cities, preserved in volcanic ashes, came to light over the last century when archaeologists dug them from their airtight tomb. The imprints and skeletons make this the most impressive ancient monument in the world. Excavators found the bones of a rich man, his fingers still clutching the keys to the treasure chests his slaves carried behind him. A thief, one hand still on a stolen purse, is nailed against the wall together with his victim. Wine stands on tables, bread lies in the oven. The skeleton of an aristocratic lady is found in the sleeping quarters of a gladiator. Graffiti proclaims love and engages in obscenities and political baiting.

Many of the finest finds of old Pompeii have been taken for exhibition to the **National Museum of Naples**. These exhibits include the spectacular animal mosaics and also the famous pornographic collection, housed in a secret cabinet where it can be viewed only with special permission.

Beyond Pompeii on the southern point of the bay are the steep cliffs of **Sorrento**,

Pompeii.

MONTE CASSINO

The Allies landed south of Sorrento on the Bay of Salerno in 1943 at their start of the liberation of Italy. The campaign was intended to divert the Germans from the landing planned later for Normandy. The first cemetery of the Italian campaign of World War II is outside Salerno where 26,000 US soldiers are buried. But the most fearsome casualties were at Cassino, the town and hilltop monastery between Naples and Rome.

Today Cassino has a population of 19,000 and is once again a tranquil agricultural centre. Thousands of war veterans make annual pilgrimages to the 70,000 graves where they walk in silent remembrance along the forest of crosses. The 18,000 Poles who sacrificed themselves in the last decisive battle are buried on Point 593, the hill for which they fought and died.

The 17,000 British are buried alongside the New Zealanders and Canadians in the outskirts of the town where they fought house-to-house and yard by yard. The

20,000 Germans rest higher up, not far from the positions around the monastery which some of their elite troops defended so tenaciously during four long battles between January and May 1944.

The fighting took place right below the Benedictine Monastery of Monte Cassino which was bombed into a ruin by the Allies in one of the most controversial actions of the war. In the words of one British general, the monastery "had become the embodiment of resistance and its tangible symbol." After the war, it was rebuilt, if not to its former beauty at least as a reasonable replica. It was founded in AD 529 by St Benedict, the father of Western monasticism, who was proclaimed patron saint of all of Europe by Pope Paul VI in 1964.

St Benedict formulated the Rule which governed monastic life from the mid-7th century. The Benedictine monks of Monte Cassino transcribed and preserved the classical works of Cicero, Horace, Ovid and Virgil which would otherwise have been lost.

The abbey also contained a great art treasure which the Germans evacuated before fighting started. The Allies carpet-bombed the abbey and the town of Cassino prior to the second battle after they decided that Germans were using it as an observation post and an ammunition dump – an assessment that proved wrong, though the Germans did put up defence positions there only after both places had been levelled by the US Air Force. Before the massive daytime air raid, the Allies dropped leaflets around the town of Cassino, warning the people to move out of the battle zone.

The first battle began on 17 January 1944 and ended with the almost complete annihilation of the United States' 34th and 36th (Texan) divisions by the German gunners. The massacre prompted one American correspondent to write that it was "the biggest disaster to American arms since Pearl Harbor."

The second battle ended with the mauling of the New Zealand 2nd and Indian 4th divisions who lost half their fighting men. The Allies took heavy losses again during the third battle, but on 11 May 1944, they broke through the Gustav line and opened the road to Rome which was liberated on 4 and 5 June.

■ **A British war cemetery.**

forlorn strips of beach below and stately Victorian hotels above. Round the point begins the **Amalfi Coast** with Italy's most panoramic cliff-top road leading south to **Salerno**.

North of Naples lies the great volcanic basin known as the **Phlegrean Fields**, a labyrinth of smouldering caves, gas-filled niches and desolate moonscapes. Somewhere here lies the entrance to Hades, the underworld of Greek mythology.

Beyond, in the far distance, lies **Caserta**, an inland town of 52,000 inhabitants just 16 miles (25 km) north of Naples. Here the spendthrift Charles III of Spain built his own version of Versailles, a palace with 1,200 rooms, 1,790 windows and so much space that American soldiers drove through it in jeeps when it was the Allied Headquarters in World War II. It was here that Lord Alexander, head of the Allied Forces, Italy, accepted the surrender of the Germans in May 1945.

Bay of Capri. Visitors from all over the Bay of Naples converge, sooner or later, on the 4-mile (7-km) island of **Capri** off the end of the Sorrentine peninsula. In the tourist season its population of about 7,000 can swell tenfold. The boats that bring them moor below the limestone cliffs at the port of **Marina Grande**. The cliffs would be intimidating but for the gentle olive trees and crawling vines along the terraced fields near the top of the crags. From the sea the town looks like a birthday cake, the top half covered by green icing and thin candles.

There is also a weekly exodus from Naples to Capri. The moment the sailor slips the mooring ropes and the hydrofoil edges out into the bay, there is an audible sigh of relief. Most of the passengers on that late Friday afternoon run to Capri have one common ambition: to escape Naples and its tooting cacophony, its bloody camorra gang wars, its army of pickpockets and petty criminals, and its general clamour and noisiness.

From the port a cable-car ferries the visitors to the lofty saddle plateau in which the town of Capri nestles. The

town's twin, **Anacapri**, on the western side of the island, can be reached either by a tortuous track or in mini-buses whose local drivers are true masters in negotiating the hairpin bends.

Isle of Sweet Do-nothing: The island has always served as a refuge for the weary. The Emperor Augustus, approaching it on his galley at dusk 2,000 years ago, imagined it could well be the mythical "Land of Sweet Do-Nothing". He and his stepson-successor Tiberius loved it so much they not only built 12 villas but turned the entire island by edict into an imperial retreat. It is the moody and ambiguous Tiberius who continues to exercise a spell over Capri. From his rocky nest he ruled the Roman Empire from 27 to 37 AD, sending orders and receiving replies from Rome by a system of signals passed from tower to tower. Half the island is named after him. From above, **Mount Tiberius** peers down placidly. There is **Tiberius's Leap** (from where the emperor supposedly hurled his enemies into the sea) and on **Tiberius's Seat** he allegedly conceived

diabolical orgies carried out in the **Baths of Tiberius** and the **Villa Jovis**, perched like a roost on the island's easternmost promontory.

Following the death of Emperor Tiberius, the island lost its influence. Frequently used as a place of exile, it became the stronghold of Saracen raiders and pirates. The infamous Saracen cut-throat Barbarossa made his headquarters on the island and built a castle. In 1656 the plague almost wiped out the entire population. It was brought from the mainland by a lock of hair from the head of a young girl who died of the disease in Naples. The lock was sent to her lover, in exile on Capri. It was at this time that the **monastery of Certosa** and the convent of the barefooted sisters of Teresa were built. At the beginning of the 19th century the island again became a strategic base, first for the British, then the French.

The Germans, headed by Scheffel and Gregorovius, sparked an invasion of Teutonic writers, poets and painters, followed at the turn of the century by a spate of Russian intellectuals headed by Maxim Gorky. Among his guests was his friend Lenin.

The great Swede, Axel Munthe, whose novel *The Story of Saint Michele* (published in 1929) made the island a literary landmark, became for many years the chief *patrone*. The Scottish writer Norman Douglas, in *South Wind*, talks of a curious religious sect which bathed naked in Capri's secluded bays and grottos. The English popular singer Gracie Fields (1898–1979) became a resident and captured the islanders' hearts.

The rediscovery in the 19th century of the **Blue Grotto** with its luminous surface (a phenomenon caused by reflected sunlight) turned Capri into a sudden excursion paradise, a trend that continues today when large numbers of boats queue outside the Grotta Azzurra.

In many ways the island is a microcosm of Italian life. The islanders speak their own dialect and, like all Italians, mistrust authority and governments. The feudal squabbles of Capri and Anacapri are typical of the intercommunity feuds that are still so much a part of Italy.

Left, Neapolitan ceramics.
Right, diving off Capri.

ALBANIA

Albania has always been one of Europe's least likely tourist destinations and since it became the last Eastern European country to throw out communism and allow foreigners in, its bankrupt economy has been laid bare for all to see. But Albania is a survivor; just scratch the drab surface of this tiny country and you will uncover something awesome and timeless: the heart and soul of the Balkans. Although what little tourist development there was has fallen into decay, for the more adventurous traveller it is still a moving, magical and mysterious land full of surprises.

The romantic image of a wild and colourful people that attracted intrepid 18th and 19th-century westerners such as Edith Durham and Lord Byron to Albania still has its truth today. Tracing their ancestry back to the Illyrians, one of the most ancient tribes of Europe, Albanians have spent virtually all their history as an invaded, occupied and oppressed people, but they have remained unbowed.

It will be a while before the country can pick up the pieces following the ruinous and savage totalitarian rule of its Stalinist dictator Enver Hoxha.

Dreaded shore: Byron described Albania as "a shore unknown, which all admire but many dread to view," and a glimpse of the rugged countryside from the aeroplane window does conjure up a fearsome prospect; but from the very moment you arrive in Albania you are an object of an intense but respectful interest. They may not be the first to start a conversation – and many Albanians speak excellent World Service English – but once introductions have been made they will tend to regard you as their guest, offering you anything from an ancient boiled sweet to a freshly-slaughtered goat for dinner. This is not just hospitality born out of curiosity but a remnant of one the ancient laws of Albania, the *kanun*, thought to have been a primitive unwritten constitution derived from the Illyrians. An Albanian's home, however poor, it decreed, "is for God and the guest". Few Albanians would claim to know much about the *kanun*, but many of its teachings are still imprinted on the cultural psyche, one reason perhaps why the national spirit has remained so strong.

Although a small country, Albania is full of contrasts. The flat plain that makes up the western coastal strip of the country is largely agricultural, where you see groups of women in conical reed hats tilling vast acres of dry earth, horse-drawn carts, and fields of maize or watermelon. Life in the bigger towns and cities can be much harsher, with drab Soviet-bloc architecture, high unemployment and poor amenities. Privatised shops are appearing, but in general give way to the markets where the unco-operatised farmers sell their produce at their own prices and the blackmarketeers display the weirdest collections of goods.

Throughout Albania, impossible to miss in both town and country, is the pillbox. Millions of these indestructible concrete pimples were built, as a result

of Hoxha's paranoia. And there they are still, carved in granite at the bottom of the most inaccessible ravine, or laid out in white-painted boulders on the top of an unclimbable mountain.

It is in those mountains, which rise up like great storm clouds on the horizon, that one can truly feel the spirit of Albania. This is wild country, the land of mountain men with dark moustaches, white felt hats, and ancient rifles slung over the shoulder. This is the Albania Byron knew and, save for the rifle, it is Albania as it has been for centuries. Where the Romans, the Turks and Stalinism could not destroy, democracy and westernisation may just succeed. A visit to Albania may be a last chance to see the living history of the Balkans.

On Albania's northern and eastern borders is the former Yugoslavia, to the south and east is Greece. To the west is the Adriatic, across which lies the country's closest western neighbour, Italy, less than 60 miles (100 km) away. It has a total area of less than 11,000 sq. miles (29,000 sq. km), a population of around 3 million and is predominantly rugged, mountainous terrain. To the north, east and south of the country are sparsely populated areas with dramatic mountain ranges. The central plain that makes up western Albania and stretches for some 200 km along the Adriatic coast is fertile and more densely populated. Albania has a Mediterranean climate with hot, dry summers and mild winters, although in the northern mountains weather conditions can be spectacularly unpredictable.

Now that private car ownership is allowed, roads in the capital, **Tirana**, are often jammed. The city's traffic controls have not kept pace with this move up from the pedestrian, the bicycle and the occasional armoured column and, at rush hour, chaos reigns. **Skanderbeg Square** is Tirana's focal point, overlooked by the dull slab of the Tirana Hotel. Named after Albania's 15th-century national hero, the square was until 1991 the site of a 40-ft (12-metre) bronze statue of Enver Hoxha. On the east side is the **Palace of Cul-**

US Air Force fighter rusts in the grounds of the castle in Gjirokaster.

ture, which houses the national library. Next to that is the **Mosque of Ethem Bey**, one of the few mosques to survive and now in regular use. To the west is the **National Historical Museum** with a good collection of artefacts from prehistory and antiquity, with some stunning mosaics, as well as evidence of a rich medieval period. To the south side is the monument to Skanderbeg, astride a horse. From here a wide, shady avenue, the Martyrs of the Nation, leads past the Datji Hotel where much of the country's unofficial business takes place. It is a good meeting place and has the best restaurant in the city.

Beyond the hotel is the **Hoxha Mausoleum**, designed by his architect son. The vast marble pyramid is expected to become an exhibition centre or even a nightclub. At the far end of the city is Tirana University and, close by, the **Archeological Museum**, with some fine Illyrian objects.

A less pompous site is the **Monument to the Martyrs** of the Struggle for National Liberation from which Hoxha

was exhumed and taken to a commoner's grave on the other side of town. With its cool, majestic view over Tirana it is a good place to contemplate how the mighty are fallen.

Around the country: Albturist, Albania's national tourist authority, organises tours to several of the country's towns and places of interest. Most towns and cities have their particular attractions and museums, but among the already established tourist itineraries are **Durrës**, Albania's principal port, with its partially excavated Roman amphitheatre and fine beaches to the south. **Saranda** is the centre of Albania's "riviera", again with fine, empty beaches and fruit groves and some exquisite wooden villas built for the former elite. Nearby are the ruins of **Buthrotum**, thought to have been built by the Trojans.

Also worth visiting is the hill town of **Kruja** with the **Skanderbeg Museum** and a Turkish bazaar. **Girokastër**, Albania's most southern city, has been designated a "museum town". Its older houses have been preserved and architecturally it retains a marked Greek character, with steep streets leading up to the remains of an old citadel. This houses the **National Museum of Arms,** with weaponry from the Stone Age to the present day – or what passes for weaponry in Albania.

Off the main tourist itinerary is **Lake Pogradec** which lies on the eastern border between the Macedonian part of former Yugoslavia and Albania. It is one of the largest lakes in the Balkans and if you can persuade a guide to take you it will not be a disappointment. The lake's Albanian coast is dotted with ancient little fishing hamlets and the area is famed for its fish cuisine and for its red wine.

Much of Albania's archaeological and ethnographic richness has yet to be fully discovered by the west, and birdwatchers, botanists, hikers and mountaineers all have treats in store as the country opens up. Meeting Albanians, however, and listening to them describe their rugged country, their rich ancestry and their isolated past, is perhaps the greatest reward of all.

Skanderbeg Square, Tirana.

FORMER YUGOSLAVIA

When television screens were lit by the fires caused by the bombing of the beautiful Adriatic port of **Dubrovnik** in 1991, many people felt deeply shocked. Here was the queen of the Adriatic, a Venetian rival that had survived centuries of attack with the motto "Freedom is worth more than gold". The ancient walled city, which enclosed two monasteries and two palaces, had survived to become a major tourist destination on Continental Europe, the star of Yugoslavia's dramatic and beautiful coast.

Yugoslavia had come late to tourism, developing after neighbouring Greece, and as a result much of it was still unspoilt. This was the nation, it was said, of seven borders, six republics, five nationalities, four religions, three languages and two alphabets (St Cyril, creator of the Cyrillic alphabet, came from the Macedonian region of the country). Just over 70 years of existence were not sufficient to make the nation gel, in spite of efforts of Marshal Tito, the wartime resistance leader and premier from 1943 until his death in 1980.

After renouncing communism, the native Slovenians, Serbs, Croatians, Boznia-Herzogovinians, Montenegrans and Macedonians, Socialists, Christians and Muslims, began battling for this delightful rocky terrain. **Mostar** in Bosnia-Herzogovina, an essential site on any tourist itinerary, with pretty minarets, churches and a much-photographed medieval bridge, was bombarded and besieged for months on end. Other beautiful sites became just so many more marks on the armies' maps.

The region's natural sites have a better chance of surviving. It has about 300 lakes and 73,400 miles (118,000 km) of rivers, among which is the **River Gacka,** declared the best in Europe for Californian trout.

In the southernmost region of Macedonia (a name neighbouring Greece claims belongs to them) is **Lake Ohrid**, shared with Albania. At 938ft (286 metres) it is one of the deepest, as well as one of the oldest, lakes in the world and round the edges of its remarkably translucent waters are a scattering of utterly peaceful monasteries and churches. Macedonia's neighbour, Monte-

negro, has some equally wild and inaccesssible places. Between the coast and the Croatian capital of **Zagreb** is **Plitvice National Park** where a terrace of 16 lakes cascades down, making it one of the most beguiling places in the country. Crayfish and trout thrive it their clear waters.

But the water most visitors have been attracted to is the Adriatic. The Dalmatian coast, with inlets and islands, is 390 miles (628 km) long as the crow flies, but the coast road, the **Adriatic Highway**, travels 744 miles (1,200 km) around its contours. Among the resorts which war has made unsafe are attractive islands such as **Primosten**, **Trogir**, **Hvar** and **Mljet**, the only place in Europe where mongooses are found in the wild.The main towns on the coast are **Zadar** and **Split**, a town of great antiquity centred on Diocletian's Palace.

To the north, in the lee of the conflict and in comparative calm is **Istria**, touching Italy. Here are the **Postojna underground caves**, the original stud farm for the Lippizaner horses of Vienna, in **Lipica**, and popular resorts such as **Porec** and **Roivinj** which both have Roman remains. ∎

Ostrog mountain monastery.

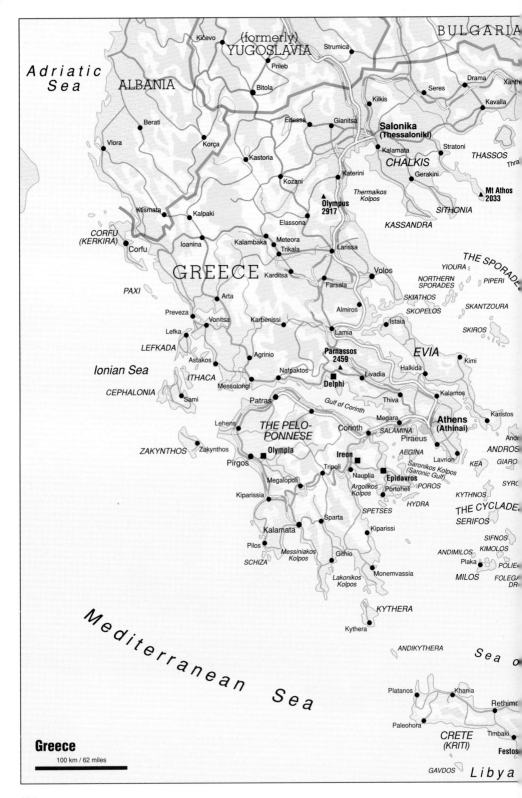

GREECE

Modern Greece, which emerged in the 19th century from 500 years of Ottoman rule, lies in a rocky pile of peninsulas and islands at the bottom of the Balkans in the eastern Mediterranean, with a language and landscape redolent of its pre-eminent place in the history of the western world. History, drama, politics, philosophy: the words as well as the concepts have their roots here.

There are several fertile plains, in Thessaly on the mainland and in the Peloponnese, the southern half of the country split from the mainland by the Corinth Canal. But by and large the country presents a rugged landscape that makes life hard: Greece is the poorest member of the Economic Community. To the north, the 51,000 sq. mile (132,000 sq. km) country borders the Balkan flashpoints of Albania, the former Yugoslavia province of Macedonia, Bulgaria and, for a few last miles, its former master, Turkey. Just over Turkey's border is Istanbul, Constantinople, capital of Byzantium and centre of Eastern Orthodox Christianity, to which the Greek Orthodox church subscribes. That is where Asia begins.

Around these rugged lands are the familiar names of the city states which vied for supremacy in the eastern Mediterranean more than 2,000 years ago: Corinth, Sparta, Mycenae, Thrace, Athens. And here are Delphi, the Parthenon and Mount Olympus, still haunted by the ancient gods.

Greece is not a hard place to find one's way around. The adventurous will take a boat from Athens' port of Piraeus and explore the delights of just a few of the hundreds of islands the gods tossed into the Aegean and Ionian seas.

Preceding pages: the sun sets over the Temple of Poseidon; changing the guard at the Tomb of the Unknown Soldier in front of the parliament building in Athens.

AROUND GREECE

At its height in the 4th century BC, Greece stretched from Italy to India, a vast empire forged by the Macedonian Philip II and his son Alexander the Great. There is not much to show of **Philippi**, founded by the king in Macedonia in northern Greece, but Ionian columns are still standing in The House of the Lion Hunt in **Pella**, on the road to Edessa, where Philip planned the conquest of all the land to the south.

The largest town in the north, and the second largest in the country is **Salonica** (Thessaloniki: pop: 710,000). It flourished as a town on the Via Egnatia between Rome and Byzantium, and St Paul preached two epistles here. It is a university town and there are several Byzantine churches, as well as the Rotunda, one of the few surviving circular Roman churches.

The 15th-century White Tower, once an Ottoman prison, now a museum, is a landmark on the waterfront. On the furthest east of three fingers of land, the Chalcidice Peninsula that stretch down into the Aegean below Salonika is **Mt Athos**, one of the country's stunning monastery sites founded by St Athanesios in AD 963.

To the south, where Macedonia stretches down into Thessaly, **Mount Olympus**, home of the ancient gods, rises to a snow-capped 9,750-feet (2,917-metre) summit, the highest point in the country. This was the home of the ancient gods and from here Zeus would let fly with his thunderbolts. In the wooded hills beneath lived the half-man, half-horse Centaurs.

The mountain is on a spur of the backbone Pindus range that penetrates down from Albania and former Yugoslavia, and nowhere is the landscape more dramatic than among the needles of **Meteora**. There are 24 rock pillars, which the ancients thought were lances hurled to the ground by an angry god (*meteora* means "things on high"). In fact the rocks were eroded by the sea, and today the pinnacles, topped by me-dieval monasteries, look completely other-worldly when seen in a sea of mist.

The main road to Meteora from **Trikala**, 18 miles (30 km) to the south, is flanked by additional monasteries. The oldest rock-topped monastery in Meteora itself dates to the 14th century, but the place had religious significance 300 years earlier than this when the first hermits and ascetics made chapels and shrines among the pillars' secret caves and crannies.

In the 14th century they moved to the summits to avoid the conflicts of the plains as Serbian emperors fought for control of the valley. Over the subsequent centuries of Turkish domination, they became a refuge and storage house for icons and manuscripts which are now on display.

Of the 24 original monasteries, only six remain and four are still inhabited: Agia Triada, Agios Stephanos, Varlaam and the Great Meteoron. The latter, founded by the monk Athanasios in the late 14th century, is the largest and most

important and serves as the core of the monastic community.

Due west, on the shores of the Ionian Sea, facing the island of **Corfu**, is **Igoumenitsa**, where the regular ferry service arrives from Brindisi in southern Italy. The service then continues down to the port of **Patras**, Greece's third largest city, in the Peloponnese. From here there are bus and train connections through to Attica and Athens in mainland Greece to the west.

The Peloponnese has been snipped off from mainland Greece by the 4-mile (6 km) **Corinth Canal** 50 miles (80 km) west of Athens. First attempts to breach the isthmus were made under the emperor Nero to speed the journey between Rome and Athens, but it didn't become a reality until 1893, shortening the journey from the Adriatic to Athens's port of Piraeus by 200 miles (320 km). Outside **Corinth** are a few remains of the old city of Corinth, which became the largest in Greece after defeating Athens in the Peleponnesian War. Every July there is a two-day festival over-

flowing with roast meat and retsina, celebrating St Paul's visit to the Corinthians in AD 51.

Acrocorinth, on a nearby hilltop, is an impressive fortress with a 1.8-mile (3-km) wall overlooking both the Saronic and Corinthian gulfs. Byzantines, Crusaders, Venetians and Turks took it by turns.

The Peloponnese is rich in ancient history. **Mikini** lies 17 miles (27 km) southwest of Corinth. In 1874 the German archaeologist Heinrich Schliemann uncovered the palace, city walls and Lion Gate of Mycenae, a 5,000-year-old city ruled over by King Agamemnon in 1400 BC, as told by Homer. Much of its treasures are now in Athens's National Archaeological Museum.

Agamemnon led the Greek forces against Achilles in the Trojan War, the subject of Homer's *Iliad* (Schlieman had come here hotfoot from western Turkey where he had just "discovered" Troy). On his return to Mycenae Agamemnon was murdered by his wife, Clytemnestra, and her lover; he was **Gypsy girl.**

338

later avenged by his son Orestes, the subject of Aeschylus's trilogy *The Oreisteia*.

There is no place better to hear Greek drama than at **Epidauros** to the southeast. There is a drama season every June and July and people flock to this theatre to hear the ancient tragedies in their original performed in this theatre of perfect acoustics. It lies apparently off the beaten track, but its reputation brings people here today much as it must have brought them across the fields and olive groves 3,000 years ago. Old Epidaurus is a port town of exceptional charm. New Epidaurus (Nea Epidhavros) is a small modern town on a hillside to the south; Greek independence was proclaimed there in 1822.

Not much is left of Athens's rival, **Sparta**. The city-state was at **Sparti**, near the modern seaside town of **Nauplia** on the Peloponnese east coast. Nauplia's impressive citadel, Palamidi, has 1,000 steps to the top.

Three miles (5 km) away there is a well-preserved, deserted city of **Mistra** at the foot of **Mount Taigetos**. Its palace and cathedral formed the setting for the coronation of the last emperor of Byzantium in 1449.

On the opposite side of the Peloponnese, 93 miles (150 km) west of Sparti, is **Olympia** where the first Olympic games were held in 776 BC. The original stadium, where Heracles and Apollo competed and where Nero won a chariot race with a 10-horse team, can still be seen. A statue of Zeus which stood in Olympia's now ruined temple of Zeus was one of the Seven Wonders of the World.

In the south of the peninsula is the town of **Kalamata**, which gives its name to large, black olives which contain the whole flavour of the country. The the west, beyond the promontories of **Methoni** and **Keroni** where Venetian castles lie in isolated splendour, is **Pilos** in Navarino Bay. Here, in 1821, the French, Russian and British fleets sunk the ships of Ibrahim Pasha – which gave a not inconsiderable helping hand towards Greek independence.

Shepherd and his flock in the Mani.

ATHENS AND DELPHI

To visit Athens is to return to the cultural womb of Western civilization. Democracy, modern drama, and the basis of 20th-century scientific investigation were born here. Today's city revolves around the poles of antiquity's Acropolis and the urban sprawl of contemporary life.

Although Athenian life reaches back into prehistory, its cultural, social, and political zeniths were reached in the 5th century BC. This Golden Age of Pericles gave future worlds the enlightening ideas of Sophocles, Euripides, Aristophanes, Thucydides, Demosthenes, Socrates, and Plato. Though the apex of Athenian supremacy lasted a fleeting 50 years, its legacy is the ancient city's most conspicuous bequest: the Parthenon, Erechtheion and Propylaea of the Acropolis.

Temple and fortress: Rising some 200 feet (61 metres) above the city, the **Acropolis** is the star attraction of Athens. As if basking in its limelight, most of the other important sights have conveniently collected at its feet.

When written with a small "a", *acropolis* simply means "upper city". Because of Greece's predominantly mountainous terrain, most ancient towns were reinforced by an acropolis which was both fortress and sanctuary.

First in grace and grandeur among all such structures in Greece, the Athenian acropolis merits its status. The **Propylaea**, its masterful entrance way, is made of marble from nearby Mt Pentelicon and stretches 164 feet (50 metres) across the western front of the hilltop. To the right stands a reconstruction of the perfect 19th-century replica of the original petite temple of **Athena Nike Apteros** (The Temple of Wingless Victory). The original was demolished by the Turks and the replica undermined by unsuspected Turkish cisterns. But the graceful beauty of its eight Ionic columns remains intact.

Passing through the gates beyond the Propylaea creates a sudden feeling of *déjà vu*. A much-fingered page of man-

kind's history, the **Parthenon** (The Virgin's Chamber) glows faintly golden, though sulphur-rich Athenian smog is slowly turning it white.

Close inspection reveals that the shafts of the Parthenon's 48 Pentelic marble columns incline slightly inwards and that not a single structural line is straight. As in the case of a very tall man who stands with a light stoop, the effect is imposing.

Originally dedicated to the worship of the virgin goddess, Athene, the Parthenon has also served as the lodgings of an emperor's mistress, the church of two Christian virgins, and, capped with a minaret, a Turkish mosque. Today this epitome of Doric architecture is one of the world's greatest temples of tourism.

In 1687, during a struggle with the Venetians, the explosion of a Turkish gun-powder magazine inside the Parthenon reduced the roof to rubble. In 1801 Lord Elgin, British Ambassador in Constantinople, recovered several statues and fragments (The Elgin Marbles) which many believe should now be returned.

Serious reconstruction of the Parthenon did not take place until the 19th century, and nowadays a glimpse of the Acropolis without scaffolding is rare.

In the shadow of the Acropolis: The most popular approach to the Acropolis is from **Plateia Syntagma** (Constitution Square), one of Athens two principal squares. Leoforos Amalias and then Leoforos Dionissiou Areopagitou lead into the 6th-century BC **Theatre of Dionysus.** In the centre of the front-row seats sat the officiating priest at the annual summer festival of the Dionysia. Here the tragedies of Aeschylus, Sophocles and Euripides were interspersed with the witty vignettes of Aristophanes to the delight of some 15,000 Athenian citizens.

Another theatre, farther along Dionissiou Areopagitou is the **Odeium of Herodes Atticus**, built in the 2nd century and dedicated to the memory of his wife. Here, from the ranks of its steep, concentric, semi-circular rows of seats, Greeks and visitors alike annually watch the Athens Festival of Music and Drama, spiritual successor to the ancient Festival of the Dionysia.

On the other side of the Acropolis from this theatre, extending south-eastwards, is the ancient **Agora**, marketplace and centre of Periclean public life. Its star attraction is the **Stoa of Attalus**, an impressive two-aisled colonnade nearly 400 feet (122 metres) long. Burnt down by invading Celts in 267, it was reconstructed in 1956 by the American School of Classical Studies in Athens, with US$1.5 million donated by the Rockefeller Foundation.

The Athenians of long ago used to stroll along its 134 superimposed columns, admiring the fine statuary and browsing in the numerous shops situated behind the columns and in an upper storey. Today's visitor can stroll along the colonnade and admire the priceless artifacts in a small museum of finds from the site.

To the east of the Stoa stands the **Tower of the Winds** looming over the remains of the Roman Agora. Dating from the 1st century BC, it served in its

day as a public clock and weathervane.

The Byzantine heritage: Overshadowed in the 4th century AD by Byzantium, the new rising star in the East, Athens's importance declined as Constantinople's rose. Sacked at the end of that century by the Goths, it remained insignificant for 15 centuries. But in 1834 it became the capital of the newly independent Greek kingdom and its latent political, social, and economic power once again came to the fore.

Nevertheless, its centuries of decline have left a conspicuous gap. Today the Byzantine era of Athens has little to say for itself architecturally, and the subsequent 400 years of Turkish domination even less. Worth visiting, however, are a handful of Byzantine churches: the oldest and best-preserved among them is the **Agii Theodori** on Plateia Klafthmonos; also noteworthy are the petite **Kapnikarea** on Odos Ermou and the **Old Metropolis** in Plateia Mitropoleos. But by far the best Byzantine mosaics are at the **Daphne Monastery**, 5 miles (8 km) out of town.

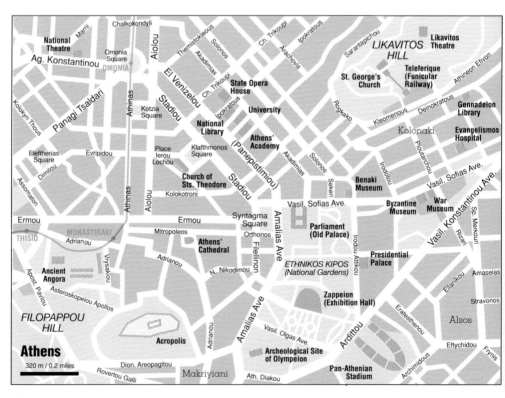

When Athens became the capital it was little more than a modest township with scarcely 5,000 citizens. The Acropolis and the labyrinthian Plaka community at its feet characterised the Athens that Lord Byron knew in the 19th century. While a lodger at 15 Odos Scholeiou (School Street), he met Theresa Makris who inspired his famous poem *Maid of Athens*.

Today the **Plaka** teams with shoppers during the day. Its small, winding streets offer pastel-framed courtyards, miniature Byzantine chapels, and picturesque tavernas. But the Plaka nights swell with the strains of the lute-like *bouzouki,* which can encourage even the most sober looking Greeks to dance.

Adjoining the Plaka is the **Monastiraki area** which houses the city's flea market. From the former Turkish mosque in Plateia Monastiraki stretch the main flea market streets of Pandrossou and Ifaistou, the streets of the coppersmiths and tinsmiths.

Leoforos Amalias runs south from Syntagma Square along the edge of the National Garden to **Hadrian's Arch**, which juxtaposes a Roman archway and a Greek superstructure in an awkward jumble of styles.

Adjacent to the Arch is the **Temple of the Olympian Zeus**, a building whose construction spanned 700 years. From the rambling ruins, it is hard to imagine that this sanctuary exceeded in magnitude all other Greek temples of its time, causing Aristotle to equate it with the Pyramids of Egypt. Only 15 of the original 104 Corinthian columns remain.

From this temple, Leoforos Olgas leads to the ancient **Stadium**, a 4th-century BC structure of Pentelic marble subsequently embellished by Herodes Atticus and completely restored in the 20th century. The first Olympic Games celebrated after a 15th-century hiatus were held here in 1896.

As an infant capital, Athens and its port of Piraeus had a combined population of less than 10,000. In the 1960s and 1970s, the years of rapid industrialization, annual growth reached 100,000 a year, and today the population of

Relaxing after a tour of the antiquities.

Greater Athens and Piraeus is approaching 4 million.

Midway between the Acropolis and Mount Lycabettus, whose summit is served by a funicular railway, is the heart of modern Athens: Syntagma, bounded on all sides by the trappings of tourism – hotels, travel agencies, banks restaurants and cafés buzzing with small talk. Modern Athens's other main square, **Omonia**, is even more lively with touts, peddlers, and all the turmoil of a central subway station. Running parallel between these two squares are the main shopping streets **Stadiou** and Odos El. Venizelou (Panepistimiou).

For nightlife that is upbeat and off the tourist-beaten track try the **Kolonaki** area on the northern slope of Lycabettus.

The Delphi Oracle: Stretching northwest from the Attica Peninsula is **Parnassus Country**, a mythical highland region rich in legend. This is the playground of Pan and his goat-like satyrs and the site of the sacred grove of the nine muses. Here is the Parnassus massif which supposedly played host to bacchanalian revels and the nocturnal dances of the Boeotian women.

On the southern slope of this 8,058-foot (2,457-metre) mountain, terraces rise to the sanctuary of **Delphi**, site of antiquity's most revered oracle. Nestled in a natural stone amphitheatre, it was for many centuries the holiest place of all for the Greeks who believed that here, where Zeus's two eagles had come together, the divine and the earthly touched at the "navel of the earth".

Delphi, 110 miles (176 km) from Athens, is best reached by crossing Boeotia via Thiva and Livadia. Halfway between Livadia and Delphi, a junction in the road known as the **Triple Way** is the spot where Oedipus, returning from Delphi, met his father, Laius, King of Thebes, and accidentally killed him.

A nearby side road leads to the beautiful Byzantine monastery of **Ossios Loukas**, one of Greece's most important. Dating from the 11th century, it is embellished with mosaics which, though less lavish than those of Daphne in Athens, are bigger and more powerful.

The site of Delphi was originally proclaimed divine because of mysterious exhalations escaping from a crevasse in the earth's surface. Prophecies associated with the escaping gas were channelled through a priestess, who was always more than 50 years old to ensure her chastity. As authoritative as they were ambiguous, her cryptic pronouncements held powerful sway over the actions of men and the fate of nations. Heads of state consistently sought the oracle's counsel. Byzas, a leader of colonists from the Greek city of Megara, founded the city of Byzantium on the strength of her advice, and from Marseille to Asia Minor the ancient kingdoms and city-states vied with each other in bringing ever richer votive offerings to the Delphi Oracle.

Encroaching religious indifference eventually caused her power to wane, and her final death knell was rung in 381 by the Christian Emperor Theodosius I who outlawed paganism (and along with it the Olympic games at Olympia) throughout the Graeco-Roman world.

A succession of mythical deities pre-

Early Byzantine Christian mural.

sided over Delphi, the last being a composite god emerging from the struggle between Apollo and Python. This crossbreed god, Pythius, funnelled his oracular prophecies through the priestess Pythia. So it is that the **Temple of the Pythian Apollo** occupies the centre of the sanctuary site and the seat of the oracle was in the centre of the Temple.

The zigzag ascent known as the **Sacred Way** meanders amongst temples, statue bases, stoas, and treasuries bearing the *ex-votos* (offerings made in pursuance of a vow) of the devoutly grateful Athenians, Arcadians, Lacedaemonians, and many more. **The Doric Treasury of Athens** is the only one intact, having been rebuilt in 1904 with much of the marble of the original structure of 490 BC.

Beyond the Temple of Apollo is the 4th-century BC **theatre** which surveys the entire sanctuary and surrounding landscape. Occasionally the ancient tragedies of Aeschylus, Sophocles, and Euripides (which often hinge on Delphic prophecy) are staged here.

Above the theatre the Stadium stretches in a state of fine preservation. In its heyday it hosted the Pythian games in honour of Apollo, and its 12 tiers of seats accommodated 7,000 spectators.

The Marmaria and museum: A short distance along the road beyond the sanctuary is the **Marmaria,** situated beneath a grove of olive trees. It embraces the **Temple of Pronaia Athena,** the **Treasury of Marseille**, and the Doric **Tholos.** Farther west are the ruins of the 4th-century **Gymnasium** later enlarged by the Romans.

To enable French archaeologists to carry on their 19th-century excavations, the village of `Delphi had to be demolished and reconstructed nearby. Between the sanctuary and the village is a **museum** which has an assortment of sculptural treasures gleaned from the various periods and outposts of ancient Greece.

The myth of Delphi and its oracle lives on in the Delphinia, the festival of the Apollo of Delphi, celebrated each year on 6 and 7 April in Athens and other towns.

The Temple at Delphi.

THE ISLANDS

Scattered across the three Greek seas – the Aegean, Mediterranean, and Ionian – are more than 1,400 islands, all chips off the mainland mountain block. Since the islands are such an integral part of Greece nobody should leave without visiting at least one.

The islands off the west coast of Greece in the Ionian Sea are wet and green, and unlike the typical parched rocky outcrops in the Aegean. In Greek they are called *Eptantisi*, the seven isles.

The largest and best known is **Corfu**, which lies just off the mainland and is around 10 hours from Athens by public transport. Its inhabitants have been welcoming visitors since Odysseus was received so warmly by Princess Nafsicaa. Although the island is a popular tourist spot, often overcrowded at **Roda**, **Astrakeri** and **Sidari** and the old harbour at **Kassiopi**, it is big enough to keep some spots hidden. Further down the west coast, **Paleokasritsa** is a busy resort, comprising a series of beautiful bays embraced by ancient jagged rocks and a backdrop of dramatic greenness. Corfu is an idyll that inspired both Lawrence Durrell, the English poet and novelist, and his brother Gerald, the naturalist.

Cephalonia and **Zakynthos** further south are best known for their Venetian built capitals, though they suffered badly in an earthquake in 1953.

On the opposite (Aegean) side of the mainland are the **Sporades**, reached from Volos. Most popular is **Skiathos**, which combines greenery with good beaches.

Skopelos next door is less popular and even more picturesque. On **Skiros** there is a statue to the English poet Rupert Brooke who died here in 1915.

The point of embarkation for most of the other islands is the **port of Piraeus** 6 miles (10 km) southwest of central Athens. Unfolding on to the Saronic Gulf and the Aegean Sea beyond, it is the Mediterranean's third largest port, outranked by Marseilles and Genoa.

Piraeus serves Athens not only busi-

ness but also pleasure-seekers. With its refreshing sea breezes, it is a frequent and welcome retreat from the stifling summer heat. The gentle arc of **Mikrolimano** (Little Bay) is a special favourite whose waterline is a string of pleasure boats and a row of open-air restaurants, and where freshly caught squid, octopus and more standard seafood fare are to be enjoyed.

The Saronic Gulf: There are a handful of islands in the Saronic Gulf, just a few hours out of Piraeus, that offer a glimpse of what awaits farther out in the Aegean.

The Saronic Gulf is the stretch of sea that links the shores of Attica on the mainland with those of the Peloponnese. Many cruise ships serve the Gulf and most offer the standard Saronic itinerary: Aegina, Poros, Hydra and Spetses.

The closest of these islands is **Aegina**, about a half-hour ferry ride away. This scenically varied island is where Zeus kept his nymph-mistress, Aegina. In 700 BC the island minted Europe's first coins, the much-coveted Turtle Drach-

Left, island cottage industry. **Right**, drying an octopus.

mas, from silver brought back from Spain. Over 2,500 years later, during a brief stint as the Greek capital, it minted the first coins of modern Greece.

Among Aegina's smattering of ruins are the 6th-century BC Doric Temple of Apollo and a theatre and stadium dating from the 2nd century BC. Unfortunately, all of these have been stripped over the centuries by greedy opportunists. By far the most interesting ruins to be found here are those of the Doric Temple of the goddess of Aphaia couched in a tranquil mountain setting surrounded by pine woods. If it looks familiar, it should, since it served as a model for the Parthenon. It is one of the best preserved island temples.

The next island out is **Poros,** which is actually two islands fused by a strip of land. This thickly wooded, limestone island is a popular weekend refuge for the Athenians. Though its Temple of Poseidon is not much to look at, the view from there is a marvellous sight. The main town is packed with pretty pastel houses and the waterfront is lined with cafés. It faces the mainland Peloponnese 1,300 ft (400 metres) away.

Hydra, about three hours out of Piraeus, is barren (except for the colourful harbour) and ideal for barefoot bohemians. Settled largely by successful seafaring merchants and blockade runners in the early 19th century, its small white houses with trimmings of primary colours are tucked among stately homes.

Hydra has no ultra-modern tourist complexes, nor even a road, so it has become a natural for the escapist instincts of artists and writers, many of whom are foreign. The tourist traps near the docks are to be avoided. Instead, a rustic mule ride to the monasteries serenely situated 984 feet (300 metres) up in the mountains provides a view of the bustling half-moon harbour below.

Only a short distance from the Peloponnesian mainland is **Spetses.** Something of an afterthought of an island, it is omitted on a number of Gulf cruises. Its main points of interest are a handful of churches and chapels and a fleet of

The colourful houses of Kalymnos.

quaint, horsedrawn cabs. It is also the birthplace of the great heroine of the 1821 revolution: Laskarina Boubolina who became a naval captain and inspired a nation.

The outer isands: Further out in the Aegean Sea are the **Cyclades**, the quintessential Greek islands where island hopping tourism at its spontaneous best. Inter-island boats and flights are frequent and reasonably priced, and the welcome mat is out at each port of call. Each island sings a different Siren song.

There are 24 inhabited islands in the Cyclades. The largest is **Naxos**, a fertile land of orchards and vineyards. Nearby are the group of tiny **Koufonissia** islands. Best known of the Cyclades are **Santorini** and **Mykonos.** The extraordinary volcanic crater of Santorini is the alleged site of lost Atlantis. The remarkable excavations at Akrotiri are a skeletal vignette of life in the 15th century BC. **Mykono**s, still dazzling after half a century of concentrated tourism, basks among whitewashed windmills and little churches. Here the chic set still set about the serious business of beach and bar life.

In the far southeast of the Aegean off the coast of Turkey are the **Dodecanese,** and though their name implies there should be 12 of them, there are in fact 14. They remained in Turkish hands until 1912, when they were taken over by the Italians, who, in 1943, gave them to the occupying Germans. They were surrendered to Britain in 1945 and returned to Greece in 1947.

The largest island is **Rhodes**, named after its abundance of rock roses. Its has a large medieval walled town whose houses and cobblestone streets are full of life.

Crete is 173 miles (277 km) long and is the largest of Greece's islands, lying 200 miles (320km) from the North African coast. The reconstructed **Minoan palace of Knossos** is one of the comparatively few reminders of Europe's oldest civilization, which was almost totally erased in 1450 BC by an earthquake and tidal waves occasioned by the eruption of Santorini's volcano.

Santorini.

«Las Señoritas de Avignon».

SPAIN

Continental Spain covers about four-fifths of the Iberian peninsula, Europe's southwest corner lying on the sunny side of the Pyrenees. The other fifth belongs to Portugal and a few square miles at its extreme tip is Gibraltar which belongs, somewhat contentiously, to Great Britain. Spain is divided into 50 provinces, one of which is the Balearic Islands in the Mediterranean while two cover the Canary Islands in the Atlantic. With an area of 195,000 sq. miles (505,000 sq. km), the country is Europe's second largest after France.

Spain is inhabited by a mix of peoples, from the industrious Barcelonans, whose history is mixed with that of their neighbours over the border in France, to the fiesta lovers of Seville and the south, who were moulded by the Moors during their 500-year occupation. Semi-autonomy has been granted to a number of the regions, so they can pursue their different cultural interests and, in the case of Galicia, Catalonia and the Basque country, use their own languages, too.

From the wet Atlantic coast in the north, which has often been compared to Scotland, to the ski slopes of the Sierra Nevada and the incomparable beaches of its popular *costas,* Spain is a country of great contrasts. It is the most mountainous country in Europe after Switzerland and much of its landscape is breathtakingly vast. It is a land of illusion: in the clear, bright air the windmills on the horizon seem close enough to touch, and nearly every journey is longer than it appears on the map. It has thousands of romantic castles and a number of splendid cities where old town quarters seem straight from the Middle Ages.

At the heart of the central plateau, or *meseta,* which covers 40 percent of the country, is Madrid. Deliberately established as the capital, it is as far from the country's celebrated seaside as you can get. On the other hand rival Barcelona, the second city, is the largest metropolis on the Mediterranean. Both these exciting cities are explored in the following chapters.

Preceding pages: windmills of La Mancha; young males show off their courage in a Pamplona bull-ring. Left, an early mural by Pablo Picasso.

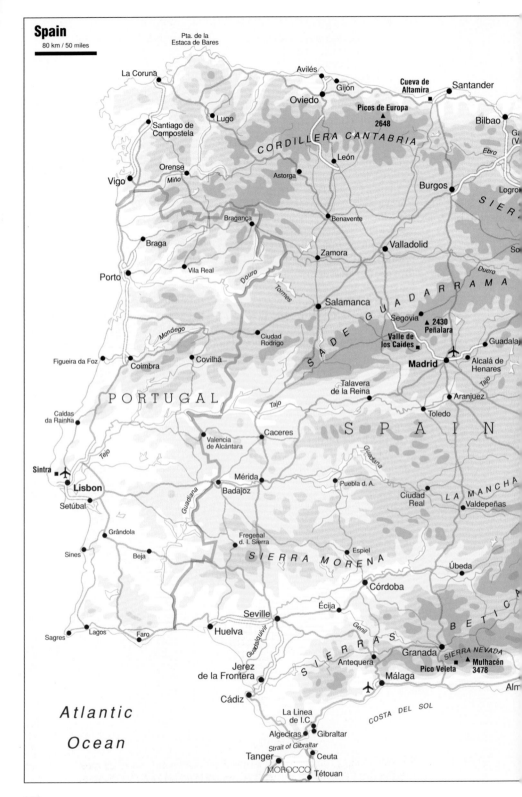

Spain

80 km / 50 miles

Pta. de la
Estaca de Bares

La Coruña

Avilés

Gijón

Cueva de
Altamira

Santander

Oviedo

Picos de Europa
▲ 2648

Bilbao

Ga
(Vi

Santiago de
Compostela

Lugo

CORDILLERA CANTABRIA

Ebro

León

SIER

Orense

Astorga

Burgos

Logro

Miño

Benavente

So

Vigo

Bragança

Zamora

Valladolid

Duero

Braga

Vila Real

Douro

Salamanca

SADE GUADARRAMA

Porto

Tormes

Segovia

▲ 2430
Peñalara

Guadalaj

Mondego

Ciudad
Rodrigo

Valle de
los Caides

Madrid

Alcalá de
Henares

Figueira da Foz

Covilhã

Coimbra

Talavera
de la Reina

Aranjuez

Tajo

PORTUGAL

Tajo

Toledo

Caldas
da Rainha

Cáceres

SPAIN

Valencia
de Alcántara

Guadiana

Tejo

Sintra

Mérida

Puebla d. A.

LA MANCHA

Lisbon

Badajoz

Ciudad
Real

Valdepeñas

Setúbal

Guadiana

Grândola

Fregenal
d. l. Sierra

Espiel

Úbeda

Sines

Beja

SIERRA MORENA

BETICA

Córdoba

Écija

Seville

Huelva

SIERRAS

Granada

SIERRA NEVADA

Sagres

Lagos

Faro

Guadalquivir

Antequera

Pico Veleta

▲ Mulhacén
3478

Jerez
de la Frontera

Genil

Málaga

Alm

Cádiz

COSTA DEL SOL

Atlantic

La Linea
de I.C.

Ocean

Algeciras

Gibraltar

Tanger

Strait of Gibraltar

Ceuta

MOROCCO

Tétouan

356

FRANCE

Moissac

Aven
Armand

Avignon

Nîmes

Arles

Aix-en-
Provence

Montpellier

Toulouse

CAMARGUE

Marseille

Canal du Midi

Béziers

Garonne

Biarritz

Bayonne

Tarbes

Carcassonne

Narbonne

Golf de Lion

Pau

Donostia
(San Sebastian)

Pamplona

Gavarnie

Pico de Aneto

ANDORRA

Perpignan

P Y R E N E E S

3404

Puymorens
1915

Andorra
la V.

Figueres

Huesca

Vic

Girona

COSTA BRAVA

Zaragoza

Ebro

Lleida

Terrassa

atayud

LA VIRGEN

Reus

Monestir
de Poblet

Barcelona

Ebro

COSTA DAURADA

Tarragona

Monreal
d. C.

RRA DE CUENCA

uenca

COSTA DEL AZAHAR

B A L E A R I C   I S L A N D S

MENORCA

Ciutadella

Maó

Castellón
de la Plana

MALLORCA

Alcúdia

Cuevas
de Arta

Sagunto

Manacor

Palma
d. M.

Cuevas
del Drach

Valencia

Golfo de
Valencia

Santanyí

Júcar

Albacete

IBIZA

S. Antoni A.

Alcoy

Ifach

Eivissa
(Ibiza)

Caravaca
d. l. Cr.

COSTA BLANCA

FORMENTERA

Alicante

Murcia

orca

COSTA

M e d i t e r r a n e a n   S e a

Cartagena

Algiers

Tizi-Ouzou

Ténès

Blida

Bouira

DAHRA

Mostaganem

Ech Cheliff

ALGERIA

Aïn-M' Lila

357

AROUND SPAIN

From the ground Spain looks like a scenic chameleon, changing its appearance continually. Over the hill, the ridges become mountains; past the bend, the mountains become a plateau. From an aeroplane it looks like a sophisticated canvas of swirling russets, greens, browns, tans, golds and amber-yellows.

The eastern and southern coasts and the Atlantic shores of Huelva and Cádiz provinces generally enjoy a Mediterranean climate. More temperate and much more humid are the northern provinces known as "wet Spain". Galicia, one of the wettest regions of Europe, has an average rainfall of 99 inches (250 cm) per year. At the other extreme Andalusia in the south, one of Europe's driest areas, averages some 12 inches (30 cm) every year.

Given Spain's size and range of topography, it is no wonder that one should speak of "climates" in the plural. While oranges are being harvested along the sunny shores of the peninsula, ski slopes are never far away. In this eccentric country it is a case of feast or famine, drought or flood. The central plateau or *meseta* is ringed by mountains which cut off moderating maritime influences. The result is a climate similar to that of central Europe but with greater swings in temperature and a good deal more sunshine.

Little remains of the Phoenician and Greek eras, but the Romans' superior architectural skills have left behind a considerable legacy: the city walls of **Tarragona**; the aqueduct of **Segovia**; the bridge over the Tagus in **Alcántara**; and the aqueduct, theatre and amphitheatre at **Mérida.**

Much of Spain's grace, sensuality, and scintillating charm derives from the Oriental legacy of the Moors. The filigree and lace of **Granada**'s Alhambra and the Generalife summer residence together form the best preserved medieval Arabic palace in the world. Córdoba, too, is blessed with gracious Arabic architecture in the arched mosque. With-

out these gifts from the east, Spain would not be Spain.

The Moors arrived in 711 and swept up through France before ebbing back to southern Spain where they stayed until they were ousted by the Catholic monarchs Ferdinand and Isabella in 1492, the year Columbus left Huelva to discover America. The Moors left their mark on castles and fortresses and in agriculture, on art and architecture, and on the language. And between the 13th and 16th centuries a blend of Moorish and Christian architecture, known as *mudéjar* evolved and was revived in the late 19th century in such buildings as the Barcelona bullring.

Most people who invade Spain from northern Europe each summer head not for the sights, but the beaches. Spain's coasts are famous. On the Mediterranean side, abutting France, is the **Costa Brava**, stretching down to **Barcelona**, where the **Costa Dorada** takes over until the wetlands of the Ebro delta. Valencia's coast is the **Costa Blanca** and as the shore turns to face south in

Left, the flamenco tradition. Right, looking towards the Alhambra's Court of the Lions.

Andalusia, it becomes the much-built-up **Costa del Sol**. Past the Strait of Gibraltar the Costa de la Luz reaches up to Cadiz and Portuguese border.

But none of the coastal resorts is far from "real" inland Spain, and the popularity of the Costa del Sol is in part due to the proximity of some of Spain's most glorious cities, including Granada, Córdoba and **Seville**, whose spring fiesta, the Feria, is the most brilliant of the country's many colourful and noisy festivals. The city was also the venue for Expo 92, which has added a new tourist site to its traditional offerings. Seville's cathedral of Santa María has the largest interior of any in the world.

Cathedrals are generally the centre of the cities' old towns or Gothic quarters. Romanesque architecture first took root in Catalonia, but reached it greatest expression in the cathedrals of **Santiago de Compostela**, one of Europe's main destinations for pilgrims for centuries. **Avila** and **Salamanca** also have good examples. Gothic cathedrals reached their zenith in **Seville**, **Burgos**, **León**, **Tarragona**, **Toledo**, **Valencia**, and **Zaragoza**, which like most cities hosted Iberians, Romans, Visigoths and Moors, plus the fictional Don Quixote who tilted at the windmills of La Mancha. Also noted for its Gothic architecture is **Vitoria**, capital of the Basque Country, which has an attractive Gothic quarter around the cathedral.

The Basque coast's most famous resort is **San Sebastián**, which has fine sandy beaches and a reputation for gastronomy. Many visitors to the Basque Country will want to see the new **Guggenheim Museum** in **Bilbao**, a great "Titanium flower" shimmering beside the quayside of the River Nervión containing many works of modern art.

"To build a castle in Spain" was a 14th-century aphorism for all manner of useless endeavours (there were some 10,000 of them then, five times the present number). But in their heyday castles served a real defensive purpose. It takes little imagination to see where the regions of Old and New Castile got their names. Today the greatest concentration of well-preserved castles is to be found in the province of **Segovia** near Madrid and in the southern region of Andalusia.

Spain's size has helped to preserve some remote wild places. Among them are the 8,660 ft (2,640 metres) **Picos de Europa** in the Cantabrian Mountains, and the **Sierra Nevada**, near Granada, which has the highest road in Europe. These are the lands of lynxes, mountain goats and eagles. The big national park is the **Coto Doñana** near Seville on the delta of the Guadalquivir. Some spectacular wildlife can be seen here in what is probably the most important bird migratory site in Europe.

Music and motion: A guitar and flounced dress, a rose in the teeth, aggressive music duelling with clicking heels and staccato castanets: the flamenco is a proud (some would say arrogant) art form which visitors rarely get to see at its spontaneous best. Its elusive quintessence is pure inspiration, known as *duende,* the fusion of motion and music, emotion and style in one quicksilver moment. Though it has *aficiona-*

Summer's end in the Picos de Europa, Cantabria.

360

dos throughout the country, flamenco belongs to the heart of Andalusia and the Spanish south.

To the Spaniards of Andalusia, flamenco and the bullfight are as personal as a love letter. Among foreigners the bullfight rarely evokes a lukewarm response; they are either fired by its excitement or disgusted by such a pageant of death. As many Spaniards see it, the *corrida* is a graceful sport requiring concentration and courage. Through intellect and sheer strength of will the *torero* must dominate the *toro bravo* as a jockey does his thoroughbred.

The tradition of the bullfight as a sport originated among knights of the Middle Ages. Until the 18th century it was practised on horseback. Then, under the Bourbon monarchs, it fell into disfavour and passed to the common folk, who fought on foot. Today the bullfight season runs from Easter to October.

Spain is a country for night owls. It is not unusual to make a dinner date for 10 or 11pm. A generally mild climate means most socialising takes place out in the streets, or in the local bars and taverns, before and after dinner.

The Spanish are adept at enjoying themselves and insist on eating well, often, and a lot. The national larder is replete with fresh seafood, suckling pig, roast lamb, and partridge; the pantry, chock-full of artichokes, olives, almonds, and oranges; the *bodega*, brimming with wines, sherries and brandies. Regional cooking is important and distinctive and gives its own special twist to these basic ingredients.

Wine is made all over the country, from **Rioja** in the north, which produces a full, oaky-flavoured red wine as well as whites, to **Jerez de la Frontera** in the horse- and cattle-breeding lands of the south, which has given its name to the fortified wine, sherry.

Spain's cities have other specialities. Córdoba is noted for leather; Granada for lace and carpets; the Balearic Islands for pearls; **Toledo** for distinctive gold-and-black metalware; and New Castile for ceramics and pottery, which is generally good everywhere.

Some prefer a pool to the sea.

MADRID AND ITS SURROUNDINGS

Madrid is virtually the geographical centre of mainland Spain. It lies about as far from any ocean as one can get in this country. At 2,150 feet (655 metres) above sea level, it is the highest capital in Europe, with a population of 3.2 million (over 4.5 million counting the hinterland). Situated on the central plateau surrounded by mountains, it has not only been climatically sheltered from maritime influences, but culturally and socially insulated as well.

The area is largely inhabited by Castilians who, like most Spaniards, set themselves apart (and often above) their fellow countrymen, considering themselves the only pure-caste Spaniards. They point out that the *castellano* they speak is the purest, most refined Spanish. The central plateau has many popular excursion destinations.

In the 10th century the future capital of Spain was a Moorish fortress named Majerit which a century later was captured by Alfonso VI, king of Castile. In 1561, during Spain's Golden Age of empire, Philip II moved his residence here from Toledo and proclaimed Madrid his new capital. Except for the brief period between 1601 and 1607 when Philip III moved to Valladolid, it has remained the capital ever since.

In 1808, the French invaded and installed Joseph Bonaparte, Napoleon's brother, on the Spanish throne. The city rose in rebellion. In his paintings *Dos de Mayo, 1808* and *Tres de Mayo, 1808*, in the Prado Museum, Goya chronicles the gruesome street battles that cost more than 1,000 lives. The resulting Peninsular War, known in Spain as the War of Independence, brought British troops to Spain's side and dragged on until 1814, when the French were finally defeated.

A little more than a century later, Madrid and Barcelona spearheaded Republican resistance to the military rebellion led by General Franco. In November 1936, three months after the Nationalist uprising against the Republic, the siege of Madrid began. The

central post office sustained 155 direct hits from Nationalist artillery fire. But the city did not succumb to the overwhelming military forces of General Franco until 28 March 1939.

Echoes of empire: Most of Madrid's sightseeing attractions are intimately linked with its history as a royal residence and centre of a vanished empire. The oldest part of the city is the area between the Palacio Real (Royal Palace, also known as the Palacio de Oriente) and the Paseo del Prado. It embraces the Plaza Mayor, the Puerta del Sol and the Morería (the old Arab quarter). By and large this area is still as it was at the beginning of the 17th century. On a map it is readily distinguished by its chaotic arrangement of narrow streets.

In its younger days the **Plaza Mayor**, a square surrounded by 17th-century townhouses, saw tournaments and bullfights, political gatherings, book burnings, and an occasional hanging or *auto da fé*. With the passing of time it has become the scene of less strenuous pas-

Left, Madrid's Royal Palace. Right, Cervantes memorial.

times such as coin and stamp fairs on a Sunday morning, theatrical productions in the summer, and an odd bazaar or fiesta hoopla.

Once the epicentre of *madrileño* life, Plaza Mayor has come to be an important focal point for visitors. More than one tourist tryst has been faithfully kept at the statue of Philip III. In spring the square blossoms with outdoor cafés, and throughout the year it is often graced by itinerant artists and street musicians.

The heart of the area is **Puerta del Sol** (Gate of the Sun), the site of a city gate which disappeared in the 16th century. Today it is Madrid's Times Square where metropolitan subway and bus lines, as well as all Spain's national highways, converge. Madrid revellers gather there to tick off the final seconds of the old year and usher in the new with the tradition of *las uvas,* the grapes. The idea is to swallow one with each stroke of the midnight clock. A tough task indeed, especially after having imbibed a little of the juice of the *uva.*

Southwest of the Plaza Mayor is an intricate maze of narrow streets whose names are frequently indicated on *azulejo* (decorated tile) plaques. This is the **Morería**, surviving soul of Moorish Madrid. Between the Plaza Mayor and the Royal Palace are many quaint, domesticated plazas, staircased streets and balconies bulging with flowers.

But perhaps the most characteristic area of old Madrid is the **Castizo neighbourhood**, which extends from Calle Toledo in the west to Calle Atocha in the east. This is where the traditions of craftsmanship, architecture, food and fiestas have been preserved best. The most popular event in the neighbourhood is the **Rastro,** the animated Saturday and Sunday flea market. If you're hoping to find a bargain, arrive before 11am, and watch out for pickpockets.

The **Royal Palace** is off the pretty Plaza de Oriente, home of the **Teatro Real** (Royal Theatre). Built between 1738 and 1764 by Italian architects in an imitation French style, the Royal Palace is not much to look at from the outside, but inside it is overwhelming. Sumptu-

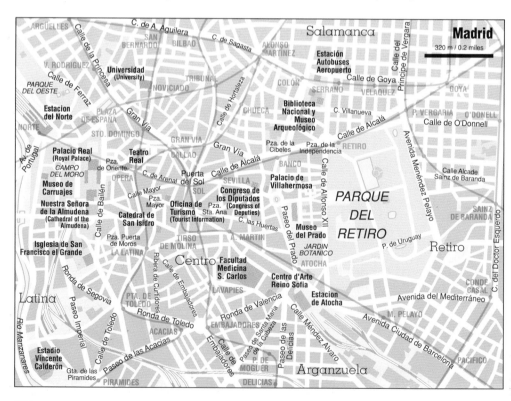

ous and elegant, it is without doubt one of the most splendid palaces in Europe. Though it has more than 2,000 rooms, only a dozen or so are open to the public. The highlights of the palace are the apartments of Charles III, the Salas Gasparini, the throne room, and the dining room. King Juan Carlos and Queen Sophia do not live there but frequently use the palace for state receptions and gala banquets.

The palace's inner courtyard is adorned with statues of the Roman emperors Trajan, Hadrian, Theodosius, and Honorius, all born in Spain. The palace's south wing was added in 1845, and the present-day complex includes a wonderfully nostalgic **Museo Cerralba** (Carriage Museum).

The **Real Fabrica de Tapices** (Royal Tapestry Factory) lies just off Avenida de Ciudad de Barcelona. Carpet and tapestry supplier to Spain's kings, the factory still makes these items as it has done since the 18th century. Several tapestry cartoons by Goya are also on display.

For a peaceful respite from sight seeing, Madrid offers several pleasant parks: **Parque del Oeste** near the university, the **Casa de Campo**, with a swimming pool, an amusement park, and the **zoo**, and **El Retiro**, the city's most popular park and a lively meeting place.

Host to the arts: Madrid has hosted many literati. Miguel Cervantes was born in 1547 in the nearby town of Alcalá de Henares, but later came to live in Madrid. In the Calle de Cervantes, No. 2, is the house where he died in 1616 and in the Plaza de España is the **Cervantes Monument**, which places the father of the modern Spanish novel in the company of his immortal literary figments – Don Quixote and Sancho Panza.

The playwrights Tirso de Molina (1584–1648) and Pedro Calderón de la Barca (1600–81) were both native *madrileños*. Not far from the Prado Museum, also in the Calle de Cervantes (No. 11) is **La Casa de Lope de Vega**, former home and now museum of the dramatist Lope de Vega (1562–1635).

The *madrileño* peck outside the Café Gijón.

From the 16th century, during Spain's Golden Age, Madrid also came into its cultural own in the field of fine arts. Diego Velázquez became a court painter in 1623. Francisco Goya, who created *Las Majas,* was installed in Madrid as court painter and director of the Madrid School from 1780 to 1824. His remains lie in the church of the **Ermita de San Antonio de la Florida**, whose dome is covered with Goya frescoes.

Few museums on earth have gathered together under one roof such an ample and awesome array of mankind's most intimate and revealing artistic imaginings as the **Prado**. The 19th-century, neoclassical structure is home to more than 6,000 paintings, including nearly all the collections of Spain's former royal families. Unfortunately, the lighting is bad, but this is understandable on learning that the building was originally designed to house a natural science museum. To make the best of the light the museum should be visited in the early afternoon.

If time allows for only one brief visit it should include Goya. His work is represented in its full range and shines at its brilliant best on its home turf. Its sarcasm can often be glaring; its sadness, devastating. No one who has seen the Prado's Goyas can fail to feel that he or she has been privy, however briefly, to the most intimate musings of the Spanish soul.

A first visit should also include the works of Spain's other celebrated artists: El Greco and Velázquez (although El Greco is probably seen to best advantage in his adopted home town of Toledo). Among the works of Velázquez not to be missed are *Las Meninas* (The Maids of Honour), *Las Handeras* (The Spinners), and *Los Borrachos* (The Drunkards).

The **Casón del Buen Retiro**, annexe to the Prado, has 19th-century work and once housed Picasso's *Guernica,* an allegory of the bombing of a village in northern Spain by the Nationalists during the Civil War. In 1992 it was moved a new showcase for modern art, the **Centro de Arte Reina Sofia** just off the

Maja Nude.

366

Paseo del Prado. This was the city hospital in the 18th century and it has been dramatically renovated to house works by Spain's 20th-century masters Dalí and Miró as well as Picasso.

Across the road from the Prado in the **Palacio de Villahermosa** is the latest addition to the city's visual feast: some 700 pictures from the collection of Baron Hans Heinrich Thyssen-Bornemisza. The works span nine centuries and include a good range of 17th-century Dutch Old Masters.

The artistic expressions of much earlier eras are housed in Madrid's beautifully arranged **Museo Arqueológico** (Archaeological Museum; Calle de Cerrano No. 13). Among its tasteful and effective exhibits are three outstanding displays: the *Dama de Baza*, a realistic goddess figure of the 4th century; the gold-crafted regalia of the Visigothic kings; and, in an underground gallery outside in the garden, a faithful reproduction of the cave paintings at Altamira.

On display at the **Museo Naval** (Maritime Museum), located at Montalban

No. 2, along the Paseo del Prado, is a curious item of great historic significance: Juan de la Cosa's map. Drawn in 1500, it was the first map to show the New World.

Much as Madrid would like to hold on to its old-world Spanish customs, the two-hour lunch followed by the restorative siesta is fast knuckling under to the pressures of time clocks and traffic jams. But one tradition that the city still clings to fast and furiously is the *paseo*, or evening stroll. The primary arena for this nightly ritual is the **Avenue de Gran Via** and the area of **Preciados** leading from it to the Puerta del Sol. Here between 7 and 9pm come Madrid's window-shoppers, movie-goers, and avid strollers. They come to see and be seen, to *merendar* (have a snack), and to sip their aperitifs.

One particular street in Madrid, *madrileños* are fond of pointing out, has more bars than all of Norway. In fact the city has more than 8,000 bars. But this is not to imply that the Spanish are a drunken lot. Their bar habit is casually

Artist at work in the Plaza Mayor.

yet cohesively woven into the social fabric. A bar is a place to meet and exchange news and views over beer or wine and some *tapas* (hors d'oeuvres).

At 11pm the fun begins in earnest. Bars, pubs and music cafés of central Madrid are packed to the brim and purring. The lively migrations from disco to jazz club to disco to pub continue as midnight passes to morning. In reference to their sprightliness and to the tradition of their nocturnal wanderings, the natives call themselves *gatos* (cats), originally a medieval compliment to the wall-scaling ability of Madrid soldiers.

Nothing has changed in the traditional allegiance of the *madrileños* to their city, as it was already noted in the 17th century by Madame d'Aulnoy. As an observer from France she wrote: "They believe Madrid to be the centre of all glory and happiness… they had rather choose to lead a mean, poor life… provided it be but in Madrid."

Day excursions: The central plateau includes many popular excursion destinations, many of which can be reached in a day trip from the capital. To the north is **Segovia**, which has a fairytale castle, a Roman aqueduct and the palace of La Granja, known as Spain's "little Versailles".

Avila is a town of dramatic medieval walls, **Burgos** is famous for its cathedral and as the birthplace of the Spanish hero El Cid, and the countryside of **La Mancha** is home of Don Quixote and his faithful sidekick Sancho Panza.

The most popular one-day excursions from Madrid are **El Escorial** and **Toledo**. The former – just 31 miles (50 km) outside Madrid – is a monstrously grandiose hybrid structure that is part palace, part monastery, part church and part pantheon. One of the most eccentric structures in Europe, it was built by Philip II in honour of San Lorenzo on whose feast day (August 10) in 1557 the Spanish won an important victory over the French at St Quentin.

Not really attractive, but undeniably impressive, El Escorial is 676 ft (206 metres) long, 528 ft (161 metres) wide, and has 183-ft (56-metre) high towers at **El Escorial.**

its four corners. It contains nearly 1,200 doors and 2,600 windows. In a country that has always built its cathedrals and monuments in an overwhelming way, El Escorial remains in a class by itself. It is an allegory for austerity rendered in grey granite.

Toledo, on the other hand, has a graceful delicate charm. Located 44 miles (70 km) south of Madrid, the patina of a steady stream of day-trippers has somewhat tarnished the city, but there are many examples of unblemished beauty tucked away in the recess of its cramped streets and steep alleyway.

As with most Spanish cities, at the top of Toledo's list of sights is the **Cathedral**, second only to the cathedral at Burgos as an example of Spanish Gothic architecture. Toledo was the capital of Visigothic Spain and from the time of the Moors to the Inquisition, it enjoyed religious tolerance. Jews, Christians, and Moors lived together peaceably and the tapestry of Toledo life was all the richer for it. Cultures and creeds played periodic leap frog: the 15th-century **Church of Santa María** was converted from a 12th-century synagogue; and the *mudéjar* architectural style invented its own cross-cultural quirks.

El Greco, who came from Crete, was captivated by Toledo and lived here from 1575 until his death in 1614. In the **Church of Santo Tomé** hangs his most celebrated painting, *The Burial of Count Orgaz*. Near the church are the **Museum and House of El Greco**.

Politically, Toledo declined when Philip II moved his capital to Madrid, but as home of the Archbishop of Toledo, Primate of Spain, it has remained the country's religious capital. The **Alcázar** (castle in Arabic) has bad memories. A 70-day siege during the Civil War left it in ruins. Subsequently rebuilt, it now houses an assortment of military memorabilia.

All these places may be visited in a day, leaving plenty of time to catch a last *copa* in one of the city's bars. In winter, you can even choose from three ski resorts within a 45-mile (70-km) radius.

Toledo.

BARCELONA

Socially, culturally and economically, Barcelona has always liked to think it outdistanced Madrid, with whom it has more than once taken up arms, the last time when it became the Republican stronghold in the 1936-39 Civil War.

Today it is the capital of the semi-autonomous region of Catalonia, with its own language. But many of the 1.75 million inhabitants are from elsewhere in Spain, many of them initially attracted by the prospects of work. This is where the industrial revolution began in Spain, to the north of the city around Poble Nou, though much of this was razed to make way for the Olympic village in 1992, when the whole city had a thorough overhaul.

From the 9th to the 15th centuries Catalonia was an autonomous state, ruled over by the Count-Kings of Catalonia-Aragon. Its seafarers were famous and its *Llibre del Consolat de Mar* was the 13th-century code of maritime law adopted by all the fleets of the Mediterranean. It was drawn up in the reign of Jaume I (James I the Conqueror) who started Catalan expansion beginning with the conquest of the Balearic Islands and Valencia.

In stature, Barcelona is smaller, shorter and broader than Madrid, It is more open to the sky and its lines are cleaner and simpler even if the port has roughened its edges. The city loves to reminisce about the time when the twisting streets and the tiny plazas behind the port were all that existed of the city. Today this area is known as the **Gothic Quarter** because of the number of 13th-to 15th-century buildings within its confines. The smartest address in the 14th century was Carrer Montcada and in a former palace is the **Picasso Museum**. The painter's father was a teacher at the local art school and most of the 700 works here are from the earlier part of Picasso's career.

The highlight of the Gothic Quarter is the **Cathedral**, built between 1298 and 1448 on the site of a Romanesque church.

The main facade, however, is 19th-century and the dome dates from 1913. Its cloisters and interior are exceptionally pretty, and one of its towers offers a view from 210 steps up.

Near the cathedral is the Gothic Quarter's administrative heart, Plaça Sant Jaume, the neoclassical **town hall** and the Gothic **Generalitat**, Catalonia's parliament, face each other across a cobbled square where the Roman forum used to be.

Columbus and the Rambla: When Christopher Columbus returned triumphantly from his first trip to America in 1492, the Catholic monarchs Ferdinand and Isabella were on hand to receive him like a king. The city was the first to hear his official account of the strange New World. Word quickly spread of the many alien products he had brought back with him and of the handful of Indians (who were quickly baptised in the Cathedral).

The palace of the count-kings of Barcelona-Aragon once stood in the **Plaça del Rei** in the Gothic Quarter. It was

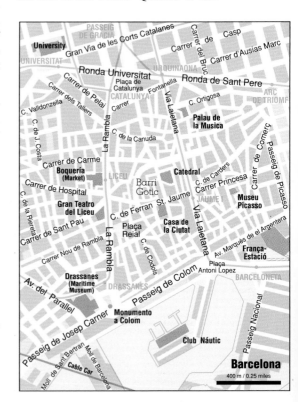

Barcelona

400 m / 0.25 miles

here that Columbus was received by the royal couple in the **Saló del Tinell**. The great hall is part of the medieval palace complex which includes the **City Museum** where foundations of the Roman city can be seen in the basement.

In honour of Barcelona's prestigious visitor, the city erected the **Columbus Monument**, which looms 197 ft (60 metres) over the seaward end of the Rambla and can be ascended for a view over the lively **port**, where a walkway extends across to a vast leisure complex and aquarium. **The Rambla** stretches from the Columbus Monument to the **Plaça de Catalunya**, the city's main square. A *rambla* is a ravine, and the unromantic truth is that this famous boulevard was once an ordinary drainage ditch. The Rambla is in fact a series of *ramblas*, most of them named after the convents that occupied the south side of the thoroughfare: the Rambla Canaletas, Rambla de los Estudios, Rambla de San José, and Rambla de los Capuchinos. This broad tree-lined boulevard marks the edge of the medieval city. On the far side is the old Bario Xines and the Raval (slum) quarter where the old hospital still stands, and the new **Museu d'Art Contemporáneo**, by Richard Meier appears so pure and white it seems shocking. The adjoining **Casa Caritat** has interesting exhibitions.

Day and night the Rambla buzzes with activity, from the selling of pets to the buying of *putas* (prostitutes). What is so unusual is the jarring juxtapositions. The **Liceo**, Barcelona's famous opera house, being rebuilt after a fire in 1994, keeps company with pornographic cinemas and brash billboards.

From the Plaça de Catalunya, the square that hosts the city's big rallies, runs the Paseo de Gràcia, a main shopping street where there are several grand art nouveau mansions. Most famous of the architects was Antoni Gaudí (1852-1926) who designed two buildings on this street, **Casa Batlló** and **La Pedrera**. Gaudí's surrealistic style has been called "Gingerbread Gothic"; these apartments have no straight walls, no right angles. When Gaudí died at the age of 74, he

The Rambla.

left behind him a number of unfinished projects. One was **Parc Güell**, a proposed garden city of 60 dwellings at the back of the city, of which only two were completed. The park contains additional Gaudí structures such as the enormous tiled cavernous strucure, fanciful stairways and fountains.

If nothing else, Gaudí did bequeath to the city of Barcelona a distinctive landmark – the **Temple of the Sagrada Familia** (Holy Family). Bulbously odd, it is a recurring motif on Barcelona postcards. Begun in 1882, construction came to a halt with Gaudí's death. In spite of the fact that Gaudí left no blueprints or specific plans for its completion,work has been in progress for a number of years to finish it to include 12 towers over 328 feet (100 metres) high and a dome 525 feet (160 metres) up. Only one of the facades was completed by Gaudí, who is buried in the crypt.

Between two hills: Rome is built on seven hills, Barcelona is built between two: **Montjuïc** and **Tibidabo**. Tibidabo, reached by funicular railway, guards the city's back and has a wonderful view over the city. It is the site of an amusement park and is especially popular for a Sunday outing.

Montjuïc, on the south side of the town, looks down over the port. This was the main site of the 1992 Olympic Games, which centred on the 1927 **Stadium** and **Palau Jordi**. At its summit is a castle built when Catalonia revolted against Philip IV in 1640, and now housing a military museum. Below it is another large amusement park and further museums located in grand buildings which were erected for the 1929 Barcelona Fair. Among them is the **Museum of Catalan Art** in the Palau Nacional, which has the finest collection of Romanesque art in Europe.

The **Miró Foundation**, a beautiful modern buidling by Josep Lluís Sert, shows the works of Joan Miró and other artists. Students of architecture will also appreciate the **Mies Van der Rohe Pavilion**. The **Spanish Village** is a collection of streets representing the architec-

Wine shop in the Gothic Quarter.

ture and handicrafts of the diverse regions of Spain, and a popular nightclub occupies the replica of Avila's walls.

On the opposite, northern side of the port in the heart of the city's largest park, **Parque de la Ciudadela**, is the **Museum of Modern Art** and a zoo whose special attraction is Snowflake, a rare albino gorilla.

On the sea side of the park is **Barceloneta**, the sailor's quarter, from where a cable car runs to Montjuïc. This area is noted for its cafés, restaurants and seafood, although the ones on the beach were torn down to make way for the Olympic village, which is now a modern housing estate stretching north to the new leisure port.

Around the city: When people of Barcelona want to go to the beach they are likely to head for the adjacent Costa Brava to the north, or the Costa Daurada to the south, with its popular resorts such as **Sitges**. The main beach of this pretty fishing village, Platja d'Or, has a 3-mile (5-km) clean sandy strand.

A place of both pilgrimage and pleasure is the serrated pinnacles of the **Montserrat Massif**, 37 miles (60 km) north of the city, which resemble a geographical rendition of the spires of the Sagrada Familia.

In the 9th century monks of the Benedictine order arrived at Montserrat and established the first monastery. In 1028 a priory was added and the religious community grew rapidly, continuing to expand until 1811 when the site was sacked by the French. The present day **monastery of Montserrat** dates from the 19th century.

From points near and far people come to Montserrat to see **La Moreneta** (the Black Madonna). Although the statue is generally accepted to be a polychrome wood from the 12th century, found by shepherds in a cave on a nearby mountainside, some still claim it to be the work of Luke brought to Spain by St Peter. Whatever her true origin may be, as the patron saint of Catalonia she commands much respect and annually prompts thousands of pilgrims to come to Montserrat to pay homage.

Sagrada Familia.

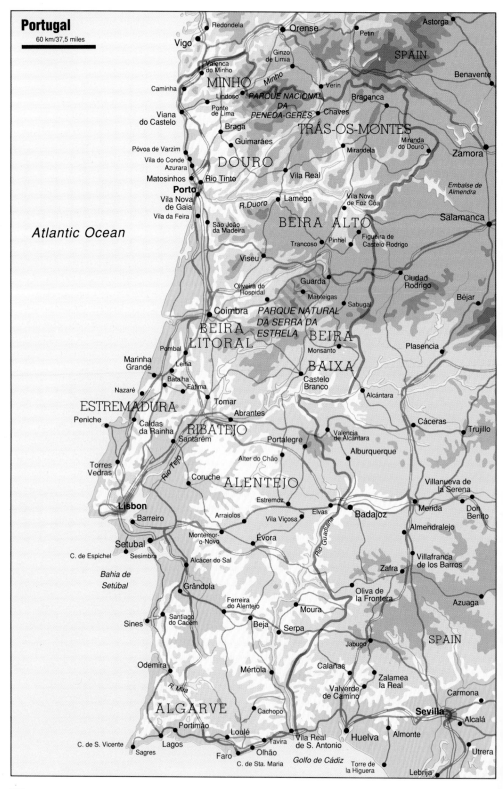

Portugal

60 km/37,5 miles

SPAIN

Atlantic Ocean

Redondela
Vigo
Orense
Petin
Astorga

Valença do Minho
Ginzo de Limia
Benavente

Caminha
MINHO
Minho
Verin
Braganca

Lindoso
PARQUE NACIONAL DA PENEDA-GERÊS
Chaves

Viana do Castelo
Ponte de Lima
Braga
TRÁS-OS-MONTES

Póvoa de Varzim
Guimarães
Mirandela
Miranda do Douro
Zamora

Vila do Conde
Azurara
DOURO
Vila Real

Matosinhos
Rio Tinto
Embalse de Almendra

Porto
Vila Nova de Gaia
Lamego
Vila Nova de Foz Côa

Vila da Feira
R.Duoro
BEIRA ALTO
Salamanca

São João da Madeira
Trancoso
Pinhel
Figueira de Castelo Rodrigo

Viseu
Ciudad Rodrigo

Oliveira do Hospidal
Guarda
Béjar

Coimbra
Manteigas
Sabugal

BEIRA LITORAL
PARQUE NATURAL DA SERRA DA ESTRELA
BEIRA

Pombal
Monsanto
BAIXA

Marinha Grande
Leiria
Plasencia

Nazaré
Batalha
Fátima
Castelo Branco

ESTREMADURA
Tomar
Alcántara

Peniche
Abrantes
Cáceres
Trujillo

Caldas da Rainha
RIBATEJO
Valencia de Alcántara

Torres Vedras
Santarém
Portalegre
Alburquerque

Alter do Chão
Villanueva de la Serena

Coruche
ALENTEJO
Estremoz

Lisbon
Arraiolos
Elvas
Badajoz
Merida
Don Benito

Barreiro
Vila Viçosa
Almendralejo

Montemor-o-Novo
Évora
Rio Guadiana

Setubal
Villafranca de los Barros

C. de Espichel
Sesimbra
Alcácer do Sal
Zafra

Bahia de Setúbal
Grândola
Oliva de la Frontera
Azuaga

Ferreira do Alentejo
Moura

Sines
Santiago do Cacém
Beja
Serpa
SPAIN

Jabugo

Odemira
Mértola
Calañas
Zalamea la Real

R. Mira
Valverde de Camino
Carmona

ALGARVE
Cachopo
Sevilla
Alcalá

Portimão
Loulé
Almonte

C. de S. Vicente
Lagos
Tavira
Vila Real de S. Antonio
Huelva
Utrera

Sagres
Faro
Olhão
Golfo de Cádiz
Torre de la Higuera
Lebrija

C. de Sta. Maria

Europe's most westerly country is in the corner of the continent: nobody passes through it because there is nowhere else to go. It is a tranquil country, underpopulated, with impressive scenery, and, although in many ways it has a Mediterranean feel, its light is more limpid and its shores are washed clean by the Atlantic tides. This is where the great navigators, da Gama and Magellan, set out from to discover new worlds. It is the land of sad songs called *fados*.

The cosmopolitan nature of the country is evident everywhere: nearly 2 million returned from former colonies when they were granted independence in the mid-1970s. Many headed for the countryside rather than the towns, and Lisbon, the capital, has a comparatively small population of less than a million out of a total population for the country of around 10 million.

Both the towns and the country are easy to get around even if Portugal was the last country in Europe to build motorways: the main one that links Lisbon with the second city of Oporto, to the north, was not opened until 1991. The Portuguese are enthusiastic drivers and, as rush-hour shows, few choose public transport, even when it is as quaint as the funiculars and trams of Lisbon. There are surprisingly few roads altogether in the country and a typical full-size road map shows the smallest lanes. The mountainous regions of the centre and north are hard work, but there never seems any reason to rush. On the northern Costa Verde, vistors can step back in time with a ride on one of several preserved steam train lines.

The country covers 35,550 sq. miles (92,100 sq. km) and its land borders Spain, of which it was part only up until the 12th century: their languages, the languages of South America, are surprisingly different. Portugal benefits from Spain's gift of three important rivers. In the north are the Minho and the Douro, which transport picturesque barges carrying barrels of port (fortified wine) down to Oporto. Lisbon lies on the Tagus, south of which is the Alentejo and the popular coast of the Algarve. The cities have a distinct flavour, and the people savour their differences. "Coimbra sings, Braga plays, Lisbon shows off and Oporto works" is one way the Portuguese sum them up.

Preceding pages: main street in Monsaraz; Mira beach.

AROUND PORTUGAL

Portugal got its name from its second city, **Oporto**, which today is synonymous with its special port wine. Majestically sited on rocky cliffs overlooking the River Douro, it was originally two cities each side of the river's mouth: Portus on the right bank, Cale on the left. And, when Alfonso Henriques united the country in the 12th century, he called his new kingdom Portucalia.

It is a stern and sober town of granite church towers and narrow streets and its Baroque treasures must be hunted out. The **Cais de Ribera** on the riverbank is the liveliest part of the city, where small shops and restaurants are built into the old city wall. Nighttimes are quiet and young people tend to head for the **Foz de Douro** suburb, older people to the coastal resort of **Espinho** where there is a casino and nightclub.

When festivities are on the calendar, however, the town livens up. At the **Alameda das Fontainhas**, a square overlooking the **Dom Luís I Bridge**, people sing and dance round bonfires, drink *vinho verde,* the refreshing, slightly sparkling local wine, and feast on roast kid and grilled sardines.

The **Church of São Francisco** in Praça do Infante Dom Henrique should be seen for its baroque splendour, while the **Salon de Arabe** in the Bourse (stock exchange) is a remarkably opulent neo-Moorish reception hall. Wines can be tasted at the **Solar do Vinho do Porto** or at any of the 60 or so port wine lodges in **Vila Nova de Gaia** on the south side of the Dom Luís I Bridge.

The Green Coast: The green wine lands of the Duoro and the Minho rivers colour the whole coast, giving it its name, the **Costa Verde.** The main resort town north of Oporto is **Viana do Castelo**, where the splendid Basilica of Santa Luzia looks down over the sweep of sandy beaches.

Inland is **Guimarães**, the first capital of Portugal, with a 10th-century castle and church of Our Lady of the Olive Tree, which has a Romanesque cloister

and good museum. The Bragança Palace can also be visited.

Braga, to the north, is the capital of the Minho and former seat of powerful bishops. Its Baroque cathedral was first built in the 12th-century by Henri of Burgundy and his wife Dona Teresa, whose tombs are nearby in the Chapel of the Kings.

Behind it in the far north east is the **Trás-os-Montes**, the most remote district in Portugal, where life was so harsh in post-war years that people emigrated to become peasant farmers in the Portuguese colonies in Africa. On its edges is the 270 sq. mile (70,000-hectare) **Peneda-Gerês National Park**, which has a series of lakes and is popular for water sports and fishing.

To the south of Oporto, perched on a hill overlooking the River Mondego, is the old university town of **Coimbra**. The tangle of narrow streets at the heart of the old town leads to the Patio das Escolas, reached through the 17th-century Porta Férrea. Behind the statue of João III, who gave his palace to the

Left, a Coimbra University student with the red ribbons of the law school. **Right**, making port barrels in Vila Nova de Gaia, Oporto.

university, is a magnificent view of the river below, and in the far corner is the library, one of the most beautiful in the world, with ceiling frescoes and intricately decorated ladders.

Luis de Camôes (1524–80), Portugal's greatest poet, was a student here, and the traditions of the university go back many centuries. Every spring there is the week-long Queima das Fitas, the "burning of the ribbons", when students ignite the ribbons they wear on their sleeves to show what faculty they belong to. University graduates also have something of a monopoly on the local *fado,* which is more serious and intellectual than the *fado* sung in Lisbon, and to show its approval the people in the audience are not supposed to clap but merely to clear their throats.

One of the country's greatest traditions is the pilgrimage at **Fátima**, situated between Coimbra and Lisbon. On 13 May 1917 three shepherd girls had a vision of the Virgin, who appeared in a glow of light over an oak tree. She asked them to pray for the peace of the world and promised to return on the 13th day of each month until October. Those are the days which have been celebrated since, and thousands come from all over the world to visit the basilica which has been built beside a colonnaded square in which up to a million people have congregated during visits by the pope.

Fátima is 12 miles (20 km) east of **Batalha**. Its beautiful Gothic abbey, the Santa Maria da Vitória monastery, is an unmistakable landmark beside the Lisbon-Oporto motorway. The ornate facade hides a simple, elegant interior. Tombs in the Founder's Chapel include João I and subsequent members of the Aviz ruling dynasty. Others, in the "Unfinished Chapels", include that of Prince Henry the Navigator (1394–1460), patron of the country's great explorers. The cloister is built in Portugal's elaborate Manueline style, named after the monarch who benefited most from South American riches. Its typical flourishes include nautical fantasy and, the symbol of Portuguese knowledge and power, the armillary sphere.

Most striking of all are the **Capelas Imperfeitas**, the Unfinished Chapels, which suffered when the royal coffers ran low.

At **Alcobaça**, just to the south, is Portugal's largest church with its finest medieval stone carvings. They tell the bizarre tale of Pedro I who exumed his skeletal queen, crowned her and made his nobles kiss her hand.

On the coast is **Nazaré** (Nazereth) , a little visited fishing village where fishermen wear stocking caps, women wear petticoats and the colourful boats are hauled up the beach by oxen.

To the south is **Torres Vedras**, a name from the history books, for it was here that the Duke of Wellington drew up defensive lines against Napoleon's troops in the Peninsular War, and succesfully halted their invasion. At one of the restored redoubts on the lines, Zambugal, there is a small museum commemorating the event.

Near Lisbon itself is **Mafra**, which started life as a Capuchin monastery and was expanded into something more palatial by João V. A craft school was

The Igreja de Jesús.

established as a result of the building works, and among its teachers was Joaquim Machado de Castro.

The resultant limestone facade is 720 feet (220 metres) long, and behind it is a church which shows off Portugal's wonderful marble, as well as six statues of saints from Italy in Carrara marble. But the high spot of the building is its beautiful baroque library of 35,000 books including the first editions of Camões' *Os Lusíadas* and the earliest edition of Homer in Greek.

Mafra is a good place to visit from Lisbon, but **Sintra**, 15 miles (25 km) northwest of the city, is a must. It has captivated everyone who has been there. At its height is the Royal Palace, used by Portugal's monarchs for 600 years. It was built by King João I at the end of the 14th century and extended by Manuel I in the 16th century, and it has Portugal's finest *azulejos* (tiles), which cover its Arab and Swan halls and the chapel.

Beautifully situated, the palace is floodlit at night and there is often a *son-et-lumière* performance in summer.

Another royal residence is at **Queluz**, an 18th-century small-scale Versailles in a rather dull town 9 miles (14 km) west of Lisbon. Among the interior's gilt and glass is a magnificxent throne room, used for a season of concerts.

A ferry ride across the Tagus from Lisbon leads to the industrial heartland of **Setúbal**, which is worth negotiating for the Church of Jesus. This was an early work of Boytec, master of the Jeronimos monastery, and its twisted rope pillars are particularly striking. There are some good primitive paintings in the museum.

Alentejo is the "land beyond the Tejo" – in other words, south of the river. Unlike northern Portugal, this is the flattest part of the country, parched planes of oak wooks and olive groves covering about one-third of it. Its main town is **Évora**, an ancient city which had its time of brilliance as a favoured residence of the kings of Burgundy and Avis dynasty; its sites, from Roman Temple of Diana to cathedral and university, are worth a day's excursion.

The Unfinished Chapels, Batalha.

LISBON

Lisbon is one of Europe's smallest capitals, with a population of around 1 million, and it can have the feeling of a big town rather than a major city. It is nevertheless a truly cosmopolitan city with evidence of former empires from Brazil to Macao.

The town is set on the right bank of the River Tagus, facing south, and is spread over seven hills, which have a number of *miradouros*, terraces and viewing points which look down over the city's rooftops. One such is the **Castelo de São Jorge**. Originally Roman, this was where the Moorish governor had his residence until 1147 when the Moors were driven out and it became the Portuguese royal palace, occupied and embellished by Kings Dinis I (1279–1325) and Manuel I (1495–1521). When the palace moved down to the river, it became a fortress, then a barracks. Ten towers and sturdy walls remain, surrounded by a moat.

The area around the castle, the **Alfama**, is the oldest part of the city, where lanes and tramlines meander up and down hill and some of the alleys are so narrow two people can barely pass. One such is Rua de São Pedro where fisherwomen sell their daily catch or eat fresh fish in the tiny front rooms that pass as restaurants. The **Sé** (cathedral) is in this part of town, a solid structure fronted by two crenellated towers and a fine rose window. Inside is the font where St Anthony of Padua, the city's unofficial patron saint, was christened in 1195. The relics of St Vincent, the city's offical patron saint, are displayed in the treasury. Opposite is **Sant Antonio de Sé**, a small church built over the room where St Anthony was born.

Regal square: The royal residence was transferred from the castle to the waterside at what is now the **Praço da Comércio**, known locally as Terreiro do Paço, Palace Terrace, after the 16th-century palace that stood here and received its waterborne visitors in sumptuous barges. The palace was just one of the casualties of the 1755 earthquake which reduced most of the city to rubble. The massive rebuilding in the aftermath was undertaken by the Marquês de Pombal, the autocratic prime minister, who didn't bother to wait for the rubble to be cleared away, but just rebuilt the new city on top. The neoclassical pink arcades of this square are typical "Pombaline Lisbon". In the centre is a statue of José I, who was the monarch during Pombal's administration. The statue is by Machada de Castro, Portugal's best-known sculptor.

In the northwest corner of this square on 1 February 1908, King Carlos I and his heir Luís Felipe were assassinated in an open landau.

Two years later a republic was declared from the balcony of the 19th-century **town hall** in the Praça do Municipio, a short stroll away to the west of the square. At its centre is a twisted column with a banded sphere, a typical Manueline architectural device and the symbol of the city.

The central archway leads through to

the **Baixa**, the downtown shopping district, a lively few blocks of old shops, tea houses and restaurants, as well as a delightful little cinema. Its Rua do Ouro and Rua da Plata, Gold and Silver Streets, give a flavour of the times when precious metals were coming back from the New World.

Up on the west side of the Baixa is the **Bairro Alto**, reached by steep lanes, a funicular or the Santa Justa Lift, a whimsical iron structure designed by the French engineer Gustave Eiffel, who gave Paris the Eiffel Tower. This immediately arrives at the **Chiado**, the smart shopping centre, which was badly damaged in a major fire in 1988. One of the city's major department stores was lost in the fire. A smart new hotel is rising from the ashes.

The 18th-century earthquake left the church of the **Carmo monastery**, then Lisbon's largest church, roofless, as it is today, and brought down the facade of the pretty little church of **São Roque**. This is a treasurehouse of gold and marble, lapiz and amethyst, and each of its eight chapels is a delight. The St John the Baptist chapel, fourth on the left, was made in Rome, blessed by the pope, transported to Lisbon in three ships and is said to be the costliest chapel in the world.

The Bairro Alto is full of restaurants and nightspots, and *fado* can be heard in its rawest as well as its most commercial forms. The city's opera house, the Italianate **Teatro de São Carlos**, built in 1792, is also here.

An evening out may well start at the **Solar do Vinho do Porto**, The Port Wine Institute in Rua São Pedro de Alcântara, a bar with a club-like atmosphere which serves a large selection of ports, red and white. The *miradoura* opposite has a grand view across the Baixa to the castle.

The Gloria funicular leads back down to the Praça de Restauradores and the neo-Manueline Rossio station, where suburban trains run to Benfica and Sintra, the first place to think of for an out-of-town excursion (*see previous chapter*). **Rossio** was once the city's main square

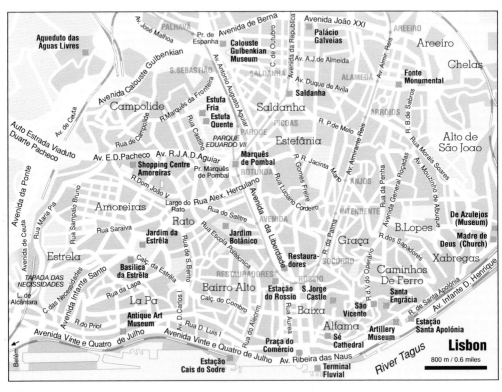

where bullfights, carnivals and and *autos da fé* took place.

Today, entertainment is confined to the **National Theatre**, built in 1840. The two large fountains in the square were brought from Paris in 1890. Today they are surrounded by colourful flower stalls.

Beyond Restauradores is the Avenida da Liberdad, the city's grand avenue where airline offices and banks line the roadside. At the top, in a square named after him, is a statue to Pombal, looking down on all he created.

Millionaire's museums: Lisbon's other benefactor was Calouste Gulbenkian, the Armenian oil magnate who was hounded out of Britain during World War II and settled in neutral Lisbon. His gift to the city is the **Fundacão Calouste Gulbenkian**, the city's principal culture centre with a large general collection and a museum of modern art. This is above the Pombal statue beside Parque Eduardo VI, where there are two fine botanical houses

The **Museu da Cidade**. the City Museum, is housed in the Palacio Pim-

The Marquês de Pombal surveys the Avenida da Liberdade.

enta at Campo Grande, a fine manorial residence built during the reign of King João V (1706–50). To the east of the city, just beyond the Alfama, is the Museo Nacional do Azulejo, a museum dedicated to Portugal's principal native art, highly coloured glazed tiles. The museum is in the splendid Madre de Deus church.

The city's other main museums are the **Museu de Arte Antiga** near the river to the west of the town, and the **Coach** and **Maritime museums** even further west, in **Belém**. The Coach museum is in the former Royal Riding School.

Although Belém (Bethelehem) is 3 miles (5 km) west of the centre of town, no visit to the city should exclude it. This is the Lisbon of the navigators, the visionaries and the soldiers of fortune. On the flat land beside the river is the **Torre de Belém**, the city's enduring landmark. It was built in 1521 to defend the harbour called Restello which used to be here and which was as the navigators' point of departure.

In 1497, at the start of his epic voyage to India, Vasco da Gama prayed in a small chapel beside the Restello, built by Henry the Navigator. The chapel was levelled shortly afterwards and in its place arose the spectacular **Mosteiro dos Jerónimos** and its church of **Santa María**.

Manuel I ordered the building in 1502 and it is a perfect symbol of the extravagant Age of Discovery. The apogee of the unique Portuguese Manueline style, the huge monastery buildings and cloisters are laced with nautical motifs, particularly the armillary sphere.

Beyond Belém the river widens into the ocean. On the same bank are the resorts of **Cascais** and **Estoril**, 30 to 45 minutes from Cais de Sodré station on Lisbon's waterfront. This is the former "Coast of Kings" which several of this century's deposed European monarchs chose for exile. They are smart resorts, with good restaurants and nightlife, Cascais catering more for the under-30s, Estoril with more elegant residential areas, and both within commuting distance of the city.

THE ALGARVE

The south-facing 95-mile (150-km) southern coastal strip of Portugal is very different from the rest of the country. Its architecture is Moorish, its vegetation is almost sub-tropical and the sea temperature in winter rarely falls below 59°F (15°C).

In the 1970s it began to take off as a tourist destination, served by the increasingly busy airport at Faro. Northern Europeans, particularly Britons, bought up the booming time-share villas and apartments and second homes that began surrounding the towns and springing up as isolated "property resorts". But there are still unspoilt villages and beaches to go with the infrastructure of golf courses, casinos, water sports and other tourist necessities.

Algarve is from the Arabic *el gharb* meaning "the west". Its western extremity is **Cape St Vincent**, described as *o fim do mundo*, the end of the world, and for centuries this was as far as Europeans' knowledge went of the geography of the earth. It is still a wild corner, where the wind has bent almond trees double. Europe's strongest lighthouse, which can be visited, has 3,000 watt bulbs and can be seen 56 miles (96 km) away. Along this coast the red earth rises in cliffs of impressive height, the highest being the 500-ft (150-metre) **Tôrre de Aspa**.

Three miles (2 km) east of Cape St Vincent at the lobster-fishing port of **Sagres**, Henry the Navigator (the Infante Dom Henrique, 1394–1460) established his school of navigation, where Vasco da Gama, Christopher Columbus and many other explorers acquired their skills. The school was housed in the Forteleza, the huge, severe-looking fortress, rebuilt in the 17th century, and the 130-ft (39-metre) compass rose Henry used to make his calculations is laid out in stone.

Henry's interest in Sagres helped open up an area that seemed to have been cut off from the rest of the country. The **Caldeirão** and **Monchique** mountain ranges stretching behind it had seen to that, while in the east the River Guadiana provided a border with Spain.

Europe's first slave market: In the exciting whirl of adventure in the 16th century, as riches were being brought back from the east, the port of **Lagos** was filled with caravelles, and it was here that the first slave market was established in Europe.

The town has a good natural harbour which the Romans used, and in Moorish times it was a trade centre with Africa. The palace of Dom Henrique has become the local hospital and crenellated defensive walls guard the harbour now used by fishing boats. A specially delightful church is the Chapel of St Antonio. Its rich, gilt baroque interior has earned it the name of the "Golden Chapel". Near the town are a number of grottoes which can be explored by boat.

Inland from Lagos is **Silves**, which as *Chelib* was the Moorish capital of the region. Then it was on a navigable part of the River Arade. Chelib was a centre for arts and learning, and at its height it

Fortaleza in Sagres.

had a population of 30,000. It fell to Sancho I of Portugal in 1189 after a six-week seige and from then on the monarchs took the title of "King of Portugal and the Algarve". Silves has a 13th-century cathedral with part of a Moorish mosque behind the altar, and its huge castle, a walled fortress with solid square Albarra towers, is one of the best Moorish buildings in Portugal. The earthquake of 1755 reduced most of the town to rubble and today the population has settled at 20,000. The **Cross of Portugal** is a 16th-century stone lacework cross on the Silves-Messines road just outside the town.

Caldas de Monchige, a spa town in the hills above Silves, makes a change from the coast. The water is supposed to have healing properties, but people also come to buy bottles of *Medronho,* a spirit distilled from the *Arbutus uneda* tree which blossoms with white or pink flowers and red berries all around the spa. In the town of **Monchique** the Carmen convent has good views over the hills and down to the coast.

South of Silves is **Lagoa**, a centre of wine growing, and the co-operative cellar is a good stopping-off point. Nearby is **Porches**, which is famous for its decorated pottery.

From Silves the River Arade slips down to the sea at **Praia da Rocha**, the best-known and longest-established resort on the coast. The wide sandy beach is backed by a clifftop promenade lined with villas and hotels.

The resort was started at the beginning of the century by the wealthy people of **Portimão**, an attractive old fishing port just over a mile (3 km) up the estuary which has become the busiest and biggest city on this western stretch of the coast. *Carinhas*, horse-drawn coaches, take tourists between the two places.

Game fishing centre: Portimão is a good shopping centre, and the tuna and sardine catches can be sampled in its many restaurants, such as the Lanterna, where smoked swordfish is a speciality and its fish soup is claimed to be the best on the coast. *Caldeirada*, a fish chowder, is

Albufeira.

often on restaurant menus, as is *cataplana*, a dish of clams and meat.

Game fishing cruisers can be hired at Portimão, or visitors can just go along to watch. This is said to be the last part of Europe where game fishing is still possible. The reefs where the sharks hunt are 12 miles (20km) offshore, about two hours out. Blue and copper sharks lie in wait, as does the tasty mako. **Ferragudo** on the eastern side of the Arad, with a fine fort overlooking the estuary, is a centre of windsurfing and surfboarding.

The morning fish market is one of the attractions of **Albufeira**, a small fishing port with steep narrow streets and a tumble of whitewashed houses, topped with Moorish cupolas. But it has been overwhelmed by the biggest resort on the Algarve coast: it is now turned over entirely to tourism, with a number of fish restaurants around the fish market, and souvenir shops spilling out on to the main shopping street, Avenida 5 de Outubro, which goes under a tunnel to reach the beach. The beach is dominated by the slab of the Sol e Mar hotel

and is crowded in high summer, but there are quieter beaches, such as **São Rafael** and **Olhos d'Água**, nearby.

Albufeira is 22 miles (36 km) west of **Faro**, the finest city on the coast and the regional capital since the 18th century. The 1755 earthquake put paid to earlier buildings, but there are many fine baroque flourishes in the town. The old town is inside what remains of its old walls and is approached through the 18th-century Arco da Vila. Like most churches in the region, the cathedral, at the centre of town beside a pleasant square, was built on the site of a Moorish mosque. It has a fine interior with a Renaissance misericordia and a lacquered organ.

Among other notable churches in the town are São Francisco, with a much gilded interior, São Pedro, with good *azulejos*, blue and white tiles, and the curious Igreja do Carmo which has a chapel decorated with human bones. The Archaeological Museum in a 16th-century convent has a good Roman collection, some of which come from the ruins of Milreu in **Estói** 7 miles (11 km) north of Faro.

The yacht basin in the centre of town shows how much Faro is linked to leisure and tourism. Some explore the islands and sandbars just off the coast. The bulk of these make up the **Parque Natural de la Formosa**, and from Faro spits continue most of the way towards the Spanish border.

The prettiest resort on the coast is the surprisingly unspoilt fishing village of **Tavira** 20 miles (32 km) east of Faro. The river Asseca on which it stands, crossed by a seven-arch Roman bridge, has long been silted up. Sparkling white with a castle, several churches, Moorish cupolas and lovely little gardens, it is the epitome of an Algarve town.

East of Tavira there are also some unspoilt places and the drive up to the hilltop castle at Castro Marim beside the River Guadiana gives a feeling of remoteness. The museum in the castle gives details of the role it played as a border point. The saltmarshes to the south are busy breeding grounds for storks and noisy black-winged stilts.

Left, the coast of Aljezur. Right, window on the world. Overpage, Catholic cleric.

INSIGHT GUIDES
TRAVEL TIPS

Simply travelling safely

American Express Travellers Cheques

- ▪ are recognised as one of the safest and most convenient ways to protect your money when travelling abroad

- ▪ are more widely accepted than any other travellers cheque brand

- ▪ are available in eleven currencies

- ▪ are supported by a 24 hour worldwide refund service and

- ▪ a 24 hour Express Helpline service provides assistance and information when travelling abroad

- ▪ are accepted in millions of shops, hotels and restaurants throughout the world

Travellers Cheques

Introduction

Getting Acquainted

The Place

In continental terms, Europe, at 10.5 million sq. km (4 million sq. miles) isn't especially large; only Australia is smaller. But it is very densely populated. Including the European portion of the Commonwealth of Independent States, its population is 670 million, giving an average of 64 people per sq. km (167 people per sq. mile). On average, 60 percent of the population is urban, rising to 95 percent in Belgium.

Continental Europe is surrounded by water on three sides: the west, north and south. Its coastline is very irregular: the many bays, peninsulas, inlets and islands combine to create a coastal length of 80,500 km (50,000 miles), longer than Africa's coast. The Alps form the most dominant physical feature and are the source of many major rivers.

The western and southern parts of Europe – which are effectively a peninsula of the greater land mass to the east – are characterised by many mountains, valleys, plateaus, and lowlands. Glacier movements during the last ice age (which ended less than 12,000 years ago) left much poorly drained land in the north and melting glaciers formed many lakes. The glaciers deepened the valleys and sharpened the peaks of the high mountains in the south, such as the Alps and Pyrenees. While the Alps rise to Mont Blanc's 3,404 metres (15,771 ft), much of the coastal Netherlands is below sea level, the water being held back by a complex system of dikes.

Time Zones

Almost all of Continental Europe lies in the Central European Time Zone, which is Greenwich Mean Time (GMT) plus one hour and US Eastern Standard Time (EST) plus six hours. Greece is an exception, being two hours ahead of GMT and seven hours ahead of EST. All countries observe Daylight Saving Time, setting their clocks one hour ahead from 28 March until 26 September, with the exception of the Netherlands which adjusts its clocks on the last Sunday in April and October.

Climate

It's difficult to generalise about the weather across a continent, but using the Alps as a rough dividing line helps.

North of the Alps you can count on cold, damp winters with grey skies. Summers are mild and often rainy. The maritime climate in the west has moderate temperatures all year round. The North Atlantic Drift, a continuation of the Gulf Stream, keeps coastal areas mild. In parts of northwestern Spain, for example, the winter/summer variation might be no more than 10–18°C (18–32°F). Rainfall is fairly even throughout the year. The continental climate in the east and north has extreme differences between winter and summer, with temperatures falling well below freezing in mid-winter.

South of the Alps, it is a different story. The Mediterranean region has dry, hot summers, averaging 22°C (72°F) in July. But the winters are mild and quite rainy, with January temperatures averaging 8°C (46°F).

A fourth category, the mountain climate, is to be found in the Alps themselves. It is variable, with temperatures ranging from minus 4°C (25°F) in January to 16°C (61°F) in July.

Vegetation & Crops

Much of western Europe was once covered by deciduous forest, but most of it has been felled to facilitate farming. Most trees are hardwoods such as oak and beech. A deep layer of brown forest soil remains, making the region quite fertile. Most of the commercial forests are in Scandinavia.

In the Mediterranean area, the drought-resistant vegetation is mainly scrub evergreen, cypress, olive and low bushes. When the soil is reddish, it means it has a high iron content. In most western European countries, about half the land is arable. Wheat is a major crop, along with barley, oats and potatoes. Citrus fruits, olives and grapes are grown in the Mediterranean. Dairy farming is everywhere, but especially in Denmark and the Netherlands. Sheep and goats are grazed on hilly areas.

Fauna

There is an abundance of small mammals such as rabbits, squirrels, moles and hedgehogs. In mountain regions and northern forests, there are wolves and foxes. Deer are found in most forested areas. Common sea fish include cod, haddock, herring and mackerel. Tuna and sardines are found in the Mediterranean.

Minerals

Considerable quantities of coal and iron ore made the Industrial Revolution possible. The best quality coal lies in Germany's Ruhr, in northern France and in southern Belgium. Europe is no longer a significant producer of iron ore, though deposits are still found in Lorraine in northeastern France and in European Russia.

Good quantities of bauxite are mined in southern France and Hungary, and potash is found in France, Germany and Spain. Many other minerals, such as lead, zinc and copper, are mined in limited quantities.

Planning the Trip

What To Wear

Two cardinal rules for travellers: travel light and dress comfortably. Don't bring things you'll only wear once or clothes you wouldn't be comfortable in for up to 24 hours (sometimes it can be that long between stops). In summer, cotton clothes with a light jacket or sweater will suffice. In winter, sturdy waterproof shoes, a warm overcoat and several layers will keep you cosy. A collapsable umbrella or a lightweight raincoat is always a good thing to carry along and comfortable walking shoes are very important.

Throughout Europe, dress is informal except for an occasional evening out at the opera, theatre or a fancy restaurant. Women should also remember to dress respectfully when visiting churches or cathedrals, especially in Italy where those wearing shorts or bare-backed dresses will be refused entry. You may be asked to cover bare arms as well.

What To Bring

Electricity

For the most part, the electric current used throughout Europe is 220 volts, 50 cycles alternating current, with the exception of some areas, particularly the rural parts of the Mediterranean countries where 110 volts is still in use. A 220-volt appliance plugged into a 110-volt socket won't do any harm but will result in low performance. A 110-volt appliance however, plugged into a 220-volt socket, may short-circuit or burn up. Therefore, travellers from the United States, Canada and parts of Southeast Asia will need adapters for their electrical appliances. Two-pin plugs are used nearly everywhere in Europe but there are variations from country to country so bring a variety of adaptors along, or just ask for a suitable adapter from your hotel.

Entry Regulations

Visas & Passports

Visa requirements vary between nationalities and change from time to time so it is wise to check with your embassy or travel agent about current regulations. A valid passport is required by all Europe-bound travellers, with the exception of citizens of several European countries who only require a national identity card. Citizens of Canada, the United Kingdom, the Republic of Ireland, the United States, Australia and New Zealand do not require a visa for a stay of up to three months in any of the countries featured in this book. Citizens of Malaysia and Singapore require a visa to enter Greece. Children under 16 require no passport if they are entered in the passport of an adult travelling with them. For people over 16, a separate document is required. Visitors requiring a visa should consult the relevant embassy or consulate in their homeland. Passports should be kept in a safe, handy place – not in your suitcase – as they are needed when crossing borders, checking into hotels or changing money.

Customs

Precise customs formalities vary from country to country but as a general rule, non-European travellers coming to the countries in this book may import the following items duty free:

All articles intended for personal use (clothing, luggage, toilet articles, photographic equipment and amateur cine cameras with film, camping and sports equipment, personal jewellery etc.) on the condition that they are re-exported and not intended for sale; food provisions required in transit; souvenirs, gifts and personal purchases whose total value does not exceed the limitations of the individual countries; 400 cigarettes or 200 small cigars (cigarillos) or 100 cigars or 500 grammes of tobacco or proportionally equivalent mixed amounts. Residents of European countries and non-residents who have stopped over for more than 24 hours in any European country are allowed half the above. All travellers are allowed one litre of spirits containing more than 22 percent alcohol or two litres of sparkling or liqueur wine or any other beverage containing less than 22 percent alcohol and two litres of still or other wine; 50 grammes of perfume; 0.25 litres of toilet water; 500–250 grammes of coffee (depending on country) or 200–100 grammes coffee extracts; 100 grammes tea or 400 grammes tea extracts.

Tobacco and alcoholic beverages are only duty free for persons over 17 years of age and coffee only for persons over 15.

Dogs and cats brought into Europe will require a veterinary Certificate of Health in the language of the respective countries of entry and certified by an official translation agency or by the Embassy or Consular Office.

Health

Inoculation certificates are only required of passengers coming from certain officially declared infected areas (normally selected African countries), or those who have been in these areas for more than five days.

Within Europe, vaccinations are not normally necessary. North of the Alps is almost always free from diseases requiring vaccination, but southern Europe has had occasional outbreaks of smallpox, cholera, typhoid and hepatitis, and in times of epidemics you cannot enter the country without the appropriate certificates. If you want vaccinations against any of these, arrange it with your doctor at least eight weeks before you go. A smallpox vaccination is invalid unless you also carry an International Vaccination Certificate. Ask your doctor for details about this.

Generally speaking, drinking and eating in the northern European countries is quite safe. In the Mediterranean countries however, some precaution is necessary. When in doubt, drink bottled water or tea and be careful to wash your hands whenever possible before handling food.

Medical fees are high throughout Europe although you can get free emergency treatment in some countries (the Netherlands, for example). Nationals of the United Kingdom can receive free or partially free medical care through the reciprocal scheme of the European Union (EU), and must obtain form No E111 from the Department of Health and Social Security Office well before departure.

In emergencies, if you require an English-speaking doctor, dentist or pharmacist, a list is supplied by the American or British consulates and, sometimes, the local tourist office. At night, on Sunday or holidays, your hotel receptionist or the police can obtain this information for you. In several of the countries listed in this guide, pharmacies operate on a rota system for Sunday and night duty. They display signs indicating the location of the nearest open shop.

Taking out a comprehensive travel insurance policy to cover yourself and your property for the entire time you are away from home is strongly recommended. Such policies can include medical costs, loss or damage to baggage or property – including traveller's cheques and money – personal accident, third party liability and cancellation and curtailment fees which can result in substantial additional costs should you alter your plans. Make sure you have the kind of policy that provides you with instant money to get replacement clothing,

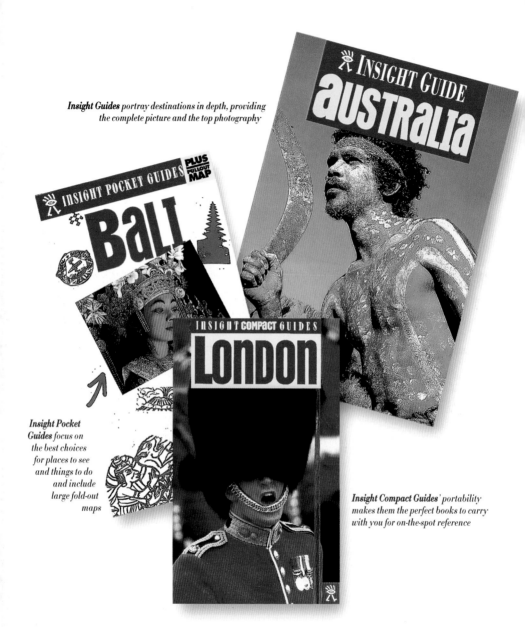

Insight Guides portray destinations in depth, providing the complete picture and the top photography

Insight Pocket Guides focus on the best choices for places to see and things to do and include large fold-out maps

Insight Compact Guides' portability makes them the perfect books to carry with you for on-the-spot reference

Three types of guide for all types of travel

INSIGHT GUIDES Different people need different kinds of information. Some want *background information* to help them prepare for the trip. Others seek *personal recommendations* from someone who knows the destination well. And others look for *compactly presented data* for on-the-spot reference. With three carefully designed series, Insight Guides offer readers the perfect choice. Insight Guides will turn your visit into an experience.

The world's largest collection of visual travel guides

Planespotting

Get a passport ✈ get some cheap tickets ✈ get a plane ✈ get some sun ✈ get a tan get some friends ✈ get another plane ✈ get some laughs ✈ get some great photos get another plane ✈ get some memories ✈ get some weird clothes ✈ get to the clubs get another plane ✈ get some more sun ✈ get some strange food ✈ get another plane get some adventure ✈ get some thrills ✈ get to the sea ✈ get another plane get to the cities ✈ get to the action ✈ get away ✈ get Young Europe Special ✈ get a life!

Young Europe Special –

✈ **YES** tickets are sold in packages of four to ten.

✈ See Europe from only £49 for the first flight coupon! This price *includes* UK airport departure tax but not any other security charges/airport taxes applicable to your selected European destinations.

Get a free info pack by:

✈ Filling in the coupon below and sending it to us FREEPOST.

✈ Calling us on **0800 214 493.**

✈ Finding us on the Internet at:

http://www.lufthansa.co.uk

What are *YOU* doing this year?

Lufthansa   British Midland   SAS

YES is available to UK and Ireland residents aged 12-26 or full-time students under 31 and can be booked via your local USIT, Campus Travel or STA Travel office.

Please send me my free YES info pack.   Lufthansa   British Midland   //// SAS

Title   Initials   Surname

Address

Postcode   Are you a full time student ? Yes ☐ No ☐ Date of birth

Please complete and return this coupon to: YES, FREEPOST LON 7242, LONDON EC1B 1PH.   INSIGHT

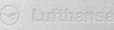

luggage or camera, without having to wait months for a reimbursement.

If you lose your passport or have it stolen, report it to the police and then to the nearest embassy or consulate. They will issue you a new passport or some emergency papers for immigration purposes. They will usually take a week or two to come through and will probably only have limited validity (extendable when you get home). Make sure you have your document number or better still, a photocopy of it (kept in a separate place) and extra passport photos as this will speed up the process considerably.

All countries maintain 24-hour emergency numbers for the police, fire brigade and ambulance services which can be found in phone directories and booths. These and other useful telephone numbers are listed in the individual entries for each country.

Currency

Most of the countries mentioned in this book do not have very strict restrictions on the amount of foreign currency brought in or out of the country. In some countries however, it is advisable to declare large amounts of incoming currency at customs if the same amount is to be exported. In Belgium, Holland, Germany, France and Switzerland unlimited amounts of local currency can be brought in and out; in the remaining countries there are certain limitations on import and export. (*See individual chapters for specifics*). As all of this information is subject to alteration, it is a good idea to check with your travel agent or bank before you depart.

Traveller's cheques are one of the easiest ways of carrying money while travelling and they have the added advantage of being fairly quickly reimbursed if lost or stolen. You are responsible for any cheques fraudulently cashed between the time of loss or theft and the time of notification, so it is important that such occurrences be reported immediately to the issuing office or to a representative agent abroad. Keep a record of the serial numbers separate from the cheques themselves and cross off each one as you use it. Fastidious record-keeping will expedite your reimbursement. In terms of easy cashing and refundability, American Express traveller's cheques are your best bet; other currencies you could consider buying traveller's cheques in are British Sterling, German Marks or Swiss Francs, all of which are usually easily negotiable for cash throughout Europe. Australian Dollar traveller's cheques are not easily convertible in Europe.

Credit cards are generally cashable at all banks and accepted in most hotels and business establishments. American Express is the most popular; holders may use it to draw cash at any American Express office in Europe.

Throughout Europe, foreign currency and traveller's cheques can be exchanged at authorised banks and official exchange agencies during their normal working hours. Before or after hours, currency can be exchanged at the exchange windows of most major train stations, airports, seaports and frontier crossings. These are generally open until late in the evening and on weekends and holidays; some are even open round-the-clock. Currency can also be exchanged on board international trains and in some post offices with foreign currency departments. Money can be changed at major hotels (four- and five-star), travel agencies and some stores, usually at a much less favourable rate. Try to use up coins before reaching the frontier, as they are often not exchangeable.

Public Holidays

Public holidays in Europe vary from country to country, within countries, from region to region and village to village. No list of public holidays could ever be complete, but below is a skeletal calendar of holidays celebrated by most of the countries listed in this book:
New Year's Day: 1 January
Easter Monday
Labour Day: 1 May
Ascension Day
Whit Monday
Assumption Day: 15 August
All Saint's Day: 1 November
Christmas Day: 25 December
Boxing or St Stephen's Day: 26 December

For exceptions to the above holidays consult the chapters of the individual countries.

Siesta: Because of the heat, most of the Mediterranean countries (Italy, Spain, Greece and the south of France) observe a siesta, which means that offices and shops are generally shut between 1pm and 4pm. This is a firmly entrenched custom in this region regardless of the temperature, although sometimes the afternoon siesta is shorter in the winter months. Most shops and offices stay open until 7 or 8pm. Public transport runs fitfully, and some bars, tobacco shops and pharmacies operate through the siesta hours, although in low gear. Doctors and dentists normally honour the siesta, but emergency services still function.

Getting There
By Air

Most visitors travel to Europe by air, either via London or direct to one of the continent's major international gateways, which include Amsterdam, Brussels, Frankfurt, Luxembourg, Paris, Rome and Zurich. Continental Europe has air links worldwide and is served by a wide choice of international carriers which run scheduled and charter flights.

If you fly from London, Heathrow and Gatwick airports provide daily connections to all major continental cities. Gatwick now has scheduled flights from more US cities than any other European airport, and receives charter flights.

The major international airport in most European countries is located in the respective capital city. Exceptions to this rule include Germany, where the main gateway is Frankfurt, and Switzerland, where travellers generally fly to Zurich or Geneva.

By Rail

Continental Europe can be reached from the Far East by the Trans-Siberian Railway via Moscow, with onward connections to Berlin, Paris and other cities. Trains and buses link Istanbul and the continent, travelling via Bulgaria and the former Yugoslavia. Motorists can use the frontier crossings of Algeciras, Spain (from Morocco); the English Channel port towns of France, Belgium and the Netherlands (from Britain); or the cities of Belgrade and Vienna (from points east).

Train and bus routes link London with inland points on the continent, with ferry crossings on the English Channel generally included in the fare. Passenger and car ferry services depart from the British ports of Harwich, Dover, Folkestone, Felixstowe and Sheerness to the Hook of Holland and Flushing in the Netherlands; Ostend and Zeebrugge in Belgium; and Dunkerque, Calais and Boulogne in France. Hovercraft services operate from Dover and Ramsgate to Ostend, Boulogne and Calais.

Practical Tips

Emergencies

Security & Crime

The usual traveller's precautions are recommended:
– Don't keep all money, credit cards or traveller's cheques in one wallet or purse; disperse them so one theft won't leave you totally penniless.
– Hold bags close and keep them fastened. Never leave them unattended.
– Have some form of identification in your wallet, because sometimes the thief will deposit your stolen wallet (minus the money, of course, but with all else intact) in a local mail box or drop it where someone might recover it. Immediately notify the local police station and your nearest consulate or embassy and see if it turns up. If you're in town long enough, check periodically at the main post office.

Weights & Measures

Continental Europe uses the metric system. Some useful conversion rates include:
1 gramme (g) = 0.04 ounces (oz)
1 kilogramme (kg) = 2.20 pounds (lb)
1 litre (l) = 1.76 pints (pt)
1 millimetre (mm) = 0.39 inches (in)
1 metre (m) = 3.28 feet (ft)
1 kilometre (km) = 0.62 miles
8 kilometres = 5 miles
For a guide to comparative clothing and shoes sizes, look under *Shopping*.

Religious Services

Most tourist information offices can supply you with a list of English-speaking religious services or, for a small charge, you can get a full listing of English-language churches in Europe from The Commonwealth and Continental Church Society, 175 Tower Bridge Road, London SE1.

Tourist Information

All of the countries listed in this guide have intensive tourist information services. Their national tourist organisations, widely represented at home and overseas, provide information before you go and once you're there. The more popular destinations are usually supplemented with a city or a regional tourist office, which dispenses more detailed information about that specific area. They are the best places to obtain city and road maps, informative brochures, schedules of cultural programmes, sightseeing guides, hotel listings and weekly magazines, all of which are available in English. Addresses of these organisations are listed under individual countries later in this guide, and all information herein can be supplemented in detail by the tourist offices of each respective country.

Embassies & Consulates

Foreign embassies and consulates are usually located in the national capitals but many foreign governments, especially those of the larger countries, maintain additional consulates or missions in other major European cities and touristic regions. These are invaluable if you lose your passport or encounter any other problems while travelling. In extreme cases, if you are without money, traveller's cheques or transport because of loss, theft or other damages, they can arrange for your passage home (usually the slowest and cheapest way) and will sometimes hold your passport as security on the loan.

Embassies and consulates are often listed in the literature distributed by the various tourist offices. When not, consult the telephone directory or refer to relevant sections in this guide.

Getting Around

Public Transport

By Air

Europe has such a dense network of airways interlinking all the countries in the continent that flying from country to country has long become a matter of ease and convenience. Airlines, both domestic and international, servicing these routes are innumerable. For more specific information, refer to chapters of individual countries.

By Rail

To move about in Europe, travellers have the choice of many types of trains – the high-speed TGV, the plush all first-class TEE, the modern Intercities, Rapidos, Talgo or Corail trains. Those with more time to spare can use the regular trains that take a less direct, but usually a more picturesque route. Almost all of the major routes offer night-train service.

The Eurail pass and the Eurail Youthpass, offered by the national railways of 16 western European countries (excluding Britain), are among the most economical ways of getting around in Europe, providing unlimited travel on all national railways and many private rail lines, steamers and ferry crossings. The Eurail pass entitles its holder to unlimited first-class travel within the validity period (from 15 days to 3 months). The Eurail Youthpass, available to travellers under 26 years of age, allows unlimited second-class travel for a period of one or two months. Both must be purchased before leaving home through a travel agent or from one of the issuing offices in your country. For more information, contact offices of CIT Tours, French National Railways, German Federal Railways or Swiss Federal Railways.

Taxi

Taxis are abundant in the larger cities and can be hailed in the streets, booked by telephone, or obtained at taxi ranks, usually at railway stations, airports and near major hotels or shopping centres. Fares differ from place to place but in general they are significantly lower (and taxis scarcer) in the small towns. All official taxis are equipped with meters – beware of those that aren't; the taxi *pirati* in Rome for example, charge two or three times the normal taxi rates for rides in their private cars. Supplements are charged for luggage, extra passengers and often for trips outside of the city limits (the airport, for example). A tip of 10 percent or rounding up the fare is customary.

Private Transport

CAR RENTAL

You can book a car from major international car rental companies in offices all over Europe in all large towns and at airports and train stations. Most of them have one-way rental policies – rent it here, leave it there. If you want to rent a car for just a day or two, the cheapest deals are offered by the smaller local car rental firms, which advertise in local papers or can be found in the telephone directory (under *Autonoleggio* in Italy, *Location des Voitures* in France, and *Autovermietung* in Germany). The local tourist office can also supply the addresses of car rental firms. If you fly to Europe and want to hire a car at the other end, ask a travel agent about inclusive Fly-Drive offers, where the price of the air ticket includes free car hire, usually for one week.

MOTORWAYS

The whole of Continental Europe is intricately laced with an extensive network of main and secondary roads. European "E" Routes, easily distinguishable by the "E" preceding the road number, make up the motorway system and provide links between all major cities and some of the lesser known towns en route. Major motorways are lined with rest stops open 24 hours a day, providing maps, information and necessary facilities, as well as intermittent emergency telephones for breakdown services.

MOTORING ADVICE

No customs documents are required for the temporary import of a motor vehicle for personal use. Foreign driving licences and car registration papers issued abroad are recognised in many countries, although the motorist planning extensive travel in Europe should get an international driving license. This can be done by applying to your local motoring organisation. Third party insurance is mandatory throughout Europe. Motorists who don't have this insurance will be obliged to take out a temporary policy at the border of each country entered. (This does not apply to rented cars.) International signs and symbols mark all roads and motorways, and traffic regulations are fairly standardized, consisting of the following basic rules:

– Drive on the right, pass on the left (passing on the right is strictly forbidden);

– The wearing of safety belts by the driver and the front-seat passenger is compulsory as is the use of crash helmets by both the driver and the passenger on a motorcycle;

– Children under 12 years can sit in the front seat only if no other seats are available;

– As a rough guide, speed limits in built-up areas are 50–60 kph (31–37 mph) or as posted. On motorways they are 100–130 kph (62–80 mph) and 40–70 kph (25–43 mph) on dual carriageways; with the exception of Germany where there is no maximum speed limit on the *Autobahn* (motorway). Speed limits on all other roads are 80–100 kph (49–62 mph).

Each country has a least one motoring club which usually operates breakdown services and which should be contacted for further information concerning motoring advisories. Driving while under the influence of alcohol carries stiff penalties in Europe and motorists with a blood-alcohol content of 0.8 percent or more are considered intoxicated. In some countries, *any* use of alcohol before or during driving is illegal and punishable by a fine.

Where to Stay

Accommodation

If your itinerary is more or less concrete and you know where you'll be and when, it's a good idea to reserve accommodation in advance, especially when travelling in the peak season (June–September). This can be done through a travel agent or, if you're flying, through the airline's hotel reservations department. The various national tourist offices can book your lodgings or provide you with a listing from which you can book directly with the establishment of your choice. When writing to these offices for information, specify the region you plan to visit. Don't forget to enclose an International Reply Coupon, available at most post offices, if you're serious about getting a response.

Although a bit inflexible (deposits can be forfeited or compensation demanded if reservations are cancelled), advance bookings save time and energy and prevent chaos when you first arrive at your destination. For the traveller without advance reservations, it's wise to check if there is any coming major event which could make accommodation hard to find. Local tourist information offices in major train stations and airports usually have hotel reservation services which, for a small fee, can successfully book you a room on the spot.

Youth Hostels are everywhere in Europe and provide one of the cheapest ways of keeping a roof over your head while travelling. For an official list write to the Youth Hostel Association, 8 St Stephen's Hill, St Albans, Herts AL1 2DY, UK. Tel: 01727 855215. For check-in you usually require a valid membership card which can be purchased at home before departure or on the spot. In most instances, addresses of youth hostels can also be acquired from the local tourist offices.

Attractions

Architecture

Europe has the world's richest variety of architectural styles, reflecting the cross-fertilisation of its many cultures.

Greek & Roman

Greek architecture is characterised by the arrangement of posts and lintels, straight lines, fluted columns and pointed porticos. The difference between Ionic, Doric and Corinthian styles depends on the width of the columns in relation to their height and the shape and decoration of their capitals. One of the best-known examples of the Doric style is the Parthenon on the Acropolis in Athens. The Erechtheum, also on the Acropolis, is Ionic. The Olympieum at Athens is Corinthian.

The arched vault is typical of Roman architecture. Out of this were developed cupolas and rotundas (rounded or elliptical structures). A fine example is the Parthenon, built by Hadrian between AD 120 and 124, and now a Christian church in Rome known as Santa Maria Rotunda.

Byzantine

This style developed in the 3rd century and lasted until the 15th. It takes its name from the ancient Greek city of Byzantium, which later became Constantinople and is today Istanbul. Characteristic of the style are the pedentives (spherical triangles formed by intersecting arches) supporting a large dome. A good example is Venice's church of St Mark.

Romanesque

This style developed in central and western Europe after the Roman empire fell in AD 467. Romanesque buildings have a central area, aisles or galleries at the sides and a raised platform or an apse. Walls are heavy, doors and windows usually small and round-arched, and columns are short and stumpy. In place of columns, square or clustered piers are sometimes used to separate the nave from the aisles. Good examples are Pisa Cathedral in Italy and the Church of the Apostles in Cologne, Germany.

Gothic

This slender and more energetic style of building, reflecting the spiritual power of the Catholic Church, began around 1150. The pointed arch is one characteristic feature; the style is also marked by large arched windows made of coloured glass and usually depicting biblical scenes. The overall impression is of verticality and lightness. The Cathedral at Chartres is a splendid example of Gothic architecture at its best. Other examples are Notre Dame in Paris, Cologne Cathedral and the cathedral in Brussels.

Renaissance

The basic idea of the Renaissance was a revival of the Roman standards combined with new materials and technologies. Florence was its birthplace and Filippo Brunelleschi, a metal worker by trade, was its initiator. If the aim during the Gothic period had been to strive towards heaven, the architects of the Renaissance strove to combine weight with elegance. Many of today's famous buildings come from this period: the church of San Giorgio Maggiore in Venice, the Escorial in Madrid and the Ecole Militaire in Paris.

Baroque

An extension of the late Renaissance style, it dominated during the 17th and 18th centuries. Starting in Rome, it travelled through Europe and adapted itself to different countries, reflecting not only different climates, materials and technical know-how but also the gradual emancipation of various royal houses from the Church. Baroque architecture, emphasising richness and splendour, can be seen as an indicator of the wealth and power of the aristocracy. Famous examples include Rome's Trevi Fountain, the Louvre in Paris, the palace and gardens at Versailles and the Karlskirche in Vienna.

Rococo

This is a more playful and more florid variant of baroque architecture and art prevalent in the late 18th century.

Empire

Empire (pronounced *om-peer* in the French manner) loosely describes the monumental, neo-classical style which arose in France from Napoleon's desire to recreate the grandeur and luxury of imperial Rome. The Chamber of Deputies in Paris exemplifies the style, which was exported to the United States in buildings such as Washington's Supreme Court.

Art Nouveau

Known as *Jugendstil* in Germany, this was a short-lived and more decorative variant of the neo-classical style at the end of the 19th century. It decorates with Japanese and Chinese motifs, exterior and interior, buildings that otherwise impress by solidity rather than sense of proportion.

Shopping

In the majority of European countries, fixed prices are normal. Only south of the Alps in Italy, Greece, Portugal and Spain can you bargain and even then, only in special self-evident cases, where wares hang from carts and stalls in flea markets and bazaars. Merchants have usually allowed for bargaining in the price of their merchandise. Shop around and compare before you buy.

Many of the larger shops and department stores throughout Europe display the "tax-free" sign, which means that travellers from non-European Union (non-EU) countries can receive a refund of the Value Added Tax or sales tax (VAT) levied on the more substantial purchases intended for export outside the EU. By filling out a tax form available at the place of purchase, you can receive a refund, amounting to as much as 25 percent of the purchase price, either upon leaving the country or by mail at your home address. Since procedures vary, it is advisable to inquire at the stores where you wish to make your purchases. This can be a useful saving since VAT in some countries can exceed 20 percent on certain items.

Tax-free shopping at airports and aboard ships, available to those leaving the country or in transit, takes on a different form: the VAT is excluded entirely from the purchase price hence eliminating the need for refunds.

Clothing Chart

WOMEN'S DRESSES/SUITS

Continental	American	British
38/34N	6	8/30
40/36N	8	10/32
42/38N	10	12/34
44/40N	12	14/36
46/42N	14	16/38
48/44N	16	18/40

WOMEN'S SHOES

Continental	American	British
36	4½	3
37	5½	4
38	6½	5
39	7½	6
40	8½	7
41	9½	8
42	10½	9

MEN'S SUITS

Continental	American	British
44	34	34
46	—	36
48	38	38
50	—	40
52	42	42
54	—	44
56	46	46

MEN'S SHIRTS

Continental	American	British
36	14	14
37	14½	14½
38	15	15
39	15½	15½
40	16	16
41	16½	16½
42	17	17

MEN'S SHOES

Continental	American	British
—	6½	6
40	7½	7
41	8½	8
42	9½	9
43	10½	10
44	11½	11

Language

In southern Europe, the *Romance* group of languages predominates, being found in France, southern Belgium, Spain, Portugal and Italy.

The *Germanic* group of languages predominates in Germany, Austria, Switzerland, the Netherlands and northern Belgium.

Slavic languages such as Russian, Czech, Slovak, Polish and Bulgarian dominate in eastern Europe.

Greece has a Hellenic language. Some old languages linger on among small groups; some Bretons in north-western France speak a variety of Celtic, and Basque is spoken by a small group on the Spanish-French border.

FRANCE

Getting Acquainted

The Place

France covers an area of 551,500 sq. km (212,960 sq. miles) and is home to more than 56 million people. Three main geographical regions exist within France: the remains of ancient mountains which make up the principal massifs; the northern and western plains and the narrow plains between the rugged younger mountains of the south and southeast. Coastal regions to the north and west are as diverse as the countryside, from the sandy dunes of the North Sea to the chalky white cliffs of Picardy and eastern Normandy which faces the English Channel. The Pyrenees make a natural barrier between France and Spain, while the Jura range is situated near Switzerland. The Alps are by far the most spectacular mountains in France. Part of the great Alpine chain which extends throughout Europe, the French Alps include the highest point, Mont Blanc, standing 4,807 metres (15,771 ft) high.

Climate

France covers an area that includes all three European climatic divisions – maritime (in the north and west); continental (inland) and Mediterranean (in the south). The Riviera has mild winters and very hot summers; the north has cold winters and mild summers. There are good ski conditions in the Alps and Pyrenees; January is the budget month for winter sports. Average maximum temperatures in Paris are 6°C (43°F) in January and 25°C (77°F) in July and on the Riviera, 12°C (54°F) in January and 27°C (81°F) in July and August.

Economy

France is one of Europe's major industrial nations; most of the great industrial concentrations lie east of a line running from Le Havre in the north to Marseille in the south, while the western regions, which have remained more agricultural, are generally less developed. Its main industries include wine, agricultural products, fashion, cars and technology.

Government

France has had 11 constitutions since 1791. Its present one, proclaimed in 1958 by Charles de Gaulle, transformed the country from a parliamentary into a presidential republic. Paris is both the head and the heart of France and more than one-sixth of the total population lives in its metropolitan area.

Planning The Trip

Health

Tap water is drinkable unless the sign *eau non potable* is displayed.

Currency

The franc is divided into 100 centimes. Although there are no restrictions on the import of foreign currency, it is advisable to sign a declaration form on arrival if you bring in more than 5,000 francs or its equivalent (about US$700) in foreign banknotes. You may need this form on departure.

In general, banking hours are Monday–Friday 8.30am–noon and 1.30–5pm. In provincial towns banks are often open Saturday but closed Monday.

Public Holidays

In addition to those holidays mentioned in the Introduction above, France recognizes Bastille Day (14 July) and Armistice Day (11 November).

Getting There

By Air

Air France is the main agent for all flights to France from America and other European countries. As well as its own services it also handles bookings for smaller operators such as Air Littoral, Air Vendée and Brit Air. These smaller operators offer direct flights from British cities to various provincial airports in France. For those travelling via the UK, British Airways has frequent flights to France from London and several regional airports.

Travellers from America and other countries can get direct flights to Paris and other major destinations, such as Nice and Lyon via Air France and most national airlines, although for long-haul passengers a charter flight via London may work out cheaper.

By Road

Bordered by Belgium and Luxembourg to the north, Germany, Switzerland and Italy to the east and Spain and the Principality of Andorra to the south, France can be reached by a number of European "E" routes. Cars cross from Britain via the Eurotunnel train from Folkestone to Calais.

By Bus: Eurolines is a consortium of almost 30 coach companies, operating in France and throughout Europe. They operate services from London (Victoria) to many major French destinations. Some (e.g. Paris) are daily, others are seasonal. One of the cheapest ways of reaching France, discounts are available for young people and senior citizens. The ticket includes the ferry crossing via Dover and National Express coaches have connections with the London departures from most major towns in the United Kingdom.

Contact: Eurolines UK, 4 Cardiff Road, Luton, Bedfordshire, LU1 1PP, tel: 0990 143219; fax: 01582 400694; or in France at the Gare Routière Internationale, 2 Avenue Charles de Gaulle, 93541 Bagnolet Cedex, tel: (01) 49 72 5151.

By Sea

Ferry services operate from the UK, the Republic of Ireland and the Channel Islands to the northern parts of France. All carry cars as well as foot passengers. Hovercraft crossings are fast, but more dependent on good weather than ferries. The Seacat catamaran service offers a quick crossing, but can only carry a limited number of cars.

By Rail

Overland trains from all major continental cities are frequent and fast. The Channel Tunnel offers fast, frequent rail services between London and Paris (journey time is three hours), and other cities.

Useful Addresses

Tourist Offices Abroad

Canada: 1981 McGill College Avenue, Suite 490, Montreal PQ H3A 2W9, Quebec, tel: 514 288 4264; fax: 514 845 4868. 30 St Patrick Street, Suite 700, Toronto M5T 3A3, Ontario, fax: 416 979 7587.

UK and Republic of Ireland: 178 Piccadilly, London WIV OAL, tel: 0891 244 123 or 0171 629 2869.

US: 444 Madison Avenue , 16th floor, New York, NY 10020, tel: 900 900 0040; fax: 212 838 7855; 645 North Michigan Avenue, Suite 630, Chicago, IL 60611, tel: 312 751 7800; fax: 312 337 6339; and 9454 Wilshire Boulevard, Beverly Hills, CA 90212, tel: 213 272 2661.

Practical Tips

Emergencies

Medical Services

Pharmacies (recognisable by the green cross) are open six days a week from 9am–noon and 2–7pm. Sunday and evening rotas are posted in all chemists' windows. The duty chemist is also officially on call at night – you will find a bell (*sonnette de nuit*) by his door. Doctors also have night and weekend rotas. They, and chemists, are listed in local newspapers under *Pharmaciens de Garde* and *Médecins de Garde*.

Business Hours

Ordinary shops open around 9am and close at 7pm, but food shops normally start at 7.30 or 8am and don't close until 7.30 or 8pm. They close for lunch at about 1pm and reopen at about 3.30 or 4pm. Large department stores, supermarkets and hypermarkets stay open until 9 or 10pm for at least one night a week. Some shops close on Monday, others don't close at midday and those in major towns are also open on Sunday mornings.

Tipping

The practice of adding 12–15 percent service charge to the bill is common in restaurants, hotels and cafés all over France. In such cases, there is no obligation to leave anything additional, although most people do so. Depending on the size of the bill, they leave about one to five francs extra. Tip room service waiters almost everywhere and wine stewards if they are helpful; taxi drivers usually get 15 percent.

Postal Services

Provincial post offices – Postes or PTTS – are generally open Monday–Friday 9am–noon and 2–5pm, Saturday 9am–noon (opening hours are posted outside); in Paris and other large cities they are generally open continuously from 8am–7pm. Exceptionally, the main post office in Paris is open 24 hours every day, at 52 Rue du Louvre, 75001 Paris.

Stamps may be purchased in post offices, cafés and tobacconists' counters. Post boxes are yellow, but at large post offices there are separate boxes for inland and foreign mail. You may receive or send money through the post office.

Telephones

The French telephone system has recently been overhauled so that all telephone numbers have 10 digits. Paris and Ile de France numbers begin with 01, while the rest of France is divided into four zones (North West 02, North East 03, South East and Corsica 04 and South West 05). Freephone numbers begin with 08 00; 08 36 numbers are charged at pre-

mium rates and 06 numbers are mobile phones.

There are two kinds of phone boxes in Paris from which you can make local and international calls: coin-operated phones, which are extremely difficult to find, and card-operated phones, which are replacing them. It may be difficult to find a telephone box that is working. Remember that you get 50 percent more call-time for your money if you ring 10.30pm–8am on weekdays and from 2pm at weekends.

A *télécarte* can be bought from kiosks, tabacs and post offices. Insert the card and follow the instructions on the screen: You can also dial from all post offices, which have both coin- and card-operated phones. To call long distance ask at one of the counters and you will be assigned a booth – you pay when your call is over. Cafés and tabacs often have public phones next to the toilets. They use coins or jetons, coin-like discs bought at the bar.

To call other countries from France, first dial the international access code (00), then the country code: Australia 61, UK 44, US and Canada 1. If using a US credit phone card, call the company's access number: Sprint, tel: 19 00 87; AT&T, tel: 19 00 11; MCI, tel: 19 00 19.

Useful numbers: operator services 13; directory enquiries 12.

Telegrams (cables) can be sent during post office hours or by telephone (24-hours); to send a telegram in English dial 05 33 4411; to send a telegram in French, tel: 3655.

Tourist Information

The French National Tourist Office (known as *Offices de Tourisme* or *Syndicats d'Initiative*) has its central office in Paris with branches in the various provinces. See *Paris* section for more details.

Getting Around

Domestic Transport

By Air

Air France, with its associate company Air Inter, operates an intensive network of routes within France. Many fly from Paris but there are also cross-country air links such as between Nice and Toulouse, Lille and Bordeaux, and Lyons and Biarritz. A number of smaller airlines also offer good services to smaller cities, towns and resorts.

By Rail

France has an excellent rail network operated by the SNCF (Société des Chemins de Fer Français), which runs trains to all parts of France and is linked to the European network. Trains have first- and second-class seats and supplements are only charged on the TVG or High Speed Train service during peak times and on the TEE, which is first-class only. Any rail ticket bought in France must be validated by using the orange automatic date-stamping machine at the entrance to the platform. Failure to do so incurs a surcharge. Carriages with "double decker" sections are for travellers who opt for scenic viewing on routes in southeast France and on some cross-country lines as well. SNCF has a central reservation office in Paris, tel: (01) 45 65 60 60 and a telephone information service in English on: (01) 45 82 08 41; in French on: (01) 45 82 50 50. The SNCF office in Paris is at 10 Place de Budapest, 75436 Paris Cedex 09. Tel: (01) 42 85 60 00, fax: (01) 42 85 63 78. Most railway stations accept payment by Visa and American Express.

By Road

France has a total road network of about 930,000 miles (1.5 million km), including over 3,000 miles (4,828 km) of motorway. Apart from the first few miles out of large cities, all motorways carry tolls. French roads are usually very crowded in summer, especially those going from Paris to the Mediterranean and Atlantic coasts. For information about current road conditions, tel: (01) 48 94 33 33, for information about routes around France contact Autoroute Information (Centre de Renseignements Autoroutes) in Paris. Tel: (01) 47 53 37 00.

Motoring Advice: All cars must carry a red warning triangle and spare bulbs for headlights. After dark, motorists have the choice of using dipped headlights or parking lights, even in rainy weather. In some areas, horns may be sounded only in dire need. Parking is increasingly difficult in towns and for parking your car in *zones bleues,* special discs have to be displayed. They're obtainable free from tourist offices, tobacco kiosks, police stations, customs offices, garages and hotels. The Automobile Club National is the umbrella organisation of France's 40-odd motoring clubs. It will assist any motorist whose own club has an agreement with it. Contact them at 8 Place de la Concorde, 75008, tel: (01) 43 12 4312; fax: (01) 47 20 8898.

On motorways, there are orange emergency telephones every 2.4 km (1.5 miles).

Waterways

Car ferries to Corsica, run in connection with SNCF rail services, sail from Marseille, Toulon and Nice. Cruises also operate on the Marne, the Canal du Midi and its extensions, and the canals of Brittany, Burgundy and the Camargue.

Public Transport

Details of routes and timetables are generally available free of charge either from bus stations (*gare routière*) which are often situated close to rail stations, or from tourist offices. They will also give details of coach tours and sightseeing excursions which are widely available.

Language

The official language is French, but three separate regional languages are spoken: Breton in Brittany, Basque in the southwest and Catalan in Roussillon (Eastern Pyrenees). A form of German is also spoken in Alsace. The first foreign language taught in schools is English, but few people speak it except in tourist resorts. Even rudimentary attempts at French will be appreciated and often break the ice for a continued conversation in English.

PARIS

Planning The Trip

Currency

Hours vary but most Paris banks are open Monday–Friday 9am–4.30pm. Bureaux de Change generally open from Monday–Saturday 9am–6pm. Both airports and train stations have currency exchange offices. All banks and Bureaux de Change in Paris charge a commission for changing money, usually about 1 percent.

Hotline numbers for lost credit cards: American Express, tel: 47 77 72 00; Diners Club, tel: 47 62 75 75; Carte Bleu/Visa, tel: 42 77 11 90.

Getting There

By Air

Paris is served by two main airports: Roissy Charles de Gaulle, about 23km (15 miles) north of the city, with two terminals (Charles de Gaulle 2 is essentially for Air France flights); and Orly

about 14 km (9 miles) to the south-east, with its two buildings, Orly-Sud and Orly-Quest.

From Roissy/Charles de Gaulle

Train: The quickest and most reliable way to get to central Paris, RER trains go direct from terminal 2 (Air France flights), or you can take the free shuttle bus (navette) from terminal 1. Trains run every 15 minutes from 5am to 11.45pm to Métro Gare du Nord or Châtelet.

The average journey time is 45 minutes.

Bus: The Roissy bus runs between the airport and Rue Scribe, near Place de l'Opéra from terminals 1 gate 30, 2A gate 10 and 2D gate 12. It runs every 15 minutes from 6am to 11pm and takes 45 minutes.

Alternatively, the Air France bus (to Métro Porte de Maillot or Charles-de-Gaulle Etoile) leaves from terminals 2A and 2B or terminal 1 arrival level gate 34. It runs every 12 minutes from 5.40am to 11pm.

Taxi: This is by far the most expensive but unquestionably the easiest solution. It can take 30 minutes to over an hour, depending on traffic. The cost appears on the meter, but a supplement is charged for each large piece of luggage, pushchair and animal.

From Orly

Train: Take the shuttle from gate H at Orly Sud or arrivals gate F at Orly Ouest to the Orly train station. The RER stops at Austerlitz, Pont St-Michel and the Quai d'Orsay. It runs every 15 minutes 5.50am–10.50pm and takes about 30 minutes to Austerlitz.

The Orlybus (to Place Denfert-Rochereau) leaves from Orly Sud gate F or Orly Ouest arrivals gate D. It runs every 10–12 minutes from 6am to 11.30pm.

The Orlyval automatic train is a shuttle to Antony (the nearest RER to Orly). It runs every 5–8 minutes from 6.30am to 9.15pm Monday to Saturday and 7am–10.55pm on Sunday, and takes 30 minutes.

Air France buses (to Invalides and Gare Montparnasse) leave from Orly Sud, gate J or Orly Ouest arrivals gate E. They run every 20 minutes from 6am to 11pm and take 30 minutes. Tickets are available from the Air France terminus.

Taxi takes 20–40 minutes.

Between Airports

An Air France bus links Roissy/Charles de Gaulle and Orly every 20 minutes from 6am to 11pm.

By Train

The main train stations in Paris are Gare du Nord (for British connections), Gare de l'Est, Gare d'Austerlitz, Gare Saint-Lazare and Gare de Lyon (for links with the Riviera, Spain and Italy).

Channel Tunnel

The 50km (30 mile) Channel Tunnel enables fast, frequent rail services between London (Waterloo) or Ashford and Paris (Gare du Nord). Le Shuttle takes cars and passengers from Folkstone to Calais on a drive on, drive off service taking 35 minutes. Le Shuttle runs 24 hours a day, all year, at least once an hour. For details, tel: 0990 353535 (UK) or 032100 6000 (France).

By Sea

Boats and hovercrafts from English ports are linked to the Gare du Nord by fast train from Calais or Boulogne and their fares are included in the cost of your ticket. Coach-boat-coach routes to Paris also exist from Victoria Station in London.

Practical Tips

Emergency Telephone Numbers

Police: 17

Fire Brigade: 18

SOS-Help: Crisis hotline, tel: 47 23 80 80 from 3–11pm (subject to change). English spoken.

Medical Services

Pharmacies with green crosses are helpful with minor ailments or finding a nurse if you need injections or special care. The Pharmacie Dhéry, 84 Champs-Elysée, tel: 4 562 02 41, is open 24 hours (Metreo: George V). Two private hospitals serve the Anglo-American community: American Hospital of Paris, 63 Bld Victor-Hugo, 92202

Neuilly, tel: (01) 46 41 2525; and the French-British Hospital of Paris, 48 Rue de Villiers, Levallois-Perret, tel: (01) 46 39 2222.

Doctor (SOS Médécins): Tel: 43 37 77 77 or 47 07 77 77.

Tourist Information

Paris's main tourist information office (Office de Tourisme de Paris/Bureau d'Accueil Central) is located at 127 Champs-Elysées, 75001 Paris (metro: George-V). For information in English, tel: 49 52 5356 daily 9am–8pm except Christmas Day, 1 January and 1 May. Other branches in the main train stations, airports and terminals.

For detailed information on Paris and surrounding areas, contact CRT 73–75 Rue Cambronne, 75015 Paris, tel: 45 67 89 41; Gare de l'Est, tel: 46 07 17 73; Gare du Nord, tel: 45 26 94 82; Gare de Lyon, tel: 43 43 33 24; Tour Eiffel, tel: 45 51 2215.

Regional Tourist Offices

These are listed as CRT (Comité Regional du Tourisme) which is the most common title, and give the individual *départements* for which information may be obtained.

CRT d'Île-de-France, 73–75 Rue Cambronne, 75015 Paris. Tel: (01) 45 67 89 41. For the *départements* of Seine-et-Marne, Yvelines, Essone, Hauts-de-Seine, Seine-St-Denis, Val-de-Marne and Val-d'Oise.

Maison de la France, 8 Avenue de l'Opéra, 75001 Paris. Tel: (01) 42 96 10 23; fax: (01) 42 86 8052.

Maison Poitou-Charentes, 68–70 Rue du Cherche-Midi, 75006 Paris. Tel: (01) 42 22 83 74. For Charente, Charente-Maritime, Deux-Sèvres and Vienne.

Maison de la Bretagne, Centre Commercial Maine-Montparnasse, 17 Rue de l'Arrivée, 75737 Paris Cedex 14. Tel: (01) 42 79 07 07. For Côtes d'Armor (formerly Côtes du Nord), Finistère, Ille-et-Vilaine and Morbihan.

Maison du Limousin, 30 Rue Caumartin, 75009 Paris. Tel: (01) 40 07 04 67. For Corrèze, Haute-Vienne and Creuse.

Consulates & Embassies

Australia: 4 Rue Jean-Rey, 75015 Paris. Tel: (01) 40 59 3300.

Canada: 35 Avenue Montaigne, 75008 Paris. Tel: (01) 44 43 29 00.

UK: 35 Rue du Faubourg St Honoré, 75008 Paris. Tel: (01) 42 66 9142.

US: 2 Rue St-Florentin, 75001 Paris. Tel: (01) 43 12 2222.

Getting Around

Orientation

Paris, capital of France, is one of the most densely populated urban centres in the world. Divided into 20 *arrondissements* (districts), greater Paris is home to 8 million people. Paris is traversed by the Seine River, dividing the city into two – the Right Bank and the Left Bank. A constant flow and interchange of citizenry from one bank to the other takes place over its 35 bridges. The larger Right Bank is home of Paris commerce and government, and is where most of the historic monuments, the great boulevards and museums can be found. The Left Bank, on the other hand, is the stronghold of the intellectual community. Although the city is now ringed by high-rise suburbs and satellite towns, its essential character has been preserved in a way few other cities have paralleled.

Public Transport

The Metro

Operates 5.30am–12.45pm; its comprehensive map and signs make it virtually impossible to get lost; the lines are identified by number and the names of their terminals. It operates in conjunction with the RER, suburban regional express trains which operate on four lines, identified as A–D. Flat fare tickets can be bought from metro stations and some tobacconists. For Metro details, tel: 08 36 08 7714.

The Paris-visite card is valid for three or five consecutive days on the metro, bus and railway in the Paris/Île de France region. It also gives discounted entry to various tourist sites; available from main metro and SNCF stations and the airports. The Formule 1 card allows an unlimited number of trips in any one day on the metro, bus and suburban trains and the night buses (it extends as far as Euro Disney). Buy it from metro offices or the Central Tourist Office in the Champs Elysées.

By Bus

City buses, which operate 6.30am–8.30pm, are efficient and on time. They are numbered and all stops have clear maps giving directions. Metro tickets are valid on the buses; one or at most two tickets are required depending on the zones travelled. You can also buy tickets from the driver.

Where to Stay

Accommodation

The Office de Tourisme de Paris on the Champs-Elysées and its branches can supply a list of hotel accommodation in every price range, or they can book you a room for a nominal fee.

Attractions

What's On

Consult *Pariscope* or *L'Officiel des Spectacles* for a guide to events in Paris. Both weekly guides are sold at newsstands. They list the current exhibitions in museums, art galleries and exhibition halls, theatre events, current films, there are also sections on night entertainment and where to eat. The tourist office's monthly *Paris Selection* also gives a choice of what's on in town.

Guides and Sightseeing Tours: First-time visitors to Paris can acquaint themselves with the city by taking the all-city sightseeing coach tour organised by Cityrama, 4 Place des Pyramides 75001, tel: (01) 44 55 6000; or Paris Vision, 214 Rue de Rivoli 75001, tel: (01) 42 60 3125. The double-decker glass-topped buses travel the tourist route covering the major landmarks. The Paris Illuminations Tour, offered by the same companies, gives a breathtaking view of Paris by night. You can also discover Paris from the deck of a glass-roofed river boat as it glides down the Seine.

Shopping

Elegant department stores such as Galeries Lafayette and Au Printemps are on the Right Bank, as are the expensive shops of the Champs-Elysées. For younger (and cheaper) fashions try the Left Bank, particularly around St Michel and St Germain boulevards.

The flea market (Marché aux Puces) opens on Saturday, Sunday and Monday (Metro stop: Porte de Clignancourt). For flowers and plants: Île de la Cité (Quai de la Corse), Monday–Saturday 8am–7.30pm (Metro stop: Cité). Other street markets are at Rue Mouffetard, and Rue Poncelet (Metro stops: Rue Poncelet and Rue Cler, respectively). Daily 9am–1pm and 4–7pm except Monday and Sunday morning.

Further Reading

General

France Today, by John Ardagh. London: Pelican.
Easy Living in France, by John P Harris. London: Arrow Books.
The French, by Theodore Zeldin. New York: Random House.
A Holiday History of France, by Ronald Hamilton. London: The Hogarth Press.
Pauper's Paris, by Miles Turner. London: Pan Books Ltd.

Other Insight Guides

Other books in the *Insight Guide* series highlight destinations in this region: *Insight Guides:* France, Burgundy, Normandy, French Riviera, Provence, Loire Valley, Brittany, Alsace and Paris. The *Insight Pocket Guide* series, designed to help readers without a lot of time plan their trips precisely, contains seven guides to destinations in France many with handy pullout maps while *Insight Compact Guides* cover Paris, Normandy, Brittany, Burgundy and Provence.

BELGIUM

Getting Acquainted

The Place

Belgium covers 30,518 sq. km (11,733 sq. miles) and has a population of more than 9.8 million. With 800 people per sq. mile, it has one of the densest populations in the world.

Brussels, its capital city, is home to about 1 million people, including over 240,000 foreign residents. Sitting between the Flemish in the north and the French in the south – Brussels is a bilingual city. All official notices and street names are in both French and Flemish (similar to Dutch). Brussels is the seat of government, residence of the monarch and chief city of the Province of Brabant.

Climate

Belgium enjoys a temperate climate influenced by the sea, so there are no extreme temperatures. December–April, the weather is relatively cool – severe cold is rare – and the temperatures are 0–6°C (32–43°F). Warm weather begins in May and continues until September with temperatures of12–22°C (54–72°F).

Economy

Belgium's capital houses the headquarters of the European Union (EU), NATO and many other private and public international organisations. Belgium and Luxembourg are the world's leading export markets in cut and industrial diamonds and sheet and reinforced glass.

Government

Belgium operates under a constitutional monarchy with two elected parliamentary chambers. The country is divided into nine provinces.

Planning the Trip

Currency

The currency is the Belgian franc, divided into 100 centimes. The smallest denomination is the 50-centime or half-franc coin, and the largest is the 5,000-franc coin. In Brussels, foreign currency can be exchanged in the North and South stations daily 7am–1pm and in the Central Station 9am–5pm or at banks 9am–noon and 2–4pm. Some banks are open at midday.

Most international credit cards are accepted everywhere. To report the loss or theft of your credit card contact the security service in Brussels, tel: 539 15 02 (24-hour service).

Public Holidays

In addition to those mentioned in the General Europe Introduction, the following holidays are recognized: Belgian National Day (21 July), Armistice Day (11 November) and Dynasty Day (15 November).

Getting There

By Air

The Belgian national airline Sabena, Air Canada, British Airways and a number of other foreign airlines link Belgium with all parts of the world. The main gateway is the Brussels National Airport at Zaventem. Located only 10 km (6 miles) from the city centre, it is linked by railway to the Central and the North stations. The rapid rail trains depart every 20 minutes from the airport and from the Central Station 6am–11pm. Additionally, the Airport–City Express travels between the airport and the South Station three times an hour.

By Rail

The majority of destinations in Belgium can be reached easily from other parts of the continent by train, and many international lines run through Belgium.

Rail/car/ferry services are available. International trains stop at the three main railway stations in Brussels: Brussels-North, Brussels-Central and Brussels-South. These stations are linked by rail and provide connections to further destinations in Belgium. For information contact: National Belgian Railways Association (NMBS), Shell Building, Ravenstein 60, Box 24, 1000 Brussels. Tel: (02) 219 28 80 (Dutch), or tel: (02) 219 26 40 (French).

By Channel Tunnel: The direct rail service from London to Brussels through the Channel Tunnel is operated by Eurostar (tel: 0345 881 811 from within the UK). The journey time is 2 hours and 40 minutes.

By Road

Bordered by the Netherlands to the north, France to the south, and Germany and Luxembourg to the east, Belgium can be reached by a number of European "E" routes, namely: E5, which links London and Cologne, via Brussels; E10: which passes through Antwerp and Brussels from Amsterdam or Paris; and E10/E40: which runs from Antwerp through Brussels to Luxembourg.

The fastest means of getting from the UK to Belgium by car is with Le Shuttle (tel: 0990 353535), the Channel Tunnel service taking cars and their passengers from Folkestone to Calais on a drive-on-drive-off system. In summer there are up to four trains an hour.

By Boat

Hovercraft, jetfoil, passenger and car ferries link the Belgian ports of Ostend, Zeebrugge and Antwerp year-round with various points in England. In connection with most crossings, there are direct train services to the main Belgian cities.

Practical Tips

Emergencies

Emergency Telephone Numbers
Police: 101.
Ambulance (Red Cross Emergency Assistance): 64 9 1122.
Accident and Fire Brigade: 100.
SOS Youth: 5129020.
Bruxelles Accueil (in all languages): 511 27 15 or 511 81 78.

Medical Services

Pharmacies close on Saturday afternoon and all day Sunday. However, in emergencies, consult the weekend editions of the local papers for the duty rotas of pharmacies, doctors, dentists and vets. Pharmacy rotas are also posted in pharmacy windows.

Business Hours

Department stores are open from 9am–6pm. Some of them close noon–2pm but remain open until 8pm. In many towns, stores open until 9pm one evening a week, usually Friday.

Tipping

Taxis, most restaurants, hairdressers, etc. very considerately include your tip in the bill, in the certainty that you couldn't fail to be impressed by the service. Ushers at some cinemas and theatres expect 20 francs for taking your ticket, while toilet attendants will make your visit a misery if you try to pass their saucer without leaving about 10 francs.

Postal Services

Post offices are open Monday–Friday 9am–6pm (large transactions will not be handled after 5pm), Saturday 9am–noon. Smaller branches may close for lunch noon–2pm, close by 4 or 5pm and close on Saturday. Mail boxes are red. The South Station post office in Brussels is open 24 hours a day.

Telephones

Telephones are automatic throughout the country. In the main towns, telephones and telegraph offices are open day and night. Only those booths showing a series of national flags accept international calls and telegrams.

Telegrams can be sent by dialing the number 1225 or via your hotel reception.

Tourist Information

The Belgian National Tourist Office has branches in all major western European capitals as well as New York, Montreal and Tokyo. Detailed tourist information in Belgium can be obtained at any of the local tourist boards of the nine national provinces, or from the Office de Promotion du Tourisme de la Communauté de Belge at Rue du Marché aux Herbes, near the Grand Place, tel: (02) 504 0390; fax: 504 0270. Information may also be obtained from Tourist Information Brussels (TIB), Town Hall, Grand Place\Grote Market, tel: 513 8940; fax: 514 4538.

A tourist information office is located at the customs hall of Brussels National Airport and tourist offices (Relais d'Accueil Touristique) are located in the North and South stations, and in the Rogier metro station. An additional guide, *Gourmet*, published and revised annually by Tourist Information Brussels (TIB), will guide visitors through the labyrinth of restaurants in Brussels.

Tourist Offices Abroad

Japan: Tameike Tokyo Building, 9F 1–14, Akasaka–1–Chome, Minatoku Tokyp. Tel: 03 3586 7041; fax: 03 35 12 3524.
UK: 29 Princes Street, London W1R 7R6. Tel: (0891) 887799; fax: (0171) 629 0454.
US: 780 Third Avenue, Suite 1501, New York, NY 10017. Tel: (0212) 7588130; fax: (0212) 3557675.

Consulates & Embassies

Australia: Guimard Center, Rue Guimard/Guimardstraat 6–8, tel: 231 0500.
Canada: Avenue de Tervuren/Tervurenlaan, tel: 741 0611.

Ireland: Rue Froissart/Froissartstraat 189, tel: 230 5337.
UK: Rue d'Arlon/Aarlenstraat 85, tel: 287 6211/287 6267.
US: Boulevard du Régent/Regentschapsstraat 25–27, tel: 508 2111.

Getting Around

Domestic Transport

By Air

Since the longest distance across the country from southeast to northwest is only 314 km (212 miles), there is not much need for domestic air services.

By Rail

Belgium has extremely good trains that cover practically the whole country. In addition, many international express services link the country with Paris, Amsterdam and many German cities. The Belgian National Railways (Société Nationale des Chemins de Fer Belges – SNCB) offers rail travellers a wide range of flat-rate excursions, mini-trips (both inside and outside of Belgium), group excursions, charter excursions and tourist packages. One of the best deals is the *B-Tourrail* ticket which is valid throughout the entire railway network for five days within a 17-day period. The TTB ticket is similar to the B-Tourrail but is also valid for bus, tram and metro. Train information may be obtained from: Belgian Railways (SNCB), 85 Rue de France, 1070 Brussels, tel: 203 3640.

By Road

Distances are relatively short and motorways serve most of the country with the exception of the mountain regions of the Ardennes. Access to all roads is free, there are no toll roads in Belgium.

Motoring Advice: In the northern part of the country, road signs appear in Dutch – in the southern part, in French. Several towns and villages have two names, one in each of the official languages, but it is important to note that road signs only show place names in the language of that particular region. Snow tyres are permitted only in exceptional weather conditions. In case of accident, with personal injury, call the emergency number 100 to request help.

The following organisations are good sources of transport information: Royal Automobile Club of Belgium (RACB), Aarlenstraat 53, B-1040 Brussels. Tel: 736 59 59.

Touring Club de Belgique (TCB), 44 Rue de la Loi, B-1040 Brussels. Tel: (02) 233 22 11.

Belgian Railways (Societé Nationale des Chemins de Fer Belges or SNCB), 85 Rue de France, 1070 Brussels. Tel: 203 3640.

Regie voor Maritiem Transport (RMT), Belliarstraat 30, 1000 Brussels. Tel: (02) 230 01 80.

Where to Stay

Accommodation

A complete list of hotels, addresses and prices is given in the *Hotel Guide*, an official brochure published by the Belgian Tourist Office.

Attractions

What's On

All information concerning cultural activities in Belgium can be obtained from the various branches of the Belgian Tourist Office, tel: 513 89 40. Tourist Information Brussels (TIB) publishes *What's On*, a weekly guide to entertainment in Belgium. Information about scheduled events in Brussels is contained in the BBA *Agenda*.

Shopping

Belgium is noted for a number of goods, among them hand-beaten copperware from Dinant; crystal from Val-Saint-Lambert of Liège; diamonds from Antwerp; handmade lace from Bruges, Brussels, Binche and Mechelen; tapestries from Mechelen, Sint-Niklaas, Brussels and Ghent, and sporting guns from Herstal, for which Liège is world famous. Credit cards are accepted everywhere and many shops offer the tourist special terms exclusive of Value Added Tax on certain types of goods.

Language

Three official languages are spoken in Belgium: Flemish, a variation of Dutch, in the north, French in the south and German in the east. German is only spoken by a small minority of people. English is widely spoken in hotels, restaurants, shops and places of business.

BRUSSELS

Planning The Trip

Currency

Exchanging currency: What some of the street establishments call commission may leave you feeling you've been mugged. The exchanges at banks and the main railway stations are the least unreasonable, otherwise ask detailed questions about rates and commission.

Credit cards and cheques: All the main international credit and charge

cards are accepted by an enormous range of businesses. Traveller's cheques are better exchanged for francs at banks, foreign exchange offices or hotels. Eurocheques can be written to a value of BF7,000 so long as you have a Eurocheque card to back them up. An automatic exchange machine can be found in the Belgian Tourist Office at Rue du Marché aux Herbes/Grasmarkt 61. It can exchange five different currencies into Belgian francs. Automatic exchange machines can be accessed by foreign Eurocheque and credit card holders, some also by the major charge-card holders.

Useful Addresses

Brussels Tourist Information, Town Hall (Hôtel de Ville), Grand Place. Tel: 513 8940. Open: Monday–Saturday 9am–6pm, Sunday (in summer) 9am–6pm, (in winter) 10am–2pm. Closed: on Sunday 1 December–28 February.

Belgian Tourist Office, 63 Rue du Marché-aux-Herbes. Tel: 504 0390. Open: Monday–Saturday (January–May, October–December) 9am–6pm, (June–September) 9am–7pm; Sunday (January–March, November–December) 1–5pm, (April, May, October) 9am–6pm (June–September) 9am–7pm.

Practical Tips

Emergencies

Emergency Telephone Numbers
Police and Gendarmerie: 101.
Accidents: 100.
Doctor: 24 hours. 479 1818 or 648 8000.
Dentist: Monday–Saturday 9am–7pm. 426 1026 or 428 5888.
Ambulances (for non-emergencies) 24 hours: 649 1122.
Pharmacies: Out-of-hours pharmacies are posted on every pharmacy. They change every week.
Fire: 100.

Business Hours

Shops are usually open Monday–Saturday 9am–6pm, although some of them close on Monday. There are few late-night shops, but the neighbourhood corner store may stay open until 9pm. Banks are open 9am–4pm or 5pm, with an hour for lunch. On Friday, department stores and many other shops stay open until 9pm.

Postal Services

Normal post office hours are Monday–Friday 9am–5pm. Some offices are open on Friday evening and Saturday morning. The office at Gare du Midi is open every day, 24 hours a day.

Telecoms

The country code for Belgium is 32. Coins of BF5 and BF20 are accepted by public telephones; "telecards" cost BF200 and BF500. To call other countries first dial the international access code 00, then the country code: Australia 61; US and Canada 1; UK 44. If using a US credit phone card, call the company's access number below: AT&T, tel: 0800 10012; MCI, tel: 0800 10012; Sprint, tel: 0800 1014.

Getting Around

Orientation

Brussels can be likened to a shallow bowl. The old heart of the city is the lower city, including the Grand Place. The upper city, strictly speaking, is the area east of the Grand Place, around Avenue Louise. But as the city has expanded, it has spread over the low hills in all directions. Brussels is a metropolitan district combining 19 local government units called *communes*, one of which is Brussels city (Bruxelles in French, Brussel in Dutch).

Public Transport

The excellent metropolitan public transport network, operated by STIB, offers tickets for single journeys, a 5-journey card bought from the driver, a 10-journey card bought from an STIB or rail station; and a 24-hour card, which can be used as often as desired on bus, tram or metro lines within the city. The 5- and 10-journey tickets must be "punched" in a platform or on-board machine, each cancellation being valid for same-direction travel by one person on the bus, tram and metro network, within a 1-hour period.

Bus/Tram: What applies to the metro applies also to these services, although buses can be reduced to near-immobility in rush-hour. The tram is usually the fastest way to travel.

By Rail

There is a fast and modern metro service consisting of two main lines which connect the eastern and western parts of the city. The underground network is supplemented by the three Pré Metro lines. Pré metro means that the completed underground tracks are also used at the present time by trams. Many metro stations contain murals, paintings or sculptures by distinguished Belgian artists. The above-ground train service is also good, but not so handy within the city limits.

By Road

Travelling by car in the city 8am–7pm, Monday–Saturday (except maybe in July), tends to be nasty, brutish and long. If you bring a car, you would do well not to use it for sightseeing. All the usual international car-hire companies, plus some local ones (try Rent-A-Car, 263 Avenue de la Couronne, tel: 649 6412), have offices in Brussels. Trams and buses always have traffic priority, as, usually, do vehicles coming from the right, unless the road is posted with orange diamond signs.

City Tours

Chatterbus (for individual – and individualistic – guides): 12 Rue des Thuyas, tel: 513 8940; De Boeck's (throughout Belgium): 8 Rue de la Colline, tel: 513 7744; and ARAU (for architecture and history): 55 Boulevard Adolphe Max, tel: 219 3345.

Shopping

There are two main shopping areas in Brussels, one in the lower city centre (Rue des Fripiers and in various shopping galleries), and the other in the upper city centre (Avenue Louise, Chaussée d'Ixelles, Boulevard de Waterloo and Avenue de la Toison d'Or). The department stores are open continuously 9am–6pm. They are closed on Sunday and public holidays, but stay open until 8pm on Friday evening.

The city has many markets.

Antique market: Grand Sablon (Grote Markt), Saturday 9am–6pm, Sunday 9am–2pm.

Flower market: Grand Place (Grote Markt), daily 8am–6pm.

Bird market: Grand Place (Grote Markt), Sunday 7am–2pm.

Flea market: Place du Jeu de Balle (Vossenplein), daily 7am–2pm.

Food and Textile market: Place Bara (Gare du Midi\Zuidstation), Sunday 5am–1pm.

Further Reading

General

***Insight Guides: Belgium* and *Brussels*.** Companions to this book, from Apa Publications' award-winning series.

***Guide Delta Bruxelles*.** Lists around 1,700 restaurants.

***The Great Beers of Belgium*.** By Michael Jackson, the world authority.

History of the Belgians by A. de Meeiis. A colourful and wide-ranging history of the Belgians.

NETHERLANDS

Getting Acquainted

The Place

The Netherlands is a small country with an area of 33,950 sq. km (13,000 sq. miles). It is situated in northwest Europe sharing borders with Belgium to the south and Germany to the east. The north and west are bordered by the North Sea. Large areas of the country consist of reclaimed land, leaving one-fifth of the country below sea-level. The areas reclaimed are extremely fertile and are known as polders.

Although the seat of government is in Den Haag (The Hague), the capital is Amsterdam.

Climate

The Netherlands has a maritime climate with pleasant summers and mild winters. Winter temperatures from December to April range from 0–8°C (30–47°F) and in the summer months of May through September temperatures range from 12–21°C (53–69°F).

The People

The country's total population is 14.8 million.

Economy

The country is one of the main agricultural producers within the EU and its economy is largely dependent on the export of vegetables, dairy products and flowers. Tourism, fishing and harbour services play a dominant role; Rotterdam is the largest cargo harbour in the world.

Government

The Netherlands is a constitutional monarchy and the present head of state is Queen Beatrix of Orange.

Planning The Trip

Currency

The Dutch monetary unit is the guilder, sometimes called a florin (or NGL). One guilder is equivalent to 100 cents. The smallest coin is the stuiver (5 cents) and the largest note is worth 1,000 guilders.

Changing money: GWK (Grenswissel-kantoren NV) is a national financial institution where you can exchange any currency and also use credit cards, travellers' cheques and Eurocheques. There are GWK offices located at 35 main railway stations in The Netherlands and at the country's borders. They are open Monday–Saturday 8am–8pm, Sunday 10am–4pm and sometimes in the evening for longer hours at main stations and airports. The office at Amsterdam Central Station is open 24 hours a day.

Change is also available at post offices (at a good rate of exchange) and banks. There can be a considerable difference in commission charged between the various institutions and at different times of night or day.

Credit cards are widely accepted at hotels, restaurants, shops, car rental companies and airlines. Access, American Express, Diners Club, Eurocard, Visa, MasterCard and JCB card are all recognised, plus many more.

Banks are open Monday–Friday 9am–4pm, Thursday 9am–7pm.

Public Holidays

In addition to those in the Introduction, The Netherlands celebrates Good Friday; Easter Sunday; the Queen's Birthday (15 April), Liberation day (5 May) and Whit Sunday.

Getting There

By Air

Most visitors from America or other parts of Europe fly into Schiphol Airport, 14 km (9 miles) southwest of Amsterdam. The airport is connected with 196 cities in 90 countries. Very regular flights link Schiphol with all major European airports, and there are several flights a week from North America, Canada and Australia. KLM is the national airline. KLM information in the UK, tel: (0181) 750 9000; in North America, tel: 1 800 374 7747.

By Train

Day and night services operate from London (Liverpool Street) to The Netherlands via the Hook of Holland – journey time is around 12 hours by ferry, 10 hours by jetfoil. There are good rail connections to all parts of the country from the main ports of arrival and very regular services to The Netherlands from Brussels, Paris, Antwerp, Cologne and Hanover.

By Channel Tunnel: The Eurostar Channel Tunnel train (tel: 0345 881881) links London to Brussels in three hours, from where there are fast connections to destinations in Holland.

By Road

Holland has an excellent network of roads and signposting is good. But, once you're in the cities, a car is often more of a hindrance than a help. From the Hook of Holland to Amsterdam, travel time is roughly 3 hours 30 minutes.

Le Shuttle: The Channel Tunnel service taking cars and their passengers from Folkstone to Calais on a drive-on-drive off system, takes 35 minutes to Calais, from where there are fast motorway connections up to Holland.

By Sea

Stena Line (tel: 01233 647 047) operates high speed ferries from Harwich to the Hook of Holland (2 services a day lasting 3 hours 40 minutes). P&O North Sea Ferries (tel: 01482 377 177) sails from Hull to Rotterdam, taking 14 hours. The Olau Line also offers two sailings a day between Sheerness and Vilissingen; Sheerness Travel Agency is one of the main east coats agencies dealing with this route (tel: 01795 666 666). There are regular ferry services between Dover and Zeebrugge, but the fastest sea route from the UK is the Jetfoil from Dover to Ostend.

Practical Tips

Emergencies

Medical Services

The standard of medical and dental services in The Netherlands is very high, and most major cities have an emergency doctor and dental service. Enquire at your hotel or consult the introductory pages to local telephone directories.

Emergency Telephone Numbers
Amsterdam (code 020)
Police: 222 222.
Ambulance: 555 555.
SOS doctor: 642 111.
SOS dentist: 791 821.

The Hague (code 070)
Police: 222 222.
Doctor: 455 300 (day) and 469 669 (night).
Dentist: 654 646.

Rotterdam (code 010)
Police: 414 1414.
Doctor: 420 1100.
Dentist: 455 2155.

Business Hours

Normal shopping hours are 8.30 or 9am–6pm or 6.30pm. Late-night shopping is usually Thursday. Food stores close at 4pm on Saturday. All shops close for one half day a week, often Monday morning.

Tipping

Service charges and VAT are included in restaurant and bar bills. An extra tip can be left for extra attention or service but this is by no means compulsory. Taxi meters also include the service charge, though it is customary to give an extra tip. A lavatory attendant is usually given 25 or 50 cents.

Postal Services

Main post offices are open Monday–Friday 8.30am–6pm, Saturday 9am–noon. Stamps are available from post offices, tobacconists, newstands and machines attached to the red and grey letter boxes.

Poste restante facilities are available at the main post office. You need a passport to collect your mail.

Telephones

Telephone boxes are green and take 25c, f1 and f2.50 coins. You find them in post offices, large stores, cafés and in some streets. Blue telephones require a pre-paid telephone card which can be purchased from Primafoon stores and other outlets. Larger post offices have booths where you can make international calls more cheaply than by hotel phone where rates may be treble.

The Telehuis at Raadhuisstraat 48, Amsterdam, handles telegrams, telexes and faxes.

The code for dialling Holland from abroad is 0031. Most telephone numbers have 10 digits (the old area code now forms part of the number, including the initial '0' which is deleted when calling from abroad). To make an international call from Holland, dial 00 + the country code: 44 for the UK and 1 for the US and Canada. AT&T, tel: 06-022 9111; Sprint, tel: 06-222 9119.

Tourist Information

Tourist information offices are clearly marked VVV and are usually just outside the railway station in every main town and city. They are a mine of information and services but there is a charge for most of them. Carry passport-sized photographs for various identity cards you may purchase.

The VVV registered address is: VVV Amsterdam Tourist Office, PO Box 3901, 1001 AS Amsterdam, The Netherlands. Tel: 020 266 444, telex: 12324.

To write to a tourist office, address the letter VVV with the town name.

Tourist Offices

Amsterdam Tourist Office: 10 Stationsplein, (white building across the road to the left outside the Central Station).

Open: Easter–June and September, Monday–Saturday 9am–11pm, Sunday 10am–5pm; July and August Monday–Sunday 9am–11pm; 1 October–Easter, Monday–Saturday 9am–5pm, Sunday 10am–1pm and 2–5.30pm. For information, tel: (0) 63 40 34 0066, Monday–Saturday 9am–7pm.

VVV Information Office: 106 Leidsestraat, Amsterdam. Open: Easter–30 September, Monday–Saturday 9am–8.30pm; 1 October–Good Friday, 10.30am–7pm, Saturday 10.30am–6.30pm, Sunday 10.30am–5.30pm.

Tourist Offices Abroad

Australia: Suite 302, 5 Elizabeth Street, Sydney, NSW 2000.
Canada: 25 Adelaide Street East, Suite 710, Toronto, Ontario M5C 1Y2, tel: 04 16 36 63 1577.
UK: PO Box 523, London SW1E 6NT, tel: 0891 200277; fax: 0171 828 7941.
US: 355 Lexington Avenue, (21st Floor), New York, NY 10017, tel: 0212 370 7367; 225 North Michigan Avenue, Suite 326, Chicago, Ill 60601, tel: 0312 8190300; 90 New Montgomery Street, Suite 305, San Francisco, CA 94105, tel: 0415 543 6772.

Getting Around

Domestic Transport

By Air

Schiphol, near Amsterdam, is The Netherlands' main airport. Amsterdam Schiphol railway station is located below the arrivals hall. Trains leave for the principal Dutch cities every 15 minutes 5.25am–0.15am, and every 60 minutes during the remaining period.

Rotterdam has a small airport served by flights from Amsterdam, London and Paris located 15 minutes from the city centre. A local bus service connects the airport and the city.

Eindhoven and Maastricht both have airports, principally for domestic flights. Domestic flights in The Netherlands are run by KLM City Hopper. For information, tel: 020 170 931.

By Rail

Netherlands Railways (Nederlandse Spoorwegen) has a network of express trains linking major cities. A fast direct train every 15 minutes links Schiphol airport and Amsterdam. There is an hourly night service between Utrecht, Amsterdam, Schiphol, The Hague, Rotterdam and vice versa. Frequently-stopping trains connect to smaller places. There are at least half-hourly services on most lines and 4–8 per hour on busier routes. It is not possible to reserve seats on these services.

For information and tickets:
Amsterdam: GVB: 1 Stationsplein, Centraal Station, tel: 020 272 727, Monday–Friday 7am–11pm, Saturday and Sunday 8am–11.30pm.
The Hague: Train services: Tel: 070 347 1681; Public transport: Tel: 06 899 1121.
Rotterdam: Train services: Tel: 010 411 7100; Public transport: Tel: 010 454 6890.
Utrecht: Train services: Tel: 030 332 555; Public transport: Tel: 030 317 031.

By Road

The Netherlands has a dense and modern toll-free road system. The smaller country roads are in excellent condition. There are 42 touristic routes of some 50–105 miles (80–170 km) some of which continue into neighbouring countries.

There are ferry services on secondary roads crossing rivers and canals. Most ferries are equipped to carry cars and in general the fares are not high. You may also be required to pay nominal fees for the use of tunnels, bridges and dams which appear frequently throughout the country.

Motoring Advice: To drive in The Netherlands, you must carry a current driving licence (an international licence is not necessary); vehicle registration document; Green Card insurance policy and a warning triangle for use in the event of an accident or breakdown.

Waterways

There are scheduled boat services from major cities throughout the country and boat tours, excursions and trips operating on the various bodies of water in Holland.

Boat Charter: Around the IJsselmeer and in the northern provinces of Groningen and Friesland, boat rental agencies offer a range of craft, some of which have living accommodation. Another area popular with those who enjoy boating is Zeeland province.

A popular way to get to know Amsterdam is by taking a canal tour. Numerous companies operate from the canal basin opposite Central Station and tickets can be booked in advance from the nearby VVV office. Tours take an hour or more; candle-lit dinner cruises are also available.

Public Transport

Tickets are sold in the form of *Nationale Strippenkaart* to be used on buses, trams, metro and the train between certain stations anywhere in Holland. The easiest place to buy the cards is at a VVV office, though they are also sold at railway stations and many newsagents and tobacconists. You can buy tickets from the bus or tram driver, but they cost more than tickets purchased in advance.

Where to Stay

Accommodation

It is wise to book in advance in the summer and the holiday season and, in the case of North Holland, during the bulb season (April–May). This is especially true of Amsterdam, where the central hotels are usually booked up June–August. However, it is worth telephoning hotels at short notice in case they have cancellations. You can book directly with the hotel – the reservations desk will invariably speak English. Alternatively, you can book in advance through: The Netherlands Reservation Centre, P.O. Box 404, NL-2200 AK Leidschendam, tel: 070-317-5456, fax: 070-320-2611.

Attractions

The NNTO publishes a brochure giving detailed information on attractions, museums and beautiful old towns, as well as a special brochure listing the year's main events. At VVV offices bearing the *i – Nederland* sign, visitors can in addition obtain information on cultural activities and even order tickets for concerts and theatre productions. Another useful source of information is the *Time Out* section of the *Holland Tribune,* an English-language periodical available at hotels and tourist offices in the provinces of North and South Holland and on all KLM flights.

Brown café notice-boards are another good source of information on local events.

Sightseeing by air: From the first Saturday in April to the last Saturday in September sightseeing flights take place on Saturday and Sunday afternoon from Schiphol by City Hopper, tel: 020 747 747. Flights view historic towns like Haarlem, Alkmaar, Edam, Volendam, Naarden or the bulb fields. Flights over south Limburg from Maastricht airport are organised by Air Service Limburg, tel: 043 645 030.

Language

Dutch is a Germanic language, which is also spoken by about 5 million Belgians. English is widely understood.

AMSTERDAM

Practical Tips

Emergencies

Medical Services
Emergency Telephone Numbers
Police: 6222222.
Ambulance: 5555555.

For urgent medical or dental treatment, contact the Central Medical Service, tel: 6642111 (SOS doctor). Open: 24 hours.

The most central hospital is the Onze Lieve Vrouse Gasthuis, Le Oosterparkstraat 197. Tel: 5999111.

The main hospital is the Academisch Medisch Centrum, Meibergdreef 9. Tel: 5669111. Both hospitals have an out-patients, and casualty ward.

Chemists (*Apotheek*) are normally open Monday–Friday 9am–5.30pm or 6pm. Late-night chemists operate on a rotating basis. For information, contact the Central Medical Service.

Postal Services

The main office is at Nieuwezijds Voorburgwal 182, behind the Royal Palace. Open: Monday–Friday 8.30am–6pm, 8pm on Thursday; Saturday 9am–noon. Parcels are handled at the post office at Oosterdokskade 3–5pm. Open: Monday–Friday 8.30am–9pm, Saturday 9am–noon. Stamps are available from post offices, tobacconists, news-stands and stamp machines attached to the red and grey letter boxes. *Poste restante* facilities are available at the main post office – you need a passport to collect your mail.

Telephones

For international calls, it's easier to go to Telehuis, Raadhuisstraat 48 (open 24 hours), where you can talk in a booth for as long as you like and pay when you finish.

Tourist Information

The main tourist office (VVV) is opposite Central Station at Stationsplein 10, tel: 6266444. Open: Easter–June and September daily 9am–11pm, Sunday 10am–5pm; July and August Monday–Sunday 9am–11pm; October–Easter Monday–Saturday 9am–5pm, Sunday 10am–1pm and 2–5.30pm. There is a VVV bureau at Leidsestraat 104.

There is a tourist information office at the airport, which is particularly useful if you have not already booked your accommodation. The GVB office, also at Stationsplein alongside the metro entrance (tel: 272727), provides information and ticket sales for local and city public transport. Open: Monday–Friday 7am–10.30pm.

Consulates

Australia: Koninginnegracht 23, 2514 AB Den Haag. Tel: 070 630983.
Canada: Sophialaan 7, 2514 JP Den Haag. Tel: 070 614111.
UK: 44 Koningslaan. Tel: 673 6245.
US: 19 Museumplein, Amsterdam. Tel: 020-664-5661.

Getting Around

Orientation

Amsterdam, capital of The Netherlands and its most populous city with 750,000 inhabitants, is on the River Amstel, supported by stilts driven 59 ft (18 metres) into the marshy ground below, enabling parts of the city to spring up where there were once only waterways. Built on a design of expanding horseshoe canals that fit one within the other, the city contains some 4,000 17th-century merchants' houses and warehouses and over 1,000 bridges. Financial and economic centre of the Netherlands, Amsterdam is part of the so-called Conurbation Holland area, which mainly comprises the provinces of North and South Holland and contains the country's major industries and its largest cities (Rotterdam and The Hague).

From the Airport

Shuttle trains leave Schiphol Airport every 15 minutes for Amsterdam Central Station during the day, and once an hour at night. Travel time is under 20 minutes. Trains also run to the RAI station and to Amsterdam Zuid for the World Trade Center, both in the south of the city. KLM operates a coach service to the city every half an hour, but it's over twice the price of the train. There is also a much cheaper public bus service linking the airport to the city.

By Road

Driving within the city is best avoided. If you do take a car, be prepared to contend with parking problems, mad cyclists, narrow canal streets (often blocked by delivery vans), the complexity of the one-way systems and trams which always have right of way. If you arrive by car, the best thing to do is leave it in a car park and go by public transport. The multi-storey Europarking at Marnixstraat 250 usually has space and is within walking distance of the city centre.

Amsterdam makes a good base for day trips. Distances to Dutch towns of interest are short: The Hague 33 miles (52 km), Utrecht 27 miles (43 km), Delft 39 miles (62 km).

By Rail

A wide and very efficient network of rail services operates throughout the country. Fast electric trains link Amsterdam with most Dutch towns on an hourly or half-hourly basis. It is well worth finding out about excursion fares, which include entrance fees to museums and other attractions, as well as the return rail fare.

Public Transport

Unless you are travelling out of the centre you are unlikely to need the buses or metro. Within the city the prominent yellow trams are easily the best means of getting around and not expensive as long as you master the ticket system. The GVB office outside the station has information on the system in English and sells the various types of tickets. You can either buy individual tickets (which is the most expensive way of travelling), Rover tickets, which are valid for 1, 2 or more days' travel, or *strippenkaart* – strip tickets, in multiples of 6, 10 or 15; the more you buy, the cheaper they come. These are valid for one hour's travel and the amount you use depends on the zones you cover.

The GVB transport office in front of Central Station provides free public transport route maps. The best general map is published by Falkplan, called *This is Amsterdam*.

Attractions

The Amsterdam Tourist Office (VVV) publishes *Amsterdam This Week,* a weekly guide to the city's art, culture, restaurants and shopping. Also available, for a nominal fee, is a weekly programme of concerts and theatres, which includes English-speaking productions. The VVV Box Office at Stationsplein 10 provides advance bookings for theatres, operas, ballets and concerts. It is open Monday–Saturday 10am–4pm and reservations must be made in person, not over the telephone. Another useful source of cultural information is the monthly magazine *Amsterdam Times*, available at hotels and tourist offices.

After dark, entertainment focuses on three main areas: Leidseplein, for lively discos and nightclubs; Rembrandtsplein for clubs, cabarets and strip shows pandering to older tastes; and the Red Light District, notorious for scantily dressed women sitting in windows and for notice-boards saying "room to hire".

On an entirely different note, you could spend the evening on a candle-lit canal cruiser, with wine and cheese or full dinner provided, or try out one of the many brown cafés, some of which provide live music.

Shopping

Bargains are a rarity but browsing is fun, particularly in the markets and the small specialist shops. For general shopping the main streets are Kalverstraat and Nieuwendijk, for exclusive boutiques try P.C. Hoofstraat and for the more off-beat shops, head to the Jordaan northwest of the centre where many of the local artists live. The VVV Tourist Office provides a series of useful shopping guides: *Art and Antiques, Beautiful and Chic, Open-air Markets* and *Between the Canals*. The leaflets give maps, route descriptions, places of interest and a list of addresses and shop specialities.

Further Reading

General

Of Dutch Ways, by Helen Colijn, Dillon Press Inc, Minneapolis, Minnesota.
Dutch Art and Architecture 1600–1800, by Jakob Rosenberg et al, Penguin, London.
The Story of Amsterdam, by Anthony Vanderheiden, Rootveldt Boeken, Amsterdam.

Other Insight Guides

Insight Guides which highlight destinations in this region are: Amsterdam and The Netherlands.

GERMANY

Getting Acquainted

The Place

At its longest point, Germany is approximately 1,000 km (620 miles) from north to south, and at its widest (Aachen to Görlitz) it measures approximately 650 km (400 miles). The population of 79.2 million people is spread over a total of 350,000 sq. km (135,150 sq. miles), with the south being more densely populated than the north. As a rule, the north is very flat and characterised by waterways and marshes, while the south embraces the mountainous part of the country. The most impressive mountains are the Harz, the Variscian mountains of the Schwarzwald (Black Forest), the Elbesandstein Mountains or Little Switzerland and the Bavarian Alps with the highest mountain, the Zugspitze (2,963 metres/9,721 ft).

Climate

The climate is temperate and the fluctuations in temperature are comparatively slight. Average temperature in January (the coldest month of the year) is around 0°C (32°F); in the mountains it is approximately minus 10°C (14°F). The winter season lasts from December to March, until May in the Alps. In summer average temperatures are around 20°C (68°F), the hottest months being June and August.

Government

Germany consists of 16 federal states. The Federal President is head of state and the government consists of the Chancellor and ministers. Legislation is delivered by the Bundestag (lower house of parliament) which consists of 662 ministers elected every 4 years. New national laws have to be confirmed by the Bundesrat (upper house of parliament) which comprises 68 federal state -representatives.

Planning The Trip

Health

People who use special medication should either bring a sufficient supply or a prescription from their own doctor. If you have to consult a doctor, contact your consulate for a list of either English-speaking doctors, or doctors who speak your native language.

In the event of an accident, dial 110 for the police, 112 for the fire brigade or 115 for an ambulance or call the Rotes Kreuz (Red Cross). All accidents resulting in injury must be reported to the police.

Currency

The German Mark (DM) is a decimal currency made up of 100 pfennigs. The coins come in denominations of 1, 2, 5, 10 and 50 pfennigs, and 1, 2, and 5 DM. The notes are in denominations of 5, 10, 20, 50, 100, 200, 500 and 1,000 DM. Money may be changed at any bank and local money changers (*Wechselstuben*) usually found in train stations, airports and in tourist areas. It is advisable to carry traveller's cheques instead of cash, as the former can be replaced if lost or stolen. Remember to keep the cheque numbers separately noted. Although the Germans are not very fond of credit cards you can pay your bills in hotels, restaurants or big department stores with American Express, Diners Club, Visa or MasterCharge cards. You may have problems, however, in smaller towns or villages. Eurocheques can be cashed practically everywhere.

Banking hours are usually 9am–3pm (Tuesday and Thursday until 6pm) with slight variations in the different federal states.

Public Holidays

In addition to those listed in the Introduction above, the following holidays are celebrated in Germany: Good Friday, National Holiday (17 June) and Unification Day (October 3). In some Catholic parts of the country, the following are also public holidays: Epiphany (6 January) and Corpus Christi Day. In the Protestant parts of West Germany, Repentance Day, usually on the last Wednesday in November, is also celebrated.

Getting There

By Air

Most air-routes into Germany lead to Frankfurt airport. Germany's other international airports are: Berlin, Bremen, Düsseldorf, Hamburg, Hanover, Cologne, Munich, Nuremberg, Saabrücken, Münster/Osnabrück, Dresden and Stuttgart. Lufthansa, the national airline, serves most of the world and has a domestic service.

By Sea

There are ferry connections from northern Germany (Hamburg and Rotterdam) to Scandinavia and the UK (Scandinavian Seaways sailings on the Harwich–Hamburg route). The port of Warnemünde has sailings to Trelleborg in Sweden.

By Rail

From northern Europe, the best train connections to the north of Germany are from the Hook of Holland in the Netherlands. Trains leave in the direction of Venlo and Emmerich.

The south of Germany is better reached via Ostend, from where trains go to Aachen and Cologne, connecting with Euro-City and Inter-City trains to the southern federal states. From the UK, ferry links with the Hook of Holland are via Harwich and with Ostend via Dover.

By Road

Bordered by Denmark to the north; the Netherlands, Belgium, Luxembourg and France to the west; Switzerland and Austria to the south; and the Czech and Slovak republics to the east, Germany can be reached by numerous European motorways.

Practical Tips

Emergencies

Pharmacies (*Apotheken*) are open 8am–6.30pm. Pharmacies carry a list of neighbouring pharmacies open during the night and on weekends.

Business Hours

Most shops are open 9.30am–6 or 6.30pm. Small shops such as bakeries, fruit and vegetable shops and butcher's shops open as early as 7am, close for 2½ hours midday, reopen around 3–6.30pm. Shops in railway stations and airports are usually open until late, some until midnight. Business hours are usually 8am–5.30pm. Government offices are open to the public 8am–noon.

Tipping

Generally, service charges and taxes are included in hotel and restaurant bills. However, satisfied customers usually leave an additional tip or at least the small change. It is also customary to tip taxi drivers and hairdressers 10 percent, and cloakroom attendants 0.50–1 DM.

° Postal Services

Post offices are generally open from 8am–6pm Monday–Friday and 8am–noon on Saturday. Station and airport post offices in all larger cities are open until late in the evening on weekdays and some are open 24 hours a day.

Telephone

In public pay phones insert coins for local calls. For long-distance calls you can also dial direct from most of the yellow public phone boxes but remember to have enough coins with you (1- and 5-DM pieces), or you may go to a post office where an operator makes the connection. Every place of any size in Germany has its own dialling code, which is listed under the local network heading. Should you have a language problem, dial 00118 (international directory enquiries). The former east German directory enquiry service is not yet standardised and differs from town to town.

Tourist Information

Anywhere in Germany where tourists are expected you should find a tourist authority or information office (marked with an "i"). Write to the office of your destination for information.

Tourist Offices Abroad

Australia: Lufthansa House, 143 Maquarie Street, 9th floor, Sydney 2000. Tel: 02 367 3890; fax: 02 36 73895.
Canada: Office National Allemand du Tourisme, 2 Fundy, Place Bonaventure, Montreal P.Q. H5A 1B8. Tel: (514) 878 9885.
UK and Ireland: 65 Curzon Street, London W1Y 7PE. Tel: (0171) 495 6129; fax: 0891 600100.
Japan: Office National Allemand du Tourisme, 175 Bloor Street East, North Tower, #604 Toronto, Ontario M4W 3R8. Tel: (416) 968 1570; fax: (416) 968 1986.
US: 122 East 42nd Street, Chanin Building, 52nd floor, New York, NY 101680072. Tel: (212) 661 7200; fax: (212) 661 7174; 11766 Wilshire Boulevard, Suite 750, Los Angeles, CA 90025. Tel: (310) 575 9799; fax: (310) 575 1565.

Embassies & Consulates

Australia: 181–183, 4th floor Kempinsk; Plaza Uhlandstrasse, Berlin D-10623. Tel: (0300) 8800880; fax: (030) 88000899.
Canada: 119 Godesberger Allee, Bonn 2, 5300. Tel: (0228) 223 1061; fax: (0228) 376525.
New Zealand: Bundeskanzlerplat 22, Bonn 1053113. Tel: (0228) 228070; fax: (0228) 221687.
UK: 5300 Bonn 1, Friedrich-Ebert-Allee 77. Tel: (0228) 344061.
US: 29 Dreichmanns Avenue, Bonn D-53170. Tel: (0228) 3391; fax: (0228) 339 2663

Getting Around

Domestic Transport

By Air

The main domestic airports are interconnected by regular Interflug, Aero Lloyd and Lufthansa services. From within Germany, Berlin can now be reached by a number of airlines including Euro Berlin and Interflug.

From Frankfurt Airport there is a 15-minute shuttle service (S15) to the main transport junction, the Hauptwache, where the suburban railway (S-Bahn) and the subway (U-Bahn) meet. From this point you can travel to just about anywhere in town by public transport. Alternatively, bus number 61 shuttles between the airport and the town centre (Sachsenhausen). Official taxis are ivory-coloured Mercedes or BMW models with a black TAXI sign on the roof.

By Rail

Two railway systems – the Deutsche Bundesbahn (DB) with a network of some 28,000 km (17,400 miles) and the Deutsche Reichsbahn (DR) with a network of approximately 15,000 km (9,320 miles). On the whole, both networks are efficient and will get you to all major places. An hourly service runs to and from more than 50 major towns and cities in the Republic by the intercity trains (IC). The new states are now included in the IC-network. IC trains do not run at night. If you wish to travel at night board a D-Zug, which travels more slowly because it makes more stops on the way. Another type of train, the E-Zug, stops even more often, but has the advantage of reaching the smaller towns. Many overnight trains have couchette cars.

Interregio (IR) trains in postmodern blue-white design transport travellers at two-hourly intervals from city to city. Euro-City (EC) trains connect major European towns and cities but are rather expensive.

By Road

Germany is renowned for its 13,600 km (8,500 miles) of motorways, the autobahnen. Autobahnen are marked with an "A" on blue signs; regional roads with a "B" on yellow signs.

Motoring Advice: If your car breaks down on the motorway use the orange telephones at the roadside. Black triangles on roadside posts indicate the direction of the next telephone.

The ADAC (Allgemeiner Deutscher Automobil Club) provides road assistance free of charge provided the damage can be repaired within half an hour. If it takes longer, you will have to pay for the repair and parts. Road assistance is also free of charge and all recovery costs will be refunded if you have an insurance certificate.

Waterways

Regular, scheduled boat services operate on most rivers, lakes and coastal waters including the Danube, Main, Moselle, Rhine and the Elbe and Weser with their estuaries, lakes Ammersee, Chiemsee, Königssee and Lake Constance; also on Kiel Fjord and from the mainland to Helgoland and the East and North Frisian islands. Special excursions are conducted on practically all navigable waters.

Public Transport

By Coach

Buses are a primary means of transport in cities and connect the smaller villages in the countryside. But there is no national coach network. The overland buses are a substitute for the railway system: wherever there are no railways, however remote there will be a bus. Information on regional buses is available at railway stations and tourist information centres.

City Buses

A widespread network of public transport systems is available in every large city. Those cities with a population of 100,000 and more offer an efficient bus system that runs frequently and usually very punctually. You can buy the bus tickets from the driver or at machines in the bus or at the bus stop. In large cities like Berlin, Hamburg, Cologne, Munich, Frankfurt and Stuttgart, the bus lines are integrated with the underground (U-Bahn) the tram, and the over-ground (S-Bahn) into one large public transport system. The same ticket may be used for all four means of transport.

By Tram

Trams (Strassenbahn) run on rails throughout the cities. The speed at which they travel allows for sightseeing, although there is the danger of getting into a traffic jam. Look out for yellow signs with a green "H" at bus and tram stops; they list the schedules.

By Underground

Underground (*U-Bahn*) stations are usually identified by a sign showing a white "U" on a blue background. Every station has detailed route maps displayed on the wall. The *S-Bahn* will transport you at about the same speed as the *U-Bahn*.

Where to Stay

Travellers should have no problem finding accommodation anywhere. In the peak season (June–August) it is advisable to book in advance if you are visiting a popular place. You may do so through the DIRG, reservation service TIBS, Yorckstrasse 23, D-79110 Freiburg. Tel: (0761) 8858150; fax: (0761) 88581.

Attractions

Most larger towns and resorts publish a "What's On" type of booklet which can be obtained from tourist office, bookstalls and hotels whenever they are available.

Shopping

Germany, being a popular tourist destination, offers lots of souvenirs. The shop to look out for is the Andenkenladen which has anything from valuable souvenirs to all sorts of knickknacks.

In practically every town you will find a *Fussgängerzone* pedestrian zone with all kinds of shops, big department stores, and small specialised shops. Cigarettes, cigars and tobacco may be bought in newspaper shops which also stock postcards, writing supplies, magazines and newspapers.

Language

The written language of Germany is High German (*Hochdeutsch*). Spoken German, however, varies in dialect from region to region. Since English is widely taught as a first foreign language in school, and due to the long presence of allied forces and their media in West Germany, the country has one of the highest percentages of at least rudimentary English skills.

Getting Acquainted

Berlin is situated in the very heart of Europe. On a map you'll find it located at approximately the same latitude as London and the same longitude as Naples. The largest city in Germany it encompasses a total land area of 883 sq. km (340 sq. miles).

Before its division in 1945, this flourishing city was both the national capital and geographical middle point of the German Empire, established in 1871. Even before German reunification on 3 October 1990, the two half-cities of East and West Berlin – including their respective administrations – had been gradually growing closer together. Since reunification it has reclaimed its status as the national capital.

At the present time there are approximately 3½ million people living in Berlin. It is predicted that by the year 2000, this number will have increased to 5 million.

Planning The Trip

Exchange Office at Bahnhof Zoo (Monday–Saturday 7.30am–10pm, Sunday 8am–7pm); the Exchange Office at Joachimstaler Str. 1 at Bahnhof Zoo (Monday–Friday 7.30am–9.30pm, Saturday 7.30am–6pm) and Tegel Airport (Monday–Sunday 8am–10pm).

Outside their normal business hours, the following banks also maintain additional hours: The Bank of Trade and Industry, Kurfürstendamm 26a (Saturday 10am–1pm); the Berlin Bank of Commerce, located in the Wertheim Department Store, Kurfürstendamm 231 (Saturday 10am–1pm and on extended Saturdays until 6pm); the Bank of Trade and Industry in KaDeWe at Wittenbergplatz (Saturday 8am–2pm and on extended Saturdays until 6pm). You'll find cash machines at bank branches all over the city.

Getting There

By Air

Berlin has three airports with regular scheduled flights: Tegel, Tempelhof and Schönefeld. Tegel, in the north, is the biggest and newest of Berlin's airports and it is from here that most of the long-haul flights leave. Schönefeld, which lies in the southeast corner of the city, still maintains links with eastern Europe. Tempelhof, close to the city centre, is the airport for domestic flights, but there are links to other European cities including London City Airport.

A regular bus service runs between Tegel and Schönefeld with stops at several points in the city centre. There is an underground station at Tempelhof which gives access to almost anywhere in the city.

By Rail

From northern Europe, the best train connections to Berlin are from Ostend in Belgium and Hook of Holland in the Netherlands.

Trains stop at three major stations. The Hauptbahnhof (Central station) is the old Ostbahnhof (East Station) in the eastern half of the city. The main station for the western part of the city is Zoologischer Garten and the other major station in the eastern part of the city is Friedrichsstrasse.

Rail Information: German Federal Railways (Bundesbahn). Tel: 212 308 3100. Recorded departure times: Tel: 11531. Arrival times: Tel: 11532. Complete Railway Service Office: Tel: 1700. Railway Information Central: Tel: 1717.

Practical Tips

Emergencies

Medical Services

Most major hospitals keep ambulances specifically for accidents and emergency rooms. There are free emergency phones in front of larger post offices and elsewhere; emergency telephones posts are common in suburbs.

Emergency Telephone Numbers
Police (Polizei): 110.
Ambulance and Fire Brigade (Notarzt und Feuerwehr): 112.
Emergency Medical Service (Ärztliche Notdienst): 310031.
Emergency Chemist's Service: 01141.
Emergency Dental Service: 01141.

Postal Services

In Berlin, most post offices are usually open Monday–Friday 8am–6pm, on Thursday until 8.30pm, and on Saturday 8am–noon.

Post offices on Friedrichsstrasse railway station and at the Palast der Republik open Monday–Saturday 6pm–midnight, Sunday 8am–midnight. The post office in Bahnhof Zoo is open; in Tegel Airport Monday–Friday 70am–9pm; in the International Congress Centre Monday–Friday 9am–1pm and 1.45–4pm.

Telephones

The dialling code for Berlin from outside the city is 030.
National Telephone Information: 010.
International Telephone Information: Tel: 0010.
Telegram Sending Service: 1131.

Tourist Information

Information is available from the Berlin Tourist Information office, Europa Centre, tel: (030) 262 6031. The office is open Monday–Saturday 8am–10.30pm, Sunday 9am–9pm.

Tourist Offices

Berlin Tourist Information office, Martin-Luther-Str. 105, Berlin 10825. Tel: 030 2626031; fax: 21232520; telex: 183356. The main information office, at the Europa-Center (Budapester Strasse entrance), is open Monday–Saturday 8am–10.30pm, Sunday 9am–9pm.

There is another information office at the Brandenburg Gate, open daily 10am–6pm, and another at Tegel Airport (main hall), open daily 8am–11pm, as well as at the Zoo train station.

The (former-East) Berlin-Information maintains its visitor centre in the converted television tower (Panoramastrasse 1), and is open Monday 1–6pm, Tuesday–Friday 8am–6pm, Saturday and Sunday 10am–6pm.

There are other information centres located in the main halls of the Bahnhof Zoo (a railway station) and the Hauptbahnhof (main station), as well as Tegel Airport and in the highrise travel agency on Alexanderplatz.

German National Tourist Office, tel: (069) 75720; fax: (069) 751930.

Getting Around

Public Transport

The Berlin transportation services (BVG) operate underground trains (U-Bahn), fast-trains (S-Bahn), bus lines, tramlines in the eastern part of the city, a well-organised network of buses running throughout the night as well as boat connections crossing the Havel River between Wannsee and Kladow. The quickest way of getting around the city is on the underground system's 10 different lines.

Further information is available around the clock by calling BVG Customer Services, tel: 030 752 7020.

By Car

There are more than 1.2 million cars cruising the streets of Berlin, and the ADAC (the German automobile association) has predicted that by the year

2000, this number will have doubled – an ecological horror for the city. If you still want to drive into the city, it is best to park your vehicle at one of the Park-and-Ride areas and hop on a bus or underground.

Useful telephone numbers:

AVD (Automobile Club of Germany) traffic information service: Tel: 240091.

ACE (Auto-Club-Europa) breakdown service: Tel: 19216

ADAC (German Automobile Association) urban breakdown service: Tel: 19211.

Weather Report: Tel: 1164.

Road Conditions: Tel: 1169.

Taxi: Tel: 210 202/261026/691001.

Attractions

The best way to get a feel for what is going on in Berlin is to take a look in either of the three city magazines *Checkpoint* (in English), *Tip* or *Zitty*. You'll find current events and performances listed under the headings Theatre, Dance, Music, Film, Cabaret, Fine Arts, etc. The Berlin brochure *Zu Gast in Berlin* and the weekly calendar which appears in the Wednesday edition of the *Tagesspiegel* will both help you to decide where to go and what to do.

Information, tickets, books, posters and brochures for various festival events and performances are also available at the Information Shop, located in the Europa-Center, Budapester Str. 48. The shop is open daily 14 March–22 November 10am–7pm; during the rest of the year hours are noon–6pm daily, except for Monday. Tel: 25489250.

Sightseeing Tours: You can hop on one of the Butterfly Lines – marked by a triangle – and end up in some of the greener, more natural places of Berlin.

During the season, excursion steamboats of the White Fleet depart from the harbour near the S-Bahn station at Treptower Park. You can get further information and book tickets in advance at the tourist agency high-rise on Alexanderplatz (Tel: 2123375); the Treptow office (Tel: 2712326); and the White Fleet Passenger Information Desk (Tel: 2728741).

Numerous enterprises organise daily tours. Tourist Information Offices will make recommendations. Tickets can be purchased directly on the bus.

Nightlife

Because Berlin is pretty much open 24 hours a day, going from a drink at a bar or two right into the thick of city nightlife is relatively effortless.

Shopping

There's only one rule that applies to shopping in Berlin: there's nothing that you can't buy. The free guide *Shopping in Berlin* is available from the Tourist Information Centre.

Further Reading

General

Germans, by George Bailey.

The Germans, by Gordon Craig.

Toward Understanding Germany, by Robert H Lowie.

Get to Know Germany, by Ian MacDonald.

New Germany at the Crossroads, by David Marsh.

Other Insight Guides

Other books in the *Insight Guide* series highlight destinations in Germany: *Insight Guides*: Germany, Berlin, Frankfurt, Hamburg, Cologne, Düsseldorf, Dresden, Munich, and The Rhine.

SWITZERLAND

Getting Acquainted

The Place

A difference in altitude of 4,000 metres over an area of only 41,295 sq. km (15,944 sq. miles) makes Switzerland one of the most geographically varied countries in Europe. At its widest point, it is only 348 km (216 miles) from east to west. Slightly more than half the country is farm land and pastures, one quarter forests and one quarter glaciers, rocks and 1,500 lakes. The highest mountain is Monte Rosa with an altitude of 4,564 metres (15,209 ft) above sea level and the lowest region is a strip of land on the banks of Lake Maggiore in Canton Ticino which is less than 193 metres (643 ft) above sea level.

Climate

Distinctions are made in Swiss weather reports between the two climatic regions of Switzerland, north of the Alps and southern Switzerland and Engadine. The weather on the different sides of the Alps may differ greatly, from Mediterranean warmth along the shores of Geneva and Ticino lakes to the most bracing high alpine weather. The average temperatures in centrally located Berne are 1°C (34°F) in the winter to 16°C (62°F) in the summer. A fact-sheet on weather and average temperatures in specific areas is available from the Swiss National Tourist Office.

For an up-to-date weather report dial 162; the report will be delivered in the language of the region you are calling from.

The People

Switzerland has a population of more than 6.4 million, about half of which are Catholic and half Protestant.

Economy

Industry and crafts, along with the tourist trade, produce the largest part of the national income and provide employment for 1 million people. Switzerland is best known for its high-precision engineering, watchmaking and jewellery, and chemical and pharmaceutical industries.

Government

Switzerland is composed of 23 cantons, three of which are politically subdivided, and each canton is a miniature state with its own constitution, its own legal system and its own government. The Federal Parliament consists of a National Council of 200 members, directly elected by the people, and the Council of States, in which each canton has equal representation in the legislative body.

Planning the Trip

Currency

The unit of currency in Switzerland is the Swiss Franc (SFr), with 100 Rappen (Rp) to a franc. There are 5, 10, 20 and 50 Rappen coins, and 1, 2 and 5 SFr coins. Notes are issued in the amounts of 10, 20, 50, 100, 500 and 1,000 francs.

There is no limit to the amount of foreign currency or other means of payment you can carry into or out of Switzerland.

Foreign currency, traveller's cheques and other means of payment can be changed into Swiss notes and coins at banks, bureaux de change, train stations, airports, travel agencies and hotels. Most Swiss banks accept Eurocheques. Travellers can often settle their bills in hotels, shops, department stores and restaurants with foreign money. (Ask for the rate of exchange; in most cases it will be slightly worse than the current rate.) It is best to carry Swiss Bankers Traveller's Cheques issued in Swiss Francs. You

can use these as you would cash and in Switzerland they can be exchanged free of charge.

Bureaux de change situated in airports and railway stations will exchange foreign cash, traveller's cheques and Eurocheques for you at the current rate. They are open 6am–9pm or 11pm.

Public Holidays

In addition to those listed in the Introduction, the following legal holidays are also observed in Switzerland: Good Friday and Switzerland National Holiday (1 August).

Getting There

By Air

The five international airports in Switzerland are: Zurich, Geneva, Basle, Lugano and Berne. Swissair and Crossair, the two Swiss airlines, connects Switzerland with 110 cities in 70 countries. The airports in Zurich and Geneva have their own train stations which are part of the national fast-train network, several trains each hour run between the airport and the main railway station. The Basle-Mulhouse airport is actually situated in France; the journey by bus from here to the Swiss train station in Basle SBB takes about 25 minutes. There are regular connections between the Zurich, Basle and Geneva international airports. Regular and charter airlines as well as local airtaxi services fly in and out of the Berne-Belp, Lugano-Agno, Gstaad-Saanen, Sion and Samedan-St Moritz airfields.

By Rail

Intercity trains connect Switzerland with all large cities in the surrounding countries. These trains have comfortable first and second class compartments and leave every hour. Intercity, fast and regional trains have direct connections to all cities and most holiday resort areas; certain trains travel directly to Swiss holiday areas. For further information contact the Swiss Tourist Information Centres (SVZ) or Swiss Federal Railways, tel: 051 220 1111.

By Road

Travellers can enter Switzerland by car from all neighbouring countries after passing through border customs on

main thoroughfares primarily motorways. In addition, there are numerous smaller border posts, but these are not necessarily open around the clock.

Motoring Advice: Motor vehicles weighing up to 3.5 tons (including trailers and caravans) are charged SFr30 per year for what is commonly referred to as the *motorway vignette* (a sticker you place on your windshield that permits you to drive on Swiss motorways). This is valid from 1 December to 31 January (14 months). They can be purchased at borders, post offices, petrol stations and garages in Switzerland and in other countries from automobile associations and Swiss Tourist Information Centres. The sticker should be fixed to the left edge of the vehicle's front windshield. Hire cars come with a valid vignette. *The Best Roads of Switzerland for 30 Francs*, from SVZ offices, has information on tolls on motorways and other roads.

Useful Addresses

Tourist Offices Abroad

Australia: 203-233 New South Head Road, PO Box 82, Edgecliff/Sydney NSW 2027. Tel: 02 326 1799.

Canada: Commerce Court West, Suite 2015, PO Box 215, Toronto, Ontario M5L 1E8. Tel: 868 0584.

UK: Swiss Centre, Swiss Court, London W1V 8EE. Tel: (0171) 734 1921; fax: (0171) 437 4577.

US: Swiss Centre, 608 Fifth Avenue, NY 10020, tel: (212) 757 5944; 222 Sepulveda Blvd, Suite 1570 El Segundo, CA 90245, tel: (310) 335 5980; fax: (310) 335 5982.

Practical Tips

Emergencies

Medical Services

All chemists have duty rota lists on their doors. Many doctors speak English and many hotels have house physicians. Doctor's fees and hospital costs are high. All hospitals have emergency wards with doctors on 24-

hour duty, as do major rail stations. **Useful emergency numbers**: In case of an accident, first dial the appropriate area code, then 144 to alert ambulances and other emergency vehicles. **Area dialling codes**: 031 (Berne); 056 (Baden); 057 (Wohlen); 061 (Basle); 064 (Aarau); 01 (Zurich); 043 (Schwyz) and 062 (Olten).
Police: 117
Fire brigade: 118
Breakdown service: 140

Business Hours

Offices are open weekdays 8am–noon and 2–6pm, closed on Saturday. Shops are usually open 8am–12.30pm and 1.30–4pm. In larger cities they are also open during lunch time. Shops are often closed Monday mornings, but they stay open until 9pm on Wednesday or Thursday.

Business hours mentioned here apply to the different service industries. There are also local and regional differences.

In large cities, banks and bureaux de change are open Monday–Friday 8.30am–4.30pm and closed on Saturday. In the countryside these hours are Monday–Friday 8.30am–noon and 2–4.30 or 5.30pm. Closed: Saturday.

Tipping

Tips are included in all hotel and restaurant bills. It is neither necessary nor expected to leave an extra tip.

Postal Services

Post offices in large cities are open 7.30am–noon and 1.45–6.30pm throughout the week. On Saturday they are open until 11am. Stamps can be purchased at post offices, postcard kiosks and stamp machines. Mailboxes are yellow and set in the wall.

Telephones

The Swiss telephone system is entirely automatic. Public telephones in post offices and booths have directories in several languages. Telephones take centime coins or the Swiss phonecard, called Taxcard, on sale at post offices, newsagents and railway stations. For directory assistance dial 113; international calls 114 or 191; information (in English) 111. For calls made at hotels, substantial service charges are levied.

Telegrams can be sent from any Swiss post office or by dialling 110. Rates can be also be obtained at this number. Lucerne's Main Telegraph Office is at Bahnhofstrasse 3a.

Tourist Information

The Swiss National Tourist Office (SNTO) maintains agencies abroad in New York City, San Francisco, London, Tokyo and Johannesburg, as well as in all major European capitals. Detailed tourist information in Switzerland may be obtained from the head office in Zurich (Bellariastrasse 38, CH-8027 Zurich, tel: 01/28811 11) or from the local tourist offices of 11 major touristic regions. The offices, located throughout the country, are known as Verkehrsbüro, Office du Tourisme or Ento Turistico. Visitors can call tourist information, tel: 120.

The Lucerne Tourist Promotion Board is located at Pilatusstrasse 14, tel: 23 52 52.

Consulates & Embassies

Lucerne

Australia: Alpenstrasse 29, 3006 Berne. Tel: 031-43 01 43.
Canada: Kirchenfeldstrasse 88, 3000 Berne. Tel: 031-44 63 81/85.
Ireland: Eigerstrasse 71, 3007 Berne. Tel: 031-46 23 53/54.
South Africa: Jungfraustrasse 1, 3005 Berne. Tel: 031-44 20 11.
UK: Thunstrasse 50, 3005 Berne. Tel: (031)352 1442; fax: (031) 352 1455.
US: Postfach 1065, Jubiläumsstrasse 93, 3005 Berne. Tel: (031) 354 7398.

Geneva

Australia: Rue de Moillebeau 56–58, 1211. Tel: 022-346200.
Canada: Avenue de Budé 10a, 1202. Tel: 022-341950.
New Zealand: Chemin du Petit-Saconnex 28 A, Case Postale 84, 1211 Geneva 19. Tel: 022-349530.
UK: Rue de Vermont 37–39, 1211. Tel: 002-343800.
US: Rue Pregny, 1292 Chambesy. Tel: 9902 11.

Getting Around

Public Transport

Offizielle Schweizer Kursbuch gives the schedules for and offers on all railways, mail buses, boats and mountain trains and the most important connections to foreign countries.

By Air

There are three international airports and over 40 smaller airfields in Switzerland, most of which organise flights over the Alps in good weather. Crossair connects Basel, Geneva and Zurich and Lugano and Berne.

By Rail

More than 5,780 km (3,400 miles) of dense, electrified railways open up the remotest sections of the country with trains every hour at least. More than 100 trains call at Zurich Airport each day. The swiftest connections are by fast, intercity trains.

Swiss Federal Railways is referred to by its initials, which vary between the official languages: SBB (German), CFF (French) and FFS (Italian). It has details of the Swiss Holiday Card in 4, 8, 15 or 30 day packages which entitles the holder to an unlimited number of journeys by train, boat and postal coach all over Switzerland.

By Road

Switzerland has a dense network of main and subsidiary roads covering over 64,600 km (40,000 miles), of which 9,350 km (5,810 miles) are highways. Twenty five major roads running over the alpine tunnels form one of the main attractions for visitors; depending on the snow, they are open from May or June to late autumn. Special rail facilities are provided for motorists wishing to transport their cars through alpine passageways.

Motoring Advice: For information on road conditions in Switzerland (road passability, etc), tel: 163. Signs along the motorways inform drivers when these broadcasts can be heard on the radio. Emergency phones are found at intervals of 1.5 km on motorways; the direction of the nearest phone is indicated by arrows. Super highways are identified with green directional signs; main roads are numbered and have blue signs.

More road information can be obtained from the Swiss National Tourist Office or any of the two Swiss Automobile clubs:

Automobile-Club der Schweiz (ACS), Wasserwerkgasse 39, CH-3000 Berne 13, tel: 031 311 7722.

Touring Club der Schweiz (TCS), Rue Pierre-Fatio 9, CH-1211 Genève, tel: 022 737 12 12.

Waterways

Regularly scheduled boats cruise all the big Swiss lakes. There are steamships to put you in a nostalgic mood on Lake Geneva, Lake Zurich, Lake Brienz and Lake Lucerne. It's also possible to take a trip along the Rhine, Rhône, Aare and Doubs rivers. Details from tourist offices.

By Coach

The alpine postal motor coach (PTT) network takes travellers through the principal mountain roads and covers regularly more than 6,800 km (4,000 miles). Some of the most spectacular stretches are included in the itinerary of the Europabus system. Conducted tours by rail, postal motor coach or private bus are regularly organised in many towns and resorts. The local tourist office can supply all necessary details.

Where to Stay

Accommodation

The *Swiss Hotel Guide*, published annually by the Swiss Hotel Association, is available from the Swiss National Tourist Office. Further information and prices can be found in the free regional and local hotel listings available from regional tourist associations.

Attractions

What's On

The Swiss National Tourist Office (SNTO) publishes an annual calendar of events including complete details on music festivals, art exhibitions, sightseeing, trade fairs and sporting events, as well as a listing of more than 100 museums and art collections available to the public.

Nightlife

Disregard the rumour that nightlife in Switzerland is pretty provincial; in larger cities you'll find a wide variety of bars, clubs, opportunities to dance and discos. Some of the well-known holiday resort areas also offer attractive places to spend an evening, as well as world-class entertainment programmes. For further, information enquire at a local tourist information centre or ask the hotel concierge.

Shopping

If you're searching for something typical and of good quality, try one of the Schweizerischen Heimatwerk (Swiss Handicraft) shops, located in many cities and well-populated areas. They are staffed by competent sales assistants. In smaller towns it's best to purchase articles directly from the source, i.e. the company or artist.

Language

Switzerland is one of the most multilingual countries in Europe with four national languages. German is spoken in central and eastern Switzerland; French in the west; Italian in the southern part of the country and 1 percent of the population speaks Romansh in south-eastern Switzerland. People who work with visitors usually speak several languages, including English.

Further Reading

General

The Alps, by Ronald W. Clark.
Switzerland, by Christopher S. Hughes.
The Swiss and their Mountains, by Sir A.H.M. Lunn.
Antiquities and Archaeology, by R. Sauter.
Why Switzerland, by Jonathan Steinberg.
Switzerland Exposed, by Jean Ziegler.

Other Insight Guides

Insight Guide: Switzerland. Companion volume to this book, from Apa Publications' award-winning series.

AUSTRIA

Getting Acquainted

The Place

Austria is the third largest landlocked country of the European continent, situated between East and West in the very heart of Europe. Three-quarters of Austria is covered by mountains, the highest being the Grossglockner at 4,138 metres (13,576 ft). Austria covers 83,887 sq. km (32,389 sq. miles).

Climate

The Alps cover most of the land in Austria and play a decisive role in determining the country's different climatic conditions. The weather on the northern edge of the Alps is Central-European for the most part, which means that even during the usually lovely summers you can expect quite a bit of precipitation. South of the Alps, in Carinthia, the climate is almost Mediterranean – warmer temperatures and less rainfall. In the Alps themselves summers are hot and winters are cold and snowy. The eastern part of the country has a continental climate. Burgenland is under the influence of the Pannonian Plain, which causes hot summers and freezing winters.

The People

Austria is inhabited by 7.6 million people. Ninety percent are members of the Roman Catholic Church and about 6 percent are Protestant. There are small Croatian, Hungarian and Slovenian minority groups in Carinthia, Styria and Burgenland.

Economy

The electronic, chemical and textile industries are flourishing; food, tourism and forestry industries are also important for the country's economy.

Government

Austria is divided into nine provinces: Vienna, Lower Austria, Burgenland, Upper Austria, Styria, Carinthia, Salzburg, Tyrol and Vorarlberg. It is a democratic republic made up of two houses which constitute the Federal Assembly.

Planning The Trip

Health

Hotels and embassies can provide lists of English-speaking doctors and dentists.

Currency

The Austrian unit of currency is the Schilling, made up of 100 Groschen. There are 1,000, 500, 100, 50 and 20 Schilling notes and 100, 50, 25, 20, 10, 5 and 1 Schilling coins.

Banks and exchange offices will change foreign currency at the current rate of the Viennese stock market exchange. Currencies not listed here are exchanged at the free market rate. There is no limit on carrying foreign money into or out of Austria, but you are only allowed to take 100,000 Austrian Schilling when you leave.

Public Holidays

In addition to those listed in the Introduction, Austria celebrates: Epiphany: 6 January; National Holiday: 26 October; Day of the Immaculate Conception: 8 December.

Getting There

By Air

Austria's national carrier, Austrian Airlines, operates daily direct services to most European capital cities from Vienna's Schwechat airport and less frequently from Salzburg, Graz, Linz, Klagenfurt and Innsbruck. Some 36 carriers, including most major European airlines, fly between Vienna and national capitals.

By Train

There are two main stations in Vienna: the Westbahnhof serves Germany, France, Belgium and Switzerland and the Südbahnhof serves Yugoslavia, Greece, Hungary and Italy.

Other major international trains are the *Prinz Eugen* (Hanover–Vienna), the *Arlberg Express* (Paris–Vienna via Switzerland) and the *Holland–Vienna Express* (Amsterdam–Vienna). Anyone wishing to arrive in style could catch the *Orient Express* on a weekly run to Budapest with stops at Innsbruck, Salzburg and Vienna.

For passenger information in Vienna, tel: (0222) 1717.

By Road

There are approximately 70 international bus lines connecting Austria to other foreign countries. There are no direct bus services from Northern Europe. Would-be bus travellers are advised to travel to Munich and change to the rail network.

Travelling to Austria by car from Northern Europe is a long and arduous journey, best achieved by travelling through Germany to take advantage of the toll-free and excellent motorway network. Beware of attempting to enter the country via the less busy alpine passes, which can be closed at night and in the winter. Motorways are free in Austria.

Practical Tips

Emergencies

Medical Services

Chemists operate a rota system for night and Sunday duty. Information about medical emergencies is available from the local police or from the telephone directory.

Emergency Telephone Numbers
Fire Brigade: 122
Police: 133
Ambulance: 144
Information: 16

Crisis Intervention Hot-line: 1770
Vienna Radio Medical Service: 141
International Aircraft Rescue Service: (02732) 70007.

Business Hours

In general, shops and businesses in Austria are open workdays from 8am–6pm and on Saturday 8am–noon. Banks are open Monday, Tuesday, Wednesday and Friday 8am–12.30pm and 1.30–3pm.

Tipping

It is usual to leave a 10–15 percent tip when the service has been good.

Postal Services

Post offices are generally open from 8am–noon and 2–6pm. A few are open on Saturday from 8–10am. The main post offices in the large cities are 24-hour. Stamps are available from post offices and tobacco kiosks. Letter boxes are yellow.

Telephones

Telephone calls may be made from the post office and telephone kiosks. Some public telephones require the use of a telephone card, obtainable from post offices.
For operator-assisted long-distance calls: 1616
Telephone enquiries local: 16
Telephone enquiries Long distance: 08

Getting Around

Domestic Transport

By Air

There are direct flights from Vienna to the cities of Graz, Klagenfurt, Linz, Salzburg and Innsbruck. For details consult airline schedules.

Vienna's Schwechat airport, tel: (0222) 711 102 231, is located 15 km (9 miles) to the east of the city (25 minutes on the motorway). It has an information booth in the arrival hall which is open 9am–10pm daily. An express bus service which operates 6am–7pm links the airport with Vienna's two main railway stations and the City Air Terminal next to the Hilton Hotel. For information, tel: (0222) 5800 2300. A train service operates between the central station and the airport every hour on the hour 7.30am–8.30pm.

By Rail

The Austrian Federal Railway System maintains about 5,800 km (3,625 miles) of track and is connected with both the Eastern and Western European railway networks. Seat reservation costs 30 Schillings. Passengers pay a surcharge on TEE and IC trains but the price of reserved seating is then contained within this additional charge.

Trains Vienna–Graz and Vienna–Salzburg depart at 1-hour intervals. Trains Vienna–Innsbruck and Vienna–Villach leave at 2-hour intervals.

Nearly all daytime trains have dining cars; night trains have sleeping compartments and couchettes. There are a number of fare reductions on offer. For information contact:
Complete Railway Service Office: 1700.
Railway Information: 1717.

By Road

Approximately 70 international bus lines connect Austria to other countries. The Austrian public bus service primarily links places not served by the railway network. Nearly all tourist areas offer bus excursions into the surrounding countryside.

Motoring Advice: There is a traffic report broadcast on Channel 3 (Ö3) every hour following the regular news edition. Programmes may be interrupted to announce especially nasty traffic conditions. In and around the city of Vienna the radio station Radio Blue Danube broadcasts regular traffic reports in English and French 7–10am, noon–2pm and 6–8pm.

The police must be called to the scene of all car accidents in which any persons are injured. Foreigners should fill out the accident form entitled *Comité Européen des Assurances*. ÖAMTC and ARBÖ maintain breakdown services along the most important thoroughfares; non-members may also take advantage of these services for a somewhat higher price than members. Useful numbers:
ÖAMTC Breakdown Service: Tel: 120.
ARBÖ Breakdown Service: Tel: 123.
ARBÖ Emergency Service: Tel: 782528.
ÖAMTC European Emergency Service: Tel: 922245.

Waterways

From the beginning of April until the end of October boats operate on regular schedules along the Danube. Vienna is connected to Budapest and Passau. There are also boats running on a regular basis on all larger lakes in Austria.

Along the stretch from Vienna to Budapest, the Donau-Dampfschiffahrts-Gesellschaft Blue Danube (the Danube Steamship Company, Handelskai 265, operates the hydrofoil to Budapest. The hydrofoil makes three trips form Vienna to Budapest and three return trips from Budapest to Vienna daily. For timetable information tel: 0222 588-800.

The Tschechoslowakische Donauschiffahrt CSPD offers a hydrofoil service between Vienna and Bratislava. Boats depart Vienna at Reichsbrücke from Wednesday to Sunday at 9pm and 9.30pm and arrive in Bratislava at 10.30am and 11pm. The hydrofoil leaves Bratislava at 5pm and 5.40pm arriving in Vienna at 6.45pm and 7.25pm.

Where to Stay

Accommodation

On just about every street in tourist-oriented towns you'll find at least one *zimmer frei*, tourist information, sign. Staff can give you a listing of local, privately-run accommodation.

Attractions

Opera, theatre and classical music performances: Austrian calendar of events, the Austrian Tourist Office Centre. Tel: (0222) 587 2000. Baroque music concert dates and literature about the *Barockstrasse*: Austrian Tourist Office Centre in Vienna 5, Margaretenstrasse 1, tel: (0222) 587 2000 and at Austrian Tourist Office agencies overseas. National Theatre Ticket Reservations: 1 Goethegasse 1. Tel: (0222) 514 440. Open: Monday–Saturday 9am–5pm.

Shopping

Austria has an abundance of high quality, valuable and hand-made articles including glassware, jewellery, chinaware and winter-sports equipment.

Language

Of the 7.6 million population, 98 percent speak German.

VIENNA

Getting Acquainted

The Place

Vienna is not only the capital of Austria, but also one of the nine federal states of the republic. Population is 1.6 million, which means that every 4th Austrian lives in Vienna. Area: ca. 160 sq. miles (400 sq. km). The city is divided into 23 districts. The standard of living is high, and since 1919 socialist governments have prevailed.

Planning The Trip

Currency

Banks are open 8am–12.30pm and 1.30–3pm Monday–Friday, and stay open until 5.30pm on Thursday. The main branches are open throughout lunch time. Eurocheques must be made out in Schilling. Most credit cards are accepted by the big hotels and main shops in the inner city.

Getting There

By Air

Schwechat Airport is about 10 miles (15 km) to the east of Vienna and can be reached by motorway in 25 minutes. There are connections to over 60 destinations all over the world and domestic flights to Graz, Linz, Salzburg, Klagenfurt and Innsbruck from Vienna Schwechat. The information desk in the arrivals lounge is open 9am–10pm.

Schwechat flight information: Tel. 711 102 233.

Airport Transport: Express Coach Services operate between the airport and the southern and western rail ter-

minals and the City Air Terminal outside the Hilton hotel 6am–7pm. During the evening and through the night, there is a bus connection after every scheduled flight arrival. A shuttle minibus service runs to the airport from every major hotel. For further information, tel: (0222) 63 60 190. Trains: Leave from Wien-Mitte (central station) every hour 7.30am–8.30pm.

By Rail

The two main railway stations linking Vienna with destinations in Europe are the *Westbahnhof* (western station) and the *Südbahnhof* (southern station). Trains from Germany, France, Belgium and Switzerland arrive at Westbahnhof, those from Greece, Hungary and Italy at Südbahnhof.

International Intercity Trains:

Prinz Eugen: Hannover–Dortmund–Frankfurt–Vienna.

Ostende-Vienna Express: Ostende–Brussels–Cologne–Vienna.

Arlberg Express: Paris–Basel–Zürich–Vienna.

Holland-Vienna Express: Amsterdam–Cologne–Vienna.

Trains carrying cars run between Vienna and Düsseldorf, Cologne and Frankfurt. During the summer months there is a ferry service on the Danube River from Passau to Vienna.

Complete Railway Service Office: Tel: 1700

Railway Information: Tel: 1717

By Road

Most visitors to Vienna from the western parts of Europe approach the town on the Westautobahn. Hotel bookings can be made at tourist information centres located at the end of the motorway. The same facilities are available when entering Vienna on the motorway coming from the south (Südautobahn).

Parking: You should try to avoid the centre of Vienna if travelling by car. There are few parking facilities in the inner city, and a network of one-way streets makes driving a nightmare. If it cannot be avoided, look out for the car parks but bear in mind that some of them are closed on weekends and during the night.

Practical Tips

Emergency Telephone Numbers
Ambulance: 40144.
Emergency Doctor: 141. Daily 7pm–7am.
Chemist: 1550.
Psychiatrist: 9, Fuchsthalergasse 18. 318419.
International Chemist: 1, Kärntner Ring 15. 512 2825.
Poisoning: 9, Lazarettgasse 14. 4343439.

Postal Services

Hauptpostamt (main post office), 1, Fleischmarkt 19. Tel: 51590. Open 24 hours.

Tourist Offices

Vienna Tourist Board
11, Obeve Augar ten-Strasse 40, tel: 211 140-1; fax: 216 8492.
Detailed information about Austria can be found at local tourist offices. The nine federal provinces maintain their own tourist boards.

Astrian National Tourist Office
Urlaubsinformation Österreich, 1040 Vienna, Margaretenstrasse 1. Tel: (222) 587 2000; fax: 588 6620.

Tourist Offices Abroad
UK: Austrian National Tourist Office, 30 St George Street, London W1R 0AL. Tel: (0171) 629 0461.
US: Austrian National Tourist Office, 500 Fifth Ave, Suite 2009-2022, New York, NY 10110, tel: (212) 944 6880; 11601 Wilshire Boulevard, Suite 2480, Los Angeles, CA 90025, tel: (213) 477 3332.

Embassies & Consulates

Australia: IV, Mattiellistrasse 2, tel: 512 8580.
Canada: I, Laurenzerberg 2, tel: 531 3830 00.

South Africa: XIX, Sandgasse 33, tel: 326 4930.
United Kingdom: III, Jauresgasse 12, tel: 716 13-0.
United States of America: IX, Boltzmanngasse 16, tel: 313 39-0.

Getting Around

A car is superfluous in Vienna. The town has an excellent urban and regional transport systems, including subway; fast subway; local and regional trains; trams and buses. For information about public transport in Vienna contact the Vienna Tourist Office, tel: (0222) 216 8492.

Shopping

The most elegant and expensive shops, as well as art galleries and antique shops, can be found in the inner city area between Hofburg, Graben and Kärntner Strasse. Opening hours for shops are Monday–Friday usually 9am–6pm, Saturday 9am–12.30pm.

Markets are held daily in almost every district in Vienna. Special markets operate only on Tuesday and Friday. The most famous of these markets is the Naschmarkt. Nearby, a flea market is set up every Saturday at 4–5, Wienzeile, Kettenbrückengasse.

Further Reading

General

Austria, Empire and Republic, by Barbara Jelavich. Cambridge University Press.
Clash of Generations, by Lavender Cassels. John Murray.
Dissolution of the Austro-Hungarian Empire, by J.W. Mason. Longman.
The End of Austria-Hungary, by L. Valani. Knopf.
The Fall of the House of Habsburgs, by Edward Crankshaw. Penguin.
The Hapsburg Monarch, by Arthur J. May. University of Pennsylvania.
Mayerling: the Facts behind the Legend, by Fritz Judtman. Harrap.
A Nervous Splendour, by Frederic Morton. Little.
Nightmare in Paradise: Vienna and its Jews, by George E. Berkley. California University Press.

Insight Guides

There are *Insight Guide* titles to both Austria and Vienna. The *Insight Compact Guide* series has titles covering Vienna and Salzburg.

BUDAPEST

Getting Acquainted

The People

Metropolitan Budapest has 2.1 million inhabitants, roughly one-fifth of the country's population. Ten percent of the population consists of ethnic minorities, the largest groups include Serbs, Croatians, Slovaks and Romanians. The city is divided into 22 districts, denoted by Roman numerals. The most important are I (Buda) and V (Pest City).

Government

The state of Hungary has existed for at least 1,000 years. The Parliamentary Republic of Hungary (Magyar Koztarsasag) came into being on 23 October 1989, the anniversary of the 1956 uprising.

Since 1989, Hungary has been a parliamentary democracy with two chambers led by a Prime Minister. The highest authority in the land is the State President, who is granted significant powers by the constitution.

Planning The Trip

Currency

The Hungarian currency is the Forint (Ft), or the HUF for Eurocheque purposes. It divides into 100 Filler. The Forint comes in 5,000, 1,000, 500, 100, 50 bills; rare are 20 and 10 Forint bills. There are also 20, 10, 5, 2 and 1 Forint coins.

Hungary is currently cheaper than Western countries, but inflation is high, 25–35 percent. The currency is frequently devalued. The Forint is not a convertible currency, so change only as much as you need. Money changers offer better exchange rates on the street. These transactions are illegal.

Traveller's cheques and credit cards: Eurocheques can be cashed in banks and most post offices to a maximum of 15,000Ft. Credit cards are widely accepted in hotels, restaurants, shops and petrol stations.

Getting There

By Air

Many airlines fly to Budapest's Ferihegy airport. Malev, Hungary's national airline, uses the Ferihegy II terminal, all others use Ferihegy I. There are regular flights to and from all European capitals and major cities, several Balkan cities, a number of Middle Eastern cities and New York.

Malev has offices around the world and desks in the main Budapest hotels. International airlines flying to Hungary have offices in the centre of Budapest.

The most reliable way to get to town is by minibus (1000 Ft in 1998). It stops at most big hotels from where you can catch a taxi. The minibus will pick you up as well. Ask your receptionist, or call 296-8555. Beware if taking a taxi from the airport. The incidence of over-charging is high.

General flight information. Arrivals tel: 296 8406; departures tel: 296 7831.

By Road

Travellers to Budapest will probably want to drive in through Vienna, from which a motorway (A4) leads almost to the crossing at Hegyeshalom. There are more crossings further to the south. If driving through Carinthia in Austria, you may want to cut through Maribor, Slovenia and drive in through Letenye.

Motorists need a valid driving licence, a sticker showing which country they're from and valid vehicle registration documents. An insurance green card isn't required, but motoring organisations recommend you bring one, together with vouchers that can get your car towed home.

Beware! There is a total drink-and-drive ban in Hungary. The legal limit is **0.0 milligrams.** There are strict rules and harsh penalties if you have been drinking anything. Up to 0.8 milligrams, there is a maximum fine of 30,000 forint (Ft); over 0.8 milligrams, prison sentences can be given (foreigners are not exempted).

By Rail

Rail travellers to Budapest usually have to change trains at the West Station in Vienna (the journey continues from the South Station, Wien-Süd). Arrival is at the Keleti pályaudvar (Eastern Railway Station) in Budapest. Some long-distance international trains have coaches going directly to Budapest: the Oostende-Vienna Express (Cologne-Frankfurt-Nürnberg-Passau-Linz); the Orient Express (Paris-Kehl-Stuttgart-Munich-Salzburg); the Wiener Waltzer (Basel-Zurich-Innsbruck-Salzburg). For the trip from one station to another you should allow at least half an hour; the Metro is a lot faster than a cab. For rail service information, tel: 322 8056.

By Sea

The Hungarian Mahart company and the Austrian DDSG-Donaureisen company operate jetfoils and hovercraft between Vienna and Budapest (and elsewhere). The trip is picturesque but not necessarily cheap. Your local travel agent should be able to help you with information. You can also write to or call: DDSG-Donaureisen, Handelskai 265, A-1021 Vienna, tel: 0222 729 2161. Or try Mahart, Belgrad rakpart, Budapest V, tel: 118 1704; fax: 118 7740.

Practical Tips

Emergencies

Doctors

Medical aid is available around the clock from the following clinics:
Falck SOS Hungary: Budapest, Kapy u.49/B. Tel: 2000100.
Stomatologiai Intézet (Central Dental Institutes; VIII, Szentkivalyi u.40. Tel: 133 0770.

Accidents

Helicopter Rescue Service, Aerocaritas, tel: 625 3130 and 625 3950.

Accidents have to be reported to the police immediately, and forms need to be filled out even for minor collisions. Report any accident – even if it wasn't your fault – immediately to Hungaria Insurance Budapest, Gvadanyi ut 69. Tel: 20 9073 0250/1.

Pharmacies (Gyogyszertar)

Almost all strong medicine is only available on prescription. Payment must be made in cash. The normal opening times are Monday–Friday 8am–8pm, Saturday 8am–2pm.

Emergency Telephone Numbers
These numbers can be dialled from any telephone:
Emergency Rescue Service: 104.
First Aid: 104 and 1111666.
Fire Brigade: 105.
Police: 107.

Business Hours

Times tend to vary, generally, shop trading hours are Monday–Friday 8am–6pm and Saturday 8am–1pm, with some shopping centres open on Sunday. Museums are open Tuesday–Sunday 10am–6pm, and mostly closed Monday.

Tipping

Gratuities are included in the price, but it's usual to add an extra 10 percent of the final sum as a tip.

Postal Services

Post offices are open Monday–Friday 8am–7pm (except in smaller towns and villages) and 8am–2pm (at the latest) on Saturday.

The post offices at the west and east train stations in Budapest are open 24 hours. At the main Post Office (8am–7pm), Budapest V. Varoshaz utca 9–11, tel: 118 5398.

Telephones

Public telephone boxes in Hungary come in three colours: use yellow and grey boxes for local calls (5F) and calls within Hungary (dialling code 06); red

for international calls. You need 5, 10 or 20F coins – and lots of them. It's a better idea to buy a phone card at the post office.

To dial internationally, press 00 and wait for the tone. Useful country codes: Australia 61; Canada and US 1; UK 44. Foreign language directory enquiries (7am–8pm); international: 199; inland: 117 2200.

Tourist Information

Tourist offices are omnipresent in Hungary, beginning with border crossings, the airport, and train stations. They provide numerous services including making hotel reservations, changing money, etc. Don't expect to always find up-to-date brochures.

If you are staying in a more expensive hotel, you will probably have a tourist office in the lobby.

A vital number in Hungary is the international Tourist Information Service TOURINFORM in Budapest, Suto utca 2, on Deak ter. Tel: 117 9800; fax: 117 9578. Use it in Budapest, or the following:
Budapest Tourist, Roosevelt ter 5. Tel: 117 3555.
Cooptourist, Kossuth L. ter 13-15. Tel: 112 1017.
IBUSZ 1 Budapest VII, Karoly Krt. 3/c. Tel: 142 3140.

Tourist Offices Abroad

Tourist information abroad on Hungary is available from either a travel agency specialising in Eastern European travel, a branch of the IBUSZ travel agent, Malév (the Hungarian airline) or the nearest Hungarian consulate or embassy.
Hungarian National Tourist Office, 46 Eaton Place, London SW1 8AL, tel: 0171 823-1032, fax: 0171 823-1459.
Hungarian National Tourist Office, 150 East 58th Street, 33rd floor, New York, NY, 10155-3398, tel: (212) 355-0240, fax: (212) 207-4103.

Embassies

British Embassy, 1054 Budapest V, Harmincad utca 6, tel: 266-2888.
US Embassy, 1054 Budapest V, Szabadsag tér 12, tel: 267-4400.

Getting Around

By Rail

The metro operates daily 4.30am–11pm. Tickets (best bought in bulk in advance) can be obtained from vending machines, at stations, at the tobacconists, at the Metro ticket offices and in travel agencies. Budapest has three metro lines; all intersect beneath Deak ter in the centre of Pest.

Hungarian Rail (MAV) has an extensive but comparatively expensive rail network.

National Information: Tel: 322 7860 or 342 9150. Daily 6am–9pm. International Information: Tel: 322 4052.

MAV customer service office: VI, Andrassy ut 35. Tel: 342 9150. Monday–Friday 9am–5pm.

By Road

The road system is quite good, and Budapest has several sections of motorway. Information on traffic conditions can be obtained from Utinform: Budapest VI, Andrassy ut 11. Tel: 322 2238. The highway code is similar to that of Western Europe, but it is absolutely forbidden to drive in Hungary after consuming any kind or quantity of alcohol.

Breakdown Services:
The *Yellow Angels* of the Hungarian Automobile Club will help you or organise any repairs. Hungarian Autoclub: Francia ut 38. Tel: 252 8000.
Camping and Caravan Club: Maria utca 32–34. Tel: 217 7248.

Car Rental: You have to be 21 and you need your driving licence and passport. Credit cards are accepted.
Avis, main office, V, Szenita ut 8. Tel: 118 4240; at the airport, tel: 157 6421.
Hertz, V, Marriott Hotel, Apaczai Csere Janos u.4, tel: 266 4344; at Airport I, tel: 157 7171.
Europcar, Budapest IX, Ulloi ut 60–62, tel: 313 1492; at Airport I, tel: 296 6680; at Airport II, tel: 296 6610.

Public Transport

Buses and Trams: In the city buses and trams cost the same as the metro and run at the same times; some trams and blue buses run at night. The lines with red numbers are express bus lines, only stopping at important traffic intersections.

Yellow buses travel long-distance routes. Most of them leave from Erzsebet ter, near Deak ter. Timetables and price lists are available daily by calling: 117 2562.

Where to Stay

Accommodation

Contact IBUSZ or the international Tourist Information Service TOURINFO in Budapest for a list of recommended hotels and a reservation service.

Attractions

What's On

The best – and most accurate – source of information is *Budapest Week*, a magazine in English by Hungarians and foreigners. Hotels and tourist agencies have monthlies containing advertising.

Sightseeing: There is the nostalgic funicular railway (Sikló) up to the Cast from the bank of the Danube, daily 7.30am–10pm; the rack railway from Sziagyi Erzébet fasor in the northwest of Buda and Buda Hill, daily 4.30am–midnight, journey time 25 minutes; and the Libegó chairlift to the Jánós-hegy observation point in the east of the city, daily 9am–5pm, 15 minutes.

Language

Hungarian belongs to the Finno-Ugric family of languages. Its only relations in Europe are Finnish and Estonian.

Further Reading

Insight Guides: Hungary and *Budapest*. Companions to this book, from Apa Publications' award-winning series.
British Travellers in Old Budapest. Emeric W. Trencsenyi (comp).
The Danube Bend, by Laszlo Cseke. 1977; originally in Hungarian.
Hungary: A Century of Economic Development. T.I. Berend and G. Ránki.
Hungary: A Short History, by C.A. Macartney.
The Paul Street Boys, by Ferenc Molnár.

WARSAW

Getting Acquainted

The Place

Poles always say their geography is their history: 120,694 sq. miles (312,680 sq. km) of flat land, most less than 600 ft (180 metres) above sea level and some below. Poland has natural frontiers only to the south – the Carpathian and Sudeten mountains – not enough to stop invaders charging through. As a result, Poland has forever been moving about and in the 18th century did not exist as a separate state. Modern Poland was drawn up after World War I.

Climate

Winter lasts only three months (December–February), but can be so severe that in many northern regions temperatures drop to minus 30°C (minus 22°F). Snow remains in the mountains until Easter. From June to August it is hot with temperatures often climbing beyond 30°C (86°F).

The People

The population of 37 million is unusually homogeneous: 98 percent Poles with just a scattering of Ukrainian, Belarussian and Jewish minorities. Poles are ardent Roman Catholics and religion has been a surrogate form of nationalism in times of subjugation.

Planning the Trip

Currency

The Polish currency is the zloty, but meteoric inflation has meant that the largest denomination note has been getting bigger and bigger. There used to be hundreds of zlotys to the dollar; by 1993 the figure was more than 10,000. It's almost a case of waiting until after a meal to change one's foreign currency to pay for it, and of course 50- and 1,000-zloty notes should not be confused in the dark.

Banks are usually open Monday–Friday mornings and in larger cities often until 5pm; the same hours apply to bureaux de change offices. There are frequently bureaux de change in hotels, conveniently open all day.

Getting There

By Air

A new terminal was added to Warsaw's Okecie International Airport in 1992 to handle the increasing number of flights both by LOT, the Polish national airline, and international carriers. There are regular direct non-stop flights to Warsaw from New York and Chicago. Domestic flights link Warsaw to at least 11 cities and towns within the country. Virtually all the major European carriers fly to Warsaw from their home bases.

By Sea

A weekly service is operated by the M/S Inowroc«aw, a freighter carrying passengers departing from either Tilbury on a Monday or Middlesbrough on a Tuesday and arriving in Gdynia on Fridays. The journey time is approximately four days. Contact: Gdynia America Shipping Lines (London) Ltd, Passenger Department, 238 City Road, London EC1V 2QL. Tel: (0171) 251 3389, fax: (0171) 250 3625. Regular passenger ferry services link the Polish ports of ;winouj,cie and Gdaøsk with Denmark, Sweden and Norway.

By Rail

There are regular daily services from London's Liverpool Street Station via the Hook of Holland and Victoria Station (via Ostend). On Saturdays (in season) charter couchettes are available on the train from Liverpool Street. Journey time from England is about 31 hours. EuroCity trains connect Warsaw with Berlin. Passengers who use this connection have links with Cologne, Wiesbaden, Karlsruhe, Hamburg, Frankfurt and Munich. All fast and express trains run on international links. Trains have 1st and 2nd class carriages, berths, sleepers and restaurant cars. Almost all international trains arrive at Warsaw Central Station, located in the city centre.

For train information in Warsaw contact: international, tel: 204512, 259942; domestic, tel: 2000361/69 and to make a seat reservation, tel: 365055.

Travelling from Germany to Poland by train is relatively cheap. It is not worth obtaining the reduced Interail Pass for people under 26 as travel within Poland is so cheap. Most trains to Poznaø and Warsaw pass through Berlin and Frankfurt am Oder. During the summer a motorrail service connects Hanover and Ilawa.

Direct trains to Poland:
Paris–Cologne–Düsseldorf–Hanover–Berlin–Poznaø–Warsaw
Cologne–Hanover–Leipzig–Wroclaw–Warsaw
Frankfurt-am-Main–Bebra–Wroclaw–Warsaw
Munich–Dresden–Wroclaw–Katowice
East-West Express: London–Hoek van Holland–Berlin–Warsaw–Moscow
Chopin Express: Vienna–Warsaw
For further information:
POLRES, Al. Jerozolimskie 4400-024 Warsaw. Tel: 022/8272588. Telex: 813636.

By Road

The main European routes across Poland are the E12 from Germany through Prague to Wroclaw, Lodz, Warsaw and Bioalystok, the E14 from Austria through the Czech Republic to Swinoujscie and on to Sweden, and the E8 from Germany through Poznan and Warsaw and on to Russia. Border formalities between Poland and Lithuania can be a nightmare.

By Coach: Regular weekly services run most of the year by luxury, air-conditioned coach with bar and toilet from the English Midlands via London, across the Channel to Poland. The journey time is around 36 hours. The Poland Express goes either from London via Amsterdam to Poznan and Warsaw; or from London or Manchester/Birmingham to Wroclaw, Katowice and Cracow.

Practical Tips

Emergencies

Medical Services

Western visitors can get medical attention in any city clinic. Treatments and hospital stays must be paid for in foreign currency. Medications prescribed by Polish doctors may be paid for in zlotys. Make sure you take out adequate medical insurance.
Emergency Telephone Numbers
Ambulance: 999
Fire: 998
Police: 997

Business Hours

Most businesses are open weekdays from 8am–7pm, but many grocery shops open their doors as early as 6am. Department stores are open until 6pm on Saturday, but most shops close somewhat earlier. Smaller shops are often closed for lunch between noon–3pm and all businesses are closed on Sunday.

Postal Services

Stamps are available wherever postcards are sold. The main post offices in large cities are open around the clock. Telegrams can be sent from many hotels.

Telephone

It is advisable to purchase one of the recently introduced phone cards. These cards (remove a corner before use) are available from post offices and kiosks. If you have to use one of the old coin-operated telephones, then you will need to buy one or more of the tokens (A = 1 unit, C = 6 units) from a post office or kiosk. The service is now generally very good. Until recently, it was often necessary in smaller towns to dial out via the operator, but now almost everywhere has its own dialling code. A leaflet listing dialling codes can be obtained at post offices.
Inland directory enquiries: 913

To call abroad from Poland, dial 00 and then the country code, eg UK 44. To call Poland from abroad, dial 00 48.

Telex and Fax

In most large hotels and main post offices you can both send and receive a telex or fax. In addition, the best hotels offer an office service including access to computers and printers.

Embassies & Consulates

Australia: ul. Estooska 3/5, 03 903 Warsaw. Tel: 6176081; fax: 617756.
Canada: ul. Matejki 1/5, 00-481 Warsaw. Tel: 298051; fax: 296457.
UK: Al. Rox 1, 00-556 Warsaw. Tel: 6281001; fax: 6252031.
US: Al. Ujazdowskie 29/31, 00-540 Warsaw. Tel: 6283041; fax: 6289326.

Getting Around

Domestic Transport

By Air

From Warsaw airport you can catch a flight at just about any time on LOT Airlines to Gdansk, Bydgoszcz, Katowice, Koszalin, Cracow, Poznan, Slupsk, Szczecin, Wroclaw and Zielona Gora. Tickets may be purchased at all LOT and Orbis branch offices. International airport, tel: 469873.

By Rail

The entire country is connected by an extensive railway network of about 16,000 miles (26,000 km). A reservation is needed on both express and regular trains. Trains are not always punctual. There are comfortable, non-stop express trains complete with dining cars running between Warsaw and Gdansk/Gydnia, Poznan and Cracow. Travelling by railway in Poland – even taking into account recent price increases – is still reasonable. Tickets are available at train stations, at Orbis or in POLRES agencies (tel: 022-365055). For information on transfers and connections, enquire at the railway station. Tel: 204512 for international rail information. Tel: 00361 for domestic rail information.

By Sea

Coastal boat tours offer the following trips 1 May–15 October: Gdansk–Sopot–Hel, Gydnia–Jastarnia, Gydnia–Helsowie, Szczecin–Swinoujscie and Miedzyzdroje. Inland boat traffic includes journeys down the Vistula (Warsaw–Gdansk), through the Masurian Lakes (Wegorzewo–Gizycko–Mikolajki–Nida–Ruciane), and along the Elblag–Ostroda Canal.

By Road

Tickets for the public transport systems can be bought at kiosks. Remember to cancel your ticket every time you transfer. Combination rail and bus tickets are available. The National Bus Network (PKS) is about 118,000 km (73,000 miles) long and composed of country, city and night buses.
Trams and trolleybuses: At every stop, and in all trams and trolleybuses, a schedule and route is posted.
Taxis: A vacant taxi has a lighted sign. The best place to hail one is in front of a hotel, station or department store.

Attractions

What's On

The dates for concerts, opera and theatre performances are in the calendar of events from the Tourist Office.
   Tours: Since the political turnaround, privately-owned small and medium-sized travel and service agencies have sprung up offering excursions and local services. Nevertheless, the former national travel agencies are still recommended. ORBIS and LOT organise city tours and excursions.

Further Reading

Atlas of Warsaw's Architecture, by J.A. Cicki Chro and A. Rottermund.
Heart of Europe: A short history of Poland, by Norman Davies.
History of Polish Culture, by Bogdan Suchodolski.
The Polish August, by Neal Ascherson.
Book of Warsaw Palaces, by T.S. Jaroszewski.
Warsaw: The Royal Way, by Jerzy Lileyko.
A Way of Hope, by Lech Walesa.
Insight Guides: Poland and Eastern Europe. Companions to this book, from Apa Publications' award-winning series.

PRAGUE

Getting Acquainted

The Place

The Czech Republic encompasses an area of 78,864 sq. km (30,450 sq. miles); Slovakia an area of 49,035 sq. km (18,933 sq. miles).

Prague is the Czech Republic's capital; Bratislava is the Capital of Slovakia. The Czech Republic shares its borders with Germany and Austria and Poland; Slovakia has Austria, Hungary, Poland and the Ukraine as neighbours. Brno is the capital of Moravia, which is part of the Czech Republic.

Climate

Warm, rainy summers and long dry winters are typical of the Czech Republic's climate. Prague receives some 476 mm (18½ inches) of rainfall per year.

Economy

The Czech Republic has opted for rapid change under a programme of economic reforms based on the free market. Slovakia, on the other hand, has opted for gradual reform; its economic problems are greater because the development of its industrial base occurred relatively recently, mostly at the whim of the central authorities in Prague.

Government

From January 1993 the federal state of Czechoslovakia ceased to exist. The revolution which took place in November 1989 brought the old quarrels between the two republics once again to the forefront. Acting without the direct mandate of the people, strong political movements in both republics negotiated the division of the country during 1992.

Planning The Trip

Entry Regulations

Customs

Visitors should note that antiques more than 50 years old can only be taken out with a special permit, which may be difficult to obtain. Most consumer goods, particularly groceries and household items, cannot be taken out of the country. When entering the country, enquire about the specific regulations and changes.

Currency

Czech crowns (Koruna or Kcs) circulate in banknotes of 10, 20, 50, 100, 500 and 1000 crowns; the coins are for 1, 2, 5 and 100 crowns. Eurocheques and credit cards are accepted. You can change money in the larger hotels, exchange offices and banks. Exchange offices and travel agencies are open weekdays until about 9pm.

Black market exchange is illegal, and hardly worthwhile.

Getting There

By Air

Prague, the Czech Republic's only international airport, has direct flights from London, New York, Frankfurt, Cologne/Bonn, Munich, Hamburg, Zurich, Geneva, Vienna, Montreal and Toronto. You can get detailed flight information from the Czech airline CSA, which has offices in many major cities.

By Train

There are direct trains to Prague from Stuttgart and Munich (an 8-hour trip), Frankfurt (10 hours), Berlin (6 hours), Hamburg (10 hours), and Vienna (6 hours).

Further information about rail travel can be obtained from the main station in English, French or German, tel: 2421 7654; or from Holesovice station, tel: 2461 5865.

By Road

There are many official border crossings with Germany and Austria. Expect some delays until border crossings are open to all vehicles from other nationalities.

By Bus: There are a great many different bus tours to the Czech Republic from Germany, Austria or Italy which include overnights.

By Sea

Groups or individuals can sail into the Czech Republic along the Elbe by boat or ship from Schmilke-Hrensko, or along the Danube from Bratislava. Ask your local travel agent for details.

Practical Tips

Emergencies

Medical Services

Emergencies are treated in every city clinic. Hospital attention has to be paid for in foreign currency, but medicine must be paid for in crowns.

Emergency Telephone Numbers
Emergency: 155
Dental Emergency Service: 2422 7663
Fire: 150
Police: 158

Chemists' shops are open during normal business hours and have information and addresses for emergency services.

Business Hours

Most shops are open 8.30am–6pm; certain specialised shops 10am–6pm. Many smaller shops close for two hours at midday. On Saturday, stores close between noon and 1pm; the large department stores, however, are an exception, staying open until 6pm.

Banks are open Monday–Friday 8am–5pm with an hour for lunch. Exchange offices work 8am–7pm daily; some remain open until 10pm. For a slightly higher commission, you can exchange money at the larger hotels (24 hours).

Tipping

In general, a service charge is included in the bill. However, it is customary to round up the sum when paying. Because prices are so cheap, satisfied foreign customers may be inclined to give the waiter more than the 10 percent service charge; local diners will probably not follow suit.

Postal Services

Stamps can usually be bought wherever postcards are sold. Ask about prices for letters and postcards when you get to the country, as postal rates are continually rising.

Orange and blue mailboxes are everywhere. Larger post offices are open Monday–Friday 8am–7pm, Saturday 8am–noon; smaller branches are open Monday–Friday 8am–1pm or 3pm. The main post office is at Jindrisska 14.

Telephone

There are two models of telephone in the Czech Republic – if they work. One takes one-crown coins and can only be used for local calls. The other will also take two- and five-crown coins, but is only of limited suitability for international calls. If you want to call abroad, your best bet is to go to a post office or hotel; the latter, of course, adds a surcharge of 20–30 percent.

In most major hotels, you can receive or send a fax or telex. First-class hotels generally make office services available to their guests.

Embassies & Consulates

UK: Thunovska 14, Prague 1. Tel: 224 510/533 370.
US: Trziste 15, Prague 1. Tel: 53 66 416.

Getting Around

Domestic Transport

By Air

From Prague, you can reach Brno, Bratislava, Karlovy Vary, Kosice, Ostrava, Sliac, Piestany and Tatry-Poprad by air. CSA (the national airline representatives) can give information about other connections. In the UK, tel: (0171) 255 1898 or 255 1366 for information about CSA flights; in the US, tel: 212 765 6545. In Prague, tel: 2421 0132 for tickets and reservations; flight information, tel: 231 7395. Central information, tel: 334 1111.

By Rail

Fare and scheduling information are available 24 hours a day in Prague, tel: 2421 7654; also on 2461 5865 Monday–Friday.

You can get train tickets at Prague Railway Station or from the Cedok office at Na prikope 18, Prague 1. Unfortunately, to do so you'll have to queue up in the morning until noon and you won't be able to pick up your tickets until the following day – after queuing once again.

If you'd rather not go through this rigmarole, try one of the many local travel agencies.

By Boat

In peak season (1 May–15 October), sight-seeing tours along the Moldau depart from Prague. Information can be obtained from the quayside on the Rasin bank at the Palacky Bridge or from one of the following tour companies: Martin Tour, tel: 2421 2473; Pragotour, tel: 232 5128 or Thomas Cook, tel: 242 28658.

Public Transport

You can buy tickets at kiosks and automatic vending machines. In buses and trams, you must cancel a new ticket every time you change vehicles. In the

underground, you can transfer as often as you wish within 90 minutes. Children and pensioners ride free.

Buses link the suburbs and the city centre, or service longer routes.

The Prague underground is a quick and convenient way to get around. You can reach all of Prague's major sights with the three lines, and it's easy to transfer from one to another. Underground stations are marked with a large 'M'. Service begins at 5am and ends at midnight. For tourists, the 24-hour ticket is a bargain.

Trams in this city are slow and old-fashioned, but offer a good way to see Prague (particularly Line 22, which runs past many tourist attractions).

After midnight, taxis are the only way to get anywhere in Prague, apart from a few night bus routes. There are plenty of taxi stands in the city centre and in front of the large hotels. Make sure the meter is switched on. You can recognise official taxis by their taxi plates and the licence number in the interior. Taxis can be ordered by phone, tel: 20 3399 or 20 6731.

Where to Stay

Accommodation

Reserving a hotel room in Prague during the peak season can be a hopeless endeavour. One alternative is to book through a travel agency.

Another option is a private room. Many agencies rent out rooms in the centre of Prague.

Attractions

What's On

There are concerts everywhere in Prague and you will be pestered by leaflets to attend. You can also book tickets for concerts and opera in the major houses through foreign travel agencies before you get to Prague.

Tickets are also available in ticket offices, agencies, hotels and information offices.

Further Reading

The Good Soldier Swejk, by Jaroslav Hasek. Penguin.
Prague Chronicles, by Ludvik Vaculik. Readers International.
Utz, by Bruce Chatwin. Picador.
We the People: The Revolution of 1989, by Timothy Garton-Ash. Granta.

Other Insight Guides

Other *Insight Guides* highlighting destinations in this region are: Eastern Europe, Czech and Slovak Republics, and Prague.

ITALY

Getting Acquainted

The Place

Likened to a high-heeled boot about to prod its triangular subject island of Sicily, Italy juts deep into the Mediterranean Sea. Another important island, Sardinia, lies some 257 km (160 miles) west of its shin. The magnificent mountain barrier of the Alps forms a northern boundary (separating Italy from France, Switzerland, Austria and the former Yugoslavia) and extends all the way down the Italian peninsula as the less elevated Appennines chain. Low-level plains, which are practically limited to the great northern oval of the Po Valley, cover a mere 23 percent of the total national area of 301,216 sq. km (116,300 sq. miles); 42 percent is hilly and 35 percent mountainous.

Climate

It is usually considerably hotter in the south than in the north where some of the Alpine heights are permanently covered with snow. The summer is hot and dry along the coast, with July and August temperatures soaring over 32°C (90°F) in Rome, Venice, Florence and Naples while it's pleasant and cool in the Alps and Appennines. Rainfall is generally low but much higher in the north than in the south. The winter is mild and damp on the Italian Riviera, cold and damp in the Po Valley and very mild in the south and Sicily. Average maximum temperatures in Milan are 5°C (41°F) in January and 29°C (84°F) in July; in Naples, 12°C (54°F) in January and 29°C (84°F) in July and August.

The People

The total population of Italy is more than 57 million, 95 percent of which are Roman Catholic.

Economy

Industry is concentrated in Milan, Turin and Genoa, and agriculture, although operating under difficult natural and economic conditions, contributes mainly olives, olive oil and wine to the export market. Tourism remains one of Italy's most important livelihoods.

Government

Italy's constitution is that of a Democratic Republic. The Head of State is the President, elected by the Parliament and the regional chamber. The country is divided into 20 different regions with Rome being the capital and the seat of government.

Planning The Trip

Currency

The sole unit of currency in Italy is the lira (plural lire). Coins are issued for units of 5 to 500 lire, notes for 500 to 100,000 lire. Up to 200,000 lire in Italian banknotes may be taken into or out of Italy. Foreign currencies may be imported in unlimited amounts but to take the equivalent of more than 300,000 lire (about US$270) out of the country, you must present a V2 declaration form (filled out upon entry) at the border. Failure to do so may result in confiscation of the amount exceeding the limit.

Traveller's cheques are recommended as they can be replaced if stolen or lost. However, commission will be charged for changing them. Most shopkeepers and restauranteurs will not change money, so it is best to change a limited amount at the airport when you arrive, especially if it is the weekend and banks are closed. Try to avoid changing money in hotels, where the commission tends to be higher than in banks.

In cities, many restaurants, hotels, shops and stores will take major credit cards (Visa, American Express, MasterCard, Diners Club and Carte

Blanche), but some petrol stations require cash. Don't bank on being able to use credit cards in country areas. Establishments which take credit cards normally have a *Carta Si* (Card Yes) notice in the window.

If your credit card has a blue and red EC sign, you can use it to obtain cash from cash machines showing a similar sign – providing you know your card's PIN number. However, remember that interest will be charged from the moment you obtain the cash, and a handling charge will be added to the final bill.

Banking: Banks are generally open 8.30am–1pm and 2.45pm–3.45pm. You can also change money at airports and main railway stations, and in the big cities there are automatic exchange machines (they take major European currencies and US dollars) and have multilingual instructions.

Public Holidays

In addition to those holidays listed in the Introduction, the following are celebrated:
Epiphany: 6 January
Liberation Day: 25 April
Corpus Christi Day
Republic Day: 2 June
Sts Peter and Paul Day: 29 June
Victory Day: 4 November
Conception Day: 8 December

Getting There
By Air
Air connections to Italy are provided by the national carrier, Alitalia, among many others. Both Rome and Milan have excellent services from many European capitals and some of the major cities including London (mainly from Heathrow but also from Gatwick).

By Rail
Frequent and fast train services link Italy with her neighbours – France, Switzerland, Austria and to a lesser extent, the former Yugoslavia. There are also several through expresses from all other major European cities, calling en route at various Italian cities.

By Road
Bordered by France and Switzerland to the northwest and Austria and the former Yugoslavia to the northeast,

Italy can be reached by a number of European routes and motorways.

The cost of travelling to Italy from the United Kingdom by scheduled coach is not much cheaper than travelling by air. National Express Eurolines run from London Victoria, via Paris and Mont Blanc, to Aosta, Turin, Genoa, Milan, Venice, Bologna, Florence and Rome.

By Boat
Sea links exist between Brindisi in the southeastern tip of Italy to Patras, Greece; between Venice and Egypt via Piraeus in Greece; and between Genoa and Malaga in Spain.

Practical Tips

Emergencies
Medical Services
Police: Tel: 113, or 112 for the armed police (*Carabinieri*).
Ambulance: Tel: 116
Public Emergency Assistance: Tel: 113.

These numbers and their services operate on a 24-hour basis, and the number 113, in the principal cities, will answer in the main foreign languages.

For more minor complaints, seek out a *farmacia*, identified by a sign displaying a red cross within a white circle. Trained pharmacists give advice and prescribe drugs, including antibiotics. Normal opening hours are 9am–1pm and 4–7pm, but outside these hours the address of the nearest *farmacia* on emergency duty will be posted in the window.

Business Hours

Shops are usually open 8.30 or 9am–1pm and 3.30 or 4–7.30 or 8pm, with some variations in the north where the lunch-break tends to be shorter and shops therefore close earlier. In most resorts and large towns, there are markets once or twice a week.

Tipping

In nearly every restaurant, a service charge is included in the bill and may be indicated as *servizio e coperto* or only as *coperto*. Tipping above this is discretionary, but much appreciated, especially when service has been good.

Taxi drivers should be tipped 10 percent. In hotels it is customary to tip the chambermaids and the head waiter at the end of your stay. Custodians of sights and museums also expect a tip (L1–2,000), particularly if they have opened something especially for your benefit.

Postal Services

Post office hours are usually 8am–1.30pm, but every town has a main post office open throughout the day. The post office can also provide such services as *raccomandata* (registered), *espresso* (express) and *via aerea* (air mail) to speed up delivery of letters.

You can receive mail addressed to Poste Restante, held at the *fermo posta* window of the main post office in every town, picking it up personally with identification.

A very fast delivery service, CAIpost, is also provided by the post office to send important documents almost all over the world in 24–48 hours.

Stamps may also be purchased from tobacco shops, which can supply information about Italian postal codes.

Telephones

Public telephones are found almost everywhere in Italy, but especially in bars, which practically double as telephone offices. From some bars, but mostly from post offices, you can call a *scatti* (ring first, pay later). Most public telephones now take phonecards (*carta telefonica*) and these are available from tobacconists or news-stands for either L5,000 or L10,000. Alternatively, you can buy a *gettone* token which costs L200 (these are sometimes given as change when buying goods) or use coins (L100, L200 or L500), depending on the type of phone. Some public telephones only accept cards.

If you have no small change, phone card or tokens, it is best to make international and collect calls from the public telephone offices (PTP). For numbers outside your area, dialling must be preceded by "0" and then the area code, which you can obtain from Information. The area codes of main cities are: Rome (06), Milan (02), Florence (055), Pisa (050), Venice (041), Turin (011), Naples (081), Como (031), Palermo (091). If you are dialling from outside Italy, you drop initial zeros.

Tourist Information

General tourist information is available at the Ente Nazionale per il Turismo (ENIT), Via Marghera, 2/6 Rome, tel: 497 1282. The ENIT also has offices on the 15th Floor, 630 Fifth Avenue in New York City, tel: 212 245 4822 and in the UK at 1 Princes Street, London W1R 8A7, tel: 0171 408 1254.

In every major town you will find the Ente Provinciale per il Turismo (EPT) or the Azienda Autonoma di Soggiorno e Turismo. For their addresses and phone numbers, check the directory or the *Yellow Pages* under "Enti". Main cities have a "travel tips" named *Tuttocittà* together with the directory.

Provincial Tourist Offices (EPT)

Rome: Via Parigi, 5. Tel: 488 3748. Open: daily Monday–Saturday 8.30am–1pm and 2–7pm.
Milan: Stazione Centrale. Tel: 669 0532. Open in Summer: 9am–12.30pm and 2–6.30pm, in winter until 6pm. Closed: Sunday. Piazza del Duomo. Tel: 809662. Open in Summer: Monday–Friday 8.45am–6.30pm and Saturday 9am–5pm, in winter: Monday–Friday 8.45am–12.30pm and 1.30–6pm, Saturday till 5pm.
Florence: Via Manzoni, 16. Tel: 23320. Open: Monday–Friday 8.30am–1.30pm and 4–6.30pm, Saturday 8.30am–1pm. More central is the Azienda Autonoma di Turismo, Provincia-Comune di Firenze, Via Cavour, 1R. Tel: 2760382. Open: Monday–Saturday 9am–2pm.
Venice: San Marco, 2. Tel: 522 6356. Open: Monday–Saturday 9am–12.30pm and 3–7pm; also an office in the station, tel: 715016. Open: daily 8am–7pm.

Getting Around

Domestic Transport

By Air

Italian mainland cities are linked by air with each other and with Sicily and Sardinia. Services are operated by Alitalia, ATI and Aermediterraniea. Bookings for all domestic flights can be made at any travel agency.
Alitalia, main office in Rome, tel: 6562 8246

By Rail

The state-owned Ferrovie delle Stato (FS) extends over the entire country and into Sicily, which is linked by train ferries across the Straits of Messina. There are also railway services in Sardinia. Trains come in five basic categories: *accelerato, diretto* and *locale* are all slow trains with many stops; *Expresso* trains are faster and *Rapido* is an express.

Public Transport

Each province in Italy has its own inter-city bus companies and each company has its own fares and lines. It is worthwhile taking buses, especially when you are going to the mountainous interior; they are generally cheaper and faster than the train.

By Road

Autostrade (expressways) are excellent and numerous. However, these are all toll roads so your ticket must be kept and given up when quitting the *autostrada*. Tolls are variable as are speed limits in Italy, calculated according to the engine capacity of the car. Get a copy of the Italian Tourist Office's *Traveler's Handbook* to familiarize yourself with these differences. Fuel discount coupons are available to tourists; so are *autostrada* toll discounts. Apply at ENIT offices abroad and at frontier crossings. For information on current road conditions, dial 194.

Motoring Advice: The Automobile Club d'Italia (ACI) has offices at all main frontier posts, offering emergency breakdown services. Throughout Italy, tel: 116 for quick towing and/or repairs. Members of the automobile associations can get help from the ACI (Italian Automobile Club); Via Marsala 8, I-00185, Rome, tel: 49981.

Attractions

What's On

All cultural information can be obtained from ENIT and EPT offices. The *Daily American* and *This Week in Rome* are particularly useful and are available from kiosks and newsstands.

Almost every town in Italy has a Touring Club Italiano (TCI) office, which provides free information about local points of interest. Telephone numbers are listed in the local telephone book.

Shopping

The flea markets and street stalls in Florence are a bargain-hunter's paradise where particularly good buys on leather goods, scarves, clothes and anything the heart desires are available. Other major cities have similar markets, albeit not as cheap. Popular souvenirs include blown glass from Venice, decorative paper from Florence, high fashion from Milan and Italian shoes anywhere. Export licenses are required for antiques, works of art and items worth over 1 million lire.

Language

Italian is the official language but French is the native language in the Val d'Aosta and German in the Alto Adige (around Bolzano). Dialects are often difficult to understand and in the Eastern Alps they are recognised as separate languages. English is not as widely spoken here as in other countries.

ROME

Getting Acquainted

The Place

Originally built on the famous seven hills, Rome has spread outwards in both directions to cover its present 1,062 sq. km (410 sq. miles), which are inhabited by around 3.5 million people. Its 2,700-year-old history is marked by some 500 churches, 58 museums and public galleries, and 32 ancient monuments.

Planning the Trip

Currency

Banking hours are 8.30am–1pm and 2.45pm–3.45pm, Monday–Friday. Currency exchange offices (cambio) normally reopen later in the afternoon and some operate on Saturday. On Sunday and holidays exchange windows at the airports and at Terminal Railway Station are open. A cambio gives a slightly better rate for hard currency than a bank.

Getting There

By Air

Rome is served by two airports: Leonardo da Vinci, commonly referred to as Fiumicino, located 30 km (18 miles) southwest of the city; and Ciampino, located 16 km (10 miles) southeast. Fiumicino mainly handles scheduled air traffic, while Ciampino is used by most charter companies.

Both airports are linked to the City Air Terminal (at Terminal Railway Station) in the centre of Rome by frequent public bus services. Telephone For flight information at Fiumicino tel: 659 53640; for Ciampino, tel: 794 941.

By Train

Most international trains arrive at Termini Station, which is connected to other parts of the city by both the A and B lines of the subway.

By Road

Rome is completely encircled by a motorway intersected by various roads leading from other Italian cities. A1 leads north to Florence; E1 leads to the west coast and Genoa; and A2 leads south to Naples. Europabus travels between London and Rome all year round.

Practical Tips

Emergencies

Medical Services

The Italian farmacia is open during shopping hours and at least one operates at night and on weekends in each district of Rome. The schedule of pharmacists on duty is posted on every pharmacy door and in the local papers.

Useful Telephone Numbers
Emergency (fire, ambulance, police): 113

Police Headquarters: 4686
Police Help and Information (in English): 461-950 or 486-609
Ambulance and Red Cross: 51 00; 24-hour medical assistance: 4826741

Telephones

Rome's main post office at Piazza San Silvestro is open 8.25am–2.30pm for ordinary postal services, till 7.40pm for urgent matters, and round the clock daily (except Saturday until 1pm) for telegram service.

To obtain telephone directory assistance, dial 176, 170 for intercontinental or long-distance; dial 15 for operator-assisted service to another European country.

Tourist Information

Main headquarters are located in Via Parigi 5, tel: 488 3748, but there is an EPT also at Termini and at the airport. Main headquarters are open: weekdays 8.15am–7pm and Saturday 8.15am–1.15pm. They provide helpful services from sightseeing suggestions to brochures and maps.

Embassies & Consulates

Canada: Via Zava 30. Tel: 445 981.
UK: Via Venti Settembre 80. Tel: 482 54 41.
US: Via Vittorio Veneto 121. Tel: 46741.

Getting Around

Public Transport

Rome has two underground railway lines (metropolitana or metro), line A and line B, which pass most of Rome's popular tourist sights. A big red letter M marks the entrance to the underground and tickets are sold at each station. A complete network of buses and trams covers the whole city, providing frequent service until midnight and a special night service (servizo notturno), details of which are given at every bus stop. Routes are well indicated on green and white signs at every bus stop (*fermata*) and the service number, starting point and destination are shown on the vehicles. Tickets (*biglietto*) must be purchased in advance at tobacconists, bars or newsstands.

Where to Stay

Accommodation

The Italian Tourist Office has up-to-date hotel information, available at the air terminal at Termini Railway Station.

Attractions

What's On

A monthly guide called *A Guest in Rome* and a weekly guide called *This Week in Rome* are among the various useful publications available from the Rome tourist offices and kiosks. Current events, timetables and sights to see are listed comprehensively.

English-speaking guides and interpreters can be hired from a variety of sources: from the main EPT office, hotels and travel agencies; from the Guides Centre located at 12 Rampa Mignanelli; in the *Yellow Pages* under "Traduzione," and in many Rome newspapers which often carry advertisements offering such services. There are also guides near most of the major tourist attractions, and portable recorders with commentaries in English can often be hired.

Nightlife

In a capital with remarkably little nightlife, the most popular custom is to linger well past midnight over dinner at the innumerable outdoor restaurants where roaming minstrels and guitarists play. The Trastevere area has small, reasonably priced restaurants and taverns and is the best place to meet the locals. The Ludovisi district around the Via Veneto has the largest number of big hotels, famous cafés, nightclubs and restaurants but most are very expensive. The city has perhaps a dozen discotheques, not all charge entrance fees, but they're usually very crowded and drinks are never cheap. A few larger establishments have dance floors and cabarets, and there's dancing in the lounges of some hotels.

Rome's *Daily News* advertises current English-language films at the Pasquino in Trastevere.

There's an outdoor opera almost every evening at the ruined Baths of Caracalla (Terme di Caracalla), an easy bus or taxi ride from the city centre. Equally popular sound and light performances are at the Forum and outside Rome in Tivoli. People-watching at the Trevi Fountain and the Spanish Steps also lasts well into the night during summer months.

Shopping

Rome's most fashionable shopping district is found between the Spanish Steps and Via del Corso, notably including Via Condotti, Via Frattina and Via Borgognona. Some of Europe's finest shops and boutiques are here but smart shoppers go elsewhere and pay considerably less for about the same quality. Via Cola di Rienzo across the Tiber River, Via Nazionale and the twisting streets near Campo de'Fiori and the Pantheon in Old Rome offer the shopper a wide selection of merchandise at reasonable prices. The *Saldi* signs often posted in shop windows mean sales. By all means avoid the appallingly expensive Via Veneto area.

Further Reading

The Italians, by Luigi Barzini. New York: Bantam Books.
Four Wonders of Italy: Rome, Florence, Venice, Naples. Allan & Unwin.
Italian Hilltowns, by Norman F Carver. Documan Press.
Art Treasures of Italy, by Bernard Denvir. Orbis Publications.
Italian Journey 1786–1788, by Johann W. von Goethe. North Point Press.
Italian Hours, by Henry James. Greenwood Press.
Twilight in Italy, *Sea and Sardinia*, *Etruscan Places*, by D.H. Lawrence. Viking Press.
The Land and People of Italy, by Frances Winwar. Harper & Row.

Other Insight Guides

Other books in the *Insight Guide* series which highlight destinations in this region are: *Insight Guides: Italy, Rome, Bay of Naples, Tuscany, Umbria, Florence, Venice, Sardinia and Sicily.*

ALBANIA

Getting Acquainted

The climate is Mediterranean, with wet winters and sunny summers.

Planning The Trip

Electricity

Electricity is 220 volt.

Entry Regulations

Visas & Passports

Albania has very limited overseas representation, but fortunately visas are obtainable on arrival at the airport or at border posts. They are not normally required for nationals of EU countries, Australia, Bulgaria, Turkey, Canada, New Zealand and the US. However, all have to pay an entry fee. All travellers require passports.

Customs

There is no limit on the amounts of foreign currency brought into the country, but local currency (Qindarks) is not obtainable overseas and cannot be exported. Alcohol, tobacco and perfume products may be brought in reasonable quantities, provided they are only for personal use.

Health

Visitors are recommended to have hepatitis, polio, tetanus and typhoid immunisations. Health services are available at state-run hospital but visitors are better off using private clinics were possible.

Getting There

Italy and Greece are the main gateways from the West into Albania, both by sea and by air, with Olympic airlines offering the most flights to Tirana.

Rinas Airport is 14 miles (23 km) north-west of Tirana. From the airport, taxis and buses are available into Tirana.

Practical Tips

Business Hours

Banks and offices are open Monday–Saturday 7am–3pm. Shops open at 7am and close at noon to 4pm, and stay open until 7pm.

Telecoms

Long-distance telephone calls can be made from the main post offices. There are no post boxes in Albania, hand your mail into the post office in person.

Changing Currency

Every town has a free currency market which operates in front of the main post office. US dollars are the preferred foreign currency. Credit cards and traveller's cheques are not accepted in Albania, apart from in the newest hotels in Tirana.

Embassies and Consulates

UK, Rruga Vaso Pasha, tel: 42849.
USA, Rruga LAbinoti, tel: 32875.

Getting Around

Public Transport

Independent travel in Albania is not recommended. There is public transport in Albania but like most other things in the country, it is a remnant of the communist past and a victim of the bankrupt present. There is a rail network but trains are sporadic and overcrowded. Buses are slightly more reliable but most are ageing articulated vehicles, imported from China. If you seriously want to travel from A to B, go by taxi. Several firms have started to operate in the main cities; you can usually find several taxis outside the main hotels – usually bright red Peugeot estates – although one fleet still keeps alive the old black Mercedes limousines once used by the communist party officials. Car-hire is not generally available.

Where to Stay

Accommodation

There are three main hotels in Tirana. Probably the best hotel is the Hotel Europapark, Boulevard Deshmorete Kombits, tel: 35035; fax: 35050. The Tirana International (tel: 34185; fax: 34188) a cheerless 300-room tower block overlooking Skanderbeg Square, is cheap. The Datja Hotel (tel: 33327), pronounced *Dytie*, is located further towards the centre of town and is highly regarded. Favoured by visiting businessmen and politicians, the Datji is a great place just to sit and watch as much of the unofficial business of the country takes place there. It has perhaps the best restaurant in Tirana, with decent imported wine and a fairly varied menu.

GREECE

Getting Acquainted

The Place

The Greek peninsula, covering an area of 131,944 sq. km (50,944 sq. miles) and containing a population of 10 million people (99.8 percent of which are Greek Orthodox), consists of mainland Greece (Attica, the Peloponnese, Central Greece, Thessaly, Epirus, Macedonia, Thrace) and the islands. The country has 15,021 km (9,334 miles) of coastline and its highest peak is the Pantheon at an altitude of 2,917 metres (9,570 ft). Geographically it belongs to Europe since it forms the most southerly extremity of the Balkan peninsula, although most Greeks don't think of themselves as Europeans. Besides the numerous islands on the Aegean Sea, Greek islands include 10 distinct island groups such as the Ionian Islands, the Cyclades, the Sporades, the Dodencanese and the group of small islands in the Saronic Gulf.

Climate

Greece has a Mediterranean climate with temperatures lowest in January and February, when it is very cold inland, and highest in July and August. It rains only in winter and nowhere in Greece does the average yearly sunshine drop below 2,000 hours. The average maximum temperature in Athens is 13°C (55°F) in January and 33°C (92°F) in July and August.

Economy

Dominant in the Mediterranean for 2,500 years, Greece now owns the world's largest tonnage of ships, over 50 million, and the second biggest merchant fleet, some 40 million tons. But overall, tourism remains its main source of income, reflected in the number of annual visitors which exceeds one half of the population during the height of the tourist season.

Government

After having tried all possible forms of government in its 4,000 years of existence, Greece elected its first socialist government in 1981. In the same year it became the 10th member of the European Union (EU).

Planning the Trip

Health

It's not advisable to drink tap water.

Currency

The monetary unit is the drachma, divided into 100 lepta. The import of Greek currency is limited to dr. 100,000. Unlimited amounts of foreign currency may be brought in but to export sums in excess of US$1,000 special arrangements must be made.

The banking hours in Athens are Monday–Friday 8am–2.30pm. The National Tourist Organization of Greece supplies a list of the banks open afternoons and Sunday.

Most major credit cards are accepted in nearly all situations in Greece, with the exception of *tavernes,* which rarely accept plastic. All banks will exchange traveller's cheques, but visitors will pay a smaller handling fee at National Bank of Greece branches.

Getting There

By Air

The Greek National Airline, Olympic Airways, and many major international airlines link Greece with all five continents. The main gateway is Hellinikon East and West Airport, 10 km (6 miles) from the centre of Athens. Hellinikon West exclusively handles domestic and international flights of Olympic Airways (tel: 969 9111), while Hellinikon East (tel: 969 4111) handles all other international airlines. Olympic Airways operates express bus services every half hour between 3.30am–8pm from West

Hellinikon to the Olympic Airways City Terminal at 96 Syngrou Avenue. Express buses also run from East Hellinikon to the City Terminal at 4 Amalias Avenue.

By Rail

There are trains connecting Thessaloniki and Athens with most major cities throughout Europe. For some destinations it may be necessary to change. Car-carrying sleeper trains connect Brussels, Dusseldorf, Cologne, Frankfurt and Stuttgart or Ljubljana in Slovenia, and from Milan on to Brindisi for the car ferry to Patras.

By Road

Bordered by the former Yugoslavia and Bulgaria to the north and Turkey to the northeast, Greece can be reached by a number of European "E" routes. The western border with Albania is closed.

By Sea

An extensive summer network of ferries links Italy with Greece. Many ferries, especially on the short routes, run all year round. Venice, Ancona, Brindisi and Bari are the Italian ports, while Corfu, Igoumenitsa and Partras serve Greece; some services go to Piraeus. The shortest routes are from Brindisi to Corfu (about 9 hours) and Patras (14 hours), the latter has a bus connection to Athens.

Practical Tips

Emergencies

Medical Services

Chemists are open during normal shop hours but a number of them stay open day and night. Duty rotas are displayed in the local newspapers and in chemists' windows, or tel: 107 for information. Free first aid treatment is available at Red Cross clinics and English-speaking doctors and dentists advertise in *This Week in Athens.*

Business Hours

Summer Store Hours: Monday, Wednesday and Saturday 8am–3pm; Tuesday, Thursday and Friday 8am–3pm and 5.30–8.30pm. Winter Store Hours: Monday and Wednesday 9am–2.30pm; Tuesday, Thursday and Friday 9am–6.30pm; Saturday 9am–3.30pm.

Tipping

Hotels, restaurants and nightclubs add 15 percent but a little extra is expected. This figure rises to 20 percent around Christmas and Easter. Round up the charge on the taxi meter to the next 10 drachma.

Postal Services

Post offices keep normal shop hours but central ones in main cities don't close for lunch. The central post office in Athens is located at 100 Aiolou Street. Letter boxes are yellow and display a postal-rates table in English.

Telephones

Local calls requiring no code or prefix can be made from the blue call boxes and from newspaper kiosks, which take phone cards. Long distance and international calls can be made from kiosks and *kafenion* in the larger cities or from telephone exchanges. The extent of the automatic dialling network is limited.

Tourist Information

The National Tourist Organization of Greece (GNTO) has offices abroad in Sydney, Montreal, Tokyo, London, New York, Los Angeles and Chicago as well as major European cities. Their head office (EOT) is in Athens at 6 Amerikas, tel: (01) 3638632, with information desks at the East Hellinikon Airport, tel: 9799 500; and at 2 Karageorgi Servias Street, tel: 3222 2545. Other tourist offices are located in the various tourist areas of Greece as well as at the major frontier crossings.

Tourist Offices Abroad

Australia: 51–57 Pitt Street, Sydney NSW 2000. Tel: 2411 663/4.
UK: 4 Conduit Street, London W1R ODJ. Tel: (0171) 734 5997.

US: 645 Fifth Avenue, Olypmic Tower, New York, NY 10022. Tel: (212) 421 5777.

Getting Around

Public Transport

By Air

Olympic Airways maintains a remarkably extensive network of internal air routes, most of which link Athens with other cities and towns plus the islands, but one or two link Thessaloniki to, for example, Crete or Rhodes. Between Athens and Thessaloniki there are about eight flights a day, more at peak holiday times.

By Rail

Greece does not have a very big railway system, but it has one main route from Athens north to Thessaloniki, where it splits. One section goes to the former Yugoslavia, another to Bulgaria and the third to Istanbul. Another rail system operates from Athens and Piraeus to the Peloponnese peninsula via Corinth. The trains are run by the Greek Railways Board (OSE) whose main offices are in Athens (1-3 Karolou Street, tel: 5240601). For train and ticket information in Athens, try 31a Venizelou St, tel: 3131 376; recorded timetables, tel: 145 (internal) and 147 (international).

By Road

Greek Railways and several private companies operate long- and medium-distance bus services in Greece. These are moderately priced and popular, so book in advance and board early – overbooking is common. Information and timetables are available from the tourist information offices. For Greek Railways' bus timetables dial 142 in Athens.

Waterways

The ferry network is both extensive and complicated with schedules constantly changing, although on trunk routes they are reliable.

Boats are run by a variety of companies and fares quoted in the brochures don't include taxes, which can add up to 10 percent of the fare. All the larger ferries carry cars and pre-booking is absolutely essential, except in the quieter winter weeks. Be warned: in August, the first two weeks see rough seas when the annual *meltemia* wind blows; and around the 15th (Assumption Day), boats are crowded with pilgrims travelling to and from Tinos.

Details and reservations can be made at any tourist agency or the various shipping and ferry offices in Athens and Piraeus. Always double-check departure times.

Private Transport

Major frontier points are open night and day. The fighting in the former Yugoslavia means that this route into Greece is not advisable. Tolls are charged on the two main motorways: Athens–Katerini and Athens–Patras.

Motoring Advice: An international driving licence is required, available at ELPA frontier offices for a small fee (you need two photos). The Automobile and Touring Club of Greece (ELPA) offers information and assistance and their vans patrol the main routes. ELPA runs a rescue service (Assistance Routiere) within a 37-mile (60-km) radius of Athens, Larissa, Patras and Thessaloniki. Tel: 104. Its main office is in Athens (24 Messoghion Street, Ampelokipi, tel: 7791 1615). The AAA is in Syntagma Square.

Attractions

What's On

Cultural information can be obtained from GNTO offices, the monthly magazine, *The Athenian*, and the glossy *This Week in Athens*, available at kiosks and hotels respectively.

Metropolitan "nightlife" in Greece, which is to say Athens and Thessaloniki, can be roughly divided into bars, live music clubs, discos, and the *boites*, *tavérnes* and clubs with live Greek music.

Shopping

The quality of Greek handicrafts is usually quite high. Cotton clothing is a well-fashioned and comfortable buy; embroidered items, handcrafted jewellery, and durable-but-crude leather goods are also favoured purchases. On higher-priced items, by all means bargain.

Language

English is the most common foreign language. French is quite widely spoken in Athens, and Italian in the Ionian Islands and Epirus.

ATHENS

Getting Acquainted

The Place

Size: 427 sq. km (265 sq. miles).

The People

Population: 4 million.

Planning the Trip

Health

Athens' tap water is perfectly safe to drink, if occasionally in short supply. Bottled water, still and fizzy, is readily available. The amount of pollution in the air, as well as the number of pesticides used in agriculture, mean that you should always wash fruit and vegetables before eating, and avoid buying food that is on open display close to a roadway.

Practical Tips

Emergencies

Medical Services

Pharmaceuticals are produced to international standards, and a rota system is used to ensure that a pharmacy is open somewhere in your part of the city at all times. Dial 107 for the pharmacy roster in Greek, or check the cards posted in pharmacy windows for the address nearest you. Most down-

town pharmacists speak English, and Greek pharmacists are often very helpful in assisting visitors with treating minor ailments such as diarrhoea, colds and sunburn.

Ideally, your travel insurance should cover airlifting out to northern Europe, if not home. If you do fall ill in Athens, seek out a reputable private doctor through your hotel, or embassy. The British and American embassies will supply a list of GPs and specialists, including dentists upon request. As with pharmacists, a telephone roster service is available, but only in Greek: tel:105.

HOSPITALS

The best private hospital and the children's hospitals are located in Ambelokipi and Maroussi, an area just north of the Hilton, and are listed here. A complete listing of the city's public hospitals can be obtained by phoning the Tourist Police on 171.

KAT Hospital, Nikis 2, Kifissia, tel: 801 4411 for accidents.

Children's Hospitals: Agia Sofia, Thivon and Mikras Assias streets, tel: 777-1811; Aglaia Kyriakou, Thivon and Levadias streets, tel: 777-5610.

Police Emergencies

In Athens the police emergency number is 100. There is also a Tourist Police number which may be more useful, tel: 171. The coastguard patrol can be reached on 108.

Postal Services

Most hotels have telephones, telex and fax facilities, and hotel operators can place international calls for you if your room lacks an IDD telephone. If you do not have access to these facilities, head for the OTE offices at 15 Stadiou Street, open 8.30am–8pm weekdays, Saturday 7.30am–2pm and 9am–1.30pm Sunday; or on Omonia Square, open 24 hours a day, seven days a week. The main post office on Syntagma Square is your best bet for mailing. They have a good selection of boxes and reinforced bags for sale at the express counter at the far end. Packages may also be sent from the post office at 60 Mitropoleos Street.

The three central telephone exchanges in Athens are at 85 Patission Square (24 hours), Omonia Square underground station and 15 Stadiou Street (both open until midnight). Calls are cheaper 9pm–5am (6am in winter). To contact the domestic operator, tel: 151/2. For the international operator, tel: 161/2.

Tourist Office

National Tourist Organization of Greece (GNTO)

The GNTO head office (EOT) is at 2 Amerikas, tel: (01) 3223 111/9, with information desks at the East Hellinikon Airport, tel: 9799 500; and 1 Karageorgi Servias Street, tel: 3222 545.

Other tourist offices are located in the various tourist areas of Greece as well as at the major frontier crossings.

Embassies & Consulates

All embassies are open Monday–Friday, usually from 8am–2pm.
Australia: 37 Dimitris Soutsou Street. Tel: 644 7303.
Canada: 4 Gennadiou Street. Tel: 725 4011.
Ireland: 7 Vasiliou Constantinou Street. Tel: 723 2771.
New Zealand: 15 An. Tsoha Street. Tel: 641 0311.
UK: 1 Ploutarchou Street. Tel: 723 6211.
US: 91 Vasilissis Sophias Avenue. Tel: 721 2951.

Getting Around

Domestic Transport

By Rail

Greek trains are a delight if you enjoy travelling for its own sake, but a frustrating experience if getting there quickly is more important. Timetables and tickets may be purchased at OSE offices located at 6 Sina Street; or 1 Karolou Street, tel: 524 0601/5; 524 0646/8. There are two stations, one serving the Peloponnese; the other, the north.

Metro: Due to extensive relics buried beneath the modern city, Athens does not have a comprehensive underground rail service. However, the one that exists runs between Piraeus and Kifissia, is clean and reliable and connects Piraeus with Monastiraki and Omonia. City centre stops are at Thisseion, Monastiraki, and Omonia. Tickets are the same as those used on buses and trolleys and are available at the stations.

By Sea

Weekly updated ferry schedules are available from the tourist information offices on Syntagma Square. Alternatively, buy the *Greek Travel Pages* from Eleftheroudakis at 4 Nikis Street behind Syntagma Square. As with the trains, investigate first (or A) class (with or without a cabin) as an option: in first class, a degree of comfort can be promised that is noticeably lacking in other parts of the ship. Book ahead from a city-centre travel agent, or phone the Piraeus Port Authority (tel: 451 1311, or 422 6000 for Zea Marina), check sailing times, and then simply arrive at the port a couple of hours before departure. Numerous ticket agencies are located adjacent to the ships, and travellers may even purchase tickets at the foot of the gangplank in many cases.

Hydrofoil: The Flying Dolphin service is speedy, but more expensive than the ferries and liable to cancellation in anything more than a stiff breeze. However, these insect-like craft, which originally ran tours up and down the Volga River, are a pleasant way to travel to the Saronic Gulf islands, especially at the 'sharp end,' which is non-smoking or, on hot days, in the stern, where there is a small deck. Trips are regular, and tickets are available either at the port or at 2 Karageorgi Servias Street, Syntagma; and 2 Xanthou Street, Kolonaki. Tel: 452 7107 for details.

By Road

Limousines, complete with chauffeur, will pick you up either from the airport or your hotel, tel: 346 7137.

Taxis: On entry, ensure that the meter is switched on and registering 1, rather than 2 which is the rate 1–5am. Don't be worried if you find yourself joined, en route, by a large cross-section of Athenian society going roughly your way. It is perfectly legal for drivers to pick up as many people as is comfortably possible, and charge them all individually. The tariff regulations are posted on cards in all taxis, with very reasonable flag down and minimum fares which double 1–5am.

There is a surcharge from airports, seaports, railway stations and bus terminals; passengers may also be charged a small fee for luggage.

Private Taxi Transfer Service: Affable Athenian cabbies are rare, and the inconvenience and sheer aggravation of finding a taxi in the city have given rise to private taxi services.

Bus: Travelling by the regular Athens blue buses is a fairly miserable way of getting around the city. They are crowded and hot, and the routes are a mystery even to long-time residents. However, they are reasonable, at under 100 drachmas per ticket. Tickets, good for trolleys as well, are sold in books of 10 from specific news kiosks and special booths at bus and metro stations, and at various non-strategic points around the city. Most bus services run until midnight.

Separate services run to air and sea ports, and these can be useful. The Express service of distinctive blue and yellow double-decker buses runs from Syntagma Square (on Amalias Avenue) to both airports at regular intervals: buy your tickets at the kiosk by the stop. The Green bus 040 runs from Filellinon Street (near Syntagma Square) to Piraeus 24 hours a day, every 20 minutes (every hour after 1am). The Orange bus runs from 14 Mavromateon Street, Areos Park, and takes approximately 1½ hours.

Trolley Bus: Though marginally more comfortable than the regular bus service, the yellow trolleys are not recommended for visitors as their routes are a mystery best left to locals.

Attractions

Greek News Weekly, published on Saturday night, is interesting and informative, with a regular "What's On" section. *The Athenian: Greece's English Language Monthly,* is just that, with features covering Greek politics, topics of interest and the arts. A mini-magazine, *This Week in Athens,* has been published for many years by the National Tourist Organization of Greece, and is available at GNTO offices.

Further Reading

Insight Guides: Greece, The Greek Islands and *Athens.* Companions to this book, from Apa Publications' award-winning series.
Greek Unorthodox, by Elizabeth Boleman-Herring. Foundation Publishing.
Greece Without Columns: The Making of the Modern Greeks, by David Holden. J.B. Lippincott Co.
A Foreign Wife, by Gillian Bouras. McPhee Gribble/Penguin Books.
A Literary Companion to Travel in Greece. Richard Stoneman (ed.). Penguin Books Ltd.
Roumeli: Travels in Northern Greece, by Patrick Leigh Fermor. Penguin Books Ltd.
Unknown Athens: Wanderings in Plaka and Elsewhere, by Liza Micheli. Dromena.

SPAIN

Getting Acquainted

The Place

Lying on the southwestern end of the European continent, Spain occupies about 85 percent of the Iberian Peninsula; Portugal, which forms its western boundary, occupies the other 15 percent. Spain is separated from France by the small Spanish/French co-principality of Andorra and the Pyrenees mountains. The total area of Spain is 504,737 sq. km (194,880 sq. miles), occupied by a total population of more than 38 million, the majority of which are Roman Catholic.

Climate

Spain is extremely hot and dry in the summer and moderate in the winter, except for bitter cold for some weeks on the central plateau. Average maximum temperatures in Madrid are 9°C (48°F) in December and January; in Malaga, 17°C (63°F) December to February and 30°C (86°F) in August.

Economy

Spain is a member of NATO, the United Nations and the EU. It is predominantly an industrial country with less than 30 percent of the population involved in agriculture. A large part of the nation's economy is derived from tourism; resort areas, like the Costa del Sol, have been the favoured holiday spots of foreign tourists for years.

Government

With Franco's death in 1975, the last dictatorship in western Europe came to an end. Spain is now a constitutional monarchy with a king as head of state and a government based on parliamentary elections. The country is divided into 15 traditional regions, marked by geographical and dialectal differences, so that the inhabitants of

each region consider themselves essentially different from each other. The two main urban centres are the capital city of Madrid in New Castile, and Barcelona on the Catalonian coast.

Planning the Trip

Currency

The monetary unit of Spain is the peseta (pta). Coins are in units of 1, 5, 25, and 100; bills in denominations of 100 to 1,000 pesetas. The import of up to 100,000 pesetas and the export of 20,000 pesetas in Spanish currency are permitted by law. Airports and main railway stations in major cities (such as Madrid) provide 24-hour currency exchange service.

Public Holidays

The overwhelmingly Roman Catholic character of Spain is reflected in its holidays which, in addition to those listed in the Introduction, include:
Epiphany: 6 January
St Joseph's Day: 19 March
Good Friday
Corpus Christi Day
St James's Day: 25 July
Feast of the Assumption: 15 August
Columbus Day: 12 October
Conception Day: 8 December
Various other saints' days are observed locally.

Getting There

By Air

The national carriers Iberia and Aviaco and many foreign airlines maintain regular flights to more than 30 international airports in Spain. Additional international charter services are provided by Spantax, Trans Europa and Air Spain and there are more than 50 other foreign charter companies which arrange periodic flights to the country.
For flight information, tel: 305 8344/45/46.
Tickets can be purchased at Iberia's local ticket offices or any travel

agency. Iberia information, tel: 411 2545; reservations, tel: 411 1011 or 411 2011.

By Rail

Major destinations in Spain are linked by direct trains to points in France and Switzerland. Three overnight through trains run to Barcelona and Madrid from Paris. A similar day train runs between Geneva and Barcelona via Lyon, Avignon, Montpellier and Perpignan. Many other trains link the Franco-Spanish border, Portugal and Italy directly with Spain.

By Road

Bordered by France and the Principality of Andorra to the north and Portugal to the west, Spain is accessible via a number of European motorways and other main roads. Regular ferry services allow drivers to enter the southern tip of Spain from Morocco and Santander from Great Britain. Main motorways are: N-I (Madrid–Irun); N-II (Madrid–Barcelona); N-III (Madrid–Valencia); N-IV (Madrid-Andalusia); N-V (Madrid–Extremadura); and N-VI (Madrid–La Coruña).

By Bus: The Estación del Sur de Autobuses at Calle Canarias 17, (tel: 468 4200) is Madrid's main bus station and most of the major bus companies covering the long-distance routes use this terminal.

By Sea

Forty-six foreign shipping companies, operating more than 50 scheduled lines, bring passengers to Spain. The Spanish companies with regularly scheduled international services are Transatlantica, Trasmediterranea, Ybarra and Naviera Aznar.

Practical Tips

Emergencies

Medical Services

Spain has countless chemist shops or *farmacias*, each identifiable by a big, white sign with a flashing green cross.

They are open approximately 9.30am–1.30pm and 5–8pm Monday–Friday; 9am–1.30pm Saturday mornings.

Useful Emergency Numbers
Police: 091
Municipal Police: 092
Emergency Medical Care: 061
Fire Department: 080 or 532 3232 in Madrid.
Red Cross Emergency: 522 2222 in Madrid.

Business Hours

Shops are open 9.30 or 10am–1.30 or 2pm and then reopen again in the afternoon from 4.30 or 5pm–8pm, or a little later in summer. Most are closed on Saturday afternoons and all day Sunday. However, major department stores are open without interruption six days a week 10am–9pm, and frequently on Sunday.

Banking: Hours vary slightly from one bank to another. Most open 8.30 or 9am–2pm weekdays and 9am–12.30 or 1pm on Saturday. All are closed Sunday and holidays. Several banks keep major branches in the business districts open until 4.30pm.

Tipping

As a guideline, tipping is frequent in bars, cafeterias and restaurants (8–10 percent), taxis (5 percent), cinema and theatre ushers (15–25 ptas), and bell-boys (according to services rendered).

Postal Services

The few existing district post offices are only open 9am–2pm on weekdays, 9am–1pm Saturday and closed Sunday. Principal post offices are open 9am–2pm and 4–7pm for general services. Post boxes are silver-coloured and in two parts – one marked *ciudad* (for local mail) and the other marked *provincias y extranjero* (for the rest of the country and abroad). Stamps are sold at post offices and at the *estancos*, or tobacconist shops.

Telephones

Coin operated telephone booths are everywhere, though it seems that more than half either don't work or have been vandalised. Assuming that

they do function, wait for the tone, deposit either 3 *duros* (silver 5-peseta coins) or a 25-peseta piece and dial the number. It is possible to place a long-distance call by depositing a handful of 25-peseta coins. You can also purchase a phone card for 1,000 pesetas at any tobacconists for use in the newer public phones.

For overseas calls, it's probably better to go to the offices of Telefónica (the Spanish telephone company), or to privately-run telephone shops where one can talk first and pay later and not have to worry about having enough coins. (If you ring from your hotel room, you will be charged a lot more than you would on a public phone.)

To make a direct overseas call, first dial 07 and then wait for another dial tone before dialling the country and city codes. It is cheaper to call before 8am and after 10pm. There are no additional discounts at weekends.

If you need operator assistance or wish to reverse the charges, tel: 008 (for Europe) or 005 (for the rest of the world).

The following numbers may be helpful – though in some cases you'll need good Spanish.
Information on Spain, tel: 003.
Information on the rest of Europe, tel: 008.
Information on the rest of the world, tel: 089.
Operator Assistance for international calls, tel: 005.
General Information, tel: 098.
Telephone company offices, tel: 002.

Tourist Information

Tourist information covering all of Spain is available at the Madrid Community Tourist Offices in the Torre de Madrid at:
Princesa, 1. Tel: 541 2325. Open: 10am–7pm.
Barajas airport. Tel: 305 8656.
Duque de Medinaceli, 2. Tel: 429 4951.
Chamartín Station, door 14, in the Main Hall. Tel: 315 9976.
Information on Madrid itself is available at Plaza Mayor, 3. Tel: 588 1636.

Tourist Offices Abroad

Canada: 2 Bloor Street West, 34th floor, Toronto, Ontario M4W 3E2, tel: (416) 961 3131.

UK: 22–3 Manchester Square, London W1M 5AP, tel: (0171) 486 8077.
US: 665 Fifth Avenue, New York City, NY 10103, tel: (212) 265 8822; 845 N. Michigan Avenue, Suite 915, Chicago, Illinois 60611, tel: (312) 944 0215/16; 8383 Wilshire Boulevard, Suite 960, 90211 Beverly Hills, California, tel: (213) 658 7188/93;

Consulates & Embassies

Australia: Plaza del Descubridor, 3. Tel: 441 9300.
Canada: Núñez de Balboa, 35. Tel: 431 4300.
UK: Fernando el Santo, 16. Tel: 319 0200.
US: Calle Serrano, 75. Tel: 577 4000.

Getting Around

Domestic Transport

By Air

Both Iberia and Aviaco operate a wide network of routes within Spain, linking all the main cities.

Iberia's main offices are at Calle Velázquez 130, 28006 Madrid, tel: 587 8787, for information and ticket sales, tel: 902 400 500. Iberia has ticket offices at Calle Velázquez 130; and in the Hotel Eurobuilding (Padre Damián) or you can purchase an air ticket at any travel agency.

Aviaco, Iberia's subsidiary airline, only services domestic flights, while Viva Air covers international routes. The planes are generally older and smaller and fly less-frequented routes. Aviaco is at Maudes 51, in Madrid, tel: 554 3600; and Viva Air at Zurbano 41, tel: 349 0600.

By Rail

The Spanish National Railways (Red Nacional de los Ferrocarriles Espanoles or RENFE) provides extensive local service within the country. There are various types of trains in Spain: Talgo, Inter-city, ELT (electric unit expresses), TER (diesel rail cars) and ordinary semi-fast and local trains. Supplementary fares are levied on all express trains. On all expresses you must either have a reserved seat or have your ticket endorsed at the station before going on board.

For information from KENFE, tel: 328 9020.

Public Transport

Spain has an excellent bus network, cheaper and more frequent than trains. On major routes and at holiday times it is advisable to buy your ticket a day or two in advance.

By Road

The cities, towns and regions of Spain are linked with nearly 144,000 km (90,000 miles) of roads and highways. If you take the minor roads, expect bad surfaces and large potholes. The number of toll roads is increasing, particularly in the north and east and around Madrid.

Petrol prices are among the highest in Europe and be warned that you won't see many petrol stations on long journeys through remoter areas.

Motoring Advice: The roadside SOS telephones are connected to the nearest police station, which sends out a breakdown van with first aid equipment. There is a small charge for work done and spare parts used. The automobile clubs of Spain are the Real Automovil Club de Espana (RACE) and the Touring Club de Espana (TCE). The following addresses and telephone numbers may be useful:
Real Automovil Club de Espana, Jose Abascal 10, Madrid. Tel: 593 3333.
Real Automovil Club de Catalunya, Santalo 8, Barcelona. Tel: 200 3311.
Touring Club de Espana, Modesto Lafuente, Madrid. Tel: 233 1004.

In the event of a breakdown in Madrid, tel: 754 3344; in Barcelona, tel: (93) 209 5737; in Valencia, tel: (96) 333 2805; in Santander, tel: (94) 223 9435.

Where to Stay

Accommodation

The complete hotel and *paradores* list, *Guia oficial de hoteles* published at Easter, is available from national tourist offices. It is advisable to book in advance, especially at popular resorts during summer or at festival times. Larger towns have Brujula offices, the official room-finding service, which charges a small fee. They have offices at stations, airports and on main roads which lead to cities.

Attractions

Information on cultural activities can be obtained at national, local and city tourist offices.

Shopping

Well-known Spanish souvenirs include damasquino jewellery, knives and swords from Toledo; ceramics from Toledo, Valencia and Seville; filigree silver from Córdoba; *botas* (wine-skin bottles), castanets, Spanish dolls and bullfight posters.

Language

The official language is Spanish (Castilian), which was originally spoken in Castile. Three other languages are used – Catalan in the northeast; Galician in the extreme northwest; and Basque along the French border in the Western Pyrenees. Of these, only Basque is unrelated to Spanish. In all tourist resorts, you'll find people who speak English in varying degrees of fluency. In the north you should find plenty of people who speak French.

MADRID

Getting Acquainted

The Place

Madrid is the highest capital in Europe (650 metres/2,130 ft), sitting in a dish in the central Iberian plateau. It is flanked to the north and east by the sierras of Somosierra and Guadarrama, and to the southeast by those of Toledo. The compact city centre is spread over hillocks, with the diminutive River Manzanares running round them to the south. In the last 20 years, huge suburbs dissected by motorways running into the centre have grown around the city.

Officially, the city has 3 million residents and the province 5–6 million. But there are many more without legal existence: the gypsies, who live in *chabolas* (shanty-towns); Moroccans, who provide cheap labour for building and, more recently, other Africans and South Americans.

Climate

Madrid has a relatively temperate climate. In autumn and spring, both extremely pleasant seasons, average temperatures range from 12–15°C (54–60°F), with a spread of 6°C (43°F) minimum to 21°C (70°F) maximum.

Planning the Trip

Currency

A surprising number of restaurants and shops don't take cards. Visa is the most widely accepted, then Access/MasterCard. You may also have difficulty paying with Eurocheques.

Telebanco cash machines (outside many banks) accept most of the usual cards, but often run out of notes at the end of the month or at weekends. If you are going out of Madrid for the day, it's best to get cash before you leave.

Banks are open Monday–Friday 9am–2pm, with a few city-centre branches open on Saturday. Outside these hours, you can change money in Barajas airport, Chamartín and Atocha railway stations, and most four and five-star hotels as well as on major central streets. Check Point, Plaza Callao 4, is open 24 hours a day.

Getting There

By Air

Most international airlines have flights to Madrid. The airport (Barajas) is 16 km (10 miles) from the city centre; buses leave for Plaza Colón every 15 minutes. A taxi will set you back about 2,000 ptas. A new 20-minute rail-link runs from Barajas to mid-town Nuevos Ministerios.

By Rail

The main train stations in Madrid are Chamartín Station; Principe Pio (Norte) Station and Atocha Station. RENFE train information and reservations, tel: 563 0202. Reservations, tel: 328 9020.

Two trains leave Paris for Spain every night: the Expreso Puerta del Sol, which has turn-of-the-century decor, couchettes, and carries cars; and the Talgo Camas/couchette, more modern and comfortable, with beds. Both arrive at Chamartín station, from where you can get the metro or a taxi to the centre.

By Bus

The two main bus stations in Madrid are Estacíon Sur de Autobuses, tel: 468 4200; and Auto Res., tel: 551 7200. For radio taxis, tel: 547 8200; teletaxis 445 9008 and for metro information in Madrid, tel: 522 5909.

By Car

The car journey from London and northern Europe takes a minimum of 24 hours (in a fast car, without an overnight break). Allow 6 hours from the Spanish border at Irún to Madrid. Burgos is a good stop-off to visit the magnificent cathedral and eat well. You need a green card, log book and bail bond, and it's advisable to carry an International Driving Licence.

For information on road conditions, tel: 900 123 505.

Practical Tips

Emergencies

Medical Services

A green or red cross identifies a chemist (*farmacia*). Outside shop hours go to a *farmacia de guardia*, listed in chemist's windows and in the newspaper.

If you need emergency medical treatment you will be taken to the *Urgencias* (casualty) at a large hospital or the local *Ambulatorios*, which are open 24 hours a day (addresses in the windows of pharmacies and in the newspapers). The Anglo-American Medical Unit, Calle Conde de Aranda 1, tel: 4351823, gives bilingual attention 24 hours a day. The Official Association of Dentists runs a 24-hour, seven-days-a-week clinic for emergency dental care, at Calle Juan Bravo 44, 6th Floor. Tel: 402 6421 or 402 6422.

Police: 091.

Business Hours

Shops are open 9.30 or 10am–1.30 or 2pm and then reopen again in the afternoon from 4.30 or 5–8pm, or a little later in summer. Most are closed on Saturday afternoon and Sunday. However, the major department stores like El Corte Inglés and Galerías Preciados are open without interruption six days a week, 10am–9pm, and frequently on Sunday, despite the protests of small shopkeepers.

Postal Services

Post offices (*correos*) are open Monday–Friday 9am–2pm and Saturday to 1pm. Alternatively (and quicker) buy stamps in an *estanco* (tobacconist) and use either a yellow or red (*express*) postbox. Telegrams are sent from post offices or tel: 522 2000. The ornate central Palacio de Correos, in Calle Alcalá opposite Cibeles fountain (8.30am–10pm) is much faster than other post offices. Most hotels have a fax service.

Telephones

You can phone from a box (they have instructions in English, but are often out of order), from bars (more expensive, but more relaxed as you don't need the right coins) or from hotels (up to four times the normal rate). There are also public phone offices (Palacio de Correos, Gran Vía 30, Puerta de Recoletos 41); major credit cards accepted, pay after the call. If you are using a US credit phone card, dial the company's access number below, then 01, and then the country code. Sprint: tel: 900 99 0013; AT&T: tel: 900 99 0011; MCI: tel: 900 99 0014.

Tourist Information Offices

Torre de Madrid, Plaza de España. Tel: 364 1876.
Chamartín railway station. Tel: 325 9976.
Barajas airport (international arrivals). Tel: 305 8656.

Embassies

UK: Calle Fernando el Santo 16. Tel: 319 0200.
US: Calle Serrano 75. Tel: 577 4000.

Getting Around

Public Transport

The Metro

The quickest way of moving around the city, the metro runs 6am–1.30am. The 10 lines (120 stations) are labelled by number, colour and final destination. Bulk buying tickets for 10 journeys saves up to 50 percent. You can get a metro map at the ticket booth.

For metro information, tel: 522 5909.

By Bus

More than 150 routes are covered by red and yellow air-conditioned buses, which run from 6am–midnight. Tickets for both are a flat price. A reduced-price ticket for 10 journeys can be bought in an *estanco* (tobacconist's/newspaper kiosk). Night services leave on the hour from Cibeles and the Puerta del Sol. Buses for out-of-town trips, belonging to various private companies, go mainly from the Estación Sur de Autobuses (Calle Canarias 17, tel: 4674200; metro: Palos de la Frontera), check first.

Buses run 6am–midnight. For municipal bus information, tel: 406 8810.

By Taxi

Taxis can be hailed with relative ease in main thoroughfares, found at a *Parada de Taxi* (taxi stand, indicated by a large white "T" against a dark blue background) or requested by phone. For taxi pick-up, call Radio-Teléfono Taxi, tel: 547 8200; Radio-Taxi Independiente, tel: 445 9008 or 448 4259; or Teletaxi, tel: 445 9008 and 448 4259.

Attractions

What's On

Perhaps the best way to get to know Madrid is to start off with a general city tour to get your bearings. Tours are available through the local tourist agencies, and the Tourist Board of the Madrid Town Council occasionally organises walking tours and excursions out of the city. For further information, contact the Patronato Municipal de Turismo at Calle Mayor 69. Tel: 588 2906/07. Open: 9am–2pm.

There are three magazines about Spain printed in English: *Lookout* and *In Spain*, both published monthly, and the Madrid weekly, *Guidepost*, which gives performance listings.

Information regarding cultural events can also be found at the Madrid Community Tourist Office in the Torre de Madrid, tel: 364 1876.

Tickets for plays, concerts, films, bullfights and soccer matches can be purchased at Galicia, Plaza del Carmen 7, tel: 531 2732 or 531 9131. Tickets for bullfights and soccer games only are sold at the small stores and booths set up along Calle Victoria, a small street off the Puerta del Sol.

Shopping

Madrid offers visitors every shopping possibility from all the regions of Spain. For craft work, leather goods, footware and furniture, try the state-run Artespaña shops (Velázquez 140; Hermosilla 14; Ramón de la Cruz 33; and at the La Vaguada shopping centre in north Madrid). Department stores and tourist shops are in the centre between Puerta del Sol and Plaza Callao, and along the Gran Vía. Select shops and international boutiques line Calle Serrano and its adjoining streets in the Salamanca area. Designer shops are in Calle Almirante, just off the Paseo de Recoletos. The streets directly to the west of Almirante lead into one of Madrid's crime zones.

Further Reading

As I Walked Out One Midsummer Morning, by L. Lee. Penguin.
A Rose for Winter, by L. Lee. Penguin.
The Assassination of Federico García Lorca, by Ian Gibson. Penguin.
Federico García Lorca: A Life, by Ian Gibson. Faber & Faber.
Barcelona, by R. Hughes. Simon & Schuster.
South from Granada, by Gerald Brenan.
The Spaniards: A Portrait of the New Spain, by John Hooper. Penguin.
Tales of the Alhambra, by Washington Irving. Miguel Sánchez.
Insight Guides: Spain, Southern Spain, Catalonia, Madrid, Barcelona and Mallorca and Ibiza. From Apa Publications' award-winning series.

PORTUGAL

Getting Acquainted

The Place

Portugal is situated in the southwest of Europe, with Spain to the north and east, the Atlantic Ocean south and west. It has an area of 88,685 sq. km, (34,215 sq. miles) and is nowhere more than 563 km (350 miles) long or 225 km (140 miles) wide. Lisbon's position on the north bank of the Tejo (Tagus) river, near its mouth on the lower part of the coast, is – to northerners – already the south. The Tejo river, which rises in Spain where it is called the Tajo, is 1,007 km long and the longest river in Iberia.

Economy

Portugal has been a member of the EU (with Spain) since 1986. The benefits of structural funds and enthusiastic international investment have brought major improvements to its infrastructure – most notably in roads and telephones. Steady liberalisation of the economy has been the pattern of recent years. Prices and salaries, which used to be low, are rising to meet the levels of richer European countries. Bureaucracy, however, remains an irritating burden.

Government

A democracy since the 25 April 1974 revolution, Portugal has been through a period of instability and a series of governments.

Planning the Trip

Currency

The *escudo*, divided into 100 *centavos*, is the basic unit of currency. The smallest denomination coin is the 1 *escudo* piece; the largest is the 200 *escudo* coin (this could change). 1,000 *escudos* is usually called a *conto*. Notes go from 500 to 10,000.

The symbol for the *escudo* is the same as for the dollar sign, but is written after the number of *escudos* (and before the number of *centavos*). Thus, 75$oo is 75 *escudos*; 75$5o is 75 *escudos* and 50 *centavos*.

It is best to change money at banks rather than hotels or travel agencies. Outside normal banking hours, there are currency exchanges at Lisbon's Santa Apolónia railway station as well as at the airports. You'll also see many cashpoints in cities and large towns. If you are driving out of town, you can use Visa cards (and sometimes charge cards) to buy fuel. A 100$oo tax is added.

Traveller's cheques are accepted in all banks and some stores, but the rate of exchange will be lower. Major credit cards can be used in the more expensive hotels, restaurants and shops.

Public Holidays

In addition to the public holidays listed in the Introduction above, the following dates are holidays in Portugal:
Anniversary of the Revolution: 25 April
Labour Day: 1 May
Portugal and Camões Day: 10 June
St Anthony's Day (Lisbon only): 13 June
Saint John's Day (especially in Oporto): 24 June
Day of the Assumption: 15 August
Republic Day: 5 October
All Saints' Day: 1 November
Restoration Day: 1 December
Day of the Immaculate Conception: 8 December

Getting There

By Air

TAP Air Portugal is Portugal's national airline and has wide international links. Many major airlines make non-stop direct flights to Lisbon from capital cities in Europe and other continents. You may also, from some countries, fly directly to Oporto in the north and Faro in the south. Links with London are particularly good. From New York and Boston there are several flights a week.

For information about train services from any station in Lisbon (or for the rest of the country) tel: 888 4025.

By Train

Nowhere in Portugal is yet linked to the superfast TGV system, but there's a busy international (and national) train service. A daily train makes the Paris–Lisbon run, and the Paris–Oporto route. Madrid–Lisbon (usually twice a day) takes around 10 hours. There are routes from northern Spain (Galicia) or southern Spain (Seville) into Portugal. These tend to be slow and time-consuming.

By Road

Good roads link Portugal with its neighbour Spain at numerous border points. Main east-west routes to Lisbon are from Seville via Beja; Badajos via Elvas; Salamanca via Viseu. Driving from England, via the Channel ferries, allow three days; or, via Plymouth–Santander or Portsmouth–Bilbao, two.

Practical Tips

Business Hours

Most stores open for business Monday–Friday 9am–1pm and about 3–7pm. Stores are open on Saturday 9am–1pm, and closed Sunday and holidays. Major banks are open Monday–Friday 8.30am–3pm and are closed Saturday, Sunday and holidays.

Tipping

A tip of 10 percent is sufficient in restaurants and for taxi drivers. Barbers and hairdressers receive the same or a little less. Theatre ushers get a tip of at least 20 *escudos*.

Postal Services

Post offices open Monday–Friday 9am–6pm; smaller branches close for lunch 12.30–2.30pm. In larger cities, the main branch may be open on weekends. Mail is delivered Monday–Friday; in the central business districts in the larger cities, it is delivered twice a day.

To buy stamps, stand in any line marked *selos*. To mail or receive packages, go to the line marked *encomendas*.

Telephones

There are plenty of pay phones in most cities. Newer phones equipped for international calls are located in city centres. Instructions are written in English and other major languages.

You can make calls – international and local – from post offices. Go to the window for a cabin assignment and pay when the call is finished. In Lisbon there is also a phone office in the Rossio, open everyday 9am–11pm; in Oporto, there is one in Praça da Liberdade (same hours). For long-distance and international calls a phone card (credifon) is recommended. These cards are available from post offices or kiosks.

Many village stores and bars have metered telephones. Phone first, pay later, but be prepared to pay more than the rate for pay phone or post office calls. Calls made from hotels are higher still.

To reach an English-speaking international operator, tel: 098 (intercontinental service) or 099 (European service). To call direct to the US or Canada, dial 097-1, plus the area code and phone number. For the UK, dial 00-44 plus the phone number, omitting the initial zero. Dial slowly.

Telephone numbers in Portugal change with infuriating frequency. To get a current number, dial 118. But be warned – that could change, too.

Telegrams and Faxes

You may place telegrams by phone (tel: 10) or from a post office. Another way to make fast contact outside Portugal is to use the fax/telecopy machines which operate in all major post offices.

Getting Around

Domestic Transport

By Air

TAP has a daily service between Lisbon and Oporto, Faro and Covilhã. Flights run several times weekly between Lisbon and Bragança, and Lisbon and Portimão.

By Rail

Trains in Portugal range from the comfortable and speedy *rápidos* to the painfully slow *regionais*. Generally the most efficient routes are the *rápido* Lisbon–Coimbra–Porto and the Lisbon–Algarve lines. Some *rápidos* have first-class carriages only; others have a very comfortable second-class as well.

The *directos*, which make more stops and travel more slowly have both first- and second-class compartments; second-class here is likely to be less comfortable than in the *rápidos*. Finally, the *semi-directos* and especially the *regionais* seem to stop every few feet and take longer than one could have believed possible.

By Road

Bus networks are private but many systems have adapted their name from the former Rodoviária Nacional so that, for example, the main bus company in the far north is now Rodoviária Entre Douro e Minho. Only the Algarve bus company dropped the word Rodoviária, calling itself Eva Transportes.

Outside the routes between major cities, the bus is often faster than the train, and the bus system is certainly more extensive. This is particularly true in the north and between the smaller towns in the Algarve and Alentejo.

There are quite a few private bus lines which tend to specialize in particular routes or areas of the country. Many travel agencies can book tickets on a private line or may even run their own.

Public Transport

Oporto's public transport is limited to buses and trams – the trams to be phased out – and Coimbra's to electric buses. Both these systems run on the same principal as Lisbon's system: you may either pay the driver a flat fee, or buy prepaid modules and validate the number required by the length of the journey. You may buy modules and get information from bus company kiosks in both Oporto and Coimbra.

Attractions

Nightlife

Nightlife in Portugal means different things to different people. For some, it's a jug of wine and a night of *fado*. For others, it's a flashy disco, or a night at the neighbourhood café.

For a list of just about everything going on in the city and larger towns consult the weekly newspaper *Sete*. Even if you can't read Portuguese, the listings are comprehensible.

Shopping

Portuguese handicrafts range from hand-carved toothpicks to wicker furniture to blankets and rugs. The most famous Portuguese handicrafts include ceramic tiles (*azulejos*) and pottery, Arraiolos rugs, and embroidery and lace work.

Language

If you speak Spanish you can read Portuguese and understand most speech. There are also slight similarities with written French. At Turismo and in virtually all hotels and many restaurants you'll find the major European languages fluently spoken.

Lisbon

Planning the Trip

Health

You can safely drink Lisbon city water, but if you have a stomach that quivers away from home then stick to mineral water.

Currency

There are many easy ways to change money in Lisbon. Traveller's cheques entail paying a commission, but the exchange rate is higher than for cash. Eurocheques are widely accepted, credit cards commonplace. There are also many cashpoints in city banks, especially in the Avenida da Liberdade. If you're driving out of town, you can quite often (but not always) use a Visa card to fill up, but garages add a 100$00 tax. There's no black market in currency.

Getting There

By Air

Lisbon's Portela Airport is on the outskirts of the city. A taxi to the city centre costs about 1500$00–2000$00. Every taxi has a meter but – watch out – is entitled to charge an excess if your luggage exceeds 30 kg (66lb). If the driver doesn't charge this item, you could pay him a 10 percent tip.

Buses to and from the airport are: Nos 44, 45 and 83. Express bus No. 91 travels direct between the airport and Santa Apolónia station, in the city centre just off the Praça do Comércio.

By Rail

Lisbon is not yet linked to the superfast TVG system, but there's a busy international (and national) train service. Trains from across Europe arrive at Santa Apolónia station.

Practical Tips

Emergencies

Medical Services

In Lisbon, there is always a pharmacy open somewhere. If you can't find one dial 118 (or get someone else to) for the *Farmácias de serviço*. Hospitals are mostly big and chronically overfull. The staff are overworked and underpaid. Some visitors head for the British Hospital, 49 Rua Saraiva de Carvalho, Tel: 395 50 67.

When you need the police, an ambulance or the fire brigade, tel:115.

Business Hours

Most shops are open 9am–1pm and 3–7pm weekdays and mornings only on Saturday. Offices often start later and finish earlier. Major banks are open Monday–Friday 8.30am–3pm. The bank at Lisbon airport is open 24 hours, as is the airport's post office. The most central post office in Lisbon, in the Restauradores, is open 8am–10pm.

Postal Services

Most post offices are open 8.30am–6pm. The central Restauradores post office is open 8am–10pm, the airport post office opens 24 hours. Stamps are *selos*: look for the gluepot to ensure they stay stuck.

Telephone

The international access code is 00. After this, dial the relevant country code: Australia 61; Canada 1; UK 44; US 1. If you are using a US phone credit card, first dial the company's access number listed below: AT&T: Tel: 05017-1288; MCI: Tel: 05017-1234; Sprint: Tel: 05017-1877. If you have problems, tel: 099 for Europe international, 098 for intercontinental and 090 for interurban. To call Portugal from overseas, get an international

line then tel: 351, followed by 1 for Lisbon. Inside Portugal, Lisbon's code is 01.

Tourist Information

Tourism/Turismo at the central Palácio Foz, Praça dos Restauradores. Tel: 346 33 14 or 346 36 58.

Consulates & Embassies

UK: Rua de São Domingo, 37. Tel: 396 11 91.

US: Avenida das Forças Armadas. Tel: 726 66 00.

All embassies are listed in the Lisbon phone book under the word *Embaixada*.

Getting Around

Domestic Transport

By Rail

Train/Metro: Santa Apolónia is the main train station for national and international rail travel. The Rossio station serves such places as Queluz and Sintra. From Cais do Sodré, on the waterfront, electric trains make the run to and from Cascais. Lisbon also has a Metro system with 24 stations on lines that fan out in a rough W from the Rossio. Above ground, stations are marked with a big M. Tickets for any distance can be bought at the ticket counter, or from a machine (which has instructions in English and French as well as Portuguese); you can also buy booklets of tickets. There's also a Campo Pequeno station, close to the bullring. The zoo, if you want to go there, is at Sete Rios station. For information tel: 355 8547.

By Road

Sterling service is provided cheaply by the numerous black-and-green cabs of Lisbon. A meter operates within the city, but it is switched off at Lisbon's city limits.

Bus/Tram: Lisbon can be packed with traffic, but the buses and trams

go everywhere at surprising speed – except during rush hours (avoid them). You can get booklets of tickets (and maybe a route map but don't count on it) from the hatch at the back of the Santa Justa Elevador in the Baixa. A week's tourist pass, for all municipal transport (buses, trams, *elevadores*, the electric cable cars) is available. Daily tours are offered to Lisbon and nearby sights by coaches parked below the park in Praça Marquês de Pombal. An antique tramcar makes daily 2-hour tours in summer from the Praça do Comércio.

Car: It's no pleasure driving in the city. For out-of-town trips there are numerous car hire companies at Lisbon airport and in the city. Avis, for example, has an office conveniently located in the garage of the Hotel Tivoli in the Avenida da Liberdade. Rental prices are cheaper than in most European countries. Petrol, however, costs more than in most countries.

Waterways

To cross the Tejo, a crucial exercise for thousands of commuters living in south bank towns, there are ferries all day from the Praça do Comércio and from the Cais do Sodré. To cross downriver, there's a ferry at Belém which goes to the small port of Porto Brandão. Some people make the trip as an outing, often to eat lunch on the other side.

Further Reading

The Portuguese: The Land and the People, by Marion Kaplan. Penguin. *They Went to Portugal*, by Rose Macaulay. Penguin.

Other Insight Guides

Insight Guide: Portugal and *Madeira* are companion volumes to this book. Also available are Insight Pocket Guides to the *Algarve* and *Portugal* and Compact Guides *Portugal*, *Lisbon* and *Madeira*.

Emanuel Ammon 209, 215
Ping Amranand 61, 32, 33, 73, 295
Anzenberger/Sagl 322/323, 324/325
Anzenberger/Satttleberger 230, 242
Anzenberger/Wiesenhofer 224/225, 226, 232
Apa Archive 150
Archives for Art and History 37R
Tony Arruza 67, 374/375, 376/377, 380, 381, 382, 383, 384, 385, 387, 388, 389, 390, 391
David Baltzer 53, 63
Gaetano Barone 56
David Beatty 339, 348
F. Lisa Beebe 344, 363, 368
Bildarchiv Preussischer Kulturbesitz 49, 318
Bildverlag Merten 14/15
Bodo Bondzio 135, 147, 245, 273
The Bridgeman Art Library 42, 112, 298, 366
Siegfried Bucher 189, 194
Douglas Corrance 69, 116, 117, 122
Pierre Couteau 78/79
John Decopoulos 31
Pete Didisheim 58
Lance Downing/Apa 99
Fritz Dressler 164
Annabel Elston 104L
Piero Fantini/Apa 286
Lee Foster/Apa 70, 153
Klaus D. Francke/Bilderberg 180, 349
Courtesy of French Tourist Office 26/27
Wolfgang Fritz 128, 132, 165, 168, 181, 191
Patrizia Giancotti 290
Wieland Giebel 167
Gontscharoff 190
Michael von Graffenried 211R
Frances Gransden 2
Albano Guatti 76/77, 305L
Archiv Gümpel 44
Manfred Hamm 9, 109, 372, 392
Harald Hauswald 158/159
Dallas & John Heaton/Apa 86/87, 297
Karl Heinz and Sabine Kraemer 171, 174, 175
Christoph Henning/Fotoarchiv 71
Michel Hetier 95, 111
Hans Höfer/Apa 234, 274/275, 281, 282L
Imagen 3 65
Catherine Karnow 59, 68, 93, 96, 97, 98, 103, 104R, 120, 123
R. Kiedrowski 20
Ingeborg Knigge 139
Wolfgang Kunz/Bilderberg 346
Dennis Lane/Apa 301R
Lyle Lawson 21, 64L, 35, 39, 92, 94L, 94R, 283
Lelli & Massotti/La Scala Archives 54/55
Till Lesser/Bilderberg 160/161, 182, 183
Magnum Picture Library 64R
Deiter Maier 233
Jean Mohr 212

Kai Ulrich Müller 166, 170
Museu Nacional de Arte Antiga, Lisbon 38
Museum of Cycladic Art 30
Ben Nakayama/Apa 187, 282R, 311, 319
Mike Newton 302
Christine Osborne 146
Jürgens Ost + Europa Photo 52R, 250/251, 260
P.A. Interpress, Warsaw 51
Erhard Pansegrau 173, 179, 193
Photo Bibliothèque Nationale, Paris 43
Polska Agencia Interpress 264
Eddy Posthuma de Boer 149
G.P. Reichelt/Apa 169
Andrej Reiser/Bilderberg 12/13, 108
Rex Features 119
Salzburg Tourist Office 246
Walter Schmitz/Bilderberg 195
Thomas Schoellhammer/Apa 280
Othmar Seehauser 74/75
Tim Sharman 252, 254/255, 258, 259, 263,265, 270L
Tony Souter 266, 269, 270R, 271, 272
Spectrum Colour Library 22
Achim Sperber/Bilderberg 237, 362
Rolf Steinberg Collection 288
Tony Stone Worldwide 18/19, 80, 102, 113, 115, 121, 124/125, 126/127, 176, 200/201, 204, 208, 217, 219, 289, 307, 310, 313, 314, 317, 321, 330/331, 332/333, 336, 337, 340, 343, 345, 347, 350/351, 352/353, 358, 369
Storto 211L
Jeremy Sutton-Hibbert 326, 327, 328
Topham Picture Source 37L, 48, 72, 151
Tourist Office of Heidelberg (Loosen Foto) 184, 188
Transglobe 230
US Press 222/223, 247
Alexander Van Phillips/Apa 84/85, 114, 137, 214, 221, 320
Paul Van Riel/Apa 106, 110, 140/141, 148, 154L,155,157, 293L
Alberto Venzago 202/203
Rolf Verres 186, 197, 198
Joseph F. Viesti 23, 354, 359, 360
Karel Vlcek 248/249
Marlies Vujovic 329
Bill Wassman 25, 67, 105, 107, 154R, 156, 196, 199, 210, 239, 240, 243, 276/277, 287, 291, 292L, 292R, 293R, 294, 296, 301L, 303, 304, 305R, 308, 309, 315, 361, 365, 371, 373
Amanda Eliza Weil 338
Wiener 134
Adam Woolfit 90
George Wright 142/143

Maps Berndtson & Berndtson

Visual Consultant V. Barl

Index

A
B
C
D
E
F
G
H

J
a
b
c
d
e
f

h
i
j
k
l